Céline

The Authorized Biography of Céline Dion

Georges-Hébert Germain

Translated by David Homel and Fred Reed

DUNDURN PRESS
TORONTO · OXFORD

Design: Scott Reid
Printer:Transcontinental Printing Inc.
Cover photograph courtesy Sony Music Canada
Photographer: Michael Thompson

Canadian Cataloguing in Publication Data

Germain, Georges-Hébert, 1944-
Celine: the authorized biography of Celine Dion

Translation of: Celine
ISBN 1-55002-318-7

1. Dion, Celine. 2. Singers — Quebec (Province) — Biography. I. Title

ML420.D592G37213 1998 782.42164'092 C98-932235-1

1 2 3 4 5 BJ 02 01 00 99 98

We acknowledge the support of the **Canada Council for the Arts** for our publishing program. We also acknowledge the support of the **Ontario Arts Council** and the **Book Publishing Industry Development Program** of the **Department of Canadian Heritage.**

Printed and bound in Canada.

Printed on recycled paper.

Thanks to Sylvain Beauregard and his web site:
Passion Celine Dion — http://www.celine-dion.net

Dundurn Press
8 Market Street
Suite 200
Toronto, Ontario, Canada
M5E 1M6

Dundurn Press
73 Lime Walk
Headington, Oxford
England
OX3 7AD

Dundurn Press
2250 Military Road
Tonawanda, NY
U.S.A. 14150

Contents

Dreams are a second life.
— Gérard de Nerval

It was only a dream
But so beautiful it came true.
— Thérèse Tanguay-Dion

For Thérèse Tanguay-Dion,
who first believed in this fairy tale

Foreword

This is the portrait of a young woman — free, independent, loving, physically and mentally stable, strong but bending. I know what she's like. I lived in her immediate entourage for over a year and spent hours talking with her, just the two of us, about everything: her loves, her sorrows, her happiness and how she's made so many other people happy. As I write this, I know she's as happy as anyone can possibly be.

People who think she's unhappy, intimidated, ill, suffering from fatigue, anorexia or bulimia, oppressed by a possessive, authoritarian, jealous husband, are wrong. They haven't seen, they don't know, they can't know.

We project our fears and dreams and fantasies onto celebrities. That's only natural. We say to ourselves, "If I were in her shoes, I'd crack up, I'd die of fear. Stage fright would just kill me." And we decide, wrongly, that these stars must be cracking up too, and dying of fear. But Céline Dion isn't cracking up. She can face enormous pressure. She loves stage fright and stress. Ambition drives her on. Not other people's ambition, but her own — her dreams that her impresario, the man of her life, René Angélil, helps her fulfill. In return, she's his lucky star, his passion, the love of his life.

It's true that for many years, he made all the decisions. If he hadn't, nothing would have happened. He found her other artists whom he trusted (and still trusts) absolutely. He found her the stages and opportunities to show off her talent. He developed an international network of contacts for her, a kind of web that spread the good news about the incomparable treasure he'd discovered seventeen years ago.

This book is their true story. It tells of their many successes, some of which took a very long time. Others were relatively easy, thanks to Lady Luck. And René and Céline have been lucky. Some of their successes are private. Others are spectacular and have been repeated in all the media.

I was never asked by them to include or not include any part of their story, or to speak to one person and not another. Céline said something to me once that I remembered. She wanted, at the end of this book, to know herself a little bit better. I think both she and René wanted to have a faithful portrait of themselves in this exciting moment of their lives, as they climbed to the top of dizzying summits, at the height of their triumph. They wanted to recognize themselves in that portrait. If they couldn't, what would be the point? Why would they want a book that wouldn't reveal who they really are, and that would just distort reality? A portrait is the reflection of a human being. But it's also a human being thinking about himself or herself.

To get to know them better, I shared their lives. During the *Falling Into You* tour, which I describe in this book in great detail, I traveled with them, I rode in the limousines and the private luxury jets. I stayed with them at the fanciest and most expensive hotels in the world. I ate in the best restaurants in Europe, America and Asia. I saw them laugh. I saw them cry and fight and kiss and tell each other, "I love you." I lived as part of the family that had formed around them, a family made up of friends, associates and fellow artists. I saw life backstage. I waited among the patient crowds to hear her sing. And I heard what the competition was saying about Céline Dion and René Angélil.

Today, they reign over an empire on which the sun never sets. Céline Dion's voice is now heard around the world. That's what René is most proud of. He took a little Canadian girl from the Quebec countryside and helped her become what she is today — a strong, independent-minded young woman who's part of all the decisions that concern her, who gives her approval to every detail of every arrangement of the songs she sings, who okays both her career plans and the layout of their Palm Beach home. She exercises complete control over her life, her art and her loves.

That's the truth. The whole truth and nothing but.

The *Falling Into You* Tour
New York, April 12, 1997

The First Sigh

She stands motionless in the hot shower, her head bowed, arms dangling at her sides, well balanced like an athlete about to jump or dive. A thick, warm cloud of steam eases its feathery fingers around her, relaxing her muscles and opening her pores, nudging her gently from sleep.

She opens her eyes and pivots her head, left and right. The full force of the spray beats against her face. The showerhead is like a microphone before her. Soon, she will break the silence that has enveloped her for the past twenty four hours. Two long nights and a whole day without the slightest sound flowing from her throat. She's resting her vocal cords so that tonight, onstage in front of twenty thousand fans, her voice will be strong and flexible.

My voice is the quickest, closest path between what I feel inside me — my emotions, my soul, my thoughts and dreams — and the world outside. When I sing, I'm part of the world. I'm the instrument that makes the world sing. I have no other reason for living, no other goal, no other happiness.

Inside the cloud of steam, she calls upon the voice that's hiding deep inside her. She breathes and sighs to awaken it gently. Slowly, her voice springs to life and stretches its wings — a voice that's been held prisoner inside her.

She has been unable to speak a single word, even to René, the man she loves, or her mother who calls every day no matter where she is. Céline answers her by tapping on the receiver with the nail of her right index finger. She always holds the phone with her left hand. One tap is yes. Two means no. At the end of the conversation, they send each other kisses. Sometimes they speak through Manon, who reads her sister's lips and transmits her questions and answers to her mother.

Like her mother, Céline has always loved the night, even when she was a little girl. She goes to bed in the wee hours of the morning. She sleeps in a cool, dark room, in complete silence. At the appointed hour, usually past noon, Manon comes in to wake her without a word, without a sound, by gently stroking her foot, her hip or her shoulders. Then she opens the curtains to let the daylight into the room. She lets Céline have a few precious last moments of sleep. Sometimes, when they've been far from home for a long time, Manon and Suzanne, her tour director, wait until she's completely awake. Then they sit on her bed and girl talk or look at magazines together. But most of the time, Céline prefers to get up by herself.

On tour, Céline hardly ever listens to music. She never turns on the radio or the television. She doesn't like TV very much. René, on the other hand, often falls asleep in front of the screen. He works in front of it and turns it on as soon as he gets up in the morning. He can spend hours tuned in to CNN and ESPN. A compulsive zapper, he sometimes watches two or three channels at the same time, as if he were afraid of missing something. He needs to know the news and sports, wherever he is. Hockey, baseball, football, boxing, horse racing, motor sports — he wants to know who won and who lost. Not Céline. She lives a cloistered existence, sometimes going several days without leaving her hotel, except to sing. The news and noise from the outside world don't interest her, except when it involves her friends and family.

*René might say to her, "*Billboard *has your album in the top spot in twenty-six countries. The US, France, Germany, England and Japan." She'll shrug her shoulders and say, "Oh, really?" He'll ask her, "Do you realize that adds up to more than twenty-four million copies worldwide?" She just shrugs it off, even if it isn't one of her silent days. She doesn't like figures or politics or business.*

Closing her eyes again, she listens to her voice as it overpowers the drumming of the water. She's always loved singing in the shower. The sound is clear, clean and sharp, like in an underground parking garage with a low ceiling where, just for fun, she might let out a whoop or two.

In New York, Doctor Gwen Korovin slid a tiny camera down her throat one day to show Céline her vocal chords at work. René was bewitched. "Look," he told Céline, "that's where your voice comes from." The glottis seemed to shiver between the folded membranes of the larynx. When Céline sang a few scales, they watched on the video monitor as her vocal chords swelled and contracted, touched and pressed against each other. The doctor explained to them that the slightest contact made them stick together. Polyps could develop at those spots, tiny mucoid tumors that could grow on the vocal chords and alter her voice. Only periods of complete and utter silence could keep those polyps from forming.

That was five years ago. At first, the silence terrorized her, as if it were a kind of emptiness that might swallow her up. Since then, Céline has learned to cherish the quiet and take refuge in it. Everything seems so much more gentle in silence. Everything moves like in slow motion: her thoughts, time, life itself. No pain and no anger can resist silence. Her voice and her ear can find peace. Her soul can be renewed.

> I guess it all depends on your nature. Some people can't stand being alone. I love solitude and silence. But when I come out of it, I'm a regular talking machine. It's all or nothing for me. Sometimes I stop and realize that I'm the only one talking and that everybody's listening to me. That's another kind of solitude.

On silent days, she looks at fashion or interior design magazines. She cuts out articles and photos and files them away in her scrapbooks with Manon. She designs dresses and costumes for her upcoming shows, inspects the plans for the house she's having built in Florida. Joanne, her interior decorator, sends her details of the project by fax. Then she sketches out a few ideas for another house she dreams of building in the Laurentian mountains, north of Montreal — a great manor house with a recording studio, extra wings for her brothers and sisters and their families, a stream and a pond with weeping willows around it and wide lawns with flower beds....

At first, she was afraid of forgetting to keep silent or talking in her sleep, which would render the whole day's efforts wasted. But she was able to follow Dr. Korovin's instructions to the letter.

She knows that René admires her strength, discipline and determination. He even says she's too much of a perfectionist. Maybe he's right. How could the free young girl she once was have become such a hardworking woman? She creates restrictions for herself and takes on new obligations and challenges. René calls her an athlete, a samurai, a marine. Sometimes she thinks he exaggerates.

She's a great pianist, he says, but she won't play in public because her playing doesn't measure up to her own standards. She could create original melodies, improvise like the best jazzman and write songs. But she won't do it because she wants to be perfect. He loves her for being that way. He loves her, period. He says it all the time. To everyone.

A lot of men are afraid to say they're in love. Not René. He tells all his friends. Sometimes he'll even say it to journalists, with their cameras and microphones. He'll declare that he's never loved a woman the way he loves me, Céline Dion. And that he'll always love me.

When he says that, she tells him, "You'd better love me forever, René Angélil." She's a perfectionist, even in love — especially in love. And if he answers, "Of course, I'm going to love you for the rest of my life," she's happy, but there's sadness too. She says to herself, in a soft voice so as not to hurt him, "I wish you'd love me for the rest of my life, René Angélil." Because she's still young, she'll probably live for many more years, longer than those she loves. Almost all of them are twice as old as she is. One day, she'll probably have to live her life without them, all alone. That's the only shadow in her life. She has everything else, and plenty of it: good health, love, fame and fortune.

Sometimes I picture myself as a little old lady. I see very clear images, visions of a kind. I work on them, I move them around like bits of film. I change my life that way. I can go back to them and touch up the sets and improve the stage direction. I adjust the lighting and end up recovering my feelings. There's no action — just emotion. I'm sitting by a window with a shawl over my shoulders, I'm looking out on a perfectly maintained garden, with lots of birds and flowers. It's a pearl-gray day, and it's raining.... Not that I'm sad; I'm just infinitely and incurably alone. I can feel it. There's no one around, neither in the garden nor in the house. There's no music. Nothing but the peaceful silence that I'll never break.

Now she's letting her voice ring out powerfully and fill the bathroom like the cloud of steam that's condensing into tiny droplets of water on the walls and the mirrors. Manon, waiting in the bedroom to dry her hair, can hear her voice. No more rasping and howling. It's music now, vocal gymnastics, a finely modulated melody. René, who's talking on the phone or busy reading the papers or watching TV, can hear it too. It she doesn't hold back, her voice will soar from the hotel window and swoop high over the city. The whole world will hear her song without words, a freshly minted melody, her own pure a cappella voice — her very first sigh. But she holds back. She keeps that song a secret, at least for now.

Falling Into You

Sometimes she wonders what city she's in. Stockholm, Seoul or New York? Is this Vancouver, Hiroshima or Milan? Montreal or Paris? For the past three years, she's lived like a nomad, always on the move, rarely spending more than four or five days in the same place. During the past year, she has sung in some thirty cities in Europe, North America, the Pacific Rim and Asia. She has lived in the most luxurious hotels, in the finest suites, in the world's finest palaces. But the bathrooms all look alike. In Los Angeles and Prague, in Miami, Bangkok and Berlin, you can always find marble, bronze, ceramic, porcelain and giant mirrors. Wrapped in a cloud of steam, between four marble walls, how can she tell where she is?

She never really sees the cities where she sings. She drives through them, most often after dark, in one of those long limousines, which are the same all over the world as they glide through the streets, smelling of buffed leather. She catches a few glimpses of where she is. A street or two, a monument, a river under a bridge, sometimes a group of faces. Sometimes she doesn't even stop at the red lights. Police motorcycles escort the limousines from the airport to the hotel to the concert hall.

She might not recognize the streets or buildings or city squares, but she can distinguish the people by the way they talk, and by their faces. She never feels lost among her admirers. She knows exactly where she is. She can recognize the crowds by their shouts and laughter. Crowds in Asia, in Europe or in America — she knows their reactions and their ovations. She'll do anything to charm them. That's her trade, her passion, her life's work.

She can hardly make out the reflection of her face and her slender, willowy body in the steamy mirror. She wraps her hair in a towel and slips into a big white dressing gown. Manon, her sister, her confidant, her follower, her lady-in-waiting — is waiting for her in the next room. She does her hair, grooms her, applies creams to her skin, makes her laugh, tells her of the time when she was small and how her older brothers and sisters fought over who got to hold her.

She makes her own breakfast. Oatmeal with brown sugar, strawberry jam, toasted French bread, three helpings of stewed pears and peanut butter. No dairy products, no carbonated beverages, no alcohol.

Manon will be with her everywhere she goes today, right up to the short stairway that leads to the stage where, a few hours from now, in front of twenty thousand fans, Céline will let her voice ring free. And her whole world will be set free.

Chapter One
A Family Affair

Céline Dion spent the first two years of her life in the arms of her mother, her father or one of her thirteen brothers and sisters. She was their joy, their toy, their idol.

She was only a few days old when her sister Ghislaine, who turned ten that summer, made an astonishing discovery. Every time she pronounced Céline's name as she held her in her arms, singing in her high-pitched, nasal, girlish voice, the baby would begin to cry. At first, Ghislaine thought that the baby didn't like the sound of her own name. Her mother had chosen the name after hearing the song "Céline," written by the French writer and singer-songwriter Hugues Aufray, who had had great success in Quebec and France during the time Céline's mother was pregnant with her. "Céline" told the story of a good-hearted, well-behaved girl, the oldest of a large family, whose mother died giving birth to the youngest. The Céline of the song sacrificed her youth to care for her brothers and sisters, and the years had passed without her ever knowing the joys of love.

Her brothers and sisters sang other names in the same tone to see what would happen. Little Céline cried just as hard. It was the note that was bothering her. The kids used to amuse themselves by making their baby sister cry until their mother put a stop to it. From then on, the children were to avoid singing any notes that would hurt the baby's delicate ears. But all the other notes were allowed. Céline grew up surrounded by all kinds of music and songs — from the radio and the record player, as well as from her parents and siblings.

Some evenings, as the supper dishes were being washed, the atmosphere in the Dion kitchen became particularly musical. The utensils, pots and pans, plates, glasses, table, fridge, range and walls became percussion instruments. Clément, Daniel and Jacques would bang away at them, while Michel, Claudette and Ghislaine, mop and dishcloth in hand, would imitate the latest hits — songs by Janis Joplin, Jimi Hendrix, the Doors and the Beatles — and tunes taken from a songbook called "La bonne chanson." There were classic French folk songs as well, such as "Frère Jacques" and "Les cloches du hameau" which they sang as a round.

Families of ten, fifteen or twenty children now are rare. But up until the Second World War, large families were common in the St. Lawrence River valley — from the new frontiers deep in the forest, practically in the wilderness, north to the Témiscamingue and Abitibi, east to the Gaspé, on to the Lower North Shore and up to Lac-Saint-Jean and the Saguenay region.

Adhémar and Thérèse Dion's family was rounded out in 1968 with the birth of the youngest, Céline. She was their fourteenth child in a little under twenty-two years, and part of the last generation of large families. To have that many children was never a dictate of religion, nor was it done out of duty or principle. Mama Dion said, "We wanted that many for the pleasure of having kids and watching them grow up."

Large families are like countries in themselves. They have long histories, kept and maintained by their oldest members. The elder brothers and sisters see the whole family grow. They rearrange family history, depending on what they can remember and what their imaginations dream up. Sometimes they'll write a whole new chapter when, for one reason or another, a forgotten episode of their childhood gets dug up from deep in their memories. That's how family legend is built.

The youngest members don't participate. They have to watch from the sidelines, fascinated by the stories. The youngest weren't there at the start. They didn't know the grandparents, and they never knew their parents young, except through photographs. They never lived in the house where, often, the family got its start. They weren't there during moments of high drama — when the stove caught fire, when the last remaining grandparent died, when their father first tangled with the oldest daughter. Family history is a legend for them, a mythology they wish they knew more about.

In the family tree, the youngest siblings are the little treasures. They're like the high point, the accomplishment of all those who came before them, as if the rest of the family were waiting for them in order to be complete. The Dions all remember the day of Céline's birth. It was Saturday afternoon, March 30, 1968, under the sign of the Ram, the Year of the Monkey. From Denise, the eldest at twenty-two, down to the twins Paul and Pauline, who would be six in four days — they all witnessed Céline's debut in this world. They heard her first words, they remember fondly the first song she sang with them, the car accident she had when she was two.

Since her birth, Céline was the center of interest for fifteen other people, who loved her, worshipped her, held her in their arms from morning till night. And when night fell, the would quarrel over who would get to have her in their bed. At four days old, on April 3, 1968, Céline Dion left Le Gardeur hospital and came home with her mother. By then, she was already a star.

As for her mother, she was angry at herself and at her husband too. She had just turned forty-one. She'd just started to have a little time for herself. Figuring that she'd done more than her fair share for the population explosion, she decided she was ready for a little free time after the twins were born. She began dreaming about what she'd do with it. She'd planned on finding a job — a paying one! — that would get her out of the house where she'd spent the last twenty-five years washing clothes, making meals, darning socks, ironing shirts. The older children could help her with the housework now. She might even get out her old violin and start making a little music with Adhémar, their daughter Claudette, their son Michel, who sang so well, and Daniel, who could play any instrument. She dreamed of the little trips she could take with Adhémar. They would go to the Gaspé, where they were from originally, and see the ocean again, then travel down the coast of Maine, maybe even all the way to Florida.

And now, here was another baby. Unplanned, unwanted. All her plans went out the window. Her life, and her husband's, and the lives of all her children would be changed.

The *Falling Into You* Tour
Paris, September 22, 1996

Departure

On a fashionable street in Paris you can find high-class hotels like the one Céline Dion and her entourage arrived at several days ago. Every day, like today, a group of people starts forming around three o'clock in the afternoon outside the hotel.

It's September. The skies are gray but the air is mild. On the upper floors of the buildings, there are narrow balconies with polished iron grillwork. Garlands of red flowers hang from them. From time to time, a curtain moves in the tall windows. Some of the people in the crowd are holding cameras with telephoto lenses trained on the windows of the hotel. Others are holding small bouquets of flowers, or a pad of paper and a pen, or an envelope that contains a letter that they intend to press into Céline's hand. They hope to come away with an autograph, or a look and a smile. Maybe they can even touch her hand or the edge of her coat.

The limousines that will whisk Céline and her entourage away are parked farther up the street. The drivers are talking among themselves, standing on the sidewalk. One of them has a receiver in his ear and a tiny microphone attached to his right wrist. From time to time, he speaks quickly into his hand, then he listens to the answer, eyes half-closed in concentration, his finger pressed against the receiver in his ear. In front of the hotel entrance, porters, car jockeys, bellhops and livery men come and go. Some of them are plugged in too.

Every time the hotel doors swing open, a murmur runs through the crowd. When Eric appears, everyone senses that the time is near. Fans in the know all recognize thirty-year-old Eric Burrows, Céline's bodyguard for the past three years. They've seen him from time to time on the Internet, on TV specials and in the pages of magazines that talk about what the stars are up to.

Eric is a tree of a man with twenty-two-inch biceps, a fifty-six-inch chest, and a shaved head who never smiles when he's on duty. He casts the same suspicious eyes on everyone — that's his job. Born in Montreal of parents from Barbados, he began his career as a football player when he was fifteen. A few years later, he had to give it up because of a knee injury. He went to Al Gregory's bodyguard school; Gregory himself was a former football player with the Montreal Alouettes of the Canadian Football League. Burrows would work out six days a week, two or three hours a day. Sunday was his only day of rest. As far as he was concerned, the hotel gyms weren't worth much in Europe in general, except in England.

Burrows takes up position in front of the hotel. He looks the crowd over. He knows that Céline Dion's fans are the nicest in the world. They are a lot more timid and well behaved than Madonna's. And he should know; he worked for her too. But there's always the paparazzi — there's nothing they won't do. They're always trying to turn over a stone and unearth some secret, in search of a photo that will make the star look bad. Tears and sadness and trivial details are their specialty. And evil-minded madmen can slip into a crowd. Some of them can become dangerously possessive and exclusive.

The tabloids will invent anything. For a year they've been saying that Céline was pregnant. Every month she supposedly has a new miscarriage. They apparently interviewed her in a hotel lobby in Los Angeles the very night she was in Milan, at Gianni Versace's fashion emporium. In the summer of 1995, six months after she married René Angélil, the tabloids had her divorcing him, even as they were sharing a perfect love in the Fiji Islands. She was in Nagoya, in Japan, the day she was allegedly spotted entering a fertility clinic in Montreal.

But her real fans can't be fooled for long. They know Céline's schedule and her work habits. They know she always gets to the concert hall long before the show for the sound check with her musicians and sound technicians. They know she'll go to the cafeteria with them, then warm up her voice with her backup singers. Then she'll proceed to her dressing room to gather her thoughts for a few minutes before stepping onstage.

Her fans also know that she usually leaves her hotel around three in the afternoon when she has a concert on the outskirts of Paris. That's why they're waiting for her now outside the hotel. She'll be leaving soon. Her fans can read the signs. The chauffeurs are in their cars, and a limousine is parked sideways at the foot of the street to block off all access. At the top of the street, policemen on foot and on motorcycles are getting ready to close the sidestreets.

Here come Manon and Gilles Hacala, her companion. He looks after the logistics of the tour — the limousines, the luggage, the reservations, the errands. Céline is behind them, escorted by Eric and René. In the five or six yards between the door of the hotel and the door of the limousine, Céline will take the time to talk to several people, smile at them, touch their hands, sign three or four autographs on pieces of cardboard or posters that are thrust toward her. Eric sticks close by. Often, he has to get involved. If someone tries to get too near to her, he'll move them aside with a firm hand. Then he urges Céline and Manon into the open door of the limousine. René gets in on the other side.

Everything happens so quickly. It's a routine that a bird-watcher would appreciate. Suddenly you see a flash of color and feathers from a thicket, and you catch the thrumming of wings. Only when it's too late do you realize that the rare species you've been waiting for came out of its cover. And then it flies out of sight.

Céline has been and gone. Now silence settles over the street. The crowd begins to disperse. But some will return tonight and wait for the precious bird to fly back to its nest. Most of the fans are young. Some are tireless autograph hunters and collectors. Every day, sometimes at the most unlikely time, they lie in wait by the luxury hotels where the sports heroes, show business personalities, top fashion models and politicians stay. Sometimes the collectors trade autographs. Two signed photos of Claudia Schiffer are worth one Prince autograph. A T-shirt with French pop singer Johnny Halliday's scrawl on it gets traded for two Sting signatures and an Elton John or a Jacques Villeneuve autograph. Three Jacques Chiracs get exchanged for one Tony Blair. Some collectors are very specialized. They follow the same star whenever they can. They already have several signed Céline Dion photos, but they want more. She's their hobby, their idol, their passion.

She adores Paris, that beautiful, refined city where she feels almost as much at home as she does in Montreal or Palm Beach. She's been coming to Paris regularly since 1982, the year she recorded her first songs. Paris was the first to love her, and it hasn't forgotten her beginnings.

Besides, the fashions are great there. Chanel, Dior, Saint-Laurent, Armani, Yamamoto. Not to mention the world's most famous jewelers and watchmakers, and the best pedicures and manicures. And she has friends there too: Eddy Marnay, Mia Dumont, Jean-Jacques Goldman, Michel Drucker, Luc Plamondon, the model Karen Mulder who's always been so sweet and kind to her. The French are faithful. When they love, it's forever.

When René asks Céline what she'd like to do if she had a year off, she always says the same thing. First, she'd like to have a child. Then she'd learn Spanish and visit some of the cities she traveled through so quickly during her tours. Barcelona, of course. And Prague, Venice, Kyoto.... She's made plenty of plans. A night at the Paris Opera, on the arm of the man she loves. A dinner for two at the Jules Verne restaurant, high atop the Eiffel Tower, with its panoramic view of the twinkling lights of Paris and the Seine river cutting through the city like a black snake. Long walks through Battery Square in New York. Shopping on the Via del Corso in Rome and the Ginza in Tokyo. And for a while, she'd like to do nothing at all, in her house in Montreal, or in the Laurentian mountains north of the city, or in Palm Beach.

But René laughs and tells her she'd never be able to sit still. She's too much like her mother. At seventy years old, she just can't stop. She works seven days a week in her restaurant in suburban Repentigny, manages her houses in Sainte-Anne-des-Lacs in the mountains and in Rosemère and travels around the world two or three times a year to see her "baby" sing.

Now the limousines are hurtling down the expressway at sunset. A single ray of sun breaks through the clouds in the autumn Paris sky, then the rain returns, soft and mild. Xavier, the chauffeur, begins complaining about the unpleasant Paris climate, even though it's his native city.

Recently, Céline has filled the Bercy Arena four times. With its sixteen thousand seats, it's the biggest concert hall in Paris. Her mother, father and Aunt Jeanne, who are going home to Quebec today, saw all four shows at the Bercy amphitheater. Céline introduced them to the crowd. Mr. Dion is more timid than his wife, and he suffers from stage fright, but as the spotlight shone upon them, he stood up and smiled and waved to the audience. Then he blew kisses to his daughter.

When Céline sang "The Power of the Dream" at the opening ceremonies of the 1997 Olympic Games, her mother wouldn't come to Atlanta. Seeing her daughter on that worldwide stage frightened her. She preferred to stay home, in Sainte-Anne-des-Lacs, and watch her on TV along with four billion viewers from all over the world.

Now the limousines are slowly driving down the tarmac at the Paris airport. They pull up next to the Lear Jet. The crew is waiting by the steps.

Céline is part of the jet set. She's met Pope John Paul II, Queen Elizabeth II of England, the President of the United States, cabinet ministers and princes, the most famous fashion designers and models in Paris, Milan, New York and Tokyo. She's on a first-name basis with the top show business stars in Europe and America. They admire her just as much as the fans who were waiting to catch a glimpse of her in front of her hotel, as much as her brothers and sisters and parents do.

Chapter Two

The Pleasures of Love

People forget over time. Everyone knows that. And their memories play tricks on them. Sometimes people have extremely detailed memories of things that never happened. Other times they forget important, even spectacular events in their childhood.

Céline's memories are helped along by stories that her brothers and sisters tell her. And her mother loves to relate the little details of her childhood. There's her brother Michel's wedding when, at age five, she first sang in public. Or that terrible time when they learned that Karine, the daughter of Celine's older sister, Liette, was stricken with cystic fibrosis. Or the accident that almost cost her her life in the spring of 1970.

It was a beautiful day. The sumacs at the edge of the property along the Assomption River had just started budding. Mrs. Dion had mobilized her sons Michel, Jacques and Daniel to clean the yard, turn the soil in the garden, rake up the dead grass, clear out the flower beds and trim the hedge. Céline, who'd turned two a month earlier, was playing in her sandbox with a trowel and shovel. A blond-haired woman pushing a baby carriage was coming up the road past the house. Figuring it was her sister Denise with her new baby Christian, Céline started crossing the road to go meet her.

In the yard, the boys heard the screeching tires and the screams of the woman. They ran out front and saw their little sister lying under the car. Michel ran to her side while Daniel, fearing the worst, tried to keep his mother away. Céline was crying. Her mother gathered her up in her arms. There was no blood and apparently nothing was broken, but the little girl had suffered bruises on her arms and head.

The driver offered $20 to Mr. Dion if he wouldn't call the police, but he insisted on taking Céline to Le Gardeur hospital. The doctors were concerned about her symptoms: she had vomited, she seemed confused and wanted to sleep, she wouldn't cry. The emergency room doctor had her transferred to Montreal's Sainte Justine children's hospital by ambulance and Michel went along with her. Mrs. Dion was fixing supper when he called to say that Céline had a fractured skull. That evening, Mrs. Dion went to see her child who was spending her first night ever away from her loving family.

Early that summer, the driver of the car that had hit her, a man named Jacques Picard, was gunned down by the Mob. By that time, Céline had fully recovered. More than a quarter century later, in 1996, when Céline wanted to make a family album that would decorate the walls of the room where her mother would sleep in her Palm Beach house, her father produced a folder with a police report. A dog-eared sheet of pink paper dated April 30, 1970 told the tale of the accident that nearly killed her.

Céline is convinced that growing up in a large family made all the difference in the world for her. The unplanned child ended up being adulated, loved, admired — the object of sibling rivalry, no doubt. As soon as her daily housework was done, her mother turned all her attention, time and energy to her youngest child. When the time was right, with the help of her brothers and sisters, she would guide Céline on her road to success.

Thérèse Tanguay, Céline's mother, was born on March 20, 1927 in Sainte-Anne-des-Monts, a small fishing village on the north shore of the Gaspé peninsula in eastern Quebec. Her mother was Antoinette Sergerie, a gentle, jolly woman. Céline knew her grandmother when she was a child. Her grandfather, Achille Tanguay, was a minor official at the parish church. Aunt Jeanne, Thérèse's older sister, remembers how he used to sing in the church, accompanied by the reed organ. Five months after Thérèse was born, in late August 1927, one windy night, a fire started — no one knows how — and half the village burned, including the Tanguays' house.

In 1931, Achille Tanguay received a parcel of free homestead land from the government in the wilderness a dozen miles from the sea. He went there in early summer with his two oldest boys—Henry, a fun-loving lad, and Lauréat, a solitary, more thoughtful young man. A hired hand, Robert Barriault, went with them. They carved out a road through the dense woods using a saw and axe, digging culverts and bracing the road surface with logs. They built a cabin on their land, along with a small barn and a shed. When the first snows fell, Achille returned for his wife and seven youngest children. And so Thérèse Tanguay, at the age of four, discovered the joys of traveling.

They went by horse cart. Everything was loaded into the long, narrow vehicle: bundles of clothing, curtains, sheets and blankets, a few sticks of furniture, barrels of smoked fish, salt pork, molasses, flour and tea. Six chickens rode in their cages. A cow followed behind.

Thérèse sat under a fur blanket with her sisters Jeanne, Annette, Jacqueline, the baby Valmont, Louis and Olivier, who'd broken a leg and was still wearing a wooden splint. When they reached the flat land where the road was better, Robert Barriault, who was driving the wagon, took Thérèse on his lap. "The way I remember it, everyone was happy that day. My mother, my father and all my brothers and sisters," recalled Céline's mother.

In Canada, homesteading has often been described as a painful process, like giving birth to a new world. Many stories speak of the poverty, the deprivation, the incredible hard work and sacrifice. The settlers were often hungry, cold, frightened, homesick. But in the Tanguay log cabin, there was nothing but happiness. They were far from civilization, deep in the woods, and the world was theirs to build as they wished. Or maybe they simply preferred to remember only the good times. There was no electricity and no running water until later on, but they had peace and quiet and complete freedom. The wilderness was their home in all its purity, generosity and splendor.

Henry, the oldest boy, a colorful character and a hard worker like his father, often returned to Sainte-Anne either on foot or in the wagon. He would set out before dawn and wouldn't return until nightfall, traveling those twenty or more miles on washboard roads.

One evening in May, the Tanguay family could hear a new sound in the air. It wasn't the distant seagulls; it was a sweeter, happier and clearer sound of music. Henry had come back from Sainte-Anne with a harmonica, and the family could hear him playing it far down the road. After supper, the children danced to the tunes he played. The next day, as soon as he went to work in the fields with his father, Thérèse picked up the harmonica. In no time, she could play the same tunes that her brother had.

A month later, Henry returned from Sainte-Anne with a fiddle. In a few weeks, Thérèse, who was only seven, mastered the instrument. She learned how to tune it and play a few tunes: the "Sainte-Anne Reel," the "Hanged Man's Reel," the "Bay St-Paul Reel" and others. It wasn't long before she was able to reproduce what she heard on the family phonograph.

When Henry got married, he found a lot across from his father's land with a lake and a mountain slope covered with hardwoods. Lauréat was next to marry and settled on a neighboring parcel. Jeanne and her new husband also found space nearby. The Tanguay family were absolute masters over their little section of the world. It was called Saint-Bernard-des-Lacs, and they loved it immensely. Achille Tanguay and his sons had created their own land out of nothing, with fields of oats, barley, buckwheat, corn and potatoes, pasture land and ponds where the animals could eat and drink and gardens that the women and girls looked after.

"That was our own private kingdom," Thérèse remembered. "It was a real paradise."

The older children taught the younger ones until the Tanguay patriarch convinced the government to build a country schoolhouse. Thérèse attended it until age thirteen, but when it came to education, she always believed that you were your own best teacher. She was convinced that self-taught individuals had a better chance of succeeding in life than those who were taught in schoolrooms.

When Henry married, he left home with his violin. For Thérèse, it was like losing a friend. One day, when she was eleven years old, her father returned from Sainte-Anne with a fiddle he'd ordered from the Eaton's catalogue. "It's the best present I ever got in my life," she said.

Then, her brother Valmont gave her a mandolin that he bought from a drunken soldier. Later, she inherited — she doesn't know from whom — a Hawaiian guitar. Every day, alone or with one of her brothers, she would make music.

The war would destroy that harmony. Suddenly, the country stopped building houses and stables and sheds and barns. The settlers weren't buying any more wood. Tanguay's sawmill fell silent. Young men weren't starting families or working the land. They were marching off to war.

It was all but impossible to maintain the Tanguay paradise. So in 1943, Achille decided to leave for La Tuque, a town in central Quebec. One of his wife's sisters, Eugénie Sergerie, lived there. In her letters she'd described the pleasures of "city life" and promised that there was plenty of work in construction. The town of La Tuque, on the Saint-Maurice River, some sixty miles from the St. Lawrence, owed its existence to the forestry industry. At the turn of the century, enormous pulp and paper plants had been built. The rivers were harnessed. As well, cheap and plentiful electricity had attracted the young aluminum industry. Though the Great Depression of the 1930s had slowed growth, things took off again during the Second World War. Achille Tanguay could make a new life for himself there and get into the house-building business. His son Henry decided to leave too.

And so, the Tanguays abandoned the land they had created with nothing but their bare hands and their spirit. Today, Saint-Bernard-des-Lacs is a ghost town, overgrown with poplars, birches and spruce. Hundreds of acres of land that were patiently and lovingly cleared and planted have returned to wilderness. The happy world of Thérèse's childhood is but a memory.

It took three days to get to La Tuque. On their first journey to Saint-Bernard-des-Lacs, the family had traveled into virgin wilderness. The world was pure and untouched. This time, they were entering the industrialized world, the noisy, busy world of machines and factories spitting out black smoke and reeking residues. They crossed the St. Lawrence River at Quebec City and took the dirt road at Saint-Roch-de-Mékinac that followed the Saint-Maurice into the north land.

Their new life was painful. They had lost their sense of freedom. In Saint-Bernard-des-Lacs, Thérèse could go wherever she wanted, pick wild strawberries, raspberries and blueberries, walk through the forest by herself to visit her brother Lauréat or to see her sister Jeanne who was like a mother to her and whose house was twenty minutes away.

In La Tuque, at 113 on Réal Street, it was another story. La Tuque was a frontier town full of prostitutes and thieves. A girl from a good family couldn't walk alone or even sit out on the porch to watch the sunset. Fortunately, Thérèse had her fiddle, her guitar and her mandolin and her voice. And she knew something that all people who discover music early in life know: happiness exists.

The *Falling Into You* Tour
Geneva, November 1, 1996

The World from Above

The Lear Jet streaks across the skies of Europe. As they leave Paris, the sun is setting. The plane turns its back on it and heads for the Alps. Before, as the pilot accelerated down the runway, Céline said a little prayer, as she does every time her plane takes off, her head bent, her hands crossed on her knees, her lips speaking words that not even René knows. Everyone in the jet fell silent and waited for her to finish before speaking. This evening, she doesn't feel like talking. She has the blues.

She stares at the red clouds against the sunset. Far below, city lights form constellations on the ground. René returned to Montreal two days earlier because he had business to attend to — the purchase of the Mirage golf course in suburban Rosemère, which he wanted to redesign and refit. He was also considering buying a floating casino in Florida. In two days, on November 3, he will be receiving a grand prize from the Association du disque et de l'industrie du spectacle et de la vidéo du Québec (ADISQ). Every autumn, ADISQ hands out its Félix awards (named for the singer-songwriter Félix Leclerc, who died in August 1988) to Quebec artists and producers in show business. The Félix awards (Céline has thirty-three of them, an absolute record) are to Quebec what the Victoires are to France (she has two), the Grammys are to the United States (she has three), or the Junos are to English Canada (she has fifteen). A special Félix award will be given to René Angélil for his overall achievement, for his masterpiece — Céline Dion.

But tonight, far from her husband's side, on board a jet cutting through the European skies, the masterpiece has the blues.

At every hour of the day or night, even when they are separated by oceans and continents, Céline and René are in constant contact. They know each other's every move. René knows that Céline is on the plane, and that Suzanne, Eric, Gilles and Manon are with her, seeing to her every need, as are Dave and Barry, who are making sure that everything goes smoothly.

René spent years putting together this team, expanding it as required. It's a kind of queen's court, a very functional family where everyone's job is to make things as pleasant as possible for the queen and to have everything run smoothly and efficiently.

"Once you've put your people where you want them," René says, "you have to trust them. It's not always easy. A lot of managers can't do it. They end up messing up promotion and marketing plans because they need to show their artist that they're the boss with all the ideas. They never let anyone else make a decision. Management is a team job. You have to know how to put your team together, and know what people can do well. You have to be the mortar between the bricks."

Born in London to Native parents, Dave Platel now lives in Toronto. He runs the offices of Five Star Artist Inc., Céline Dion's international marketing company. He's René's right-hand man. As an associate manager, he's part of every decision. He knows Céline's constantly changing schedule by heart. Dave loves order. He's efficient and fast.

Merchandising in show business has become very important in recent years, generating revenue that is sometimes greater than the show itself. It involves on-site promotion and sales of all kinds of articles (books, programs, T-shirts, caps, signed photos and various knickknacks) bearing the artist's name or face.

Barry Garber is Céline's "Minister of Foreign Affairs" and booking agent. He has planned and coordinated the Falling Into You *tour. Since 1990, with local producers, he has made the arrangements for every Céline Dion show. He is also in charge of protocol. This morning, just to make sure that everything runs as it should, he spoke to a representative of the British producer John Giddings, who acts as their representative everywhere in Europe except for the French-speaking countries. Céline and her entourage will be met at the Geneva airport. Everything is ready at the Arena. The musicians came in the night before from Ghent, in Belgium, where Céline sang two days earlier. The technicians have set up the stage and installed the lighting board programmed by the engineers. Céline's dressing room has been decorated with flowers, her knickknacks and lucky charms. The caterers are preparing the meal she'll eat this evening with the entire team ... except for René.*

Almost every day, more activities are added to an already overbooked schedule. A talk show here, a meeting there with a minister of culture, a movie producer, a fashion designer, the mayor of some large city, a radio interview, a photo session. She never knows what she's going to be doing next. She trusts Dave and Barry because they have René's trust. She knows they've thought it over, that they've weighed the pros and cons of every job she's asked to do. But she doesn't want to look too far ahead. She doesn't want to hear about career strategies. To her, only action counts. She likes the heat of the action so she doesn't have to think. "I'll sing and you take care of the rest. Everything else. Just make sure I'll be able to sing for the rest of my life." That's the agreement she made with René Angélil at the very beginning of her career.

He and the media and their friends often remind her of that agreement. But she doesn't remember anything about it. "I don't recall saying that. Maybe you were reading my mind. In any case, it all comes down to the same thing." And she loves him more for it because he can read between her lines and anticipate her desires. And she's always operated as if that agreement did exist between them. She's always done what he asks her to do. For a long time, she never balked or even asked why. But for the past several years, she's been voicing her opinion. And sometimes hers and his don't jibe.

Last night on the phone, she and René quarreled. She let René talk on. She said nothing, but he could tell by the way she tapped on the receiver that she wasn't happy. In early December, he told her, between one important show at Wembley and another in Las Vegas, that she should record a TV show in Paris to be broadcast on New Year's Eve. She had wrapped herself in her perfect silence. Several times he had to ask her, "Céline, or you there? Are you listening to me?" She struck the receiver once with her nail. "Yes, I'm here." And he went on, telling her that Michel Drucker would be the host of the show, that it would be one of the year's best, that she'd be the centerpiece and that she'd be singing with Charlebois and Delon. She knew it would be an extraordinary show. She loves Charlebois, Drucker, Delon, and she loves Paris.

But she was in a bad mood. She felt cold and dry. And she purposefully hurt the man she loved. Why? Because she was mad at him for being so far away. When he wished her good night, she felt there was sadness in his voice, and maybe even a little anger and impatience. After she hung up, she was unhappy too. She told herself she'd spoiled everything. She should have understood. René couldn't be there. He was busy somewhere else. There was the special award he was to receive, and it terrified him.

Three days ago, she recorded a few measures of "Ce n'était qu'un rêve" in her dressing room. Mégo was on the piano, and a stationary camera stood before them. She was still wearing the long white skirt she'd had on when she'd gone back onstage for her encore. She was exhausted but ecstatic. She had gone all-out to rouse the conservative Geneva fans, and it had finally responded with a moving ovation. She sang the first couplet and chorus of "Ce n'était qu'un rêve," the song written for her by her mother and her brother Jacques. It was thanks to that song that René Angélil discovered her in 1981. With her eyes on the camera, she added this message: every day she loved him more. He was her manager, her man.

That footage was shown in Montreal during the presentation of the special Félix award. René was very moved. In his world, nothing is more important than being recognized by one's family and friends. He told her over the phone that he was afraid of the awards ceremony. For sixteen years, she'd always looked to him for what to say and what to do. He'd admitted, three days ago, that he was at a loss. For the first time in their lives together, he asked her for advice.

"Be yourself," she told him. But there was one problem. When a man's at a loss, often he doesn't know who he is any more. Céline realized that she has much more experience than he does when it comes to being in public. She knows how to talk to people, to the cameras, to crowds, and she knows infinitely better than he does how to receive praise and offer it in return.

Still, she always misses him when he's not there, especially if she had a truly extraordinary performance. Like this very night in Geneva, when she charmed the crowd and when they finally rewarded her with a tremendous standing ovation. She likes these moments of improvisation more and more. When there's a contact between her and her audience, it's direct and very intimate. She doesn't need the music any more, or even the words. She likes venturing out on the tightrope, all alone, high above the admiring crowd.

But if René's not there to see her, how will he know how brilliant she was? Suzanne, Mégo, Dave or Barry might tell him about those great moments, but it's not the same. And she won't boast of her performance. She thinks it's vulgar to brag about yourself; only small minds do that. And no words can ever sum up the beauty of a crowd rising in applause.

She likes to hear about her own successes only from him. He always goes over each of her shows with her, detail by detail. Even at the very beginning, in small Quebec towns like Val d'Or, Rimouski or Chicoutimi, he would come into the room she shared with her mother and describe the evening. He would point out the highlights as well as the mistakes. That's what Céline's missing tonight. His point of view on the Geneva show.

When I'm onstage, everything seems so unreal to me. I'm in

control, of course. I have absolute control. It makes my head spin. I know what I'm doing at every second, the way a race car driver feels. But just like the driver, I have no time to take in the scenery. Everything's happening too fast.

For Céline, going onstage is like a two-hour ride on a runaway train. René saves the fleeting images of her shows for her. He is her mirror, her memory. When he tours with her, he spends every night in the concert hall with the crowd. He watches the show as if it were his first time. Sometimes he chooses a seat high in the balcony. He'll sit next to Denis Savage, the sound engineer, whose console is like an island of lights in the middle of the crowd. Other times, he'll position himself close to the stage, or in the middle of the house. He watches everything, both onstage and in the crowd. He observes how people react, whether they hold back or follow Céline. He takes no notes, but he remembers everything. He can tell you which song during a concert in Norway left the crowd cold, while two months later in Australia, that same song had the audience begging for more.

She'll miss René tonight when she returns to the hotel, takes off her makeup and tries to sleep without him. She loves talking to him, though not just about anything. No golf, no hockey, and especially no news from the Billboard *charts. There are parts of his life that she has no intention of getting to know. She doesn't follow him into his world. She likes the fact that part of his life is his alone — his life with his cousin Paul Sara, his friends Marc Verreault, Pierre Lacroix, Jacques Des Marais, Guy Cloutier, Rosaire Archambault, Aldo Giampaolo, Roch Cloutier. He's very close to his friends. He calls them on their birthdays, buys them gifts, brings them to Las Vegas or Paris. Every day, wherever he is, he calls Marc Verreault, his alter ego. Verreault owns a circus that tours eastern Canada in the summer. He runs a team of ex-hockey stars, and he takes them around the world during the winter.*

René's friends love playing golf. They go to Las Vegas for their favorite sport. They have their secret code: they call Las Vegas "the House." Their nicknames are "Champ" and "Chief" and "Old Man." They have a special handshake. They crisscross the United States and Canada to see the decisive baseball or hockey games or the big boxing cards. They love show business and the city lights. Like René, most of them are gamblers. They'll bet on anything. Just for fun, to add spice to life. For Céline, the friendship among them is something wonderful.

With René, she likes to talk about life's little things. She likes to tell him she loves him when there are other people around. And she likes to make him cry. When he's very happy, that's when he cries.

Chapter Three
The Dion Tribe

One day in August 1944, Henry Tanguay, Thérèse's older brother who was working at the Aluminum Company of Canada in La Tuque, came home and told the family about a coincidence. At work, he'd met a guy with a Gaspé accent who looked exactly like Robert Barriault, his father's hired hand from Saint-Bernard-des-Lacs.

"Didn't you ask him his name?"

"But I didn't know him!"

"If you'd have known him, you fool, you wouldn't have needed to ask him. When you don't know someone — that's when you ask them their name!"

The next day, he asked the young man who he was. Adhémar Dion, he told him. He came from Les Méchins, in the Gaspé.

"I *do* know him," Achille Tanguay said. "He's Charles Dion and Ernestine Barriault's boy. They're all musicians in that family."

Charles Dion, Adhémar's father, was a workingman, who was unreliable and quick to fight. He had a weakness for alcohol and lived hand-to-mouth, wandering from one lumber camp to another with his brothers at the northernmost edges of civilization. He'd just come into La Tuque with his family.

Achille Tanguay was so happy to hook up with a childhood friend again that he decided to go visit the Dions with all of his family. "Tell him we'll be right over," he said to Henry. And when Thérèse returned from the Saint-Joseph-du-Lac hospital where she worked as a nurse's aide, he told her, "Bring your fiddle with you. I want Charles Dion to see that my daughter knows music."

The idea of playing her violin in front of total strangers filled Thérèse with terror. She'd always played alone. Music was something private for her, her way of expressing her emotions. "But back then," she recalled, "the children did what the parents told them to."

The Dion's house was a depressing place. Nothing on the walls, no decorations, nothing comfortable, no armchairs or sofa, not even enough straight chairs to seat everyone.

"Adhémar was the only boy there with anything going for him," Thérèse remembered, even if her first impression wasn't very good. "He seemed stuck-up to me. He was wearing a white shirt and pressed trousers even though it wasn't Sunday."

Urged on by their parents, Thérèse and Adhémar started to play music. Timidly, at first. Adhémar was a remarkably good accordion player. He knew all the tunes that Thérèse could play, and plenty of others she'd never heard of, like "The Mockingbird" and the "Sainte-Anne Reel."

As he was leaving, Achille Tanguay invited the Dions to their place. The next day, Adhémar showed up with his fiddle. He soon made it a habit to spend evenings at the Tanguay house.

Adhémar had developed a good sense of responsibility. Since his father was so unreliable, he'd had to look after the family himself and do his best to keep his younger brothers and sisters fed. At seventeen, he'd gone up to work at the dam-building site in Rapide-Blanc. Then he'd found work at Shawinigan Water and Power, and after that, the aluminum smelter. In the end, his family followed him to La Tuque.

When Adhémar and Thérèse played their instruments, he would look at her and smile. That's what did the trick: his smile, their music, a very private thing that they shared.

That autumn, despite her parents' disapproval, Thérèse, with her sisters and their girlfriends, attended a big dance. She met Adhémar there. He told her that he liked her a lot, but that he was leaving for the Abitibi region where he'd found a job that paid more than the smelter. "I'll wait for you," Thérèse told him. So she went back to playing solos on her violin. When Adhémar returned at Easter, he had bought her a ring. Secretly, they got engaged. Later, Thérèse showed up with the ring on her finger and showed it to her parents.

They got married on June 20, 1945, the same time as her brother, Valmont, did. She had turned eighteen on March 20. Adhémar celebrated his twenty-third birthday on the second of that same month. The wedding took place at the Hotel Royal, then the young couple took the train to Quebec City for their honeymoon.

In the summer of 1950, Adhémar found construction work in Montreal. The family, which already included four children — Denise, Clément, Claudette and Liette — moved to the big city. Later, they settled in Charlemagne, a country town just east of Montreal, where the Assomption and Prairies rivers come together. Adhémar rented a little house on Sacred Heart Street. It was in terrible shape, no better than a shack, and he planned to renovate it completely. He wasn't very skillful when it came to the finishing touches, but he knew how to build a house from the ground up.

The children were never hungry, or cold, or ashamed. Thérèse and Adhémar worked hard. They never asked for help from anyone. But there were no frills. Thérèse cut her husband's and her children's hair to save money. She took in her sisters' dresses at the waist for her own use. She made a new coat for Clément out of Adhémar's old one. The following year, Michel would wear it, then Jacques, then Daniel.

Adhémar walked to work. No matter the weather, he would cross the Bout-de-l'Ile Bridge to save a dollar a week, which he put aside for a special purpose. Everyone in that family always had plans for something new and different. Thérèse and Adhémar wanted to build their own house. And they did it, once they managed to get the tools and materials on credit from some of the local merchants. Every evening after supper, and on weekends, they both worked on their project with help from the older children.

Their family looked after the Dion grandparents, who didn't thrive on city life either. Besides looking after his large family, Adhémar took on the responsibility for his parents. His alcoholic father would disappear for days or even weeks at a time, and his mother was too timid and gentle to complain. Before long, she became ill.

Late in November 1957, Charles Dion's car was hit by a train a hundred yards from the house that Adhémar had built. He couldn't go on living by the site where his father had met such a horrible death, so Adhémar had to pull up stakes again.

There were ten children in the family. After Michel, the fifth, along came Louise, Jacques, Daniel, Ghislaine and Linda. In the fall of 1959, they all moved into a house at 130 Notre Dame Street, on the banks of the Assomption River in Charlemagne. The final four children —

Manon, the twins Paul and Pauline and Céline — spent their childhood in that house. Doctor Emile McDuff delivered Céline, as well as the nine other Dion children born in Charlemagne.

The house on busy Notre Dame Street was an old, steep-roofed building, with two bull's-eye windows and a wraparound porch. The spacious kitchen was built off the side, like in many old farmhouses. When you went in the front door, on the left was the simple living room. On the right was a parlor, used only for special occasions. The left bull's-eye window illuminated the girls' room. On the closet door hung a full-length mirror. The girl used it to practice imitating the popular French singers of the time—Mireille Mathieu, Dalida and Ginette Reno. That mirror was Céline Dion's first stage.

At the beginning of the 1970s, Adhémar left his construction job and began to work as an inspector for a meatpacking business owned by a farmers' co-op. To earn a little spending money, he played accordion for a folk group that worked weddings and family get-togethers. The following year, he put together his own band — Thérèse played fiddle (a new one she'd just bought), Jacques was on guitar, Clément on drums and Daniel on organ. "A. Dion & his Band," it was called. Denise, Claudette and Ghislaine handled the vocals. They played mostly folk music, but sometimes they threw in some current pop tunes like Janis Joplin's "Me and Bobby McGee" and Barbra Streisand's "The Way We Were." The Dion family made an appearance on the *Soirée Canadienne*, a folk music variety show. But two years later, Thérèse and Adhémar hung up their instruments, and Clément gave up his seat behind the drums to Ghislaine.

With Jacques on guitar, Daniel on drums, Michel on percussion and Ghislaine (who was only sixteen and had decided to call herself Penelope) doing the vocals, they formed a new group with a family friend, Michel Desjardins, who played bass. Though their playlist wasn't very original, it was eclectic. They could bang out Afro-Cubans, sambas, cha-chas, not to mention rock and rhythm and blues. For a whole year, they played every Thursday, Friday, Saturday and Sunday at the Bord-de-l'Eau, a club in Charlemagne. They went into debt to buy new instruments (including a Gibson Les Paul guitar) and a band bus. And, of course, the group had its own T-shirts.

And Céline was their number one fan.

Céline often sang for her mother, father and siblings. In the evening after supper, they would urge her to climb onto the kitchen table and would press an imaginary microphone into her hand — usually a spoon or a pencil. She would sing for an entire hour. But she never dared perform outside the house. If someone knocked on the door, she would stop singing.

Her first public appearance was at her brother Michel's wedding on August 18, 1973, when she was five years old. She sang a folk tune, "Du fil, des aiguilles et du coton," that France Castel had made popular again, then Hubert Giraud's "Mamy blue" which had been such a success for Roger Whittaker. She wore a hat and gloves, and a tulle dress. The night before, she'd rehearsed with her mother. When the time came, she stepped up next to the piano, played by her brother Daniel, who could play anything. A smile was frozen on her face and her eyes were downcast. But as soon as she started singing, her stage fright disappeared. She felt as though she were being carried far away by a magic breath of wind. For the first time in her life, Céline felt how good it could be to be watched and listened to. All that day, she sang and danced. When night fell, she refused to leave the party as long as the music was playing.

Two weeks later, she had to leave behind her wonderful, carefree world. On the first Tuesday of September 1973, Céline Dion began kindergarten. She was miserable. She'd always been with adults and older children. What fun was it to get to know the insignificant little creatures in her class?

It was worse the next year when she started first grade. Her life had been turned upside down. Her mother had found work in a store called American Salvage in the east end of Montreal. She sold boots, slickers, rainwear and other such articles. Every day, Céline ate lunch at her sister Louise's house on Pierre Street and she slept there when her mother had to work Thursday and Friday nights. Louise's house was modern, clean, polished and comfortable. And Louise was very nice to her. But in the evening, all alone in her bed, Céline would cry. She knew that if she were back home, she'd be in the kitchen with her mother and Manon and Pauline. And even if she were sent to bed, there would be the familiar noises and voices and smells, the world that she knew. She would have heard the band coming home from its gig. She would have overheard them describing how the evening went, how the show was, as they made themselves a snack. Both at Louise's house and at school, she felt as though she were in exile, away from her comforting life.

Thérèse was absolutely consumed with guilt. In the mornings, when she took the bus to work, she would wonder if she wasn't ruining her daughter's life. She bought her a green bicycle so she could get to school more easily. At lunchtime, at least, Céline could spend time with her brothers and sisters. They were her friends, her best audience, the center of her world.

One night, she had a dream. She was going home after school. Running home, as usual. Suddenly, everything went into slow motion. Her strides got longer, as if she were bouncing on a trampoline. It was a strange feeling, but it made her extraordinarily happy. For days, she floated on air. She still remembers that dream and it's still a source of happiness and energy for her.

Nowadays, when Céline looks back at her childhood, she has only pleasant memories. Except for the terrible day when they discovered that Liette's daughter Karine, who was only two months old, had cystic fibrosis. It happened on a Sunday. That afternoon, Liette, the Dion's fourth child, came to the house with her daughter. The little girl had been suffering from diarrhea for three straight days. When Mrs. Dion took her in her arms, she noticed that the baby's skin had a strange smell. The child was bathed in a sour-smelling sweat. The next day, Liette went back to see the doctor. He had Karine sent to the Sainte-Justine children's hospital by ambulance. There, Liette was told that her daughter was suffering from an incurable illness, and that she might not live more than a few weeks. They decided to have her baptized immediately.

First identified in 1938, cystic fibrosis is a terrible disease. A child will develop it only if both parents carry the gene that causes it. Mrs. Dion found out that one of her cousins living in the United States had seven children, and that two of them had contracted the disease. The fibrosis attacks the lungs, digestive system, and the glands that secrete tears, sweat and saliva. A thick, viscous mucus membrane develops in the lungs, making breathing difficult and creating an ideal environment for infection. The heart has to work harder, and it soon succumbs to fatigue. The lungs wear out and slowly deteriorate. In the digestive system, mucus stops the flow of enzymes from the pancreas, necessary for normal digestion. Children stricken with cystic fibrosis have constant intestinal problems. Even if they eat heartily, they stay thin and stunted, and their growth is never normal.

Céline had just turned nine, and she was strongly affected by what was happening to baby Karine. She heard her parents say that, according to the doctors, Karine would never have the chance to grow up, that she'd have to take pills every day, that she probably wouldn't live very much longer. Perhaps because of all that, Karine was the first child Céline felt close to. But Karine wasn't like other children. She grew into a very serious little girl who already knew that life could be terrible at times. For Céline, Karine was a reminder that the world could be a hard and unforgiving place.

That summer, Adhémar left the meatpacking business and took a job as a guard at Berthelet, a reform school for young delinquents. With his daughter Claudette, he bought a restaurant-bar in Le Gardeur called the Vieux Baril, the old barrel. For years, the Dion children sang there. At the beginning, though, it was another story. The place was practically deserted. Paul, who was fifteen by then, decided to buy an electric organ and start playing there to create a little atmosphere. The Vieux Baril quickly became a popular meeting place. And it was also part of the Dion family home.

Céline saw her first real shows at the Vieux Baril. She faced her first audiences there, and had her first public successes on its stage. Sometimes they found her at four in the morning, asleep in a booth. Her mother told her, "You can stay up as late as you want, as long as you can get up the next morning for school." And so, remembering her promise, and not wanting to miss out on the pleasures of late-night music, she dragged herself off to school every morning, no matter how tired she was.

Her teachers remembered that Céline, especially during the first periods, had a hard time keeping her eyes open. She couldn't follow the rest of the class and learned almost nothing. "It was like she came from another planet," one of her teachers said. "She didn't talk much. She didn't mix with the other kids."

She was too busy dreaming.

She hated school with a passion and was bored silly. No subject held any appeal for her. She couldn't wait for the class to be over. What good was arithmetic, history or geography? She imagined herself onstage, in the recording studio, facing the audiences.

Often, her mother would catch her standing in front of the television, imitating female vocalists. Or upstairs in the girls' room, with the mirror. She knew all the songs of local sensation Ginette Reno by heart. One day, Adhémar noticed that she wasn't just following the melody; she was singing in harmony. She was truly redesigning the song. Her brother Michel, who was also her godfather, told her that one day they'd sing together on TV.

With the Dion children's band having dissolved, Michel formed a new group called The Show, which had some success playing the nightclub circuit. They recorded two 45s, and one of their songs climbed almost to the top of the hit parade.

One fall evening, the Dion parents traveled to the small Quebec town of Saint-Jean-de-Matha with Céline and the twins to see The Show. The group was warming up for a tour around Quebec. Since those were the days of flashy band suits, Mrs. Dion sewed a long white jacket for Michel with satin lapels and trim. Céline watched her brother with open-mouthed admiration. He was The Show's lead singer. His voice was strong and full, he had a great sense of rhythm and he moved well onstage. He did all the talking for the group and everyone's attention was focused on him. Céline insisted on staying until the end of the last set. As long as there was action — something to see and listen to — she wouldn't leave.

She had memorized an incredible number of songs. At the Vieux Baril, people were so astounded by her repertoire that they paid her for their special requests. Her parents were amazed to discover that she could now face the public with no fear.

When the Vieux Baril burned down, it was a personal disaster for Céline. She had gotten used to the crowds, the applause, the laughter and cheering, and she now couldn't do without the attention. Her mother understood completely. She hadn't succeeded with Claudette and Ghislaine. She was determined to succeed with Céline.

Thérèse Tanguay-Dion always had a very clear idea of what show business was. When she felt her daughter was ready, she approached the man whom she considered to be the most important producer and the best manager — the man who was responsible for the career of Ginette Reno. And in Céline's opinion, Ginette Reno was the world's greatest artist.

The *Falling Into You* Tour
Seoul, February 21, 1997

The Press Conference

As Céline says her secret prayer as the DC-8 lifts off from Nagoya en route to Seoul, the plane banks sharply. For a moment, it seems to hang motionless in the air. Then comes an instant of panic: how could anything that heavy stay up in the sky? What would keep it from crashing into the water below?

Céline is terrified. Though the flight proceeds normally, she still feels nervous and scared. Now they are flying over Osaka, the coast of Sanin, and the Sea of Japan, on the way to South Korea. She has only one desire: to turn around and go home. Yet the DC-8 offers every possible luxury. Céline has a spacious room with a double bed, a washroom and a shower. For the rest of the team, there are two large salons, a comfortable sofa and bunks. It is dark when the airplane touches down in Seoul, on a glistening, wet runway. Everyone is feeling the tension by now.

The airport is dark and deserted. Cold drafts blow through it. Suzanne, Manon, Eric and Dave try to shield Céline from the wind. They wrap an extra scarf around her. The city looks like a lumbering metal maelstrom. Eleven million people live here. Everything seems disorganized and hectic. Barry Garber has been warned that there would be terrible traffic jams, and that it might take them an hour and a half to get to the Hilton. At eight o'clock, Céline is to give a major press conference at the hotel.

There is bedlam at the Hilton. The limousines have to nudge through the crowd. Eric grabs her by the waist and heads for the elevators. It's like Moses parting the Red Sea. He manages to escort her to her penthouse suite that stretches over two floors. It affords a breathtaking view of the famous Hansam Tower and of the nearby mountains scored with superhighways, resembling streams of lava.

Fifteen minutes later, Céline steps into the meeting room. More than a hundred journalists from all over the Far East have been awaiting her for over an hour. There are banners and giant posters with the Falling Into You *album cover. Long tables, covered with green carpet, have been arranged in a semicircle. Microphones and cameras represent TV stations from seven Asian countries: South Korea, Taiwan, the Philippines, Thailand, Hong Kong, Singapore and Malaysia.*

Standing at the podium, looking very slender in her golden Chanel jacket, Céline smiles as the cameras flash. The press conference is a kind of consolation prize Sony is offering to the countries that Céline hasn't had time to visit on this tour. It also is, as Martin T. Davis, vice-president of Sony's operations in Hong Kong says, a way of saluting the people of the Far East. "Céline Dion will be spending more time in Asia," he promises.

Canada's ambassador to Seoul makes a short speech, presents Céline with a Team Canada sweatshirt, and declares her an honorary member of the team. Mr. Hun Bang, a native of Seoul who has long played violin in Quebec folksinger Gilles Vigneault's band, and who is involved with the producers of Céline's show, handles the translation from French to Korean. English, Chinese and Thai are also spoken.

Sony representatives from half a dozen countries steps forward to present Céline with platinum records. Finally, at nine o'clock, the press conference begins. It is a formal affair with a host. Journalists wanting to ask questions have to identify themselves first.

There are the usual empty, repetitive questions. The kind she's heard over and over again, everywhere, for the past two years. Does Céline really want to have a baby? Can she say a few words about her husband? Is she anorexic? She answers in a pleasant voice despite her fatigue and hunger, and despite the sense of foreboding that has filled her since their arrival in Korea.

Then, finally, a young man speaking hesitant English asks a question that has some depth: "What keeps you going?" Céline stops to think. Then she speaks of her parents, describing how hard they have always worked, how they have built the house they raised their children in, how they have found happiness and a sense of stability in their work. "I was brought up that way," she added. "Besides, every time I stop working, believe it or not, I get sick. To tell the truth, the thing that motivates me and keeps me going is the need to feel good about myself. And I never feel good about myself when I'm not doing anything."

She makes the reporters laugh when she admits that she's always believed she had a lucky star to guide her. A kind of guardian angel. She tells them about her idea of happiness. The happiness of traveling and seeing the world, discovering the similarities behind the many small differences. There is another kind of happiness too that sometimes, for no apparent reason, lifts up her heart and soul. "Real happiness," she says, "might have something to do with doing your job well. But it's not always earned, it's not always fair. There are some people that happiness just doesn't want to touch." That's her way of talking about her niece Karine, about cystic fibrosis and those other incurable childhood diseases. So many questions haunt her: why do some children die of hunger and cold? Why are some born feeble? Why are others born with no chance of survival?

Someone asks her which are her favorite songs. "They're like my children," she answered immediately. "I think that my mother loved each of her fourteen children with equal affection. The same thing goes for my songs. They all have a way of reaching out and touching people, and sometimes even changing their lives. Maybe they just add a little hope and light to their day. My songs can go anywhere: into the bedroom, in the kitchen early in the morning with the smell of toast and coffee, in elevators, in cars speeding down the expressways. Music is like water," Céline adds. "And it's like fire, too. It can spread."

When Dave Platel steps up to announce the end of the press conference, she thanks the journalists and the people from Sony who have organized the event. "We have grown up together, you and I," she says. "I owe my success to you."

She is dead tired. She is escorted from the room as the crowd applauds heartily. Next, she finds herself in a smaller salon where she is to meet some key people from Sony. She is to leave her hand imprints in a block of plaster and sign it with a knife. The plaster has already started to harden. She is willing to try again. "A job worth doing is worth doing well," she says for the half-dozen cameras that remain. But there is no more plaster, and no more time either. She has to hurry off to do a radio interview about her family, René, her travels, Paris, her opinions about fashion and the child she wants to have. Then there will be a photo session with some fans from Seoul who have won a contest.

It is almost midnight when Dave steps in again, politely but firmly. He tears Céline away from her fans, telling them that she needs to rest, that she has a big show tomorrow night. She expresses a few regrets, then lets herself be escorted to the hotel restaurant that has stayed open late especially for her and her party — her sister Manon, her brother Michel, Suzanne Gingue, Gilles Hacala, Dave Platel, Barry Garber, Eric Burrows and Patrick

Angélil, René's son, who have arranged the menu and ordered the wines, and Meursault and Vosne-Romanée. On a tour, these private moments are always reassuring.

They talk about the panic attack she had leaving Nagoya, the terrible traffic jams in Seoul, the memorable press conference and the enormous suite where Céline will sleep, all by herself. And, of course, they talk about René. Patrick imitates him: his hand gestures, his voice, his laughter. Everyone laughs as Patrick describes him gardening or hunting or changing a tire.

Then Céline says how much she loves him.

Chapter Four
The Angélil Clan

René Angélil was born on January 16, 1942, at 7760 Saint Denis Street, in the working-class, French-speaking Montreal neighborhood of Villeray. His father Joseph Angélil was a tailor. He immigrated to Canada three years before René's birth with his older brother. Born in Damascus, in Syria, the Angélil brothers lived several years in Beirut, then in Paris. In Montreal, a marriage was quickly arranged between Joseph and Alice Sara (also of Syrian origin), who was fifteen years younger than her groom. They had two children: René and André.

René's father often spoke of Beirut as a magnificent place, "the world's most beautiful stage," he called it. He described the Corniche, the seaside promenade, that overlooked the beaches of Saint George's Bay just beneath the old city. He told his children that it was a city of great beauty and refinement. At the day's end, the natives would make their way down to the seafront from the souks, the Martyrs' Square and the Grand Sérail, and watch the sun set over the Mediterranean. There were swaying palm trees and music, and all the sweetness life could offer. Joseph Angélil dreamed of returning to that city one day with his wife and sons.

He loved to sing. His tenor voice was strong and tuneful. Every Sunday, he sang at the Holy Savior church. He worked in a shop located on what's now Alexandre-DeSève Street. The place no longer exists, and in its place sit the offices and studios of the television station, Télé-Métropole.

Joseph Angélil took his responsibilities seriously, and he believed in duty. A reserved and extremely religious man, he never spoke in anger. His French was strongly accented with his Arab origins. Though she was much younger than her husband, Alice was a strong-headed woman, a natural leader in all things. She spoke Arabic, English and French perfectly well. René was very attached to her. "My mother and I always thought the same way about things," he recalled. "She always understood me, even when I did things I wasn't supposed to."

The Angélils led a simple life. Their traditions, their culture and their personal characters made them a united family that was very attached to the Lebanese community in Montreal. The Angélils and the Saras ate Lebanese meals every other day, and neither family drank alcohol, even on holidays. They talked constantly, endless discussions about everything. For the Angélil family, talking was an art. And it was important to be right.

Almost every evening on Saint Denis Street, and later at 7860 Casgrain, where the family moved and where René spent his childhood and teenage years, the Angélils and Saras, including all their aunts and uncles, would play cards. Poker, canasta and baccarat. They would use matches or tokens as chips; sometimes pennies. They organized round-robin tournaments: couple against couple, or the men against the women.

Grandma Sara had a special talent for cards. She could remember entire games and point out where players had made mistakes. Games were serious business. You had to respect the rules, and win according to the rules. Otherwise, you were cheating. The children learned to play cards, backgammon and dice games from an early age. At five years old, René knew all about cards: the role that luck played, the strategies, how to bluff. He learned that sometimes you have to fake and pretend, and create the illusion that you were better off or even worse off than you really were.

On Sundays, the Angélils would go for car rides, as many people did back then. René and his brother André would sit quietly in the back. They would go to Ottawa, to Quebec City, to the Richelieu Valley or Plattsburgh, New York. One Easter, they went all the way to New York City. In his silent way, René's father was showing him the world.

René was eight when Joseph Angélil took him to the Montreal Forum to see his favorite hockey player, Maurice Richard. They were paying homage to Richard that night. He was presented with a Chrysler with the number nine on the license plate in honor of the hockey player's number. A few days later, when he was with his father on Saint Denis

Street, René spotted Richard stopped at a red light in his brand-new Chrysler. "That changed my life," he said. For the first time, the boy made the connection between reality and the world of stardom. He understood that the stars weren't necessarily inaccessible or untouchable. If he hadn't been so shy, he could have approached his idol.

There wasn't much music at the house. Just a few old records of Arab music that his father would listen to—strange melodies in a foreign language. He got his music from school or church. Of course, there was always the hit parade every evening at dinnertime on CKVL. Afterward, at seven o'clock, before the card games, the family said the Rosary together.

When he was nine, René joined the choral group at Saint Vincent Ferrier school. There, he met Pierre Labelle, who lived right across the street from him. The choral's director took the group's repertory from old folk songs, and Labelle thought there was nothing more boring than that. "Give me jazz and rock," Labelle said. He was born in Windsor, across from Detroit. His father once played in the Detroit Symphony Orchestra. Now he accompanied French stars like Charles Aznavour, Charles Trenet and others when they toured Canada. He also conducted the orchestra at the Mercier Theater on Saint Catherine Street, known for its very popular variety shows.

The two boys, Labelle and Angélil, began to hang out at the Mercier Theater and in other clubs where Labelle's father was working. During rehearsals, they would play around backstage and in the wings. They even got to watch some of the shows from the orchestra pit. They were there when many TV stars got their start on the humble stages of the variety shows.

School was easy for René. He skipped seventh grade and went straight into high school at André Grasset. Two years later, René and Pierre were still classmates at another school, Saint Viateur, in the same Villeray neighborhood.

Like his uncle who drew the posters for the Odeon theater chain, Pierre Labelle wanted to be an artist and a designer. He would take René down to Saint Catherine, Saint Denis and Mount Royal streets to see what his uncle had painted for the fronts of the movie houses. René envied his friend's enthusiasm and sense of the future. He himself was thirteen or fourteen years old, and he didn't know what he wanted to do with his life. He only knew he didn't want to work in a shop like his father, or in a factory. He would have liked to be a singer, but unfortunately he'd inherited the kind of voice that was nice enough, but thin and without much substance.

At the time, among popular French-Canadian singers, doing French-language covers of American hits was the thing to do. All the disc jockeys and many artists and impresarios took on American-sounding names. Every Sunday at noon, the CKVL AM radio station broadcast a show called *Billy Monroe's Diamonds in the Rough — Les Découvertes de Billy Monroe.* Coming live from the Chateau Theater on Saint Denis Street, the show was a kind of amateur hour. Pierre and René decided to sign up. They chose Paul Anka's "Diana" as their song. Anka was from Ottawa, and at the end of the 1950s, he had had a series of world-topping hits.

On a Sunday morning, off-air and with no audience, the contestants had to go through a first tryout. Labelle and Angélil showed up, messed up the words, and were eliminated.

"Better luck next time," they were told.

They'd been so sure of themselves when they'd gone down to the Chateau that they'd told all their friends, who'd filled the Chateau, waiting for their two heroes After all, wasn't the point of it all to impress the girls and their friends? Meanwhile, Pierre and René, shamefaced, strolled up and down Saint Denis, waiting for the show to end. They quarreled (and still don't agree) over who messed up.

When René went into his final year of high school, the teacher in charge of discipline would not let him run for student council president because he was too much of a troublemaker — a school clown and cutup. With the chance for power gone, he teamed up with a guy named Gilles Petit. One by one, they recruited the wildest, most undisciplined — but often most imaginative — guys in the school and chose a candidate to campaign for. Their candidate got elected. René loved being campaign manager. He wasn't on the frontlines, and would never be student body president. But from the back rooms, he exercised and enjoyed his power. "The secret of politics," he told Labelle, "isn't to get elected — it's to get control."

Both the stage and the arena are places where glory is to be won. René played basketball, baseball and hockey. He was good at indoor sports too: pool, bowling and especially ping-pong. Ping-pong is a fast game using reflexes, and teaching himself to use his left as well as his right hand, he soon beat everyone in his school. It was hard to beat René, especially since he played effortlessly and showed no emotion, speaking slowly in a voice you could hardly hear. "The secret of ping-pong," he told Labelle, "isn't how fast you move, it's how you control the ball."

Gilles Petit, René's candidate, who'd become student body president, produced a show at the school with his friend Jean Beaulne. The two boys had gotten together with René and Pierre to sing a popular song from the time, "In the Still of the Night," originally done by a quartet called The Satins. Their performance went over very well. René told his friends that they should try their luck again with Billy Monroe, this time with a song by The Teardrops, "I Promise," a sugar-sweet tune in the middle of which the lead singer confesses his love while the backup chorus chimes in with a series of doo-wop's.

On Sunday morning, at the Chateau, Pierre, Jean, Gilles and René rehearsed with the house band. This time, they didn't tell anyone. The organizers asked them to find a name, and as he leafed through the sports section of *Montréal-Matin*, Gilles Petit noticed the name of a Quebec City minor league hockey team called the Baronnets. The name sounded good, and it worked well in both French and English. It became their group's name.

They won the contest and shared the incredible sum of $20 dollars. That same Sunday, they went to the Casa Loma on Saint Catherine Street, where Jean Simon also ran a "diamond in the rough" contest. They won again, with the same song. That evening, they performed at the El Dorado, where Georges Tremblay ran a three-piece band with piano, bass and drums. Once again, they won the contest. Three victories in a single day! On Monday, René Angélil made sure the whole school knew about their exploit. What good was success if no one knew about it?

In the fall, René began business school at the University of Montreal. He was the youngest, and probably the most experienced, of the students there. But three months later, he was bored silly. With Labelle, Beaulne and Petit, he continued taking part in amateur singing contests. They'd learned two Coasters songs: "Along Came Jones" and "Charlie Brown." Little by little, they built up a repertory of a dozen songs, including "Little Darling" by the Four Diamonds, "Love Is a Many-Splendored Thing" by the Four Aces, "Never Forgot" by the Three Bars, "I Promise," "Diana," and others.

They learned a thing or two from Georges Tremblay, who helped them smooth out their harmonies. They met Roland Séguin, a more serious man with classical tastes. He was too technical for them, but Angélil never forgot a comment he made. "He told us that if we wanted to succeed in the business, we shouldn't think about money. If you go into it because you like it, because singing brings you happiness, then go ahead. You might just make some money along the way."

But money didn't interest Angélil and his friends. At their age, fame was much more fun. They were seventeen, they wanted to be popular with the girls and make it on their charm. After all, wasn't that what show business was all about?

One day, a producer saw them in a contest and offered them a gig in Grand-Mère, a small town in the isolated middle part of Quebec. Three days, a hundred dollars, plus food and a room at the Saint Maurice Hotel. A regular gold mine! Angélil was the coordinator — he accepted or refused offers, controlled the schedule and negotiated the fees.

In the summer of 1960, he took a job at the Bank of Montreal. He liked the position and felt at home in the orderly world of numbers. When it was time for school again, he realized he wasn't interested. He began to skip classes. He played cards for hours on end in the cafeteria, learning how to bet. His parents and his aunts and uncles would bet pennies and nickels, and their losses or gains wouldn't change their lives. But in business school, Angélil had developed a taste for high stakes; he liked the feeling of taking risks.

By Christmas time, he had quit school. For several weeks, he was too afraid to admit it to his parents. Every day, he left home, his books under his arm. His father would tell him that with his talent and intelligence, he could easily become an accountant or a lawyer if he wanted to. Why not both? "Finish business school. Afterward, if you like, you can try out for the bar. I'll help you." Day after day, René sank deeper into the lie. He knew that one day the gap between his father and him would be too deep to bridge.

He went back to the Bank of Montreal and was rewarded with a full-time job. Gilles Petit had started selling insurance. Jean Beaulne was working with his father in his TV shop. Pierre Labelle was drawing movie posters in his uncle's shop.

Soon the Baronnets had their own poster, created from black-and-white photos taken in a drugstore machine on Saint Catherine Street. They were singing almost every weekend, most of the time in the Laurentian Mountains north of the city, in small towns like Saint-Canut, Mont-Rolland, Saint-Sauveur, Saint-Jérôme and Sainte-Marguerite-du-Lac-Masson. Three shows a night on Fridays and Saturdays. They never made much money, but they were slowly building a reputation.

In the middle of May in 1961, an artist's agent by the name of Gordie Wilson offered the Baronnets top billing at the Feuille d'Erable, a very popular club in Montreal's northern suburbs. Joseph Angélil went there to watch the group sing. He realized that night that his son would never be an accountant or a lawyer. He applauded, of course; sometimes he even laughed at the jokes. But he was obviously disappointed that René had quit his studies. He let him know as much in his gentle way, without scolding him, accepting the world as it was, but without hiding his disappointment either. And that troubled his son all the more. It weighed upon them both. René realized he'd disappointed the man whom he loved and admired most in the world; at the same time, he was angry with his father. It's hard to love someone you've disappointed.

By day he worked at the bank, administering the Baronnets' young career, negotiating, rehearsing, singing two or three evenings a week. But he came down with mononucleosis and had to put everything on hold for three months. Alone all day at home, he listened to the records that his friend Labelle brought him. For the first time in his life, he got interested in such French singer-songwriters as Charles Aznavour, Gilbert Bécaud and especially Jacques Brel. He loved Brel's intensity in songs like "Ne me quitte pas" and "Quand on n'a que l'amour." He watched a lot of TV, a companion that never let him down. He discovered Perry Mason, the lawyer with the heart of gold and the nerves of steel, the benevolent avenger played by the iron-faced Raymond Burr who could figure out the most twisted plots, and after the most convoluted legal squabbling, could expose the criminal, let the truth shine through, then apply the law to its fullest.

Perry Mason was the kind of hero Angélil appreciated. He couldn't say the same for those athletic adventurers such as Jungle Jim or the Saint or even James Bond. Once again, he thought of going back to law school. He had everything needed to be a good lawyer. He liked using words. Most of all, he liked being right.

But once his health returned, the siren song of show business rang out louder than ever, and law school went out the window. To his father's great consternation, René decided not to return to the Bank of Montreal, and to go into singing full-time instead. He convinced Labelle and Beaulne to do the same.

But Gilles Petit didn't go along. As far as he was concerned, being a singing artist wasn't a stable profession. He gave up show business and went into insurance. By the fall, the Baronnets were in the American Guild of Variety Artists directory (the AGVA later became the Musicians' Guild). The Baronnets were establishing a presence on the club scene. There were more and better paying jobs, but they decided they needed a professional agent.

One day, they got together at the Select restaurant on the corner of Saint Denis and Saint Catherine. All the artists' agents had their offices in that neighborhood. Each of them had his own contacts in a couple of dozen clubs and cabarets where his artists played. The Baronnets knew most of the biggest agents — at least by name. René went to see Roy Cooper, Jean tried his luck with Johnny Reed, and Pierre renewed his acquaintance with Gordie Wilson, who had put them on the Feuille d'Erable stage the spring before. Two hours later, the guys met again at the Select and discovered, to their delight and surprise, that they had all accepted different jobs for the coming weekend. They liked Johnny Reed's proposal best: the Central Hotel in suburban Chomedey. The other two dates would have to be canceled. Wilson and Cooper, none too happy, advised them that they'd better find a good manager.

"A manager?" they questioned.

"Call it an impresario, if you like. Someone who'll take care of your song list, your bookings, your travel and your finances. Even your look."

Cooper had told René about a guy he knew very well; he'd make a great manager. The guy's name was Ben Kaye. He used to work for a concert organization and brought American pop singers like Bobby Rydell and Bobby Vinton to Montreal on a regular basis.

The contact was made. On Thanksgiving weekend, Ben Kaye went to see the Baronnets in Chomedey. Kaye was a small man with a quick eye and a sidelong smile. He spoke French with a strong English accent. To make himself look older, he always had a cigar in his hand. The three Baronnets were mightily impressed and sure they were now in good hands. The way they saw it, Ben Kaye was just as good as Colonel Parker, the man who had masterminded Elvis Presley's career, and whom all managers everywhere worshipped.

They agreed on all the important points right away. Ben Kaye would sort through the offers, work on the selection of material, expand the group's territory and seek record deals to command higher prices. For that work, he would take twenty-five percent of what they made. Right off the bat, he told them that show business involved a lot of wheeling and dealing. When he called Ottawa to book the Baronnets, he claimed that they'd just torn down the house in Quebec City. And vice versa. "You've got to impress the public" was his motto. Soon the Baronnets were very much in demand. Their material wasn't very original, but they had a sound of their own.

Labelle had a fine tenor voice. Beaulne sang bass and was gifted with a sense of rhythm. Angélil's voice was as thin as a reed, but he was extremely charming. He was a natural onstage. He liked to talk and make the audience laugh. And the audience liked listening to him, and he always took care of the onstage presentations. Ben Kaye noticed he was a hit with women.

"Talk to the women," he would advise René. "Charm them."

René had another gift too: he was a believer. He believed that everything was possible, that one day, with or without the Baronnets, he'd step onto the world's most prestigious stages. Take Les Jérolas — that pair of entertainers from Quebec. They were on the *Ed Sullivan Show*. Why not the Baronnets?

In 1962, Ben Kaye got them a booking in a Puerto Rico hotel popular with vacationers from Quebec. The Baronnets spent two weeks there, and no doubt did nothing to change the island's musical tastes. But René Angélil had an experience there that was to mark him for life.

The *Falling Into You* Tour
Frankfurt, October 16, 1996

The Hotel

He never tells her where he'll be seated, but she knows he's somewhere out there in the darkness, somewhere deep in the audience, where her eyes can't see, watching her every minute of the two-hour show. When she sings "Pour que tu m'aimes encore," she sings it for him, every time. The song reminds her of the Edith Piaf number, "L'Hymne à l'amour." The same theme, the same structure — a woman consumed with love.

Recently, René introduced her to Edith Piaf's world. Before Piaf, she mostly listened to black American singers like Aretha Franklin, Tina Turner, Ella Fitzgerald and Sarah Vaughn. She knew dozens of their songs by heart. She even learned to sing like them, for her own pleasure. All singers do that: they listen to one another, and sometimes imitate or parody each other. In their voices, you can hear echoes of other singers they've loved. Céline's good friend Mia Dumont, Eddy Marnay's wife, once told Céline that every time she heard Mariah Carey or Whitney Houston, she couldn't help thinking of her. "You've changed their style," Mia told Céline. "Now they're imitating you." But Céline reminded her that those two singers had changed her style too. "You always learn from your colleagues. If you copy, copy from the best."

A few days earlier, in Paris, René called her into the living room of their suite at the hotel. A documentary about Edith Piaf was on TV. There was original footage from the old days, all in black and white, along with recent interviews with people who had known her and who were still alive. The film showed Piaf as a tiny woman, a street child of Paris, a whirlpool of emotion, and you could feel the incredible energy that flowed from her and her voice, and the strange, jerky way she had of moving. The documentary described how she had influenced great songwriters like Eddy Marnay, and discovered a host of talented artists in France, including Yves Montand, Georges Moustaki, Claude Léveillé and Eddie Constantine. Céline was captivated by Piaf's voice and its heartrending inflections. That's what Céline looks for in another singer: intensity, as if the voice was greater than the singer, as if it didn't belong to her any more. That happens to Céline sometimes. Her voice takes on a life of its own, it goes beyond her, it takes over her. What she hopes for every time she sings is not to master her voice, but to lose control of it. She wants her voice to possess her.

Céline was captivated by the love story between Edith Piaf and Marcel Cerdan, the boxing champion who died at the height of his glory. Piaf was devastated afterward! The next day, René bought the video of Claude Lelouch's film "Edith and Marcel," along with every book he could find about Edith Piaf and every record she'd ever made. Céline listened to them religiously:

J'irais jusqu'au bout du monde
Je me ferais teindre en blonde
Si tu me le demandais.

(I'd go to the ends of the earth
I'd change my face, my hair
If you asked me to.)
— "L'Hymne à l'amour,"
Edith Piaf and Marguerite Monnot

Piaf's song captured the same passion, the same obsessive, possessive, all-consuming love, and the same determination that she found in the Jean-Jacques Goldman song he'd written for her, "Pour que tu m'aimes encore." She'd sung that song all around the world—in the United States, in Australia, in Scandanavia, in Japan—always in the original French version:

J'irai chercher ton âme dans les froids dans les flammes
Je te jetterai des sorts pour que tu m'aimes encore.

(I'd search for your soul in ice in flame
I'd cast spells to make you love me again.)
— "Pour que tu m'aimes encore,"
Jean-Jacques Goldman

When Céline walks into a hotel room for the first time, she always goes to the window and looks down upon the city. Often she thinks about the strange man in "Le blues du businessman," a song written by Luc Plamondon and Michel Berger. Like her, the businessman lives in great palaces and always travels first class. He's a great success. He has everything it takes to be happy. But he's still dissatisfied because he wishes he could be someone else — an actor, an author "to rewrite my life," an artist "to say why I exist." Unlike the businessman in the song, she's always known what she wanted to do: sing. And that's what she did. She's happy and fulfilled. She never led a tortured life like Edith Piaf. She's surrounded by people who love her. She's never had unhappy love affairs with painful good-byes. Great sadness has never touched her — except for when her niece Karine died.

I owe a lot to Karine. Though she didn't know it, she opened my eyes to many things. She made me realize how much suffering and pain there can be in the world, and how much of it is unfair. If it weren't for her, I would not have seen that hidden side of life.

People say that you have to suffer in order to sing with your soul. A journalist once wrote that, despite her powerful voice, Céline Dion could never become a real star because she'd never suffered, she'd never been mistreated by life. The journalist said that real stars (like Edith Piaf) were always lonely people who'd suffered from the cruelties of life. This opinion bothered Céline. She began wondering whether she should wish for some calamity in her life so she could become an even greater singer.

That critic maintained that Céline had only one voice. No bad experiences. No deep-seated pain she could convey to her art. She'd never go anywhere. That was back in 1991, seven years ago, just after her record Unison *came out.*

In the meantime, Céline Dion's voice has been around the world. And wherever she sings, people agree that her voice can communicate every emotion and awaken deep feelings in every member of the audience. Everyone agrees that her voice has known "ice and flame." Somehow, she's acquired great knowledge and wisdom about life, and experience.

Céline and René have lived out their wildest dreams — but not the way they thought they would. When you set out on a long journey, you don't always end up where you thought you were going. But what does it really matter? The journey is what counts — not the destination. As you travel like a wanderer, you carry your dreams with you. They're like a horizon you keep moving toward, day after day.

Chapter Five

The Man Who Loved Gambling

In Puerto Rico, for the first time in his life, René Angélil walked into a gambling casino. For the first time in his life, he won. Then he lost it all.

The Baronnets were fed, housed and paid $375 a week to sing at the Caribbe Hilton. Once the booking had been signed, a few weeks before, Angélil started dreaming of the casino. Ben Kaye, who accompanied the Baronnets and who knew about his passion for gambling, strongly advised him never to set foot in a casino of any kind. But Angélil knew that no one and nothing could stop him from what he wanted to do.

They arrived in Puerto Rico late on a Tuesday afternoon. They were to start their gig the following Thursday. The routine wasn't hard to take. By day, there was sea and sun and sand. The evenings were spent wining and dining, and dancing with the prettiest girls on the island.

The manager of the Caribbe Hilton picked the Baronnets up at the airport. Once he was satisfied that the baggage was in good hands, Angélil slipped away. He grabbed a taxi and told the driver to take him to the casino nearest to the Hilton. A few minutes later, overcome with anticipation, he walked into La Concha. He strolled among the roulette wheels and one-armed bandits, then sat down at a blackjack table. "I'll bet $20, no more, no less," he promised himself. "Whether I lose or win, I'll get the hell out of here."

In no time, he'd won more than $100. He went back to the Caribbe Hilton, and he insisted that his friends return to La Concha with him. Beaulne and Ben Kaye agreed, and in less than an hour, they'd lost everything. They were stunned and crushed by their defeat, until Ben decided to go and asked manager Carlos Gomez for an advance for their gig. In the meantime, René went back to the room he was sharing with Pierre Labelle. Labelle was sitting on the bed, writing to his girlfriend, using as a model the hot-blooded love letters that *Playboy* published back then. René tried to think of a system that would let him win every time. There is a way of playing called a martingale, which consists of betting twice the losses suffered on the last bet. Bolder and less experienced, René's idea was to gamble twice his previous bet, whether they were losses or gains.

"We're going to be hanging around this place for the next few days," he told his friends. "If we want to have any fun, we'd better make some money."

With Jean Beaulne as the dealer, and using matchsticks instead of chips, René set out to show that his system was unbeatable. And relatively simple too. You bet one dollar, then two, then four, then eight, and so forth. Sooner or later, you have to win. Then you put your profits aside and start again. For example, if you lose the first six bets, you end up with a deficit of 1 + 2 + 4 + 8 + 16 + 32 = $63. The seventh bet is worth $64. If you win that one, and finish with a profit of one dollar. Or you lose (1 + 2 + 4 + 8 + 16 + 32 + 64 =$127), so you bet $128. In Puerto Rican casinos, the maximum bet is $200. Therefore, if a player loses eight consecutive bets, he will be unable to double up his bet again.

"The chances of losing eight times in a row are miniscule," Angélil stated.

"Miniscule," Beaulne and Kaye agreed.

"If not non-existent," Labelle added. He too was convinced.

The next day, Ben Kaye got his hands on a $150 advance. Labelle entrusted Angélil with the $200 he had, in the unlikely event that he'd have to double up eight straight bets. At the casino, Angélil sat down at a blackjack table with his silent friends at his side. And the impossible happened: he lost eight consecutive bets.

The guys hung out at the casino, eating the chicken sandwiches and drinking the ginger ale that the establishment gave the players for free. René couldn't believe what had happened. He succeeded in convincing Ben Kaye to request the remaining money they were owed for their shows — $225 — and divided it equally. Ben, Jean and Pierre ate and drank to their hearts' content, while Angélil went back to the casino and lost what he had left.

"Blackjack, like all games of chance, is based on sequences," Angélil says now. "You can win ten times in a row or lose a dozen times straight. I paid dearly to figure that much out. The mistake I made was winning the first time I played. I'll always believe that I can beat the bank. That has to happen sooner or later. You have to be there at the right time and have placed a hefty bet. That's what fascinates me about gambling. Anything can happen at any time. I'll never stop believing that."

In June of 1963, Ben Kaye got the Baronnets a two-week booking at the King's Club in Dallas. He'd written the club owner a letter praising his new group, and claiming that they were "the best thing to come out of Canada" since Robert Goulet, the crooner who made it big in the United States. Kaye even described the Baronnets' triumphant tour in France. They hadn't been outside Canada more than three or four times—for the Puerto Rican engagement and for a few club dates in Plattsburgh, New York and Burlington, Vermont.

The agent came and picked them up at the airport. "If you're half as good as your manager said in his letter," he told the group, "then you'll be number one in no time. And not just in Dallas."

The Baronnets had prepared a medley of French songs that most Americans knew. Tunes like "Les feuilles mortes," sung by Yves Montand, who had just finished filming *The Billionaire* with Marilyn Monroe. There was Edith Piaf's "La vie en rose" and "Mais c'est magnifique" and "C'est si bon," popularized in the US by Eartha Kitt.

They wore long coats like the Four Aces, though they were but a pale imitation of that group. They tried to reproduce their sound as faithfully as possible, copying their stage presence and harmonies. But they soon switched their allegiance.

Suddenly, in the spring of 1964, a hot new group came out of Liverpool, England. The Beatles were the talk of the industry. Their songs flooded the pop music world like a great tidal wave. Angélil bought their records and listened to them night and day. The Baronnets decided to do several of their songs in French.

The Baronnets completely changed their style, their look and their sound, trading in their long coats, à la Four Aces, for British fashions from the Mersey. They let their hair grow like their new idols. Just as the Beatles literally wiped the Four Aces off the map, the Baronnets were to rise above singers like Michel Louvain and Donald Lautrec who, in Quebec, had dominated the pop charts.

They immediately released four French versions of Beatles' hits, including "Hold Me Tight" ("Serre-moi fort") and "It Won't Be Long" ("Ça recommence"), which were boffo hits. When it came to record sales, at times, the Baronnets were selling more than the Beatles. Ben Kaye organized a tour across Ontario and Quebec. The Baronnets were making big money and spending it as fast as they could, living high on the hog, going from gig to gig in a pink Thunderbird convertible.

In the town of Alma, they met a man named Guy Cloutier. Though only twenty-three years old, he owned a record store. He was a colorful character, intelligent, hilarious, crazy about music, sports (he'd starred for the local minor hockey team) and girls. He and Angélil quickly became fast friends. Cloutier sold his store and moved to Montreal, and stayed with the Angélil family for several months. Along with Ben Kaye, he worked on promoting the Baronnets. But he wanted to sing too. He recorded a few titles, including a version of the hit song "Donna," which did quite well.

Angélil liked to work with Ben Kaye on the group's management, almost as much — or more — than he liked being on stage. Beaulne loved the manager's job too. They took care of another group, the Bel Cantos, who gave the Baronnets a serious run for their money in the mid-1960s. Needless to say, this caused tension and arguments between Kaye, Angélil and Labelle. In 1966, Beaulne was replaced by bass player Jean-Guy Chapados.

For the past several years, Angélil had a girlfriend named Denise Duquette. He'd met her in 1961 at a dance hall, the Buffet Versailles, where the Baronnets were a frequent attraction. Like all rock stars at the time, he wanted to keep his love life secret. He didn't want to get married, figuring it wouldn't be good for his career, and that he would lose his other girlfriends scattered here and there. Denise let him live his life the way he wanted to, which was the "in" thing at the time, and René liked having her in his life. She was very cool, very beautiful, never complicated, and had no faults, except that she liked the orderly life and country living a little too much. Not like Angélil, who preferred city life, especially late at night, and the games city people play.

In the fall, she came to live at René Angélil's parents' house. On December 11, 1966, mostly to please his parents, and so that she could keep on living with them, Denise and René got married. Labelle, Chapados and Cloutier didn't find out until several months later, when René announced that his wife was pregnant.

Two months later, on March 13, Jean Beaulne was back with the group. The Baronnets made their return to the Café de l'Est with a full-fledged orchestra, new songs, well-rehearsed stage patter that linked the songs and a few comic routines. The next morning, René woke up very late. The first night of their show had been a huge success, and he couldn't wait for the evening to come.

Around six o'clock, his father went into the bathroom, clutching his chest. His wife watched him, worried. When they heard him fall, René had to knock down the door. Joseph Angélil had died of a massive heart attack, without disturbing anyone else, just as he had lived.

When his father died, René realized that he'd never been close to him. He bitterly regretted never taking the time to tell him how much he loved and admired him, and that he realized how disappointed he'd been. They'd never really spoken ever since René had chosen a career in show business. He traveled frequently across Quebec, to Florida and to Nassau with his wife and his friends, but he rarely saw his father.

But even as a boy, René had felt closer to his mother than to his father. She was the one with the sense of humor in the family. Like René, she liked gambling, she liked talking — and she loved to have the last word.

The *Falling Into You* Tour
Dublin, June 12, 1997

To the Stadium

The River Liffey doesn't exactly flow proudly into the sea. It simply dumps its thick, khaki-colored water into it. From the empty lots that stretch around The Point theater, where Céline had performed the year before, you can smell the river's heavy odors — hops, pulp and paper, sawdust, grease — the smells of Dublin that mix in with the sea, and that make your head spin.

There's always a lot of wind around The Point. The winds of Ireland are sweeping the entire world these days. No other small country — the population is hardly four million — has had such an impact on the world's art and cultural scene. Ireland is very much in fashion nowadays. In literature, there's Seamus Heaney, the 1995 Nobel Prize. In the movies, there's Liam Neeson, Gabriel Byrne and Gerry Conlon. Music is that country's main export with Enya, her sister Maïre Brennan and her fabulous group Clannad, the melancholy Cranberries, the world-beating U2, Sinéad O'Connor, Mary Black, the Chieftains, the Corrs, etc.

The Corrs, three sisters and their brother, explore traditional Celtic folk music. They add pop and rock to it to create something new. They were the warm-up band for Céline Dion on last year's portion of the tour, playing for audiences all across Germany, Scandanavia, Belgium, Holland, England and Scotland.

The Irish are among the greatest consumers of cultural products in the world — their own and others'. All through 1996, Céline stayed at the top of the charts in Ireland, just as she had elsewhere in Europe. Not only was her last record in English a runaway success (Falling Into You)*, but her French release* (D'eux) *was too, with songs like "Je sais pas" and "Pour que tu m'aimes encore," which played constantly on radios throughout the United Kingdom. No group or singer had ever maintained a streak like that. Céline Dion had linked Ireland with French culture once more.*

As soon as the plane touches down, Gilles Hacala tells the crew that Céline and her entourage will be at Lansdowne Road in less than a half hour. Around five o'clock in the afternoon, the crowd of young people around the stadium where the show is to be held spots the limousines. Without slowing down, the long black cars disappear into the enormous building where the technicians are finishing the stage setup. Eric moves through the stadium, looking under the seats in the first few rows, evaluating the exits, calculating the distances. Meanwhile, the musicians are proceeding with the sound check.

In the field, by the buses, stand ten trucks, each one nearly fifteen yards long. They came from London with all the tour equipment — 200,000 pounds of material, including floodlights, projectors, tape recorders, miles of electric wire and cables, cathode-ray screens, computers, consoles for monitoring the images and for doing the sound mix, loud-speakers, smoke machines, spotlights and microphones, cameras, clothes, the technicians' and the musicians' baggage, guitars, drum kits, keyboards, plates and cooking pots, utensils, and tools of all kinds.

When they get to a new place, the first person Céline and Manon usually see is their brother Michel, his gray hair pulled back in a ponytail, walkie-talkie in hand. He shows the drivers where to park their vehicles, then goes and kisses his sisters. Michel is a reassuring and familiar presence. When he's there, it means that the Dion team has taken possession of the concert hall, and they can relax now. He's the tour director's assistant, in charge of the musicians and their instruments. He's their shepherd. This morning, he escorts the musicians to their hotel, makes sure everyone has the right room and the right suitcase, and sets down the schedule for the day.

Since dawn, Lansdowne Road has been a busy construction site. The action there is positively frenetic. Seen from behind, the stage looks something like a giant ship about to set sail, with its scaffolding, hanging cables, tall masts, great hull and crisscrossing bridges and catwalks. The crew is putting on the finishing touches. Each type of technician wears a different color. The carpenters wear black T-shirts, the cameramen are in blue, the soundmen in green, the lighting people wear yellow.

They arrive in Dublin at night. They slept in the tour buses on the English highways, then on the Irish Sea aboard the ferry. The buses are regular houses on wheels, with living rooms both front and back, wide, comfortable sofas, music, television, beds, storage space, a library, a selection of videos, games, a microwave oven, and all anyone would want to eat and drink.

A small army of over fifty men and women from Quebec accompany Céline in her travels around the globe. They're a very close-knit group, very united and well organized. They fall into a natural hierarchy made up of three separate societies: technicians, musicians and Céline's personal attendants. In every city and every country, support staff is added, including various suppliers and providers of services, members of the media and drivers.

The technicians, presided over by Ian Donald and Jean-François Canuel, are responsible for setting up the infrastructures — the stage, all the sound and lighting effects, the dressing rooms, transporting the equipment, instruments and costumes and preparing meals. These technicians include specialists in electricity and electronics, mechanics, pursers, drivers, equipment handlers, restaurant workers and cooks. Their work is often done early in the morning, late in the evening, or at night. They're the backstage crew people never see. At the rear of the hall, at the very back of the main floor, they've set up their enormous soundboards and light boards. Tonight, Denis Savage, the sound engineer, and Yves Aucoin (known as "Lapin") the lighting man, will be doing the honors. Their two boards are like the control tower, the master switch.

Denis Savage knows the show by heart, even if he hardly ever sees it, because he's too busy listening to it. Often his head is turned to the right, with his left ear glued to the stage. From time to time, he'll give a deep, satisfied smile. Or if he doesn't like what he's hearing, he might frown with a puzzled, worried look. Then he'll push a button or move a lever. He's after perfection in sound.

François ("Frankie") Desjardins creates the sound environment by placing clusters of loudspeakers and room mikes at strategic points to make the sound equal in all parts of the hall. Every venue has its own acoustics and resonance. There's a complex and ever-changing geometry of echoes and reverberation that the crowd will alter just by being there. Sometimes he will install relay loudspeakers from which the music will flow a minute fraction of a second sooner (or later) than the main loudspeakers, creating a unified sound.

The type of music also has to be taken into account. A hall isn't prepared the same way for Metallica, a symphony orchestra or Céline Dion. Every sound is custom made. "The important thing with Céline," says Frankie, "is to be able to hear her voice clearly in all parts of the hall. Within her range, everything has to be crystal clear."

Lapin and Gatien, his assistant, the two men who take care of the lighting, are placed behind Denis and Frankie. Sometimes, they're actually above them, sitting on a platform on top of a scaffold. From this position, they can see the stage with its two giant screens that show video clips and images from the show itself. Offstage, on one side, is an incredibly messy and complicated scene: there are screens, computers, bundles of electric cables. On the other side, down a little stairway leading to an exit, is a tiny electronics workshop. That's where you'll find Jeff Dubois, who does the maintenance on the musical instruments. To his right is Daniel Baron's console. He takes care of the stage sound, which is what Céline and her musicians will hear during the performance. Behind him is another small electronics workshop, a storehouse full of fuses, batteries, alligator clips and tiny welding torches. A few steps further on is a kind of a tent where Louise (better known as Loulou) Labranche has hung changes of clothes for Céline. There's the long skirt and blouse she'll wear for her encores, carefully folded white towels, a hairbrush, face creams and powder. All around are enormous cases and humming machinery, a smokemaker, a bellows, Guy Vignola's console, the sequencers. Somewhere — sometimes he's underneath the stage or behind the large black curtain that serves as the backdrop — you'll find Yves "Kiwi" Lefebvre's outpost. During the show, Lefebvre will flash pictures taken by a variety of fixed and mobile cameras onto the two screens.

White arrows, taped to the floor, lead from Céline's dressing room to the stage. In dark spots, glowing cables are stretched along the railing. The path that Céline will take from her dressing room to the Dublin stage will be well lit. Soon she will meet the people of the Irish capital. She loves them above all the rest. They're sentimental, they have great spirit, they love the passion and magic of music. She loves them best of all because ten years ago, on April 30, 1988, she had an experience in Dublin that changed her career — and her life.

Chapter Six
Loser Takes All

In the fall of 1967, at the height of flower power, while his generation was floating on a psychedelic cloud to the sounds of the Beatles' *Sgt. Pepper's Lonely Hearts Club Band*, Jimi Hendrix's "Purple Haze" and Janis Joplin's "Ball and Chain," René Angélil of the Baronnets had locked himself in his room at his mother's house in Montreal. He was busy compiling statistics, working on another system to help him win at blackjack. He intended to take Las Vegas by storm and break the bank. And he was deadly serious.

He had bought himself a roulette wheel and a stack of graph paper. Lost in the mysterious world of figures, he began noting the results from each turn of the wheel. For weeks on end, day in and day out, the click of the roulette wheel could be heard on Casgrain Street. Then, one day, René told his mother and his wife that he'd finally discovered an absolutely unbeatable system.

He then tried to convince three of his friends — Pierre Labelle and the drummer and bass player from the Baronnets — to invest $1000 each. The opportunity would make them all rich men in no time at all. René was absolutely sure he could beat the Las Vegas dealers. Any man who believed that had to be very headstrong and naive. But these young men were so sure that they'd make a lot of money that they even tried to hire someone to help them bring back all the cash.

Angélil considered his brother André. He was a serious type, a married man, with no interest in gambling. He worked at *Montréal-Matin* as sales director for the Montreal region. Every Saturday afternoon, André would stop by to see his mother. René waited for him there to make him the offer that, he thought, André couldn't refuse. But Mrs. Angélil had tipped him off. "Your brother René's lost his mind," she told him.

René had gone off the deep end. He'd always been a little wild. He was a dreamer, a visionary. He believed you had to try the impossible, make things happen, dance with Lady Luck, find something that had never been done before. You couldn't be happy with things the way they were. He told his younger brother André what he wanted him to do. "I found a foolproof way of making money," he said. "All we need is patience and the courage to try it out."

A few days, or a week at most, is all they would need to spend in Las Vegas. René had written a few pages describing his system. "I'm so sure it will work that I'm willing to repay anyone who buys into it and doesn't win," he declared.

But his brother would have nothing to do with it. He laughed off the whole thing. It was a stinging rejection for René, who thought he could convince anyone to do anything. René loved mystifying people with head-spinning schemes. That's what life was — a game of chance. At the time, he considered himself to be a hustler. With his friend Marc Verreault, he would hang out in the bowling alleys and poolrooms downtown. His favorite trick was to act as though he were a first-time player. Then he'd line up the bets with other would-be hustlers and beat them all, one by one.

Convincing people to see things his way has always been a game for him. He's always wanted people to think and act the way he did. As immigrants from the Middle East, the Angélil and Sara families were unlike their neighbors. They had a distinctive accent, and just walking into their house, you could see by the style of decoration, and the books and records, that these people were different. It was especially evident when you went into the kitchen, where the smell of Syrian and Lebanese cooking permeated the air. René always invited his friends to try out the delicately spiced dishes that his mother and aunts prepared. Unlike many children of immigrants, he never tried to hide what made him different. Just the opposite: he was sure that everyone would like Syrian food, and the spirit of gambling and gaming that was so strong in his family.

Then, to his surprise, his own brother told him he would have nothing to do with his foolproof scheme. But the three other investors didn't give up. Their dreams were too strong. Labelle wanted to have his own recording studio. The bass player had already drawn up the menu for the Italian restaurant he would open. And the drummer had already chosen the name for his new music school.

So they set off to Las Vegas. They went to Caesar's Palace, the world's largest and most prestigious casino. They had $3,000 in their pockets. According to Angélil's calculations, with his system, they should make an average of $1,400 every half hour. By spelling each other, they should easily pile up over $10,000 in winnings each day. They'd go back to Montreal rich men.

It took them a few days to lose it all. Strangely, Angélil wasn't discouraged. Like an explorer who still hadn't discovered the hidden treasure, but who still believed he could reach it, he was just as excited and motivated as before. He wanted to keep on searching for the error in his system. He would perfect it until one day, sooner or later, he'd be able to break the bank.

Caesar's Palace would always be one of the most important places in his world. But in January 1968, his wife Denise gave birth to a son, Patrick. René put away his roulette wheel and, for a time, stopped thinking about gambling. He was too busy learning how to be a father.

The Baronnets' star was not shining nearly so brightly. The current music scene featured a veritable landslide of new groups: the Classels, the Hou-Lops, the Excentriques, Caesar and his Romans, the White Gloves, the Sultans, the Bel Cantos. Each group tried to pass itself off as the clone of an American group. Angélil and Labelle went on performing for a while. They acted in two B-movies: "L'Apparition" and "Après-Ski." Slowly, they turned away from singing and added comic routines to their act. Labelle turned out to be an excellent stand-up comic, and Angélil played his straight man. He began to realize that he didn't have what it took to be a true stage performer. He could never forget the intoxication of the spotlights, but sooner or later, he'd have to do without them. Maybe Lady Luck would smile on him in some other endeavor.

He teamed up with his friend Guy Cloutier. A few years earlier, Cloutier had discovered a boy wonder who would take Quebec by storm — a young man by the name of René Simard who had a remarkable voice and extraordinary charisma. Guy Cloutier's offices were situated right across from the television station Télé-Métropole, in the same building as the Musicians' Guild. Cloutier's company also looked after Johnny Farago, Patrick Zabé and a popular songstress by the name of Anne-Renée, a very pretty, blue-eyed blonde, the picture of feminine elegance.

The *Falling Into You* Tour
Fukuoka, February 11, 1997

Onstage

When Céline walks into a concert hall prior to a performance, the emotions always run high. She's the last piece in a giant jigsaw puzzle that makes everything come together. Most of the time, she doesn't even take off her jacket or boots. She doesn't even bother stopping at her dressing room. She goes right to the stage. She walks back and forth across it, looks over the empty hall, gives a kiss and a hug to the technicians who are doing the sound check and fine-tuning the lighting effects.

In Fukuoka, she steps out of the limousine, goes to say hello to the technicians who are already hard at work, and kisses Loulou, in charge of her wardrobe. Then she disappears. She has slipped into one of the giant folds of the large black curtain that provides the backdrop for the stage. She plays hide-and-seek with Manon, Michel and Loulou. The musicians don't even know she is there. They are fooling around to pass the time until the show begins.

Dominique Messier starts it all, laying down the rhythm on drums, gently at first, then adding a stronger beat. Mégo slips in sensual piano phrasings to complement Coutu's chirpy guitar. Marc Langis's bass provides a rich groundwork for their improvisations. There's nothing like musicians jamming before a big show. Paul Picard chimes in with percussion, and Frulla's keyboards soar high above the other instruments. It is pure music, wild and free.

The hundred or so technicians putting the finishing touches on the stage and the concert hall stop to listen. Just when the backup singers are getting into it, Céline steps from her hiding place and adds her voice to theirs. Then she walks right to center stage, laughing, telling the musicians how good they are and singing along as they improvise. She is wearing a long, sea-green cashmere coat, high boots and a scarf. When she looks out at the main floor and the balconies, Fukuoka's Marine Messe seems damp, cold and depressing. Like all empty concert halls, it is not a very friendly place. Then she looks behind at the stage; everything is exactly as it should be.

The stage set has become perfectly familiar to her. It never changes from show to show — the boards of the stage, the black curtain at the back, all the rest. In Osaka, two days ago, it was the same. In Nagoya and Seoul, it will be just the way it is tonight. She could walk around that stage with her eyes closed. She could find the banister that leads to the hidden stairs. Halfway down, on the left, there will be a light. To the right, the Plexiglas shield that protects Dominique Messier's drums. At the foot of the stairs to the left, attached to the banister will be a little shelf with a box of Kleenex and a bottle of water. Everything is exactly where it should be. For months to come, this will be the world she knows best, the most reassuring place in a constantly changing landscape. The dressing room varies from one concert hall to the next. She rarely sleeps more than three nights in the same bed. But since last winter, the stage and the people who work on it have been the same.

She greets her six musicians, three backup singers, and all her technicians one at a time. She calls them "sweetheart," "my love," "honey." She asks after their sick mother or their pregnant wife. She does it because it's the human thing to do, and because she needs the contact.

All big stars are, to some degree, the product of how the media and the public see them. They inevitably end up looking like what their fans want them to be. Whether they're aware of it or not, they begin to act like the image people have of them. Right from the start, everyone seemed to agree that Céline Dion was the nicest star on the scene, that she was direct and uncomplicated, approachable, and concerned with others. And she really is that way. That's her nature, the way she was brought up. But she's become even more that way because that's how the media and the public see her. That's the way they want her to be.

A journalist named Geneviève Saint-Germain once wrote, "What if her kindness were nothing but a weapon? What if it were simply her way of protecting herself, her shield, her shell? Maybe it's just her way of controlling people."

It does me good to kiss my friends and tell them I love them. It reassures me. I do it as much for myself as for them. I admit it. But I'm not trying to control anybody outside of myself. I learned early on to be polite and kind to people. My parents taught me that, and so did everyone I worked with when I started out in the business, like René and Mia. It's part of my nature now. I love the people I work with. That's why we work together — because we love each other.

She stops by the combination console and workshop that belongs to Daniel Baron. He hands her a set of headphones. Baron has prepared a personalized channel for all the musicians and backup singers. Through it, he can broadcast a continuous flow of information as the show progresses. There's the ticktock of the metronome that sets down the beat at the beginning of every song. There's the little beep that cues the prerecorded parts that Guy Vignola controls. There's a signal for everyone onstage so that they can follow the rhythm and integrate the sounds they produce in a perfectly harmonious way. These headphones fit snugly. They are much more accurate and unobtrusive than the old-fashioned monitors.

When Céline steps onstage, Claude Plante gives her a mike. He stands close by during the entire performance, just out of sight, ready to help if she needs it. When she leaves the stage, his hand will reach out, from the same place, and at the same height, to lead her to the stairway.

Chapter Seven
A Lesson Well Learned

In October 1970, the ex-Baronnets were playing at a club called Le Patriote on Saint Catherine Street. They shared the bill with Quebec comediennes Clémence Desrochers and Françoise Lemieux in a review created by Desrochers, *La Belle Amanchure.* Those were the days when the cabaret scene and the folk clubs began to come together. In Quebec, the Quiet Revolution was on, democracy was on the upswing, and the Catholic Church was losing its power over day-to-day life.

Michel Constantineau, who produced the show, thought that his *Belle Amanchure* would bring together all the different elements of the Montreal club scene. But political events proved him wrong. Bombs went off, and a British diplomat and a Quebec government minister were kidnapped. A group known as the Front de Libération du Québec (FLQ) issued a violent call for radical social change. The October Crisis had begun, a series of events that shook all of Canada. Intimidated by the FLQ and by the Canadian government soldiers who patrolled the streets, people stayed home. Like all other public activities, show business suffered.

In *La Belle Amanchure,* Angélil played, among other roles, a candidate who believed in the independence of Quebec and who wanted to change the world. Some nights, he performed for no more than twenty people. On Sunday evenings, the actors and musicians divvied up the take. It never added up to more than $125 each; sometimes it was as little as $75. Meanwhile, Angélil was betting ten or twenty times his weekly salary. He never mentioned his bad habit to anyone because he knew that what he was doing was insane. He had all but lost control of his life. He was both ecstatic and in deep pain, consumed with remorse and completely fulfilled. He had fallen in love with the singer Anne-Renée. He had left his wife Denise and their son Patrick. He had hurt them both, and he hated himself for it. But he was no longer in control of himself.

One Sunday evening, he bet everything he had — more than $2000 — on the Canadiens hockey team, who were playing the Buffalo Sabres at the Montreal Forum. He was counting on winning that bet and paying off his debts. He was even hoping to stop gambling. Every time he stepped offstage, he would get on the telephone to find out the score. In the middle of the show, while Clémence Desrochers was doing a solo, he learned that Marc Tardif had scored on Roger Crozier, the Sabres' goalie. It was one to nothing for the Canadiens. He went back onstage with a smile on his lips. Twenty minutes later, he ducked into his dressing room just in time to hear the end of the game. A minute before the final buzzer, the Sabres' Gilbert Perreault got one past Canadiens' goalie Charlie Hodge, tying the score and ruining Angélil. But he had to get back onstage again. His job was to make the audience laugh in a sketch called, ironically enough, "The Card Game."

His mother helped him. She signed for him at the bank, first making him promise never to bet with bookies anymore, and never to borrow from loan sharks. René kept his word. But his love of gambling did not die.

A short time later, he and Labelle went their separate ways. Labelle wanted to stage one-man shows. Angélil was getting more and more interested in managing artists and producing records and was working more often with Cloutier. His friend was still as involved as ever with the young René Simard, who had become Quebec's pet, a large-scale star. "You've got to get him out of here," Angélil kept telling Cloutier. "You've got to find him other gigs in English Canada and the States."

But how?

In 1974, they had an incredible stroke of luck. At fourteen years of age, René Simard went to the Yamaha Popular Song Festival in Tokyo with Cloutier and Angélil, where he won first prize. Frank Sinatra himself presented the trophy. Angélil and Cloutier finally thought they'd hit the big time. René Simard became an overnight sensation in the Land of the Rising Sun. He even recorded a song in Japanese which enjoyed a lot of radio play. When they got back to Canada, Angélil and Cloutier, master promoters, played up the event for all it was worth. They'd worked with Ben Kaye. They knew they had to play to the public.

The first prize in Tokyo boosted Simard's status within Quebec considerably. But René Angélil's dream was the United States. Cloutier had the same ambition, even if he hardly spoke English. Their Mecca was Las Vegas; their idol, Elvis Presley. They knew the King's songs and legend by heart, and they'd seen all his movies. Cloutier had even met him once in Las Vegas for thirty seconds, when he'd been photographed standing next to Elvis. He'd even shaken his hand.

But the two managers hadn't been able to do much with Simard's international success. They didn't have the contacts or the know-how. They made bad decisions and serious mistakes. During a monster promo campaign in Quebec that they orchestrated, Angélil told a journalist from *Time* magazine that René Simard had sold more records in Quebec than the Beatles and Elvis Presley put together. That was true — for a few weeks. Angélil hadn't exactly told a lie, he'd just bent the truth a little. The *Wall Street Journal* repeated Angélil's words on the front page, adding a caricature of Simard. The following week, researchers from the *Mike Douglas Show* tried to contact him. Next thing they knew, CBS Records was showing interest. Guy and René smelled big bucks. They got in touch with the Beatles' lawyer in New York, Walter Haford. From that point on, they lost control of the events they themselves had set in motion.

Not only did René Angélil love the Beatles' songs, he admired their machine, their marketing, their image, their career, their legend. He was probably more a fan of Brian Epstein and George Martin, their agent and record producer, than he was of the four lads from Liverpool.

A setting was chosen for the business meeting: the very chic, very expensive, very snobbish Twenty-One Club in New York. When it came time to talk money, Haford announced that Angélil and Cloutier wouldn't settle for less than one million dollars for the privilege of recording the Simard boy. In 1974, and for a singer who was totally unknown in the United States, the amount was completely staggering. The head honchos at CBS Records didn't bat an eye. They were icy and polished, and when the meal was over, they told Haford that they needed to think about it. They never called back. In fact, they never returned any of the many calls put through by the Beatles' lawyer or by Simard's two managers.

It didn't take long for Angélil and Cloutier to realize that they'd made a big mistake. When an artist is just breaking into the big time, he's in no position to demand anything from anyone. All he can hope for is that his record company will look after him well, get involved with his music, and create a promotion and marketing strategy. When they believe in someone, the decision makers from the big multinational show business corporations can push their favorite artists with incredible effect. They have the machine, the know-how and virtually unlimited money and methods.

Too late, Angélil recalled what Roland Séguin had told the Baronnets when they were just starting out in the business: "Don't ever let yourself be led by money."

Angélil and Cloutier decided to produce René Simard's English-language record themselves, and to launch it on the American market. It never amounted to much. That was the second lesson they learned: if you want to hit a big market, you have to have a big machine. You have to have the contacts. No one can take America by storm all on his own.

Angélil had plenty of time to mull over the mistakes he'd made. He'd learned that if he wanted to play in the big leagues, he'd first have to find allies— people who believed in what he believed in—who were competent, hardworking people who believed in the artist's talent.

He was thirty years old. It seemed he had everything a man could want. He had two sons: Patrick, who lived with his mother Denise, whom he could see whenever he wanted to, and Jean-Pierre — with Anne-Renée — who was born in the spring of 1975. But something was missing. A goal, a project, an artist. Sometimes, when he thought about the future, he began to feel very anxious.

The *Falling Into You* Tour
Stockholm, October 25, 1996

Sound Check

Every singer in the world has dreamed the same dream: to stand one day at the top of a great spiral staircase as her fans look on adoringly, then, slowly and gracefully, descend toward them, singing the most moving song that's ever been sung.

In 1990, as she was preparing her first English show, the success of her Unison *album had given her a little room to dream. Céline Dion revealed her future projects to the media. She told them how she pictured herself in a musical comedy, going down a long stairway, wearing a dress decked out in spangles, flowing skirts and flounces. Or tap dancing with Fred Astaire, when he was young and handsome, in a Hollywood movie. Or playing in a Broadway musical. Some people laughed at the time. But Angélil encouraged her to put her dreams into words. "Go all out," he said. "Don't be afraid."*

Now, six years later, as she is designing the opening of the Falling Into You *show, she remembers that great spiral staircase. She will stand at the very top for the opening, "The Power of Love." Exactly what René had suggested. For about twenty seconds, she will sing the first two couplets of the song in darkness. When she comes to the chorus — "Cause I'm your lady, and you are my man" — she wants a wind to blow. Not just a little breeze, but a gale-force blast that will fill the hall and hit everyone head-on, blowing back their hair. Then she'll pick up the first chorus again in intense light, and close-ups of her face will appear on the two side screens.*

Lapin, the lighting engineer, works with her on the concept of that set. He listens to her and smiles, as he always does. "You're starting too strong," he says. "We can never keep it up. If you want the people in the upper balcony to feel a gust of wind, it would knock over everybody in the first rows."

Céline laughs.

"Everybody has a bad idea once in a while," she concedes.

Lots of times, just for fun, just to laugh at herself, she recalls that ridiculous idea she shared with Lapin when they started working on the show.

> I think you can't help but get bad ideas when you start working on a show or a record or anything else. I think you even have to pursue those kinds of ideas. You have to go ahead and have all the possible and impossible ideas you can. Ideas that'll never work, insignificant ones, crazy ones, twisted and plain dumb ones. Then you start making choices, and save not necessarily the ideas you love the most, but ones that are very personal, so you can share them with the world. People come to the show to hear songs they know. But they want something new too, something unexpected and fresh.

They keep the staircase idea. It turns out to be a very steep ramp that splits the stage in two. Halfway down, on the left, stands the kind of lamppost you see in Paris. On each side are seats for the musicians. Jeff sets out their instruments, which he has already tuned. On one side, Paul Picard's congas, bongos, cymbals and bells are at the very top of the ramp. A little further down is the podium and the backup singers' mikes; they belong to Rachelle Jeanty, Terry Bradford and Elise Duguay. At the very bottom is Mégo's piano. On the other side, from the top, there's Dominique Messier's drums surrounded by numerous microphones and enclosed by a sheet of clear Plexiglas. Then come Yves Frulla's keyboards, Marc Langis's bass and string bass and André Coutu's guitars. In addition, there are a dozen video screens, some dark and others displaying live or pretaped images.

Light is the essential building material for creating stage effects. Smoke produced by the machines behind the stage captures the light. Smoke is Lapin's art museum. He uses the smoke the way a painter uses a canvas. He sketches and projects his colors on it, creating all kinds of striking visual effects — whirlpools, caves, and spirals with contrasting forms and colors. Sometimes patterns are produced on it that make you think of the century's greatest artists, like Picasso or Victor Vasarely. In the middle of these visual effects is Céline. Sometimes he surrounds her with clouds and makes golden rain fall upon her. Other times, he flashes lightning across her face. But she never sees Lapin's work, because she's part of it. She's at the very heart of the magic kaleidoscope.

When Céline steps onto the stage of the Globe, Lapin lights the concert hall so that she can see the rows of colored seats and the steep balconies. His spotlights follow her eyes and soar to the top rafters of the building, where multicolored banners hang. She laughs out loud. She blows kisses towards the light board where Denis and Lapin sit. Through the monitor in her ear, she hears the many echoes and voices of the concert hall. Then she sings a few notes:

Everything you are
Everything you'll be.
"Seduces Me,"
Dan Hill and John Sheard

She closes her eyes and lets herself follow the sound of her voice into the dark hall — the ghost of her voice, its echo, its reflection. An empty hall always makes a voice sound hollow and metallic. There's too much reverberation. But the fans that will soon fill the Globe will absorb that echo. They will soften and dampen the sound, and will add their own shouting and applause. Céline's mike will capture it all and she'll hear the crowd noise along with her own voice. Daniel is always working to clarify the sound that she's receiving. Throughout the performance, his eyes will be glued on her, ready to make adjustments at any time, either soften the sound or make it more intense.

And all that I am
And all that I'll be
Means nothing at all
If you can't be with me.

It is almost dark at four o'clock in the afternoon when Céline comes to the Globe for the sound check. Night comes early this time of year, but Céline doesn't mind. She loves the night. It's her time, the time when she feels free and strong and protected. Tonight, in Stockholm, there's an exhilarating kind of joy. Everyone feels it, and everyone knows more or less where it comes from. Last year, Céline sang here, and later, after the show, she told the musicians that she wanted to go out to a club with them. They discovered a disco in the old part of Stockholm, near Lake Mälaren, and they spent the better part of the night there.

Céline feels like drinking — something strong. Frulla told her to try tequila. She danced until four o'clock in the morning, and for the first time in her life, she was tipsy. The band was worried. After the third tequila, they tried to get her to stop, but she answered that she never did things halfway. She ordered a fourth, then a fifth, then a sixth. They lost track. They only remember how worried they were. They were thinking of how René would react when he found out that they'd let Céline drink in a smoky bar. He'd tell the guys that they'd let him down by letting Céline go overboard.

In the bar, everyone recognized her, and men and women both came and danced around her. The Swedish men surrounded her, handsome, big-boned, elegant, blond and polished — and drunk too, no doubt. It was quite a night. Céline was floating on air, dancing to disco music.

She woke up in great shape the next afternoon. She loved that night — all of it. But she hasn't drunk anything since, except for a glass of red wine, and even then, very rarely. When Angélil found out about her escapade, he laughed. Mostly, he laughed at how concerned the band members had been.

Every sigh in the night
Every tear that you cry
Seduces me.

Suddenly she stops singing. "Hey, Dark Viber!" she calls (her nickname for Yves Frulla), "you remember that bar where we went dancing last year?"

Tonight, Céline knows the show is going to be magic. She can feel a certain something in the air. You never know when it's going to happen. That's the beauty of show business: the unexpected can always happen. And there are some nights — like tonight — when the magic just pours down!

Chapter Eight

The First Skirmishes

Ever since things hadn't worked out in the United States, a failure for which Angélil felt largely responsible, the fifteen-year friendship between him and Guy Cloutier began to sour. With Anne-Renée urging him on, Angélil began demanding a larger share of the company's profits. Cloutier, who had discovered the Simard wonder boy and had created a business that was growing like gangbusters, offered his associate only 15 or 20 percent. In the spring of 1977, Angélil left Cloutier's production company, taking with him pop singer Johnny Farago, whose career wasn't exactly successful. But ironically, a few months later, on August 16, Farago's luck changed for the better when his model, his inspiration, his idol died. That was none other than Elvis Presley.

Angélil and Farago went to the King's funeral in Memphis. By showing their driver's licenses, they were able to pass themselves off as Canadian journalists, and they were able to get on the buses that drove the accredited media into the cemetery. They mingled with Elvis's family and friends, followed the funeral procession and watched as the King's coffin was lowered into the ground. Angélil was in a trance. He loved everything about Elvis: his voice, his look and the cult that surrounded him. He admired the sheer bigness of the operation — the hundreds of thousands of admirers in fan clubs around the world, the myriads of Elvis impersonators, his tremendous success, and even his decadence. The Elvis legend had so much to teach a man like Angélil. He knew that Presley never learned how to be truly happy; but he admired even his unhappiness. Oh, the mysteries of life! Here was a man who was unhappy in the midst of all his riches and glory. Angélil knew that Colonel Parker had made some big mistakes. He kept Elvis confined to the United States and refused all bookings elsewhere in the world, even though people clamored for him everywhere — from Germany to Japan to Mexico. Toward the end, Elvis performed almost exclusively in Las Vegas. His career stagnated and his life was essentially over. All that remained was the legend, the greatest one in show business.

A few months earlier, in December 1976, René had attended one of the King's last shows at the Las Vegas Hotel. Anne-Renée was there, pregnant with their second child, Anne-Marie, who would be born the following June. Guy Cloutier was there too, with his wife and René Simard. They were sitting in the first row. Presley had laid eyes upon them several times, and each time, it was a revelation.

Angélil knew very well that he could never reach the heights he was aiming for with an entertainer like Farago. Sooner or later, he'd have to find something else. He was thirty-five years old, with three children and an ambitious, intelligent wife who wasn't going to stand for a husband who was only the manager of a second-rate artist. She was pushing him to look elsewhere, to find something new.

Over the Christmas holidays, René Angélil went to Acapulco with Anne-Renée and their two children, Jean-Pierre and Anne-Marie. Farago was singing at the El Presidente Hotel, a popular spot at the time for French Canadians. One evening, a hush swept over the room as Ginette Reno came in. She went over and sat down at the Angélils' table. Though she was only thirty-one, she'd been a well-established star in French Canada for over fifteen years, and she was well known in English Canada as well. Her voice was rich and powerful, and she could bring out emotions in people like no one else could. She was also quite the character. She spoke freely of her problems with obesity, her numerous broken hearts, her deep-seated fears and phobias.

That evening, she asked René Angélil to manage her career. Although he knew that she had a reputation in the business for creating problems with her agents and managers and that being her impresario would be no easy task, René accepted immediately. He respected her talent and success, and he liked her larger-than-life quality. She might have been eccentric, but at least she had heart, guts and a voice to match. And it also made Anne-Renée happy.

As soon as he got back to Quebec, he went to see one of Ginette's shows. For the first time in his life, he heard a song that truly moved him. It was "Je ne suis qu'une chanson," with words and music by Diane Juster. He was sure it would be Reno's next hit, but she told him that the song was for live shows only. Angélil insisted on recording it. He had new arrangements done, reserved a studio, hired musicians and virtually forced Ginette Reno to record it.

During the 1978–79 season, the album that Angélil produced sold more than 350,000 copies in the province of Quebec alone — an absolute record. He realized that this unprecedented success would be difficult to beat — a challenge not only for other artists and producers, but for himself too. How could he ever bring together all the ingredients and create another enormous success like that again?

Meanwhile, he wasn't going to sit around and just savor the success. He keep up the promotion and get a tour going. Angélil negotiated to produce two television specials in Quebec, and also approached producers in France. and showed them a videotape of Ginette Reno.

The French producers were genuinely impressed, yet no one was willing to actually put out the album. Jean-Michel Fava of CBS told Angélil that Reno's songs, especially "Je ne suis qu'une chanson," were magnificent, but they weren't right for France.

Through Fava, Angélil met pianist Fred Farrugia who introduced him to Eddy Marnay. Marnay was working with Mireille Mathieu and Nana Mouskouri at the time, and had already written material for the greats: Yves Montand, Michel Legrand and Edith Piaf. He had also penned the original words for Barbra Streisand's French-language record, "Je m'appelle Barbra."

"René came to me just as I was changing my life," Marnay recalls.

He had just gotten divorced, and at the time, was living in a tiny apartment in the Beaubourg neighborhood in central Paris. A mattress on the floor, a shutter on two sawhorses for a writing table, boxes of books. Rich and famous, and very free, Marnay was living the student life at age fifty-eight. Bald-headed, with a sparkle in his eyes, a kind of power emanated from him that comes from being truly happy. The year before, he had met a young woman named Suzanne Mia Dumont who was working for the Quebec government and doing music promotion in Europe. Ever since then, Eddy and Mia were hardly ever apart.

René and he hit it off right away. Marnay was born and raised in

Algeria, and perhaps he found in Angélil a little of his Mediterranean past. In Marnay's little apartment, René played "Je ne suis qu'une chanson" for him and Reno's videotape. Marnay was enchanted.

"When can I see her?" he asked.

"She's singing next Tuesday in Quebec City."

"I'll be there."

The following Tuesday, Angélil, who'd returned two days before, picked up Marnay at Mirabel Airport and took him that same evening to the Grand Théâtre de Québec, where Ginette was singing. He was totally bewitched by Ginette Reno's performance. At first he'd had doubts: she was too heavy and her accent was all wrong. But Eddy had worked with plenty of artists who started out with disadvantages. When Nana Mouskouri had come begging him to write her some songs, she was forty-five pounds overweight, wore Coke-bottle glasses, had a thick accent, and she couldn't even put together a sentence. With Reno, Marnay was sure of one thing: her voice stimulated him.

Marnay wrote several original songs for Ginette Reno and found others for her in Canada and France. At the end of the summer of 1978, while the demos were being prepared in Montreal, Marnay asked Angélil if he'd be interested in teaming up with French publisher and producer Claude Pascal, who'd had enormous success with Nicole Croisille's version of "Femme."

A few days later, the new company was a reality. There were three producers: Pascal, Marnay and Reno, with the latter represented by Angélil. Each would have a third of the profits. Angélil was plenty proud of the deal he'd made.

Ginette left for a month's vacation with her lover, Alain Charbonneau. While she was away, Angélil put the finishing touches on a tour he was organizing for the fall of 1980 through Quebec, Ontario and the Atlantic provinces, and then on to Paris to record the new album. But when Ginette came back from vacation, things had completely changed. Alain Charbonneau, who had become her fiancé, insisted on sharing the management duties with Angélil — and that included his 20 percent commission. It was the classic story, and all but inevitable. The bonds between a manager and his artist can be very strong, very close and completely exclusive. A jealous lover often won't accept the fact that another man is looking after the career of the woman he loves. The history of show business is full of terrible conflicts between managers and spouses.

Angélil's answer came quickly. He didn't want any associates. Ginette Reno was in a difficult position. She offered him a one-time payment of

$15,000 for the preparation and production work he'd done for the album they were about to record in Paris. That wounded Angélil's pride, and he refused. A few days later, Ginette Reno won five Félixes at the ADISQ awards. Angélil was both frustrated and proud. He was responsible for a good part of her success, yet he wouldn't be enjoying it with her. He had put Reno in contact with a French songwriter and producer, but he wouldn't see the pleasure — and the rewards — that it would bring.

Lady Luck seemed to have left Angélil. He made a quick trip to Las Vegas, where he spent three days losing money. He began to understand that life was made up of series and sequences — runs of good and bad luck. In gambling, like in the rest of life, there are hot and cold streaks. And René Angélil was on a losing streak. He didn't feel like playing anymore; he'd lost faith.

He began considering getting out of show business altogether. He would study law instead. Anne-Renée backed him up in that choice. She was co-hosting a show called *Les Tannants* on French TV and making enough money to support the family. He'd always dreamed of being a criminal lawyer like Perry Mason. He'd talked it over with friends like Marc Verreault, Paul Sara and Jacques Des Marais, who was a lawyer himself. They understood and approved of his decision. There was nothing more he could get out of show business. Or so he thought.

The *Falling Into You* Tour
Brussels, June 20, 1997

The Crowd

To do his job well, Patrick, René Angélil's oldest son, has to know like the back of his hand the places where Céline performs. And that includes colossal arenas and amphitheaters like the Stade du Roi-Beaudoin in Brussels, Belgium. It's four o'clock in the afternoon, and despite the steady rain, the crowd has begun to stream in. Mostly young people fill the field level. They'll watch — participate in, really — the show standing up. They'll dance and sing and react to every note with intense joy. It will be a spectacle to see.

There's nothing like a crowd on its feet to make a show really take off. That's why all performers try to get the audience out of their seats. When people are standing, they're much more receptive than when they're sitting down. When a concert hall is too comfortable, it can be a tough place to play. People slump down in their seats and wait. They watch the show like they're watching TV. Almost everywhere in Europe, people stand on the main floor because there aren't any seats. And that changes everything.

Some people are carrying umbrellas and wearing raincoats that shine in the lights, making for a very colorful landscape. Others have binoculars around their necks, and some are holding rectangular plastic and cardboard boxes — periscopes so they can see over the top of the crowd. The party has begun. The music is very loud: Jamiroquai, the Stone Roses, Oasis, an old Rolling Stones' hit, a Cabrel song. By six o'clock, the stands have started to fill up. There are now more than sixty thousand fans in the stadium.

Early this morning, Patrick began to familiarize himself with the place: the passageways, the safety exits, the light and sound areas, the service sheds, the staircases, the corridors and hallways, the catwalks and walkways that run under the stands. He introduced himself to the security people who run messages and control the doors. He can move freely throughout the stadium and in all its storage areas.

When the time comes, he'll go and fetch the lucky winners of a contest who've come all the way from Montreal to meet Céline Dion. He'll escort them through the corridors to meet her. They'll be photographed with her, and she'll ask them what's new back home. Some of them will giggle, while others will cry with happiness. Then Patrick will take them back into the stadium. A few minutes before the show begins, he'll escort invited guests and members of the entourage to their reserved seats. Finding your way in a stadium or crowded amphitheater is never easy. There are barriers everywhere and locked doors. On the main floor where the light and sound boards are located, it's easy to get swept away in a human tide. Patrick loves that world: the currents, the movements, the surges. After all, he's an expert scuba diver!

Everyone in the crew and the entourage — nearly one hundred people — wear a pass around their necks. A brightly colored plastic badge with Céline's picture and the words "Falling Into You around the World" that form a halo around her head is the last of a series of passes since the tour will be over in a few days. The design of the pass had to be changed several times so that it couldn't be forged.

Fan club members have their passes too and special buttons that Patrick hands out so that they can recognize each other. Excellent seats are always reserved for them. Patrick helps them find their way through the corridors, and sometimes, before or after the show, they can catch a glimpse of Céline or even speak to her.

Like Sylvia the accountant and Dave, Barry and René — who always have hundreds of calls to make, Patrick has his office in a makeshift cabin behind the stage. He stays there during the entire show, and actually rarely sees any of it. Neither does Sylvia. Nor Manon who looks after the souvenir counters. Nor Loulou who oversees the wardrobe. Nor Kiwi and Vignola who are busy with their monitors and their computers. Nor the dozen or so technicians who look after the stage, the technical operations, the materials and the musical instruments. Nor the girls who work for Snakatak, preparing the food that will be put on board the buses in which the technicians and musicians will travel tonight. While the show is in progress, some thirty people are at work in the shadows, in the belly of the beast that is the concert hall, each one busy with his or her job. The show could not go on without them.

Chapter Nine
It Was Only a Dream

A melody had been running through Thérèse Dion's head. One evening, when the children were in bed with the house tidied up, she sat down at the kitchen table with her cigarettes, a pencil and a few sheets of lined paper torn from one of Céline's school notebooks. She began to hum a melody, and the words came to her quite naturally.

Dans un grand jardin enchanté
Tout à coup je me suis retrouvée
Une harpe, des violons jouaient
Des anges.

(I awoke in an enchanted garden
Suddenly there I was
Angels were playing music
Violins, a harp.)

She went to bed happy that night; she had found something she liked. But when she read what she'd written the next morning, she wasn't satisfied at all. She began working on her song again. Around the middle of the afternoon, her son Jacques stopped by the house. Thérèse explained the problem to him. Like his older brother Daniel, Jacques had an incredible ear for music and an extraordinary memory for sound. He could recall the scores for every instrument in a recording he'd heard only two or three times. When he left the house, he had Thérèse's melody in his head too. Returning a few hours later, he had polished the music, but something still didn't work in the chorus. Céline, who was washing the dinner dishes, listened to it and wrinkled her nose.

"Find something better, then, if you're so smart," her mother told her.

Fifteen minutes later, Céline told Jacques and her mother that she'd found something. She'd found the missing link between the chorus and the verses. The next day, they recorded the song in the kitchen, with Jacques accompanying Céline on the guitar.

Back then, Céline had a manager, Paul Lévesque. He handled the rock group Mahogany Rush, whose virtuoso guitarist Frank Marino was often compared to Jimi Hendrix. Lévesque also managed the group Eclipse; Michel Dion had joined them to form The Show. Lévesque first heard about Céline through his carpenter, who was Ghislaine Dion's father-in-law. But he wasn't interested in meeting her. In Quebec, they already had a singing child star, René Simard, and Lévesque's tastes ran more toward male, guitar-powered, American-style rock and roll. He had no use for sweet-sounding ballads.

All the same, in the summer of 1980, he went to see Céline sing at the Repentigny Golf Club. He was astonished. Céline was doing remakes of songs by Ginette Reno and Olivia Newton-John, popular tunes among the younger set. "She probably didn't understand a single word of those songs," Lévesque recalled. "After all, she was only twelve. But she really knew how to sing. She knew how to move people. And she had energy enough to bring down the house."

A family meeting was quickly called, and a management contract was signed between the two parties on December 5, 1980. Lévesque, though only twenty-eight, was orderly, careful and responsible. He respected the rules, the established values and the traditional way things were done. He promised to find Céline a good record company, a competent producer — everything she needed to become a star. But from the start, there was a basic cultural incompatibility between the Dion family and Lévesque which made everything complicated. He was shocked by the disorderly way that the Dions lived. They went to bed late, even Céline. She often missed school, and no one in the family seemed to care. As far as the law was concerned, Céline's young career was not allowed to interfere with her studies in any way. Lévesque was worried. What if the teachers at her school complained of her truancy? What if that led to his contract with the family being cancelled? He decided to send a registered letter to the Dion parents urging them to make sure their daughter went to classes every day. Obviously, that didn't help relations between the two parties.

Nonetheless, Lévesque had demos made for three songs: "Chante-la ta chanson," (a remake of a Jean Lapointe tune) "Ce n'était qu'un rêve" and "Grand-maman" (the last two written by Céline's mother Thérèse). The demos were produced by Georges Tremblay at the Pélo Studio in Longueuil, a Montreal suburb. But Lévesque was unable to get anywhere with these demos; no record company was interested. Actually, Lévesque didn't know how to place his artist. He didn't know what material to put in her repertoire and what category she belonged to. During that winter, at Mrs. Dion's urging, he finally agreed to contact René Angélil, and he sent him the demos. But Angélil never responded.

In the spring of 1981, Michel Dion called Angélil about Céline's demos. Angélil knew Michel Dion from the days when the latter was the singer for The Show. Angélil knew that the Dions were a musical family, and that Michel was nobody's fool when it came to popular music. René promised Michel that he'd listen to the demos, but when Michel told him that the tape contained songs sung by his twelve-year-old sister, Angélil reminded him, "We've already got a girl who's a singing child star."

Michel Dion was ready for that. He told Angélil that Céline was completely different from Nathalie Simard, René Simard's sister. "There are only three songs on the tape. It'll take ten minutes of your time. And it might change your life," Michel said.

Angélil had all but given up on show business after the rejection by Ginette Reno, and he was seriously considering becoming a lawyer. But he had nothing to lose, so he listened to the tape. Ten minutes later, he called Michel back and asked if his sister could come and see him.

"When?" Michel asked.

"Now."

They set a meeting for that same afternoon. Around two o'clock, the Dion girl showed up with her mother. Céline was a tiny little thing, painfully shy, badly dressed, not very pretty, with buck teeth, a pointy chin and very thick eyebrows. But her eyes were extraordinary — big brown eyes brimming over with intelligence that took in everything. Angélil spoke to her gently. The little girl said, hoping to please him, that her favorite singer was Ginette Reno, and that she knew all Reno's songs by heart, and that she'd even seen her once at the Place-des-Arts in Montreal.

He asked her to act as though she were on stage at the Place-des-Arts. She told him she was used to singing with a microphone, or an imitation of one. Angélil handed her a pencil. Céline stood up, took a few steps back and began to sing "Ce n'était qu'un rêve" ("It Was Only a Dream"). It was as though she were standing on the stage of a world-class hall. It was as if she really *was* at the Place-des-Arts. Her eyes were focused on the upper balconies above Angélil's head. He sat there at his desk and couldn't believe his eyes or his ears. That little girl had everything: the instincts, a powerful voice, a presence.

Angélil started to cry. The voice he heard was incredibly touching. He was so impressed that when the girl stopped singing, he couldn't even speak or remember her name. Was it Christine or Céline or Cécile?

Angélil decided then and there that he'd never be a lawyer. He told Mrs. Dion, "If you trust me, I guarantee you that in five years, your daughter will be a big star in Quebec and France." He didn't dare say "throughout the world." No one in French Canada had real contacts in the big leagues of American show business. No one in Quebec had a machine powerful enough to launch an artist onto the international scene. The only frame of reference was Ginette Reno. She was a huge hit in Quebec and might still become a big star in France.

Angélil had long thought that there had to be a way to reach the big markets on Broadway, in Hollywood and Las Vegas. For instance, hockey players such as Guy Lafleur, Jean Béliveau and Maurice Richard were popular with Americans. But in show business, except for the odd breakthrough in France (often the result of government backing), Quebec artists never made it big outside of their home province.

Mrs. Dion wasn't surprised by Angélil's enthusiasm — in fact she seemed to have expected it. She talked about her family, about her kids who were already performing and even about the Vieux Baril nightclub where Céline had first started.

Suddenly there was a knock at the door.

"That must be Gilles Cadieux," Mrs. Dion said to Angélil. "I asked him to come. I wanted you two to talk."

Cadieux was Paul Lévesque's associate, with whom the Dion parents had signed a five-year management contract in their daughter's name. Though he was disappointed to discover that there was someone else involved with Céline, Angélil got along quite well with Cadieux. But he did make one thing absolutely clear. If he, Angélil, were going to look after Céline Dion, he would have to be free to draw up her career strategy and make promotional plans for her without having to justify or argue his decisions with anyone.

He played "Ce n'était qu'un rêve" for Anne-Renée and she was bowled over too. "You're good at what you do," she told him. "If you think this kid's got talent, then show the world. The decisions are yours to make."

A few days later, Angélil met Paul Lévesque to seal the deal. He had contracts prepared by his lawyer friend Jacques Des Marais, and he got down to work. The little Dion girl was his lifesaver, his last chance, his wild card.

He would bet everything on Céline, his lucky number. Since she was a lot younger than he was, he could spend his life in show business, in his country. He had more experience than all the other managers he knew. He'd been on stage, he knew the nightclubs, the recording studios, the world of records. He had contacts in France and everything he needed to succeed. He'd have been able to put Ginette Reno in the big leagues, if only she'd trusted him.

Only a few weeks earlier, he was ready to leave show business. Reno was a rejection for Angélil, but in the long run, it had beneficial results. If Ginette Reno had stayed with him, he would have never been able to accept the providential offer he was made several weeks later. That offer laid the groundwork for the young singer who was soon to not only take Reno's place, but bring him the kind of success that surpassed even his wildest dreams.

Angélil asked pianist Daniel Hétu to redo "Ce n'était qu'un rêve" in the studio so he could have Eddy Marnay listen to it. The two men hadn't seen each other since their break-up with Ginette Reno, but René believed that their friendship hadn't been compromised. "Eddy is the most sensible, intelligent person I've ever known," he said to Anne-Renée. "I'm sure he's going to love Céline."

When he talked to Marnay on the phone, he didn't tell him that this extraordinary singer he'd just discovered was only twelve. He was afraid, and not without good reason, that Marnay would think he was grasping at straws. He described her moving her voice, its strength, its unique quality. Eddy listened and said, "I'll be in Montreal in two weeks. I'll listen to your singer then."

When Angélil picked up Marnay at Mirabel Airport and drove him straight to his office, on the elevator ride up, he confessed that his discovery was only twelve. Then he played the recording of "Ce n'était qu'un rêve" that Daniel Hétu had prepared. Marnay was won over.

Marnay was wildly enthusiastic. Not only did the strength of her voice impress him, but so did its content, its vibration, the emotion it aroused in him. "I've never heard so much feeling and experience in such a young voice," he remarked. "Her voice is still too tight and a little nasal in the higher register, but that's to be expected at her age. We can correct it."

The fact that Céline came to Angélil with an original song impressed him too. It's difficult sometimes to judge how good a singer is when she's doing a song that's already been recorded by other people. The young Céline Dion had actually created "Ce n'était qu'un rêve," revealing true musical talent in the process. Many singers with great voices can't ever create their own songs. They imitate, they copy, they parody other singers. Eddy Marnay quickly saw that Céline had real creative talent. She wasn't imitating anyone.

"In her voice, we heard the true image of her soul," he would say later.

That evening, he told Mia, "This is a turning point in my life."

Together, the idea for a song came to them. It was called "La voix du bon Dieu" — "The Voice of Heaven." The next morning, Eddy called Angélil, who was still in bed, and told him he had written a song the previous night. He had the words and the beginning of the music.

Les mots pour consoler, les mots pour l'amitié
Ils sont encore plus beaux quand on peut les chanter.
C'est un philtre magique
Ce don de la musique
C'est un très grand cadeau que le ciel nous a fait.
On a tous a peu la voix du bon Dieu
Quand on rend les gens heureux.

(Word of comfort, words of friendship
Are more beautiful still when they're sung.
The gift of music
Is a magic potion
A wondrous gift bestowed by heaven.
The voice from above is within us all
When we make other people happy.)

"With that song," Marnay declared, "I wanted to put Céline on a higher level right from the start and give her a high-class image in people's minds. The way I saw it, I was taking responsibility for a kind of treasure that came more from the Lord than from men."

Angélil reacted the same way. And so did Paul Lévesque, who had sought out the best record producer for her. "She has a way of making that happen," Marnay said. "Not only because of her voice, but because of her very being. Among all the people who've worked with her, no one has ever tried to take that away from her."

Angélil treated her like a star from the very start. He knew he couldn't make her sing just anything. Everything she recorded would have to be distinct, different, exceptional.

When he was a schoolboy in Algiers, Eddy Marnay wanted to be a singer. He studied voice for some fifteen years. He had a good sound and good pitch, but his voice didn't arouse people. So he began writing for other singers.

Céline was definitely impressed by this polished, cultivated man who spoke in such fine French. She realized she could learn a lot from him: singing, life, the French language, even good manners. She drank in his every word.

Céline reminded Marnay of Barbra Streisand. He had known her when she was a young, inexperienced girl, a real diamond in the rough. She was older than Céline, but she had that same inexhaustable hunger for knowledge. In Paris, Barbra kept asking Marnay questions about the city's architecture and its famous inhabitants like the writer Victor Hugo, and political figures like Napoleon and Haussman, and actresses like Sarah Bernhardt. Céline, too, wanted to learn.

"She had a magnificent voice, and she could already master it in a most remarkable way," Marnay remembered. "And she had another quality: she knew how to listen. She simply wanted to learn how to sing better."

Céline loved singing and was a musician at heart, but she would sometimes forget to articulate and correctly pronounce her phrases. Marnay picked up on it right away. Sometimes she drowned the words beneath the music and her singing style. He decided to teach her how to weigh her words and evaluate their meaning. Some were to be clearly separated, while others were only bridges between two ideas or were there just because of their sound. "If you breathe before this one, its emotion will be stronger. If you hold this word as long as you can, you'll get a dreamy effect."

He showed her how to use breathing and pauses to shape a piece of music. He taught her how to give words their meaning and full emotional content and link them to the music so they would sound just right, so that the vowels and consonants would carry the note and make it vibrate longer — to marry the colors of the music.

Céline was now a lot more extroverted and a lot less reserved than that shy, scared little girl he'd first met. He was charmed by the unconditional love she had for her mother. Often, when someone asked Céline a question, she would defer to her mother. When she did give an opinion, she immediately checked her mother's reaction.

Marnay start composing, stimulated by "the Voice of Heaven" and by Thérèse and Adhémar Dion, that enterprising, intrepid couple who had raised a family of fourteen. Marnay had never seen or even heard of such a thing: fourteen children! The Dions had enough energy to have fourteen more. They loved life unequivocally and they had a passion for action. He listened to their stories for hours on end. They were fascinated with him as well. A foreigner, let alone a Frenchman, had never shown them any interest before. But Marnay wanted to know everything about them: the parents' lives when they were young, how they'd met, how many times they'd moved. One evening, Mrs. Dion let slip that she and her husband — with the older kids' help, of course — had built the house where they lived. Marnay leapt to his feet, took his head in his hands and wondered out loud, "My God, this is fabulous! And the woman writes songs on top of it all!"

The first press release ever issued about Céline Dion was published in the spring of 1981. It revealed that she'd turned thirteen on March 30, and that besides singing, her favorite activities were horseback riding, waterskiing and fashion.

"She is working with an excellent team," the press release said. "Her two managers, Gilles Cadieux and Paul Lévesque, keep tabs on her, while her producers, Daniel Hétu and René Angélil, are teaching her all the ins and outs of the trade."

Céline was being talked about in public even before she had a true show business existence. She still didn't have a song on the market. She'd never been heard on the radio, never been seen on TV.

Lévesque enrolled her in drama classes with Yolande Guérard, an experienced, classically trained singer who was a little on the old-fashioned side. But Angélil set his sights on wider horizons. He talked about Paris, and Hollywood, and Broadway. The Dions dreamed along with him. They trusted him.

You could feel his influence in the next press release. Céline spoke in her own words, and said she was broadening her education to be able to work in the movies and play in musicals. "I want to learn how to step onstage and make that stage my own."

Angélil realized he had to position her — he had to provide her with truly original material. With the help of his wife Anne-Renée, Mia, and Marnay, he discovered a new niche: the world of teenagers.

"Her songs reach out in different directions," the press release said, "though most of them speak openly about teenagers and their daily lives, their happiness, their pain and most of all, their hopes."

That was the way René Angélil worked. He was counting his chickens before they were hatched. The songs he described weren't even written yet. Marnay was working on them that spring in 1981. He was trying to understand what went on in the head and heart of a thirteen-year-old child.

In reality, René Angélil was slowly becoming Céline's manager. Officially, he was still only the record producer. Since Lévesque was busy with his rock groups, Angélil insisted on sharing management duties for Céline's career. He wanted to be the only decision-maker and strategist. Lévesque hesitated, but finally agreed to share the job.

The *Falling Into You* Tour
Cardiff, November 11, 1996

The Canteen

About two hours before she steps onstage, Céline goes to the makeshift canteen. The place is filled with fifty or so people: musicians, technicians, the whole crew. There's no seating plan, and no head table. Everyone can sit where they want to, wherever there's room at the tables that seat eight. There's something for every taste: meat and fish prepared in a variety of ways, vegetarian dishes, Chinese food, pizza, pasta. Not to mention the decadent desserts. The big favorite is the sticky toffee pudding. Céline, the perfect wife, won't let René touch it because, as she says, "once you dive into it, my love, you never come up."

This food-on-the-run is provided by Snakatak, a caterer from a city in the north of England called Sheffield. The biggest names use Snakatak when they tour Europe. Sting, Paul McCartney, Elton John, Tina Turner and plenty of others. They know what all the musicians like to eat. Five girls and two guys do the work. Their cooking is modern, light, very tasty and extraordinarily eclectic. There's always someone in the band or on the crew who doesn't eat meat. Terry Bradford, one of Céline's backup singers who lived on junk food for twenty years, got converted to natural, macrobiotic food. Now he eats only raw things — grains, vegetables and organic fruit that haven't undergone any chemical or industrial processing. The Snakatak people fix special dishes for him that contain nothing that's ever been cooked, including rice.

A group on tour is like a tightly knit community, and the canteen is its social center. It's like the marketplace or the main square where all the important things happen. It's where big news is announced first. During the 1995 tour, the crew was having dessert when René Angélil announced the 1996 tour. In mid-November of 1996, in the midst of that same tour, René told them that this biography of Céline — the only one she's authorized — was in the works. That same evening, Céline, Manon and Loulou gave presents to two crew members who had just become fathers: Eric and Christophe, French equipment handlers. Two days later, In Manchester, England, they all celebrated the thirty-fifth birthday of guitarist André Coutu. There was a cake and candles and whipped cream in a can, which they squirted all over the birthday boy. And there were presents too. When his girlfriend, who'd flown in unannounced from Montreal, strolled into the dining hall, Céline began to sing, "Happy Birthday, dear André!"

When Robert Goldman, brother of songwriter Jean-Jacques and his business manager, came to meet with Angélil in Brussels, they spent over an hour locked in private discussion in the canteen. René was parked in front of a tray of Snakatak cakes; Robert nursed a cup of herbal tea. When Mégo needs to consult René (or vice versa) about changes to the show, or adjustments to the introduction, or because a song isn't working the way it should, they use a canteen table as their workplace. They grab seats at the end, and no one disturbs them.

If Céline has something on her mind — if she wants to thank or chew out the crew — it'll happen around those tables. One evening in Nuremberg, Germany, she stood up in the middle of the meal and demanded silence. She pointed out how hard she was working so the tour would go well, how she was depriving herself of a lot of things, in order to protect her voice, and she reminded everyone that she'd asked them not to smoke in the corridors, around the stage, in the offices or the canteen. And she'd meant it. The moment was very emotional. Everyone felt like a team, on the same mission, a crew all working for the same goal. Needless to say, no one ever smoked anywhere around her again.

One time — was it in Cleveland, Brisbane or Buffalo? — someone wondered out loud who had composed "Twist and Shout," a song the Beatles had recorded, and that both Bruce Springsteen and Céline had done in their respective shows. Even René, who knew a lot about the history of rock and roll, couldn't remember. In the end, drummer Dominique Messier, came up with the answer: the Isley Brothers. Céline got up and began to sing:

Come on and twist a little closer
And let me know you're mine.

One evening in London, along with Ossi Burger, wife of the head of Sony-UK, she sang a medley of old Jewish folk songs. Everyone was very touched.

The canteen is where news from home gets traded. "Back in Canada, it's snowing," someone reports. "The Canadiens lost again." A Canadian journalist passing through Cardiff brings newspapers from home. There are (in general) extremely flattering reviews of the November 1995 show in Paris that was filmed by Pulicino and shown the previous Sunday on CBC.

In the weekend section of the Journal de Montréal, *there is a portrait of René Angélil and a detailed article on the ADISQ awards, where he had received the special achievement prize. The article describes the giant screen at Montreal's Molson Centre: after Yvon Deschamps' introduction, the image of Paul Anka appeared (Anka's songs were among the first covered by the Baronnets). From Hollywood, New York and Paris, the praise poured in — from Tommy Motola, the big boss of Sony-USA and Mariah Carey's ex-husband, and several other top show business figures. From her dressing room in Geneva, via videotape, Céline sang a few measures of their favorite song, "Ce n'était qu'un rêve," then she told him once again, in front of the multitude at the Molson Centre, how much she loved him. She called him "my manager, my man, my love."*

Of course, the article says nothing about how lost René felt, and how he suffered from stage fright. As he stepped onto the Molson Centre stage, as thousands watched at home on their TV screens, he wondered what he was going to say. He thanked the Lord, his luck, his mother, his family, his friends, everyone who'd helped Céline's career along the way. He looked very much at ease as he spoke, but inside, he was trembling with fear.

In the process, he forgot to thank the Dion family. He never forgave himself for that mistake. Without them, nothing would have ever been possible. He is still mad at himself. The newspaper article, though very flattering, only serves to remind him of his poor performance.

He tells everyone at the table, musicians and technicians alike, "I should have thanked the Dions. Without them, none of this would have been possible."

But they are scarcely listening. They are too busy reading the sports or the entertainment pages, or the gossip column. They have spent six months on the road, and they are hungry for news from home. Communications are always possible through fax or e-mail, but it's not the same. There's nothing like a daily paper from home to lift your spirits.

The Corrs, the warm-up band, have finished their meal when Céline's crew come into the canteen. In less than an hour, the Corrs will hit the stage and give a thirty-five minute show. Then there will be an intermission. At five minutes after nine, Céline well step on the stage. Meanwhile, she's talking and laughing and having supper. Vegetable soup and spaghetti with pesto sauce. And a glass of plain water.

Chapter Ten
The Voice of Heaven

By the summer of 1981, Angélil had begun acting as Céline Dion's only manager. He wanted Michel Jasmin to be the first to present Céline to the Quebec public. At the time, Jasmin hosted the biggest talk show on Quebec television. He had started out in radio when he was still very young, and he quickly became the number one disc jockey. He loved the wild life, especially night life — the faster the better. When both his legs had been crushed in an auto accident and the doctors told him he'd never walk again, he decided to prove them wrong. He ended up on his feet again, and even started playing golf. Since then, he was much admired as a symbol of courage and perseverance.

In mid-June, Mia Dumont contacted Jasmin's head researcher, René-Pierre Beaudry, and convinced him to come to Angélil's office, along with Michel Jasmin. Céline hadn't recorded anything yet, but Angélil knew that every time she'd sing to the camera, she'd win over new fans. Jasmin had a way of bringing out the best in his guests while projecting a natural kind of authority. When he told his audience to listen, they listened.

René played "Ce n'était qu'un rêve" for Jasmin and Beaudry who immediately promised to put Céline on their show. That was quite an accomplishment for René, and he was very proud of himself. When he called Céline to give her the good news, the entire household exploded with excitement. That very day, Mrs. Dion began making a pink dress for her daughter — "pink's your favorite color, it suits you so well, child" — gathered at the waist with bouffant sleeves. Three long nights' work. She located some pink silk stockings to go with it. No pink shoes could be found, so Mrs. Dion bought red ones and dyed them.

Céline went on Michel Jasmin's show on June 19, 1981, just as her 45 "Ce n'était qu'un rêve" hit the stores. Angélil arrived very early with Céline and her mother. He introduced them to Jasmin himself, René-Pierre Beaudry, Pierre Sainte-Marie, the director, the floor manager, the cameramen, the make-up girl, the hair stylist and so forth.

Céline was terribly nervous. During rehearsals, she couldn't bring herself to look at the wide, cold eye of the camera that stared at her mercilessly. "You've got to dive right in," René told her. "Don't look at the monitor. Look at the camera. Act like your mother's watching you through it, she's on the other side of it. She's listening to you, and she loves you."

Céline felt like he was asking her to jump off a cliff. She was afraid of forgetting the words to the song, and afraid her voice would break. For good luck, she wanted to knock on wood, but there wasn't any in the studio. She spotted a briar pipe in an ashtray, and she touched that.

But once she started singing, her nervousness disappeared. She looked straight into the camera, knowing that through it, at least one million people were watching and listening to her. And they liked what they heard. For a fleeting, marvelous moment, she was completely happy. Several times, she let her eyes come to rest on the studio audience. In the dark hall, she saw her mother, father, brothers and sisters, who were watching her adoringly. She felt as if they were singing along with her.

She finished with a broad smile. The floor manager gave the audience the "applause" signal. But on her way to the armchair and the little table where Michel Jasmin awaited her, her stage fright returned. She knew how to sing. But when it came to answering questions from a professional interviewer — that was another kettle of fish. She didn't know what to say.

Her shyness made her sound brusque and arrogant. Jasmin innocently asked her if she'd ever taken singing lessons; she answered no. Would you like to do that? he asked. She looked at him in astonishment, as if to say that she didn't need any. She said, "No," and shrugged her shoulders. Then she said she was from suburban Repentigny, and not the country town of Charlemagne, a place no one knew. Angélil was watching the show from the control room, and his first thought was that people in Charlemagne who knew the Dions wouldn't be happy. Fortunately, Michel Jasmin helped set the record straight. But the

Charlemagne locals probably thought that Céline was putting their little village down.

After the recording, the entire Dion family crammed into the living room of their house to watch the show. Céline was still nervous. She hated looking at herself. She didn't like her face: her teeth stuck out too far, her eyebrows were too thick, her nose was too big. She hated her accent and the sound of her voice when she answered Michel Jasmin's questions.

But when she sang, her voice was strong and true. She was used to hearing herself that way. She'd spent hours singing, recording herself, then listening to the results. She didn't like her nasal tone, and she'd tried to correct it. She'd succeeded, at least some of the time, but there were still echoes of that tone in the higher notes.

For René Angélil, this television appearance launched Céline Dion's career, even though it hadn't gone very well. Céline had sung well — that much was true — and she'd demonstrated that she had an extraordinary voice. But in the charm and openness department, she had a long way to go. Anne-Renée had spent years in television production, and she set out to teach Céline the tricks of the trade.

On that same show, fate had assembled a wide variety of guests. There was Fernand Gignac (the owner of the briar pipe), singer Bruce Huard, who'd starred for the defunct group the Sultans and had given it up when he discovered God, and there was also Rodger Brulotte, public relations director for the Montreal Expos baseball team. After Céline had sung, Brulotte told Angélil how wonderful he thought she was. Thinking fast, Angélil asked him whether he thought Céline could sing the national anthem at an upcoming Expos game.

During the summer of 1981, Céline Dion did the honors several times at Montreal's Olympic Stadium. She even had a special Expos uniform made for her. Just before the first game, the announcer told the crowd that the US and Canadian national anthems would be sung by "a thirteen-year-old girl, Céline Dion." Microphone in hand, she ran onto the field, up to the mound. Facing the crowd, the players and the TV cameras, she belted out "O Canada" and "The Star Spangled Banner." She had no idea what the words of the second song meant since she'd learned them by heart. But she wasn't afraid. The crowd and the cameras didn't scare her. The anthems moved her and her voice soared.

That summer, some twenty-five thousand copies of "Ce n'était qu'un rêve" were sold. Besides the album of original songs that Eddie Marnay was furiously working on, Angélil decided to put out another record of Christmas songs. He wanted to prove that Céline wasn't just another child singing star, but a true singer with a magical voice and original material.

But that took money, and René Angélil had none. He used to have good contacts at the Canadian Imperial Bank of Commerce when his cousin Paul Sara, at age twenty-two, was the youngest branch manager in Canada. When René was a member of the Baronnets and later, when he worked with Guy Cloutier, he had done business with Paul Sara — you had to keep it in the family. Little by little, the two cousins had become friends. Paul had offered René some much-needed help when the latter was managing Ginette Reno's career. But by the time Céline had come into René's life, Paul had left the world of banking and was now administering franchise restaurants.

Angélil considered gambling, but over the past months, he had had terrible luck every time he set foot in a casino. His need for money was real, and he preferred not to take anymore risks. To produce Céline's first record, he decided to mortgage his house on Victory Street, in suburban Laval. He also went to his friend Denys Bergeron to get a $30,000 advance from Trans-Canada distributors. With those resources, he was able to record the first two Céline Dion albums in four nights at the Saint Charles and Celebrity studios.

Suzanne Mia Dumont, Eddy Marnay's fiancée, formed a PR firm called Communimage. Naturally, Angélil and Marnay gave her the public relations contract for Céline. Mia was to organize and orchestrate the two-record launch that fall.

She was also promoting Gilles Vigneault and Fabienne Thibault, who had a more "cultural" and intellectual style. They had very structured ways of thinking about songs and songwriting, and they liked to discuss their role in society and how an artist should act. Young Céline Dion had no particular philosophy or ideology. She had great dreams that were sometimes a little vague, and burning ambition. She would be the great voice that would sing quality songs.

On October 31, 1981, she was featured on page one of the entertainment section in the daily paper *La Presse* in an article written by journalist Denis Lavoie. "Céline Dion, at thirteen: Will she be the next Judy Garland?" the headline asked. For the first time, the whole story was told: her musical family, her thirteen brothers and sisters, a father who built his own house outside Montreal, a mother who wrote songs and sewed dresses, her meeting with René Angélil and with Eddy Marnay, her talent, intelligence and determination.

The article quoted Marnay at great length. It spoke of his astonishment when he first heard Céline's voice. He called her a "treasure" and said that she possessed a rare magnetism that isn't acquired through experience. She was born with it.

Like everyone else, Lavoie compared her to the other child singing stars of the time, like Nathalie Simard. But there was a difference. The Simard girl's audience was the very young market, whereas Céline Dion seemed to appeal to a wide range of ages, including adults.

"Right from the start," Mia Dumont remembers, "Céline always had the best of everything. Even if she was practically unknown in 1981, Angélil made it possible for her to record two albums and have them launched in a first-class style. He had Céline team up with some great songwriters. For *La Voix du bon Dieu* ('The Voice of Heaven'), he insisted that the launch be a major event, even if his artist was not yet a household name."

He rented the Portage room at the Bonaventure Hotel in downtown Montreal. On Monday, November 9, Mia had invited the newspapers, radio, TV, music industry people, distributors, record store owners — more than 150 people. They served canapés and wine, and each guest was presented with a bouquet of mimosa, a press kit and a copy of the album. On the front of the press kit, Marnay had written, "Thank you, Céline, for letting me hear the Voice of Heaven. I'm no prophet, but I believe that you'll ride the rainbow, and that the sun will shine on you forever. With all my love."

The album jacket presented two sides of Céline's personality. On the back, a well-behaved, gentle child whose eyes were averted, as if she were carefully listening to someone. There was sparkle in those big dark eyes, and a pout on her lips. Her cheeks were round like a child's, and her hair fell freely onto her pink sweater. But on the front of the jacket, there was a made-up young woman. In her long fingers, with pink, polished nails, she held a flowery parasol that rested on her shoulder. Her straight-on gaze depicted a self-assured, conquering look. The record cover showed her two sides: the girl-child attentively listening to someone, and the young woman who had mastered her image as well as she'd mastered her voice.

Céline has always loved to pose, especially for her brothers and sisters, charming and captivating them. The Dion family albums contain photos of a young girl in very sophisticated poses, very studied, no doubt inspired by the fashion magazines her sisters would bring home. These poses are all the more impressive because they were taken candidly, without Céline's knowledge.

Mia and René wanted Céline to sing with an orchestra, a new idea at the time. René wanted people to know she was a true artist and could sing for the most demanding audiences.

Three weeks later, in early December, Angélil launched *Céline Chante Noël.* During the winter of 1981-82, the two albums sold several tens of thousands of copies. Soon Angélil would have the funds to pay back his debts and the mortgage he'd taken out on his house. But he preferred to invest the profits in his young singer's career. On March 30, 1982, the day Céline turned fourteen, he founded TBS Productions, their first business venture. The name came from a trip to Japan he'd taken with Guy Cloutier and René Simard. In the Far East, TBS was the biggest TV station — a young, dynamic and very large enterprise. "I was aiming for the top," he said. "That's why I picked the name."

Anne-René was winding up her season with "Les Tannants." She decided to quit the TV hosting business and devote herself full-time to Céline's career, along with René. Born Manon Kirouac, Anne-Renée started out in show business at a very young age. By the time she was thirteen, she was touring the province of Quebec almost continually. Her mother went with her to every engagement. She had done countless hours of TV, cut several records, and she knew everyone in show business and television. She knew the trade inside out, and she had a lot to offer Céline, including small but important pieces of advice about how to look at the camera or the crowd and how to hold the microphone.

When she sang on Michel Jasmin's show, Céline kept changing the mike from one hand to the other. Sometimes she held it too high, in front of her mouth. "If you want to get your song across," Anne-Renée told her, "you have to look people in the eye and stop playing with your microphone." She had Céline rehearse and encouraged her when she made progress. Together, they did simulated interviews. She reminded Céline that sometimes the interviewer wasn't very good, and that she'd have to take the initiative. She'd have to say what she wanted to say, even if no one asked her, in order to get her message across. But for the longest time, Céline was intimidated by interviews.

Anne-Renée also took her to clothing shops and hair salons. Céline loved fashion; to her that world was almost as attractive as the world of music. When she was a little girl, she would watch her mother sew and crochet and knit. She cut out patterns from magazines and designed dresses and coats. She loved wearing her older sisters' high heels and fancy dresses. Whenever they could, they would buy her clothes and sweaters and shoes. With Anne-Renée, she discovered the world of high fashion, and she learned to tell the difference between designers. She learned how to appreciate style, recognize quality, distinguish between originals and fakes and between beautiful and bland. It became a passion for her.

When it came to communicating with the media, René and Anne-

Renée split the work. She took care of the highbrow media, the FM radio stations and the mainstream press. He looked after the less sophisticated media, the AM radio and the tabloids. He went with Céline on interviews. He introduced her to directors and hosts. He was charming, he had irresistible natural authority, he was calm and intelligent. People listened to him. But he was so extravagant in his claims about Céline that journalists began to talk more about his outlandish expectations and blind faith in her, and less about her voice.

He noticed how ill at ease she became whenever he talked about her talent. She began interrupting him in the middle of an enthusiastic description to tell him he was exaggerating, and that she wasn't as extraordinary as he wanted to make people believe. He would laugh. When they were alone, he'd tell her politely that they were together in this adventure, and that they shouldn't be playing against each other's interests. She understood, and agreed. From now on, when he spoke with a journalist or TV producer, she would step aside so he could sing her praises.

He changed his approach too. He always found a way to leave her alone with journalists and interviewers. Over the past few months, with a big boost from Anne-Renée, Céline had all but gotten over her shyness. She discovered she liked talking. She was open, honest and free in her conversation. And charming too. She wasn't the prettiest girl anyone had ever seen. But everyone who met her remembered her lively spirit, her intelligence, her spontaneity — and her eyes.

The *Falling Into You* Tour
Berlin, June 24, 1997

The Daily Constitutional

The clouds hurry through a low sky, and the woods heavy with summer rain give off a heady smell of ferns and humus. As they do every night, the crew marches out of the dining hall to take a half hour walk around the concert hall. They call it the "geriatric stroll" because the older members of the crew had popularized it. The pace is very slow, which is good for digestion and for clearing the head.

Paul Picard, forty-six years old, otherwise known as Mr. Geriatric or the Great Shepherd, usually decides where the group will go for its evening stroll. Most of the time, the musicians like Messier, Frulla and Langis participate. Sometimes, Denis Savage and Rachelle Jeanty take part. Some of the crew, like backup singer Terry Bradford, never go out. He'll stay in his room, listen to music or watch TV. On the odd occasion, he'll spend a few hours in a jazz club with Eric and Rachelle.

At the beginning of the Falling Into You tour two years ago, the geriatric strollers usually found themselves on busy downtown streets in the cities where they played. That was because Céline was still singing in smaller theaters with only several thousand seats. Then she started playing amphitheaters in southern United States. Later, she moved on to bigger and bigger venues. By June 1997, she was performing in Europe's largest stadiums (eight shows with more than 400,000 spectators) in seven cities (Dublin, twice in London,

Amsterdam, Copenhagen, Brussels, Berlin and Zurich). These gigantic thirty-five thousand- to seventy-thousand-seat venues are usually found in industrial suburbs, like London's Earls Court or Brussels' Roi-Beaudoin stadium. Sometimes, the hall will be out in the middle of nowhere, like Amsterdam's Zuid-oost, which looks something like a spaceship in the middle of a field. Other times, the amphitheater will be in a forest preserve, like Berlin's Waldbühne, where Céline will be singing tonight, with Australia's Human Nature, who has been the warm-up band for all the shows on this tour.

The Waldbühne was built by Adolf Hitler for the 1936 Olympic Games. It's one of the oldest amphitheaters in Europe and one of the few to blend in with the landscape. The grandstands merge with the hills, and the steep aisles are bordered by flowering hedges. It is surrounded by forests. From the hilltops, there's an excellent view of the stage far below, under its protective canvas canopy. On the other side, he tower of a nuclear power plant with its ominous vapor plume looms above the green trees.

On their stroll today the geriatric walkers move carefully through the forest. The trails are muddy; it had been raining steadily since the tour began, though not at the moment. In Copenhagen, Brussels, Amsterdam and here in Berlin, the technicians had to assemble the stage in the pouring rain. But each time, at the exact moment when Céline arrived for the sound check, a miracle occurred. In Amsterdam, the sun came out for the first time in two days. The same thing happened in Copenhagen, where so much rain had fallen on the orchestra level of Parken Stadium that the plastic seats had to be drilled to drain the enormous puddle. Not a single drop fell during those two concerts. The technicians began calling Céline "Miracle Dion."

As they stroll along, the group admire the landscape. The forest reminds them of New England — the same kinds of maples, the same lush ferns. Messier almost steps on an exotic flower that turns out to be a lady's slipper.

When they return from their constitutional, Céline sometimes asks them to describe what they've seen and done. She likes to know about the different landscapes. The crew has a game: they make up all kinds of inconceivable adventures, or tell her about unusual encounters with Madonna, Mother Teresa, Tiger Woods or Elvis Presley. However, nothing usually happens.

But once, in Denver, the wind shifted dramatically while they were out and the Rocky Mountain air nearly froze them. In Boston, one evening, a friendly stray dog tagged along with them and insisted on following them into the concert hall. In Lyon, France, a Doberman that seemed lost and dangerously skittish forced them to beat a hasty retreat. In Amsterdam, they got soaked to the skin. In Melbourne, Australia, they were accosted by an expatriate Canadian who recognized Rachelle's Montreal Jazz Festival T-shirt.

Sometimes they talk, but most of the time they walk along in silence.

Everyone is lost in thought. Often, on the way back, they blend in with the crowds around the stadium and they have to show their passes to get in. The groupies watch them enviously as they file through the stage door.

When the strollers return to the Waldbühne, they come upon a lovely sight. In the large, sun-dappled clearing that had only recently been soaked with rain, Mégo is leading the rehearsal of the thirty-voice choir (eighteen women and twelve men) that will sing two tunes with Céline that evening: "Call the Man" and "The Power of the Dream."

Chapter Eleven
Bound for Glory

René Angélil went to the Dions' house. Over the past months, trust had grown between him and the family, as they found themselves appreciating the work he'd done for Céline. Their daughter had been on television several times, she'd sung at Olympic Stadium, she'd recorded twelve original songs and a Christmas album. She was beginning to develop a following, and she already had contacts in France, where doors were starting to open up for her.

Angélil needed one final card in his deck: he wanted the Dions to allow their daughter's career to be managed by René Angélil. Lévesque would be forced to share the management contract. Mr. Dion got on the phone and very firmly told Lévesque that he wanted nothing more to do with him. Lévesque had no choice. An artist can't be legally forced to work with an impresario whom she no longer trusts.

He knew full well that relations between Lévesque and the Dion family were at a stalemate, and that his rival was in no position to manage Céline Dion's career by himself. He didn't have the contacts or the expertise.

But before Angélil could open his mouth, Lévesque's lawyer demanded for her client $75,000 cash plus 50 percent of gross revenue for the life of the contract. Angélil didn't have a penny to his name. After ten minutes of negotiations, Angélil stood up and told Lévesque that he wasn't offering any more than a quarter of his share — 6.25 percent.

In the end, Lévesque accepted Angélil's proposal. Angélil now had absolute control over Céline Dion's career. "That's the first thing you have to get," he said. "If you don't have control, then you're just carrying out other people's orders. That doesn't appeal to me."

Céline trusted René completely. He would soon become more than a manager for her. He would be her comrade-in-arms, the one she dreamed and schemed with, an experienced and loyal adviser with a vast knowledge of the show business world. A brilliant strategist, an able and clever negotiator, a confessed gambler fascinated by power, René Angélil would have made an excellent politician.

He knew the legends behind the showbiz greats: Elvis, the Beatles, Jacques Brel, Sinatra, Edith Piaf, Streisand. He knew their life stories — their ups and downs, their climb to stardom, their mistakes. He was fascinated by their managers, too, the ones who actually built their careers: Colonel Parker, Brian Epstein and Louis Leplée, who knew Piaf when she was a twenty-year-old waif and who urged her on to glory. He told Céline about the adventures of his heroes — how they'd won glory for themselves and how it had changed them in return.

Glory would be their only true goal, their grand design, and everything they did would be for that objective. Not only would they attain glory, they would also master it. And that would be a lot more difficult.

"At the time, Céline was singing songs that were bigger than she was," Mia Dumont recalled. "Her talent hadn't quite blossomed, but she was elevated by complex and wonderful lyrics full of meaning, material that Eddy was writing for her. His songs let her open up and develop her talent."

Céline was listening to a lot of American music. Often, all alone in front of the mirror in an upstairs room, a hairbrush or a pen in her hand for a microphone, she would sing Aretha Franklin or Stevie Wonder songs, faithfully reproducing their intonations. She was singing with her soul, without worrying about what the words meant.

She'd developed a regular obsession for *Flashdance*. She'd seen the movie so often she knew it by heart, scene by scene. The film told the story of a poor beautiful girl, a welder by trade, very much on her own. Her dream was to dance one day in a Broadway musical. She studied by herself until one day she meets an older lady who once had been the prima ballerina in a classical ballet company. She told the younger woman that she had enough talent, but that she needed to find the balance, harmony, beauty and strength to succeed inside herself. She had to learn without the benefit of schools; she had to not accept other people's vision of her. The older woman told her, "If you give up your dream, you die."

Céline loved that story about raw talent and wild ambition, and the necessity for absolute freedom. Best of all, there was the music. One song in particular struck her. She practiced it hundreds of times in front of the mirror, then a cappella for her brothers and sisters. Then she sang it for René, Eddy and Mia. The song was "What a Feeling." She swore one day that she'd sing it onstage.

The *Falling Into You* Tour
Bandar Seri Begawan, February 23, 1997

Prelude to the Stage

*Tropical heat is always good for the voice. After the February tour of the big Asian cities with their cold, dusty wind, everyone was feeling tired, and Bandar Seri Begawan seemed like a warm, sweetly perfumed oasis, a lovely moment of relaxation before the hustle and bustle of the Grammy awards. Céline was nominated in four categories: Song of the Year ("Because You Loved Me"), Best Pop-Rock Album, Best Pop-Rock Singer (along with Shawn Colvin, Gloria Estefan, Toni Braxton and Jewel) and Best Album (*Falling Into You*).*

Brunei is a curious little country in the northern part of the island of Borneo, very green and, thanks to oil, immensely rich. The capital, Bandar Seri Begawan, has fewer than 100,000 people. There are whole villages built entirely on stilts, charming places where the musicians, who are staying at the Sheraton, go exploring. They see no bars, and there is no beer or wine in the restaurants. Officially, there isn't a drop of alcohol in the whole country. It promises to be a restful stop.

The sultan of Brunei is reputed to be the richest man in the world. He offered Céline and her entourage two enormous mansions whose opulent architecture seemed straight out of Gone with the Wind. *The houses come complete with magnificent gardens filled with birds. The sweet songs of the birds can be heard through the open windows. And, for good measure, there are families of monkeys. A luxurious jungle stretches beyond the grounds.*

Yesterday afternoon, along with Suzanne, Eric, Dave, Barry, Manon and Gilles, a very quiet Céline toured the property in a golf cart. They encountered a variety of cats (Suzanne is crazy about cats) and a monkey family, with which they mingled. Céline's friends were very much impressed by the beauty of the surroundings and the wealth of the setting, with its swimming pool, tennis courts, gym and auditorium. But Céline wasn't using her voice. She pointed and opened her eyes wide whenever she saw something new and astonishing.

At one point, the two golf carts clipped each other and the passengers acted as though they'd just had been in a terrible car accident. Eric lay on the ground, with Céline sprawled over him, and the rest of the crew scattered every which way. Gilles took pictures of the imaginary carnage. Céline loves these little games.

Later, one of the princes drove them in a cart to see his car collection. There were Bentleys, Ferraris, Maclarens, Rolls Royces, Bugatis and Lamborghinis. Some were new models, and others were antiques from the 1920s and 1930s.

In the evening, Céline and her entourage made their way to the castle where four of the sultan's children, two boys and two girls, awaited them. Out of politeness, but also because she wanted to talk to the children, Céline broke her silence. In the great hall filled with knickknacks and statuettes, she sat with her back to the giant bay window, which overlooked a lawn as big as half a dozen football fields — the sultan's private polo grounds. The two girls, twelve and fifteen years old, were intimidated, despite the hefty diamonds that decorated their fingers and hair. The younger boy, who must have been six, was a natural actor and not at all reserved like his older sisters. He played "Here's the church, here's the steeple" with Céline for an audience of twenty charmed adults.

Then Céline told them how she'd once lost her voice on the stage of a big theater in Paris. The children listened with undivided attention. The little boy, who was sitting at her feet, took her hand when she described how she'd cried backstage at the Zenith Theater because she'd lost her voice.

"Did you ever find it?" he asked.

"I had to look for a long time," Céline answered. "Luckily, the people in the theater helped out."

"Did they close all the windows and all the doors?"

"They did that too. Then they looked under their seats, in their pockets and their purses. They found little bits of my voice everywhere."

"Even in their own mouths?"

"Even in their own mouths, and their ears. We put the pieces back together. Then everyone sang along with me."

The little prince knew that they'd left reality behind, and that they were now in fantasy. He wasn't fooled by the story, but he loved it just the same.

Everyone took pictures. Cool, refreshing juices were served. Somehow, Céline struck up a friendship with one of the sultan's wives. They talked and laughed together, and held hands as if they had been friends for a long time. Dave Platel and Barry Garber were ecstatic.

"She makes friends wherever she goes," they observed.

That's one of Céline Dion's great talents. Without asking why, she approaches people. She enters their lives and goes straight to their hearts. She moves them and makes them laugh. And she loves them, without asking why. Blindly. She almost always is the initiator. But she only expressed certain thoughts and feelings. She would never tell the sultan's family and friends that she was scared to death about the show she'll be giving tomorrow night. Even if she did, they wouldn't believe her. They all know she's sung in the world's top concert halls and won over the most demanding audiences.

The invitation to Brunei had been extended for some time now. René loved the idea. "Do you realize," he told everyone who'd listen, "just how few people have ever been invited by the sultan of Brunei? Tina Turner, and Sting, and Elton John." But he'd had to refuse. Céline was singing in Seoul, South Korea on February 21, and at the Grammys in New York on the 26th. The technicians wouldn't have time to set up the stage. "What does that matter?" the sultan's representatives asked Barry Garber. They'd tracked him down from Montreal to London to Oslo, "We'll build an exact replica of the stage. The same dimensions, with all the equipment. We'll have the screens, the cameras, the consoles. Everything." René wasn't convinced. "Céline has to rest," he said. The sultan's people made them an irresistable offer. "I'd never dare ask that much," he admitted, "not even for a giant stadium." But he still wasn't sure. Finally, the sultan's representatives promised that a private DC-8 would pick her and her entourage up in Seoul, on to Brunei, and return them to New York immediately after the show. All for an audience of three hundred. That's what's bothering Céline tonight. Her show is designed for big concert halls. She's not used to nightclubs and cabarets where the audience eats and drinks and talks during the performance. And she's never enjoyed singing for captive audiences.

I always get the feeling I'm disturbing people. Everyone is talking, laughing and having fun. Then I show up with my big speakers and my lights. Maybe they don't particularly want to listen to me. Maybe they have a lot more important things to say to each other.

Lapin sees it as a good omen. He knows that when Céline is worried, when she's tired or in a bad mood, she gives the best performance. She works twice as hard.

Chapter Twelve
Great Beginnings

Right from the start, René gave Eddy Marnay a prominent role. He wanted him to meet the journalists because he expressed himself so well. He always had a lot to say about Céline's exceptional voice, her sense of discipline and her ability to memorize words and music. Journalists loved Marnay; he was charming, patient and polite in that European way. They could easily quote him in their articles without having to rewrite or massage his words. He spoke intelligently and meaningfully.

Along with René, Marnay was responsible for the directing duties for the first album. He had written most of the material, suggested the accompanying music and chose the orchestrator. It was up to him to make things happen in France, where he was an established, well-known songwriter.

But it wasn't as easy as he'd hoped.

"The market is always so uptight in Paris," he explained to René. "When you offer a project or a new idea to the French, they always say no. Especially if it's from abroad. It's different in Canada. Canadians always start with a positive attitude."

There was another problem. The French music industry had no control over Céline. She came from somewhere else. She already had an artistic vision. No one in the record companies or the media could change her image. She couldn't be shaped or manipulated or controlled. She wanted to win over the French, yet she refused to give them any power over her. That's why, according to Marnay, it took her so long to really break through in France. But Angélil was obstinate. He wasn't going to let anyone in France take over the artistic direction.

Marnay won at least one concession from a record company. Pathé-Marconi would put out a 45 of "Ce n'était qu'un rêve," the song Mrs. Dion had written for her daughter, to which he had made some minor changes. For Marnay, the song had a powerful symbolic value. "Mrs. Dion must have said to herself, 'I don't want my daughter making it with somebody else's song, a song that's already been sung.' The whole adventure started with her. Both René and I wanted to respect her wishes."

Marnay knew, as did everyone else, that this song wasn't the usual commercial variety. It wouldn't have tremendous popular appeal in France. It wasn't going to take the market by storm. And, in fact, it didn't sell well. But as far as Eddy Marnay was concerned, Céline needed to start with a strong base and roots that everyone could respect.

Though the Pathé-Marconi people had agreed to launch the song they didn't believe in, they weren't ready to put out the *La Voix du Bon Dieu* album in France — even if it had sold more than 100,000 copies in French Canada. According to the French record company, the album needed two or three more really strong songs. As for the Christmas album, they wanted nothing to do with it.

Pathé-Marconi complained that the songs on *La Voix du Bon Dieu* weren't commercial enough. They didn't like Céline's accent or intonation. And her social image — daughter of a big family of working-class origins — was too similar, they said, to that of Mireille Mathieu.

"That's not true," Marnay retorted. "She doesn't sound like Mathieu at all. And even if she did, what of it? Mireille Mathieu sounded like Edith Piaf when she started out. Nobody, except for a few journalists, ever complained. She ended up finding her own voice. Céline Dion has a young voice, and it's extremely promising."

Marnay had been given a mission by René and Céline, but it began to look as though he couldn't carry it out. "I was in bad shape, confused, angry and humiliated" he admitted. "I started looking for a way out, for some kind of strategy. I was obsessed. I had to find *the* song that would win over the French!"

Then, a pretty melody written by Jean-Pierre Lang and Rolland Vincent popped into his head. He walked for hours through the streets of

Paris with the melody running through his head. He thought of Céline and realized she was leaving her childhood behind. That's where he would find the material to write her the song she needed.

"I thought back to my teenage years," he says. "It was like visiting a psychiatrist! I was Céline's age again. I was in Algeria before the war, in that idyllic world that Albert Camus knew when he was young. I used to spend entire days on the beach with my friends. Girls back then would intimidate us, and dazzle us and arouse the flames of unforgettable, marvelous first love — with all the hesitations, taboos and confusion that comes when those emotions are first awakened. I was always in love back then, and so were all my pals. Sometimes we admitted it — but never around the girls. We told them that a friendship like ours was sacred. Almost a half century later, I realized that ever since the beginning of time, things have always been that way between boys and girls. In the wink of an eye, you emerge from childhood and cross that barrier from friendship to romance and love. There's no reason why Céline wouldn't have experienced that, or at least dreamed of it."

Marnay wanted to get to know her better. He returned to Montreal and spent hours with the Dions. He talked and laughed with Céline. He wanted to capture her feelings, her dreams, and guess what she would have written if she could have. "I wanted to understand her thoughts and emotions. I tried to tune in to her frequency, of a girl awakening to love."

Céline may have been only fourteen, but she was very mature for her age. She had always mixed with people older than she was. She was very close to her family, much closer than young teenagers usually are. She was beginning to be known in Quebec, and with her career came a highly organized, busy professional life. Yet when it came to real experiences, she was still a very protected little girl. She had no way of expressing herself or analyzing what was happening inside her. Unlike most girls her age, she wasn't obsessed with dreams of personal freedom and emancipation.

Sometimes she would spend several days with her sister Claudette in Verdun, a working-class Montreal suburb. Sylvain, a boy who lived in the neighborhood, began to get interested in her. He was shy and very good-looking. One day, they kissed by the front door. Was she in love? Céline wondered. Did he love her? She searched her heart for clues. She wanted to love and be loved in return. But was it love she felt, or just the desire for love?

Céline was a well-behaved girl. In her head and her heart, she wanted everything to be in proper order. She always told her parents and her siblings what was on her mind. But she couldn't figure out what she felt for Sylvain. "I would observe her," Marnay remembers, "and that mixture of emotions inspired me to write 'D'amour ou d'amitié.' There is impatience and doubt in that song, and the desire to understand and know more about the world."

Et je suis comme une île
En plein océan.
On dirait que mon coeur
Est trop grand
"D'amour ou d'amitié,"
Eddy Marnay, Rolland Vincent and
Jean-Pierre Lang

(I'm like an island
In the midst of the sea.
They say that my heart
Is too big for me.)

At fourteen years old, she would much rather sing than fall in love.

Eddy discovered two more fine melodies, and he set his words to their music. One song was called "Tellement j'ai d'amour pour toi" ("The Love I Have for You") the other, "Visa pour les beaux jours" ("Visa for Happiness"). According to the agreement with Pathé-Marconi, in the summer of 1982, they began work on a new album that would be released simultaneously in Quebec and France.

On July 1, 1982, Céline's brothers and sisters, and a few wives and husbands, went to Mirabel Airport to wish Céline "bon voyage." Her mother, Anne-Renée and René were also on the plane. Céline was excited, but a little sad too. The evening before, she called Sylvain to tell him she was leaving for Paris, and that she didn't know when she'd be back. It would be better if he didn't wait for her. He didn't sound surprised. She was sorry that she'd never loved him. She had wanted so much to be in love — more than she'd wanted to be loved in return.

By then, Céline and René had good friends in Paris. There were Eddy and Mia, of course, but also Guy and Dodo who had a little restaurant on the rue Cadet in the ninth *arrondissement* of Paris. "Chez Guy et Dodo" was a warm, comforting little cocoon in the midst of bustling Paris. Almost every evening, you could find Guy's mother there, his son Thierry and a large circle of friends that quickly grew bigger. Céline's songs were first heard in this neighborhood restaurant in Paris.

A rough-and-ready fellow named Guy Morali had been the lead singer for the Scorpions, a group that was starting out in France around the time that the Baronnets were all the rage in Quebec. Angélil and Morali became fast friends. They both loved good food and drink, and they didn't mind a little outrageous behavior from time to time — like driving the wrong way around the huge Parisian traffic circles in Morali's beat-up jalopy.

Guy and Dodo had come to spend Christmas in Montreal in 1981. Night after night, in the little town of Charlemagne, they sang and played music, with Adhémar on accordion and Thérèse on the fiddle. Thanks to Céline and René, the Dion family's fortune had really taken off. They started out as a humble, hard-working family, and now, as if by magic, they were part of another world, partying with Parisians.

Though she was still hesitant and awkward in front of the journalists and their cameras, Céline was completely at ease and sure of herself in a recording studio. At the Family Sound studio, Céline recorded three songs from her new album. The first was "D'amour ou d'amitié." Next came "Tellement j'ai d'amour pour toi," the heart-felt confession of a teenage girl to her mother. More than a dozen people crowded into the studio to watch her sing. "Do you want us to leave you alone?" Angélil asked. But Céline preferred to sing in front of an audience: René and Anne-Renée, Eddy and Mia, composer Hubert Giraud, arranger Guy Mattéoni, Guy and Dodo, the technicians and the record company people. She stood in the middle of the studio, eyes on the control room. Then she turned to her mother and sang.

Il peut couler du temps
Sur tes cheveux d'argent,
Je serai une enfant
Jusqu'à mon dernier jour.
Tellement j'ai d'amour pour toi

"Tellement j'ai d'amour pour toi,"
Eddy Marnay and Hubert Giraud

(Time may color
Your silver hair gray,
But I'll always be your child
To my final day.
That's how much love I have for you.)

When the recording was over, everyone was so touched they had to wait another hour before trying the third song, "Visa pour les beaux jours."

Three weeks later, she recorded six more songs at the Saint Charles studio. The album *Tellement j'ai d'amour pour toi* came out in the fall of 1982. Eddy Marnay had written eight songs, working with his usual associates. "Le piano fantôme" was penned by Luc Plamondon and François Cousineau.

Céline's material was completely original and personal. Marnay's songs were tailor-made for a very special fourteen-year-old girl who sang of her desire to know about love, and of her attachment to her mother. Marnay wrote it, and Céline experienced it, spoke of it, sang it. He dug deep inside her to find his inspiration.

> Ecoutez-moi:
> Je veux garder ce monde-là
> Où je suis libre de marcher
> Avec des flots de rêves
> Entre les yeux
>
> "Ecoutez-moi,"
> Eddy Marnay and André Propp

> (Listen to me:
> I want to keep this world
> Where I can walk free
> With an ocean of dreams
> In my eyes.)

Shortly after Labor Day, René Angélil and Mrs. Dion paid a visit to the principal of Céline's school. They wanted a special program drawn up for her. With the tours, TV appearances and upcoming promotions, she wouldn't be able to attend school the way other children did.

Angélil was convinced that the experience Céline was gaining was at least as enriching as school. She already had a career, an impresario, an accountant, songwriters, composers and arrangers. She would travel and see the world. He knew she was extremely intelligent, perhaps too much so to find sitting in front of a blackboard very enlightening. He had watched her learn entire songs — words and music both — in a matter of minutes. She understood how the world was organized and what made it tick.

While the other girls and boys in her class spent the summer in Charlemagne or the surrounding countryside riding their bikes, watching TV or working at part-time jobs in fast-food outlets or plant nurseries, she had gone to Paris where she'd cut an album with professional artists. She had sung on dozens of stages across Quebec and been interviewed by journalists. Her songs were playing on the radio every day. She was making more money in one month than her father did in a whole year. In Quebec, she was already a star on the way up.

And there she sat, trembling in front of the principal, her mother and René. She had no doubt that René would convince the principal to let her leave school. No one could resist René's intelligent and calm strength. But when the principal took out her folder and handed her report card to her impresario, she thought she would die of shame. She probably had the worst marks in the class. Most of them were below average; some were closer to zero.

What would René think of her pathetic schoolwork? He was so intelligent and well educated. He spoke English and French perfectly, he knew math, history and geography. Céline's parents always spoke of him with the greatest respect and admiration. He had class, they said.

Céline lowered her eyes and bit her lip. She was mortified, humiliated. René must think that his little singer was pretty empty-headed, she said to herself. She was ashamed, but at the same time, she was excited. Soon she'd be out of that horrible school, and she'd never look back! She wouldn't miss anyone because she didn't have any friends there. The only happy memories she had were the times Mrs. Sénéchal asked her to clean the blackboard after class. She'd take the brush and run it over the surface carefully, never missing a spot. Sometimes the teacher would use the time to show her how to calculate a square root or do percentages. But she never understood what good that would do her for the rest of her life.

René put her report card down on the principal's desk. Laughing, he pointed out that Céline probably couldn't learn any less than she was already learning at school. She was ashamed, but she knew that when she sang, the man she admired so much was moved, sometimes to the point of tears. She realized she had a kind of power over him, and already she was thinking of ways to solidify and increase it.

Once she told Angélil that she wanted only one thing from life — to sing — until her dying day. She saw how her older sisters Claudette and Ghislaine had to struggle to be able to sing. She knew how much trouble her brother Michel was having with his group, The Show. Very early on, Angélil made it clear to her just what kind of power an impresario could have over an artist's career. "You sing," he told her, "and I'll take care of the rest. I'll find you original material, writers and composers who'll work for you. I'll rent the theaters, I'll sign the deals with the promoters, I'll hire the press people and the translators. You don't have to worry about a thing."

From that moment on, he made it his duty and his mission to make sure that Céline could spend her lifetime singing. And in the best conditions, with the best musicians, for the largest audiences possible. He realized he would have to do some long-term planning.

"If I look after her future, I'll be looking after my own," he told Anne-Renée.

This was no time to quibble over expenses, or worry about his income. He never haggled over how much Céline would be paid to sing on TV or at the Olympic Stadium in Montreal. That would come later. First, the artist had to be established. The media and the public had to learn who she was. She needed all the exposure she could get. He was absolutely sure that one day she'd be a star. Her stardom was his only goal. His sole obsession. He wasn't just looking for fleeting success. He wanted to build a career for her the way a skyscraper is built — solidly, from the ground up, a structure that's made to last.

Then something totally unexpected happened, something that gave his plans a giant boost.

The *Falling Into You* Tour
Copenhagen, June 22, 1997

Vocal Gymnastics I

The room where Céline will do her vocalizing sits at the top of the grandstands of Parken Stadium. The large bay windows overlook the back of the stage and the orchestra pit. It's six-thirty in the evening. With a little help from the sun, which finally put in an appearance after two days off, the stadium will be dry by the time Human Nature warms up the house in less than two hours.

There's a lot of action around the lighting boards and soundboards where Denis Savage and Lapin are busy programming their consoles. Poor Lapin is a little out of sorts. At this latitude — fifty-five degrees, forty-three minutes north — and this time of year — June 22 — night won't fall before the end of the show. And it won't be a dark night either, but only a filter of darkness that will dampen the sun. Those beautiful effects that he's gone to such trouble to design will end up looking rather washed out. "It's like trying to play chamber music in a steel mill," he complains. But soundman Denis Savage is happy. In an outdoor venue, if the wind isn't too strong, the sound is always purer and clearer, with no echo.

Performing outdoors does have other drawbacks. Céline and the backup singers can attest to that. Once in Denver, it was so windy that they all nearly suffocated. The smoke from Lapin's smoke machines blew back onto the stage, camouflaging the lighting effects, which rapidly changed from bright to invisible.

The sun was setting on the mountains. The view was magnificent, but it was wasted. The wind whistled into the microphones and distorted the sound. During the sound check, it blasted Céline's face. But here in Parken Stadium, the orchestra pit and the stage are well protected by the high grandstands and an arching half roof. Gatien Ouellet, Lapin's assistant, has just unrolled a long section of fabric over the proscenium arch, and the wind hardly stirs it at all.

Céline warms up her voice. For the past five years, she hasn't gone on stage without doing her warm-up and stretching exercises for a good half hour. Her trainer, Dr. Riley, convinced her to adopt the routine. He created it himself, and it's been used by a large number of singers, whether they're working in rock, pop, jazz or opera, including Luciano Pavarotti. Every two months or so, Céline visits Dr. Riley in New York. They work standing up, in a tiny studio. Pressing her with his weight against the wall, or making her cross her arms and throw her head back, he has her sing scales. With Dr. Riley, she discovered the pleasure of studying, training and hard work. She's a much better student now than she was back in school when she struggled through algebra and irregular verbs.

Dr. Gwen Korovin, her ear, nose and throat specialist, has the office next to Dr. Riley's. She studies voice physiology with him. The larynx, a hollow organ situated at the very top of the trachea, is the main vocal organ, a kind of vibrating box. The vocal cords are twin muscles located on both sides of the larynx, which is actually a box of rigid cartilage. The tension and movements of the cords determine the register and depth of the sound. But the sound itself has no form. The singer's mouth and tongue create words and understandable notes by shaping them. The skull, along with the sinus cavities, acts a little like an echo chamber, similar to the body of a violin or guitar, and it determines the tone. Using various techniques, a singer can sing from the head or the diaphragm, and the voice can be refined in the process. This is where Dr. Riley comes in.

He showed Céline how to position her tongue and cheeks to make the sound as pleasing as possible when it flows out of her mouth. He had her work on her articulation, phonation and voicing. He taught her how to use the different resonators in her chest and face.

At first, Céline sang through her nose. Over time, she had developed flawed vocal techniques. Dr. Riley's job was to get her to shed them. He proposed a battery of daily exercises, but the results wouldn't be audible for another five years.

"Five years!" René had exclaimed in disbelief.

He would have understood if she had refused. It was as if a doctor were proposing a slimming-down diet, the results of which wouldn't be visible for five years.

"You'll do the exercises every day," Dr. Riley went on. "The rest of the time, when you're onstage or in the studio, don't think about them so you won't lose your passion. But every day, take the time to do the exercises. And in five years, you'll see the difference."

Every day, except during periods of silence, no matter how tired she was or how bad she felt, she followed his instructions to the letter.

Now it's five years later. Every day, she can see and hear the results. Dr. Riley helped her undertake the long, slow transformation that changed her voice and her life. He helped her develop the fullness of her voice — its quality, richness, texture and projection. Her voice is sharper and clearer now with greater shades of feeling. Its sound is fuller and more complete. Céline has perfect control over it as well. She can bend and inflect it. She can move smoothly from one sound to the next almost effortlessly.

Her exercises aren't that much different from what athletes do before a big game. She works on breathing and stretching, bending and massaging, and her entire system relaxes. Then her vocal cords get involved and she produces pure sound without concern for notes or words. Her voice seems to wander through the scales. It will fall silent, resume again, then she'll vocalize a note and hold it for what seems like an eternity. She'll place her fingers on her nose to feel the vibration. That same note slips slowly into her throat, while she holds it like a bird of prey. It reaches her belly, deep inside her, then emerges slowly and emerges from her mouth like the flight of doves.

Céline walks through her dressing room with her arms crossed. She takes a sip of warm, honeyed water. She looks out the bay window and spots Yves Frulla behind the stage, far below, standing behind his keyboard, running his fingers up and down the unplugged instrument. Guitarist André Coutu is shaking his hands, getting the tension out, massaging and relaxing his fingers. She casts her dreamy eyes over the stadium. It's just beginning to fill up.

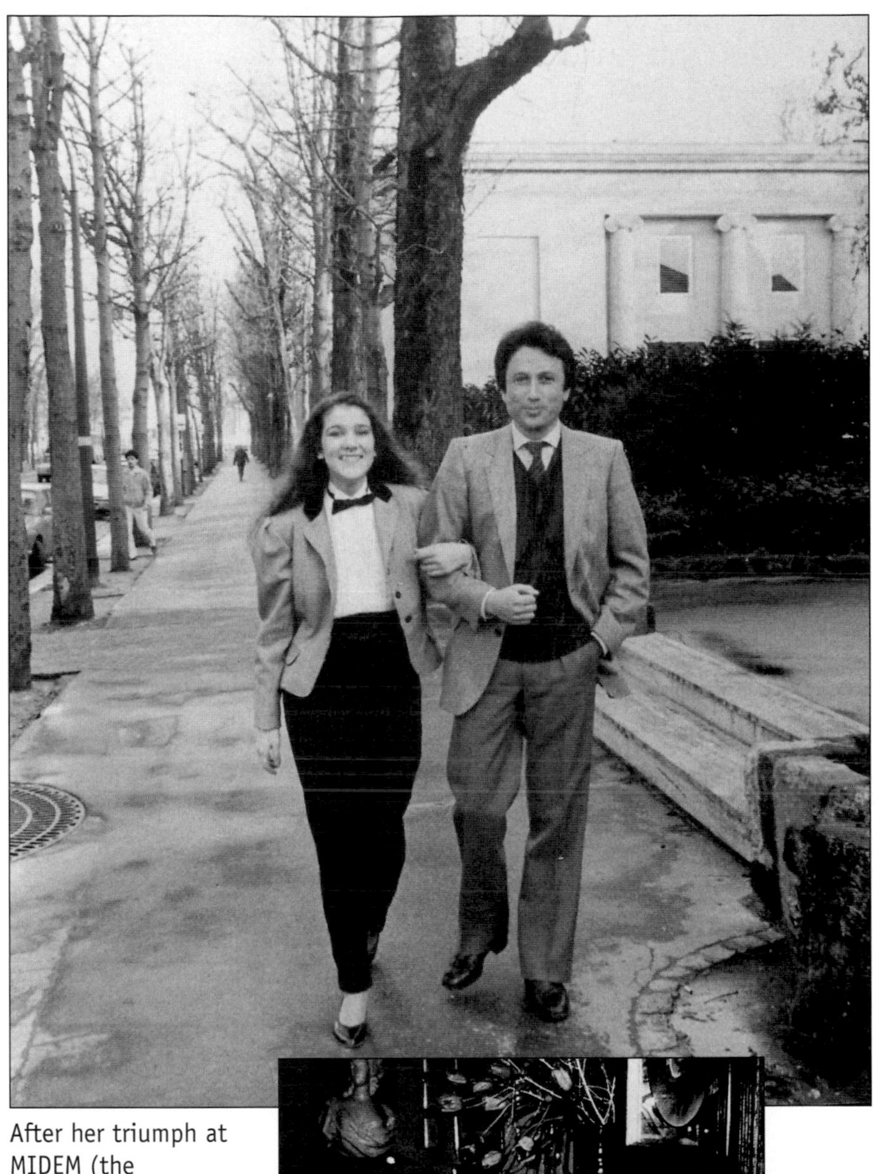

After her triumph at MIDEM (the internationally known music convention held annually in France) with "D'amour ou d'amitié" ("Love or Friendship"), she is invited to appear on the popular French TV show *Champs-Élysées*, hosted by Michel Drucker.

Representing France, she won the grand prize in the Tokyo Festival, out of 1900 contestants.

Spokesperson for the Canadian Association for Cystic Fibrosis, she is among the leading personalities of Quebec show business.

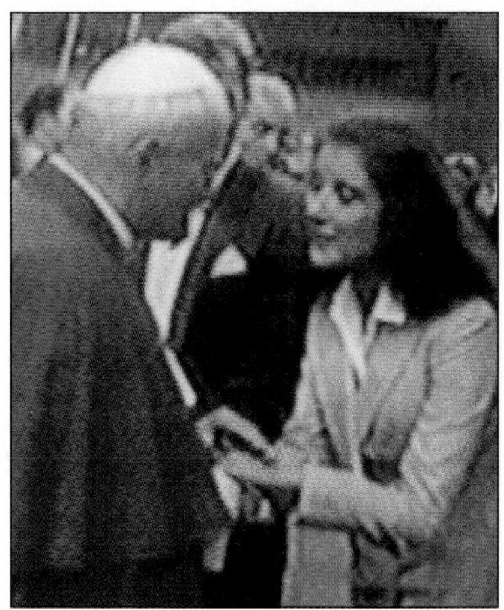

A historic moment in her career.

Along with Eddy Marnay, press agent Mia Dumont remains, to this day, close to the star.

Each year, Céline dominates the ADISQ (Quebec music awards). For fifteen years, she has been recognized as the greatest singer in Quebec.

Celine's image was still not fully developed, but, a recognized star, she was in full control of her gift.

Despite the enormous success and the professional demands of her first albums, Céline remained close to her parents.

Céline felt truly at home at the restaurant Chez Guy et Dodo, on rue Cadet in Paris.

Naturally candid and open, Céline meets her first fans.

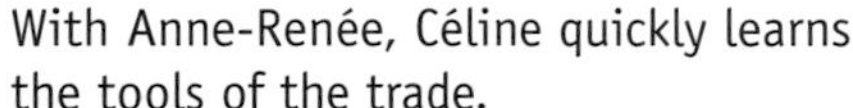

With Anne-Renée, Céline quickly learns the tools of the trade.

The Dion clan. First row, left to right: Louise, mother, Thérèse, Céline, Adhémar Dion and Denise; standing: Manon, Pauline, Linda, Michel, Daniel, Clément, Paul, Jacques, Liette, Claudette and Ghislaine.

Mother Dion wrote Céline's first song, "Ce n'etait qu'un reve." ("It's Nothing But a Dream").

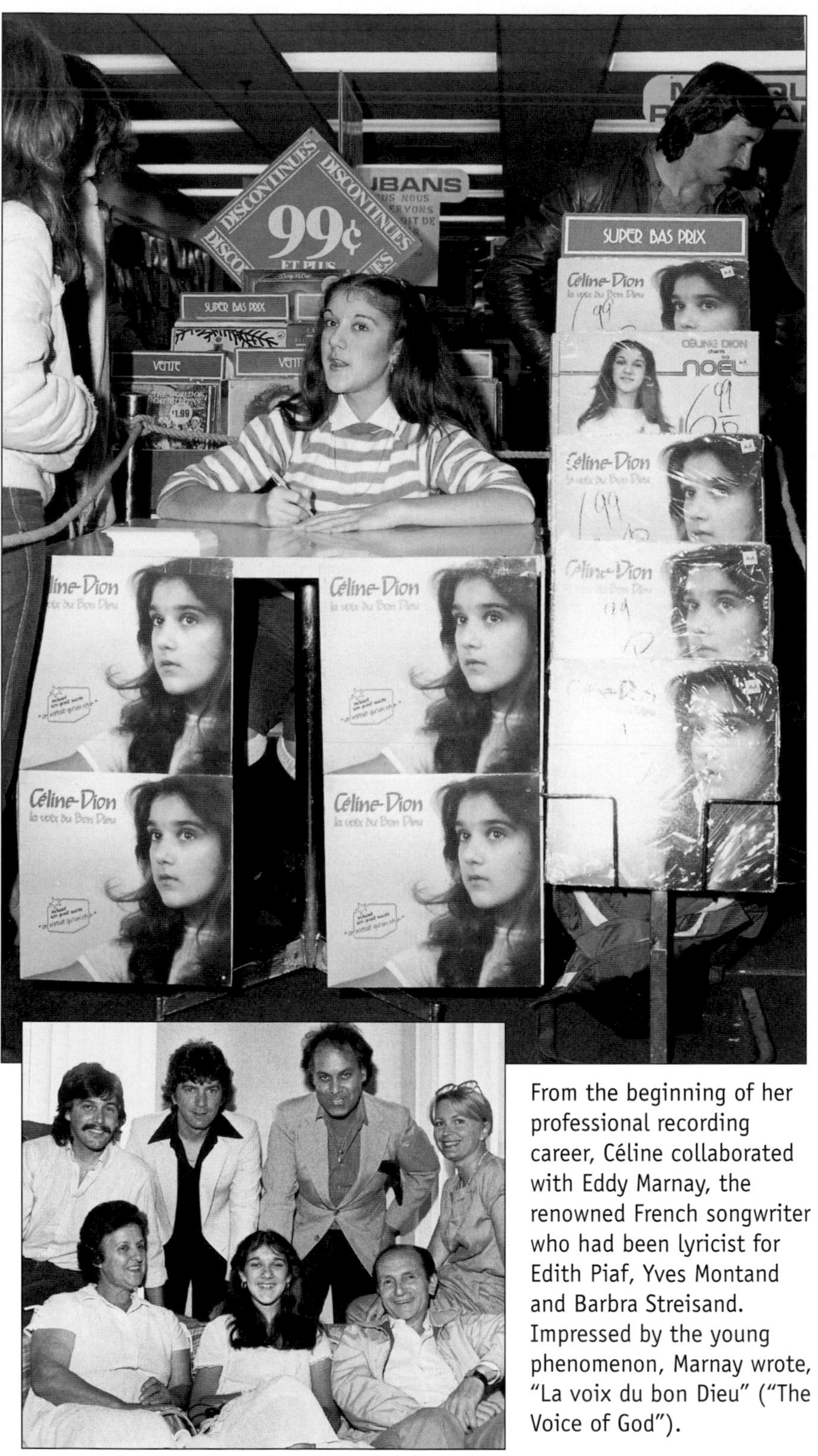

From the beginning of her professional recording career, Céline collaborated with Eddy Marnay, the renowned French songwriter who had been lyricist for Edith Piaf, Yves Montand and Barbra Streisand. Impressed by the young phenomenon, Marnay wrote, "La voix du bon Dieu" ("The Voice of God").

Céline's immense talent attracted the attention of music professionals early on.

René Angélil convinced Denis Bergeron of Trans-Canada (here with his daughter Martine and his wife Christine Lamer) to financially back Céline's first studio work.

During the era of the Baronnets, of which he was a member, René got a taste of fame and fortune.

Alice Sara and Joseph Angélil, both of Arabic background, settled in Villeray, a Montreal suburb, where René and his brother André spent their youth and acquired a strong sense of family.

René discovered the world of music through church, where his father sang, and through school, where he was part of a musical band.

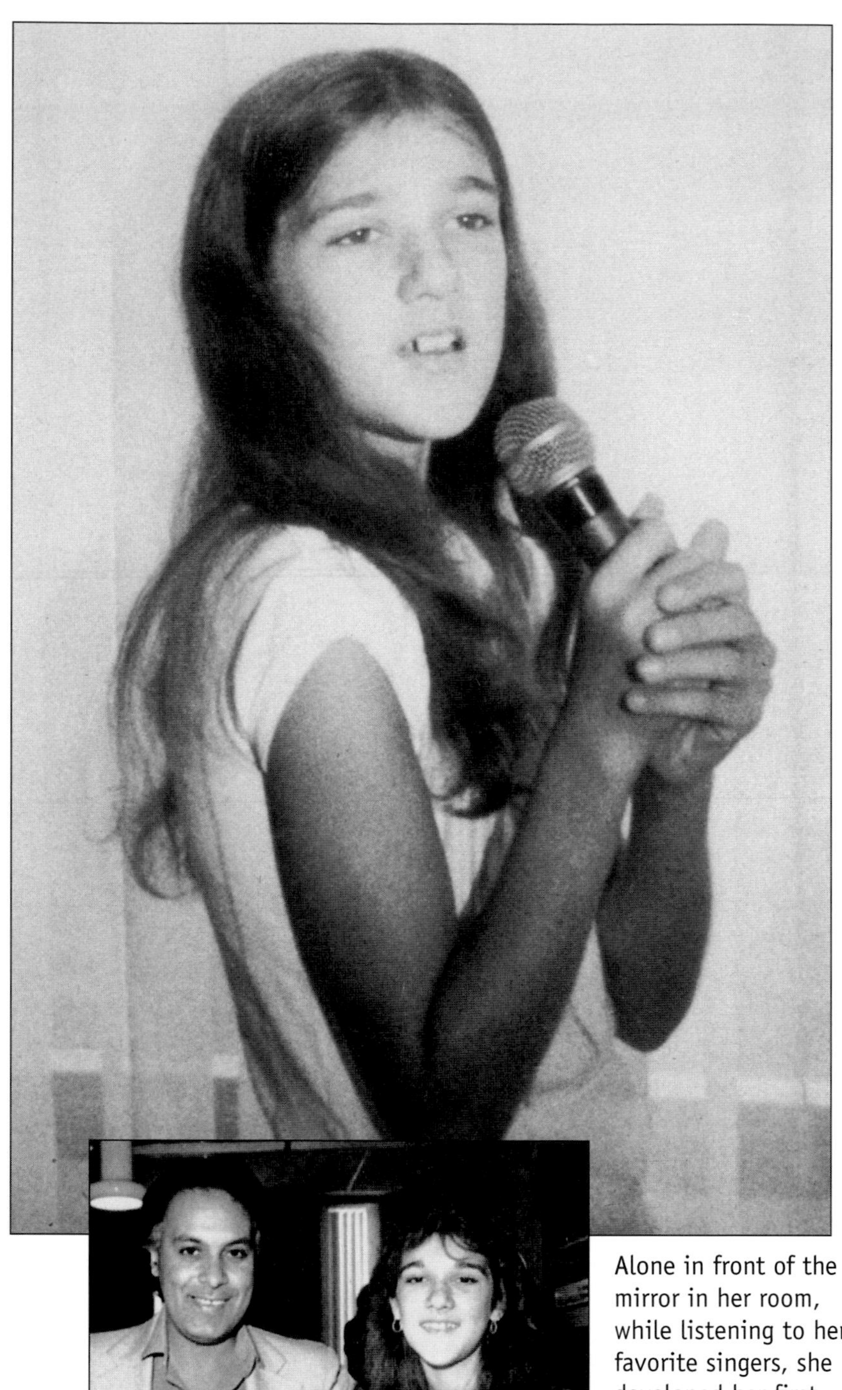

Alone in front of the mirror in her room, while listening to her favorite singers, she developed her first stage image before meeting René Angélil.

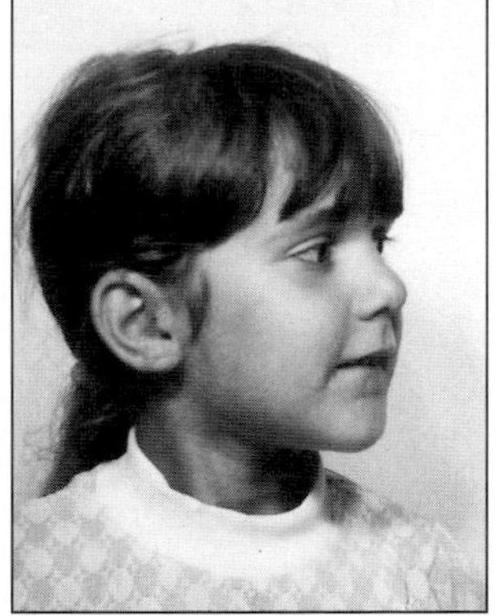

Her sister Claudette was her godmother and her brother Michel was her godfather. They already had launched singing careers. They were Céline's first idols.

School always felt like prison to her.

The Early Years

Montréal, 1982

Music was very much a part of Céline's childhood. Her family was her first audience.

At age six, she sometimes did her homework at the cabaret Vieux Baril (the Old Barrel), owned by her parents.

The Olympia is a legendary show business venue, where Céline performed for five weeks. Her show includes a mascarade, with public participation, in which Céline disguises herself as a flamenco dancer.

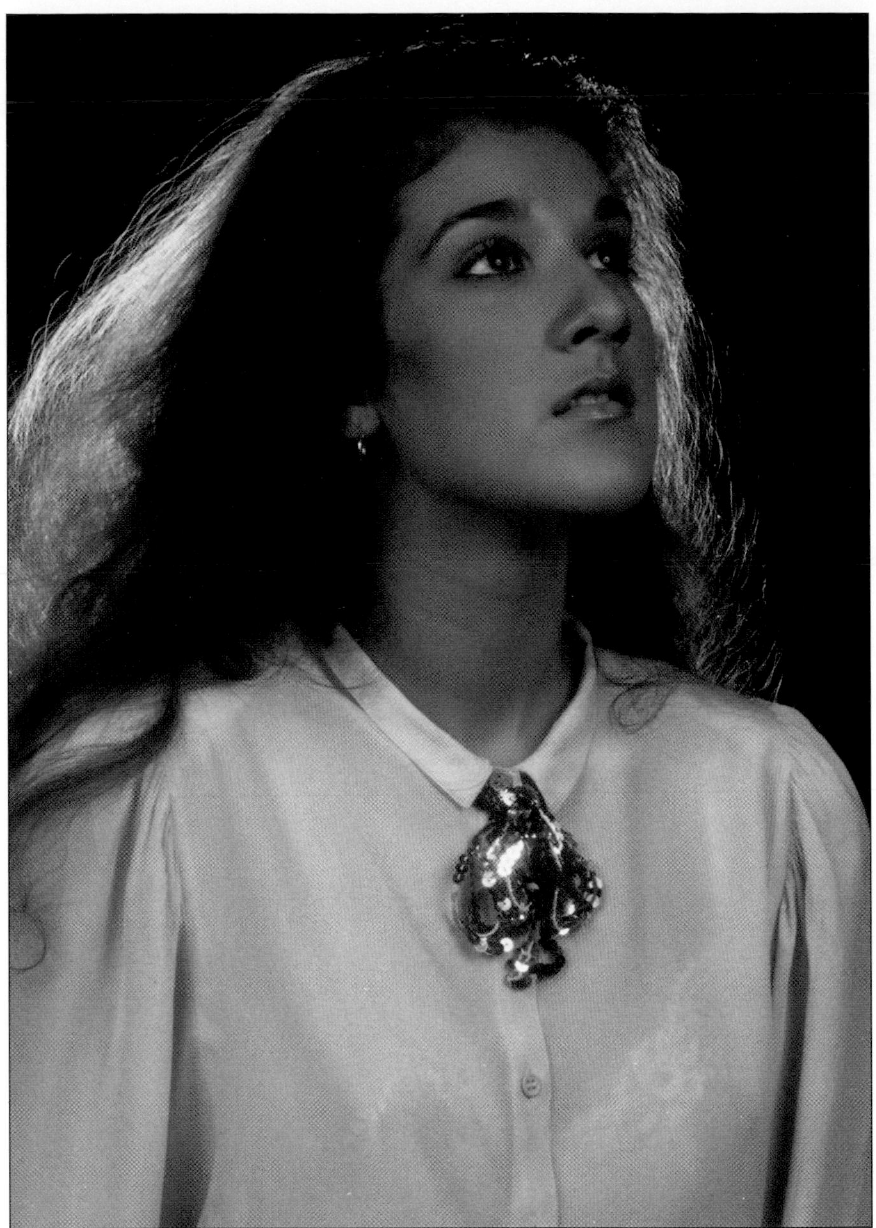

At sixteen, Céline was already an established star in Quebec and France.

Chapter Thirteen

In the Land of the Rising Sun

One September evening around dinnertime, Eddy Marnay called from Paris to say that the song "Tellement j'ai d'amour pour toi" had been selected to represent France in a big international contest the next month in Japan. Céline answered the phone. Eddy's news was so fabulous and unexpected that she didn't know what to say. "Yes, all right … I don't really know … I'll have to ask Mom," she stammered. Mrs. Dion spoke to Eddy and Céline heard her say that she agreed. Her daughter could go to Japan to sing, and she would go with her.

No sooner had she hung up than the phone rang again. It was René Angélil. He had all the details: the figures, the dates, the names. It was the Thirteenth Yamaha World Popular Song Festival in Tokyo. Thirty songs had been selected out of the 1,907 submitted by forty-nine countries.

They quickly began preparations for their Japanese trip. René, his friend Ben Kaye and Mia Dumont would accompany Céline and her mother. Eddy would meet them in Tokyo.

But two days before his scheduled departure, Eddy developed a bad case of neuritis in his back. He consulted a doctor, a chiropractor, a massage therapist, an osteopath and an acupuncture specialist. The next day, he couldn't even walk. Mia rushed to Paris to his side, while Céline set out for Japan with her mother, Angélil and Ben Kaye.

Mrs. Dion was a hard-working woman who believed that if you wanted something, you had to earn it. And now here she was, about to jet off to Japan to see a new country, sleep in big hotels and meet interesting people. A few minutes before going through the gate at the airport, she put her hand into her pocket and pulled out a pack of cigarettes. Without thinking twice, she handed them to her son Paul. "Here, smoke them, throw them away, eat them, do whatever you want with them, just get them out of my sight!" She hasn't touched a cigarette since. Céline was relieved. She'd always hated it when her mother smoked.

Céline and her mother were not very adventurous when it came to eating. Mrs. Dion was a good enough cook, but she made old-fashioned, country dishes: meatloaf and meat pies, boiled dinners, that sort of thing. It was good, wholesome food, but not spicy enough, at least as far as Angélil was concerned. In a restaurant, even at Guy and Dodo's in Paris, the Dions never ate anything but chicken and steak frites. In Montreal and Paris, René would take them to Lebanese restaurants and show them how to eat *hummus, baba ghanooj* and *shawarma.* He tried to get them interested in gambling too, anything was new.

On board the flight to Tokyo, the passengers could choose between Western fare (chicken, what else?) and Japanese food. Céline and her mother ordered the chicken, while Angélil chose the tempura, sushi and sashimi. Just as the Dions suspected, he tried to get them to taste his dinner. There was no doubt in his mind: If they tried it, they'd like it. Of course, they wouldn't try it. But he made them promise that if Céline won the contest, they'd eat whatever the Japanese offered them — even if it meant raw fish!

One night, in the restaurant at the hotel, Céline asked for a tea. Ben Kaye stood up and started dancing and singing "tea for two." Céline joined him, and they put on a real show. Everybody was laughing. Since that time, every now and then, Ben would send a postcard with the words "tea for two" to remind Céline of this happy moment of their lives.

The first round of the Yamaha Festival took place on Friday and Saturday, October 29 and 30. Céline was to appear on the Friday. Each contestant chose a number at random to determine his or her singing order. Céline ended up with five, pronounced "go" in Japanese. She performed well, received warm applause from the audience and good marks from the judges. She was one of the final ten selected for the grand finale that would take place on Sunday afternoon in Tokyo's Budokan Hall, a large amphitheater, with a seating capacity of twelve thousand, located in a magnificent park near the Imperial Palace. For the final performance, she also drew number five — "go." This time, though, because she was much closer to her goal, she felt tense and nervous.

She stood as she waited her turn so that her white cotton dress that her mother made her wouldn't get wrinkled. She noticed a coin lying at the foot of the narrow stairway that she would soon climb to go onstage. She picked it up. It had the number five on it, so she decided to keep it, just for luck. But her dress had no pockets. Instead, she slipped it in her shoe just before she ascended the steps. And as she moved toward the spotlights to sing "Tellement j'ai d'amour pour toi," she could feel the five-yen coin, her good luck charm, under the arch of her right foot.

It was the first time she'd ever sung before such a large audience. Besides the twelve thousand people who filled the Budokan, there were tens of millions of viewers watching the Yamaha Festival on television.

René had a phone installed in front of the stage. He called Eddy and Mia in Paris so they could listen to Céline and hear the crowd's reaction. He called them an hour later as the chairman of the jury stepped forward to announce the winner. In Paris, where dawn was just breaking, Mia and Eddy heard "Céline Dion" and the crowd going wild.

Céline ended up sharing the grand prize with Mexican singer Yoshio. But she earned another distinction. Impressed by her talent and charisma, the sixty-two musicians gave her the Orchestra's Special Award.

A few days after the festival, at a special gala, Céline sang five songs for an audience of ambassadors and high Japanese government officials. At the banquet that followed, she sat with her mother at the head table. After a heavily spiced soup that she managed to choke down, what she dreaded might happen, did. She was served raw fish with herbs, a little rice and all kinds of strange sauces. She remembered what she'd promised René on board the plane. Figuring it was something like the chickpea paste she'd eaten in Lebanese restaurants, Céline took a whole mouthful of hot wasabi mustard. She thought her head would explode. Through her tears, she watched anxious-looking faces swim in and out of focus. When her head cleared, everyone was standing around her. They brought her damp towels to cool her brow and handkerchiefs to blow her nose. She was offered water, sake, Coca-Cola, even sugar. Once she got her wits about her, she explained through her interpreter what had happened. Everyone burst out laughing. A waiter asked if she wanted a steak. She said no. Instead, she took the chopsticks awkwardly between her fingers and guided the sushis and sashimis onto her plate. As the Japanese looked on in intent silence, she chewed her raw tuna and seemed to enjoy it.

Suddenly she was the queen of the party. Her tablemates were relieved and happy, and went on at great length to praise the wonders of Japanese cooking. They bombarded her with questions about her family, her country, the snow and the wide-open spaces. She was delighted.

On the trip, she spent hours with her mother asking her questions about her youth, how she'd met Adhémar Dion and when she'd first started having children. It was her way of getting to know herself by discovering her family history.

With her mother's encouragement, she wrote down in her diary everything that happened every day of the trip. She described her impressions of Japan, the tatami mats, the temples, the pomp and circumstance, the perfectly raked gardens, the good manners of the people, the soothing orderliness of their culture. She would have liked to have said how much the country was like her, but she couldn't find the words. After a few lines of description, she drifted into a melodramatic fantasy that moved her to tears.

Just like the young René Simard in 1974, the victory in Tokyo turned Céline Dion into a major star in Quebec. The next morning, she was front-page news in the papers, and talked about on radio and TV. People were intrigued. Céline had sold more than 100,000 copies of her first album, but she was relatively unknown outside of show business and the recording industry. Who was this fourteen-year-old Quebec girl, and why had she represented France in a major international competition? The tabloids set off in search of the answers. Where did she come from? How old was she really? What color were her eyes? What did she like to do? Who was her boyfriend?

When she returned in November, a crowd greeted her at the airport. There were loads of flowers, stuffed frogs and teddy bears, cameras and microphones. René Lévesque, the premier of Quebec at the time, insisted on meeting her personally and congratulating her in the name of all Quebeckers. A few days later, at the Montreal Forum, she was part of a show to help rescue the airline company Québecair. Some ten thousand people gave her a deafening ovation when she came onstage. The next day, she was back on page one. Not only had she won the prize in Tokyo, but she'd charmed the Forum with her openness and the amazing power of her voice. In only one and a half years, she'd become an important figure in Quebec.

There was no better time to launch the record she'd cut that summer. It was called *Tellement j'ai d'amour pour toi*, and, not surprisingly, it sold more than 125,000 copies in a few months. Angélil was happy, of course. He could pay off his debts. And do some gambling too. But he couldn't help thinking about the record 350,000 copies that Ginette Reno had set several years earlier with *Je ne suis qu'une chanson.* He told everyone that Céline Dion would one day beat that record. So what if it would be hard to beat. He was up for the challenge! Céline would succeed beyond the borders of Quebec, and before long, she'd be a star in France. He'd show the doubting Thomases!

"If you want something to happen," Angélil said, "you have to believe in it, you have to talk it up, you have to act as if it couldn't *not* happen. You have to be absolutely convinced that things are going to happen just the way you say they are. When I said that Céline would be a big star, I never doubted it for a moment. Doubt is your worst enemy. It destroys you. A manager has to believe. And make other people believe."

Céline had changed her vision of what an artist was or should be. She wasn't at all self-centered like most of the stars Angélil had known. At first he thought it was her youth and because she'd been raised in a big family, which doesn't usually engender selfishness. And even though Céline had been the baby of the family, and was constantly inundated with attention and affection, she was not spoiled or selfish. In fact, maybe it was because of all the attention she received that she grew up without a deep-seated craving for it.

The *Falling Into You* Tour
Sydney, March 24, 1996

Vocal Gymnastics II

Céline had never been to the opera in her life, though she had heard the century's great voices on record. And she knew the buildings. La Scala in Milan and the Opéra-Bastille in Paris. The only opera she'd seen was on film, Bizet's Carmen *directed by the extraordinary Francesco Rosi. She'd always dreamed of seeing* La Traviata *or* Turandot *or* Don Giovanni *live, in a real opera house. "I'll do it one day," she thought, "when I have a little time."*

When they found out that they were going to Australia, Mégo, her pianist, suggested they go to the Sydney Opera House, one of modern architecture's most beautiful buildings. From a distance, it looks like a giant ship under full sail. The city itself is spacious and green, with the Blue Mountains on one side and the deep blue Pacific on the other.

"There's no opera playing at the Opera House," Mégo told her the day they arrived.

But they went anyway. Beethoven's Fifth Symphony was to be performed, and Barry Garber was able to make arrangements for all to attend the sold out performance. Céline was so thrilled that she could barely sit still. She tapped out the rhythm and sang along with the violins, oboes and piano. She cried with joy. The next day was a silence day, but she still felt the power of that music within her.

I don't always listen to the same kinds of music, even if it's music I deeply love. I can't say I really studied Aretha Franklin, Ella Fitzgerald, Barbra Streisand or Edith Piaf. I listened to them two or three times. But I know they all influenced me, they changed my life, each in her own way. Streisand probably more than the others.

I don't know much about Beethoven. That night in Sydney came as a shock. When I concentrate, I can still feel the music. And feel the joy the way I did that night. That kind of music stimulates me and makes me want to sing much more than any prize or award I might receive. It moves me almost as much as applause or an ovation, but in a different, private way.

The next day, she kept the sound check going for longer than usual, improvising with Frulla and Langis just for the fun of it. When the geriatric strollers leave the dining hall for their constitutional, she goes off by herself to do her vocalizing.

The second exercise barely involves her vocal cords at all. She keeps her voice in her mouth, right on her lips. That technique produces a vibrating sound, the kind of noise people make when they're cold, or when a child wants to imitate an airplane.

That exercise tells me what state my voice is in and the state of my nerves. Because it takes a lot of control, if I'm not in good shape, I'll find out right away. It's a little like an X-ray.

Céline's little vocal plane buzzes through the windowless room, a kind of bunker with concrete block walls. Then it fades into the distance.

Today, I feel good. I feel my voice close to me. Usually, when I have my period, it's not as clear, or that's how it sounds to me. But not today. Why? Who knows. There's always something mysterious to it. Some days, my voice is dull. It doesn't want to listen to me or answer when I call it. It tries to get away from me. When that happens, I go into a room with it and lock the door, whether I'm at the hotel or in my dressing room. I talk to my voice, I struggle with it, I pamper, I caress it, and in the end, it always listens to me.

The first time René mentioned singing lessons to her, her feelings were hurt. "So he thinks I can't sing either!" she said to herself bitterly. Still, she agreed. That was in Paris in 1982, when she was recording some of the songs for the second album at Family Sound studios.

Eddy Marnay took her to see an old woman who was a long-time friend of his. Tosca Marmor had been teaching opera singers of both sexes for more than a half century. After Marnay did the introductions, he left them alone. Céline was terribly intimidated. The old lady closed the curtains, sat down at the piano and the two of them sang scales for a good half hour. Then she made Céline sing one short phrase from an Italian composer over and over again. Marmor listened but didn't react, showing no emotion at all. When the time was up, she bid Céline good-bye without giving her a single word of advice.

The first session was a lesson in doubt and uncertainty. As the days went by, Céline began to wonder if she really did have a voice. She realized that those doubts would never end. In the end, she surrendered to the old lady's harsh brand of charm. After all, she valued anyone who could teach her something.

> I don't remember exactly what I was thinking at the time, but I do remember that I decided I had to trust the people I was working with. Nowadays, I know enough about show business to be able to give an informed opinion. Sometimes I question a decision, and I want people to explain why they're doing what they're doing. But in a business like ours, you can't have two captains of a ship.

She began bringing flowers for Tosca. She chose white and yellow ones to try to light up the room, which she thought was too dark. Tosca went to the cupboard and took out a scratched glass vase and filled it with water. Together, they arranged the flowers. One summer day, as the old lady was placing the vase on a low table, her sleeve rode up and Céline saw numbers tattooed on her wrist. She was so upset that she could hardly do her exercises.

That day, Tosca compared emotions to wild animals that a singer has to learn how to tame and master.

"Don't let them carry you away. But don't be afraid of them either. You must get used to them, then dominate them."

More than fifteen years have gone by since that day. Tonight, Céline will sing on the other side of the world. She often thinks about Tosca, one of the dear friends that she's lost.

Chapter Fourteen
On a French Roller Coaster

Though the Yamaha prize in Tokyo had a big effect in her hometown, the same couldn't be said for France. Since the album *La Voix du Bon Dieu* hadn't been released over there, Céline Dion was still completely unknown in 1983 in the land of the Eiffel Tower. Pathé-Marconi seemed to be behind her. They'd released a new 45, "D'amour ou d'amitié" with "Visa pour les beaux jours" on the flip side. The record went absolutely nowhere. Radio stations weren't interested in it. Neither was the public, who'd never been given the chance to hear Céline's voice. Much to Angélil and Marnay's anger and dismay, Pathé-Marconi kept putting off the release of the album.

Angélil was convinced that Céline would get her breakthrough if only the public could hear her. Desperately, he looked for some kind of stage for her — a singing engagement, a television performance, anything. Finally, he found what he was looking for.

On January 23, as a young hopeful, Céline represented Canada in the city of Cannes, on the French Riviera, at MIDEM (the Marché international du disque et de l'édition musicale), the most important trade show for the music industry. Pathé-Marconi put up posters and banners with the name of their new star in big letters.

At MIDEM she performed "D'amour ou d'amitié" in front of

3,500 music professionals, including a relatively unknown French singer- songwriter by the name of Jean-Jacques Goldman. The professionals who applauded Céline in Cannes were to become her most attentive and helpful audience. They were a kind of family for her and a source of comfort. These people can be the most difficult audience on earth. They've seen and heard it all. But if a singer can win them over, she can win over the world.

She got off to a strong start. The programmers of RTL, one of France's largest and most influential radio stations, which was closely associated with MIDEM, decided to make "D'amour ou d'amitié" their favorite song. The following week, they played it several times a day. Soon, other radio stations in the country followed suit.

Six days after MIDEM gala, on January 29, Céline was invited to appear on Michel Drucker's TV show *Champs-Elysées.* It's Europe's biggest variety show, watched by the French, Belgians, Swiss, Germans, Italians and Spanish.

Céline's team was growing fast. She had her own circle of show business professionals — what's called an entourage — a group of gentlemen and ladies-in-waiting that was growing in proportion to her success. After her stunning triumph at MIDEM competition, several new people joined her staff, including Françoise Haïck, the head of promotion at Pathé-Marconi, and Thérèse Zeidman, PR person for the Editions Claude Pascal. Along with Anne-Renée and Mia, they helped her choose her wardrobe and plan the answers to the questions that Michel Drucker and other journalists would ask.

Everyone was very nervous. Two hours before the television appearance, they were still wondering whether Céline should wear the same dress she did in Tokyo, or the black pants and white blouse that Françoise had bought for her, or the jacket that Anne-Renée loved but that drove the cameramen and the lighting people crazy.

On the big night, they got together as they always did at Guy and Dodo's restaurant, on the rue Cadet in Paris. Guy Morali, Céline and René left there at the very last minute. René, who was at the wheel, was tense and nervous. At the Champs-Elysées traffic circle, they had a fender bender. Without a second thought, he told Morali, "You take care of it." Then he grabbed Céline by the hand and dodged the oncoming cars as Morali tried to placate the irate driver. Five minutes later, a taxi dropped them off at the *Champs-Elysées* studio where Mrs. Dion, Eddy, Mia and the rest of the crew were waiting for them anxiously.

They had rehearsed the day before. Before the rehearsal, Thérèse Zeidman explained to Céline that she should be able to tell if Drucker was favorably impressed by her rehearsal by the way he acted. "After you sing, if he comes to you and touches you, if he puts his hand on your shoulder, that means he liked what you did. If he talks to you, then you've hit the jackpot." After the rehearsal, Drucker hugged her, then told her he wanted to ask her a few questions on his show. "But that doesn't mean you've won the battle," René warned. "You've got to keep impressing him. This guy's been hanging out with all the big showbiz types for years. You have to really make him feel something."

Finally, the time had come. To open the show, Drucker paid tribute to the great French actor Louis de Funès, who had just died. Then he reminded the audience that Céline Dion had been the revelation of the recent MIDEM competition. "She's going to go far," he said, looking straight into the camera. "Remember the name Céline Dion." René was sitting right next to her. He whispered in her ear, "You're the best. This place belongs to you. Everybody loves you." Then he urged her gently out of the shadows.

She stepped onto the giant set. Black pants, a white shirt, a swallowtail jacket. Then she sang "Ce n'était qu'un rêve." René stayed backstage and watched on a screen. Everyone else — her parents, Mia, Eddy — were sitting in the audience. "She was a little awkward, and she still had her baby fat," Drucker remembered. "But she sang with such power and emotion that you would have sworn she was a lot more experienced."

After Céline finished, Drucker went over to her, took her in his arms again and told her, in front of all of Europe, what a beautiful voice she had. He held her hand during the closing seconds of the show.

Angélil was in seventh heaven. But at the moment, he was in desperate need of money. Cutting a record in Paris cost a fortune — there were hotels, airplane tickets, restaurants, rental cars and telephone calls to be paid for. And because he was out of money, he was afraid of making the mistake of accepting, just for some quick cash, a booking for Céline that could turn out to be disastrous for her career. And for his career as well, since in his mind, hers and his were one and the same. "If you want to plan for the long term," he said to himself, "you have to have money. Or at least act as if you do. You have to bluff others, and bluff yourself, make yourself believe that you have what it takes."

He developed a very simple strategy. Whenever he was called upon to consider an offer for Céline, he would act as though he had a million dollars in his pocket. But at the beginning of March, notices of bankruptcy began to appear in the Montreal papers. René Angélil, "virtual" millionaire, living at 9255 Joseph Melançon Street in Montreal, was admitting that he was broke. A few weeks later, a promoter named Pierre Parent offered him $250,000 for Céline to tour the province of Quebec. It was very tempting. Some thirty shows in twenty cities, standing room only. Pierre Parent knew about Angélil's precarious financial situation, but to his amazement, René refused the offer.

"It's too soon," he told Parent. "Céline has some stage experience, but I'm afraid she'd burn out if I sent her on a tour that big."

On the other hand, René knew he had other aces up his sleeve. Finally, in April, Pathé-Marconi released Céline Dion's first record in French, *Du soleil au coeur* (*A Heart Full of Sunshine*). She had just turned fifteen. Her future looked bright, as did Angélil's. In less than two months, 350,000 copies of "D'amour ou d'amitié" were sold. The record spent the summer on top of the hit parade.

Eddy Marnay had discovered the ideal way to get his inspiration. Through the summer, he continued developing his descriptive diary, his careful exploration of the soul and imagination of a young teenage girl. As soon as he penned a few lines, he would call her. Once he telephoned from Mirabel Airport; he didn't want to wait until he got into town. "Listen to this," he told her.

> Si je dois courir le monde
> Mes pas me ramèneront
> Toujours sur les chemins de ma maison
>
> "Les chemins de ma maison,"
> Eddy Marnay and Patrick Lemaître

> (If I have to roam
> My feet will lead me back
> Always on the pathway to my home.)

The words came to Marnay in the airplane between Paris and Montreal. He had begun thinking of Céline as his inspiration, his muse, his subject matter. She had started a life of travel, first throughout Quebec, then to Europe. Marnay knew her very well by now. He knew she was attracted by the bright lights and the romance of the stage, yet she missed her family and those she loved the most tremendously. No doubt she'd understood by now that the price of her success was to slowly lose contact with those who'd known her from birth — her first and most loving audience. She would have to leave the family circle and live like an exile, on her own. Marnay knew that Céline would be spending a lot more time in France. He'd been told a few days earlier that she'd be a special guest that autumn at the Pathé-Marconi annual meeting in Paris, where she'd receive a gold record for having sold 500,000 copies of "D'amour ou d'amitié." By the time the airplane touched down at Mirabel, the song "Les chemins de ma maison" was all but written.

"In those days," remembered Eddy Marnay, "she and I were one. We lived through each other and for each other. She knew I was observing her. She was like a model posing for a painter: fully trusting, completely honest, obedient and attentive. Her sense of trust was magnificent. She was sure of herself, her talent and her strength."

Her next album, *Les chemins de ma maison,* was produced with greater technical and financial resources. There was a full orchestra conducted by Alain Noreau, with woodwinds, strings, backup singers and sophisticated arrangements. In early June, five songs were recorded at the Saint Charles studio in the Montreal suburb of Longueuil. Five more songs were committed to vinyl at the end of the month at the Montmartre studios in Paris in the middle of a heat wave. Pathé-Marconi's PR people invited journalists to the recording sessions. *Marie-France* and *Podium,* teen magazines, wrote enthusiastic articles about Céline, praising her "impressive voice, its depth and musicality."

Meanwhile, back in Montreal that summer, producer Frank Duval was preparing a special about Céline Dion for Radio-Canada, the French-language public television network. The show was called *La naissance d'une étoile, — A Star is Born.* It was the first real portrait of the young singer. Duval filmed her in the studio, onstage, with her family. He met the important people in her life. To illustrate "D'amour ou d'amitié," he used a very charming dramatization. She was shown sitting in a Porsche next to hockey player Gilbert Delorme from the Montreal Canadiens team, whom she called "meltingly cute." As they drove down a country road, she was to lean her head on his shoulder. After the filming was done, she asked René to set up a rendez-vous with the handsome stickhandler. For several days, she dreamed of him, and talked only about him to her sisters and mother. The date never took place. Either René never passed the message on to Delorme, or Delorme declined the invitation.

Angélil kept things on track. He carefully considered every new offer, imagining how he would handle it if he had a million dollars in his pocket. In the spring of 1983, Céline sang with the Montreal Symphony Orchestra at the annual Quebec Cystic Fibrosis Association gala, which she once again headed up. That summer, she performed several outdoor concerts in resorts. On Saturday night, July 30, she sang at the La Ronde amusement park in Montreal. Frank Duval's cameras were there, along with some 45,000 people, that summer's biggest crowd.

René Angélil's reputation as a hard bargainer dates back to that concert. He had some lively discussions with La Ronde management who were acting as the show's promoters. Angélil thought that the floating stage was too far (some thirty yards) from the grandstands on the shore. The audience would be blinded by the bright lights from the amusement park, which would literally overpower the stage. Angélil demanded that the stage be moved fifteen yards closer. Céline needed more intimate contact with the audience, he insisted. That was her strength. The park management replied that it would cost $6,000 to move the stage. Divers would have to be hired to lift its anchors, and then it would have to be towed and reanchored. Angélil wouldn't back down. "Céline Dion sings only in the best conditions. Otherwise, she doesn't sing." The stage was moved closer.

The show was a triumph. And so was the next one, two weeks later, in a country town called Roberval, during the festivities for the crossing of Lac Saint-Jean, one of the great swimming events of the season. Céline attracted fifteen thousand paying customers to that performance.

On September 7, TV personality Michel Jasmin presented her with two gold records: the first was for sales of 100,000 copies in Canada of *Tellement j'ai d'amour pour toi*; the other was for sales of 500,000 copies of the song "D'amour ou d'amitié" in both France and Quebec. On that same day, the album *Les chemins de ma maison* was released simultaneously in Paris and Montreal.

On the record jacket, Eddy Marnay wrote: "This is a precious album, Céline. It's the last memory of your childhood that you'll leave with us. From now on, you'll be singing of your life as a woman. May that life be full of the same music and the same magic."

In October, a celebration was organized for the opening of a new theater in Montreal. Several top artists were invited, including Céline Dion. The theater was named after Félix Leclerc, a singer-songwriter, writer and poet from Quebec. René Angélil knew that the intellectuals and cultural types who would patronize that theater didn't have much respect for Céline Dion because she was too commercial and too popular for their taste. They distrusted her success and found it had come too easily. In other words, they were jealous. She would be performing for an openly hostile audience, one that thought she was too corny. They said as much too, in magazines and newspapers. They didn't think she fit on the stage of a theater like that one. "That's fine with me," Angélil decided. "She has to broaden her appeal."

Financially, the performance wasn't very rewarding. But artistically, it was. Céline sang a Félix Leclerc song called "Bozo." It was the story of a poor, simple-minded guy who falls desperately in love, and who's caught in a web of impossible dreams. That night, she revealed a new and surprising side of her talent and personality. Not only could she sing songs expressly written for her, she could also do justice to the more difficult classics.

A few days later, at the 1983 ADISQ ceremonies, she received four awards: Album of the Year, Female Singer of the Year, Most Popular Artist on the International Scene and Revelation of the Year. She wept openly — tears of joy — every time she went onstage to receive her trophies.

Angélil produced a Christmas album for children. There were three story songs by Yvan Ducharme, the Jacques Brel song "Un enfant" and an Eddy Marnay original called "A quatre pas d'ici" about the imaginary world of small children. It was Eddy's idea to get the whole Dion family together to sing with Céline. When you counted the parents, brothers and sisters, cousins, husbands and wives, aunts and uncles and nieces and nephews, that added up to a forty-voice chorus, directed by Alain Noreau.

In show business, one success usually leads to another. Not only are prizes a good indicator of popularity, they also stimulate sales. The four ADISQ awards boosted Céline's fortunes. By Christmas, more than 100,000 people in Quebec had bought the album *Les chemins de ma maison.* In France, Céline went back on Michel Drucker's show, and also made an appearance on *Atout coeur,* hosted by Patrick Sabatier. In that country, "D'amour et d'amitié" had sold over 700,000 copies.

The money finally started rolling in, but it rolled out just as fast. "If you want your rocket to take off," Angélil liked to say, "you have to use the very best fuel."

The *Falling Into You* Tour
Portland, March 29, 1996

Vocal Gymnastics III

The third voice exercise is a group one. Today, in the Rose Garden Theater, Céline and her backup singers are making an inventory of all the different textures that their voices can produce. They move quickly from crystal to sandpaper — they get rough and gritty, then they become smooth and sound like a caress and then break off again with the suddenness of a gunshot.

To finish up, they pant and sing the sound "eeee" and "ahhh" and "oou" as high as they can, high enough to shatter glass, hitting each note hard, then quickly changing their rhythm and tone. There's no way to describe that whirl of sound. Their voices mingle. Elise's voice is high, Rachelle's is bluesy and sultry, Céline's is supple and powerful.

They've been on the road for more than a year. At first, the show depended a lot on improvisation, but now it runs as smooth as silk. Two or three songs have been replaced, and sometimes the order changes. But in general, every evening they sing the same notes, the same words and repeat the same movements. Their routine might turn into sterile repetition if not for the physical pleasure they get from singing and from keeping their voices flexible and finely toned like the best athletes.

World-class performers, like marathon runners, are junkies of a kind. Their bodies crave physical exertion and secrete endorphins, a natural substance that acts something like the drug morphine. It inhibits pain and produces a euphoric feeling. As the tour progresses, Céline and her singers work their voices ever harder. They sing even when they're not onstage. Without even realizing it, their exercise sessions grow a little longer every day.

You can't yield to temptation. You can't work too hard, even if you want to. Sometimes you have to leave a little undone. Hold back on your pleasure, and not go all the way. Sometimes my voice calls me, but I don't answer. The next time we meet, the pleasure will be greater for both of us. My voice has a memory of its own. When I'm on tour and singing the same songs, I push a lot less. I sing without thinking, and I never need to remind myself to hit one note harder than another.

"Céline rarely forces her voice," says sound engineer Denis Savage. "She knows how to breathe and give the most of herself without risking injury."

To keep from straining her voice, she has to stay in superb shape. Holding back can take a lot of energy. Mastering her voice demands concentration. When Céline gets tired, you can feel her effort. The musicians and sound people pay complete attention to her voice during every performances. They can sense the pain and fear and fatigue. An imperfection, or a break can sometimes appear on the highest notes. The effect is beautiful and very sensual. And disturbing too. It's as though her voice could break at any minute.

Maybe it's just a coincidence, but last night I had a dream I've been dreaming for years. I'm on the roof of a very tall building, probably in some American city, New York, maybe, or Chicago. There's a great crowd of people down below, shouting at me not to jump. I'm trying to tell them that I have no intention of jumping. I'm up on the building just for the view, and I want them to stop worrying. But they don't hear me, or they're not listening. They're running every which way, going completely hysterical. They flood into the building, thousands of them, like ants, and they take the elevator to stop me or save me, I can't tell which. They come onto the roof and run toward me, still shouting. They tell me to be careful. But this time I don't listen to them. I leap over the edge. I fall for what seems like an eternity. Beneath me, the city is empty. No one watches me fall. I go on falling forever. I try to scream, but no sound comes out of my mouth. I always wake up before I hit the ground.

At first, the dream terrified me. Now it intrigues me instead. I wonder what it means.

I used to have another similar dream that lasted for years. Except that in this dream, I didn't fall. I flew. I was with my brothers and my sisters, my mother and my father. I can't really say where, nowhere in particular, in the middle of a field. Suddenly I noticed that they were all looking at me, and that they looked surprised. Then I realized I was flying. I told them to come with me, but they just looked at me. They were growing smaller and smaller. They weren't following me. I was all alone, very high in the sky, and I was very cold. I called to my brothers and sisters, but no one heard my voice, not even me. That's because I had no voice anymore.

Céline is at the Rose Garden Theater tonight because last year, in August, she was forced to cancel the show. She'd gotten sick two days earlier in San Francisco. The doctors were unanimous and absolutely sure. "Too much stress," they told her. "You need immediate rest." That's what they told René in the spring of 1992 when he suffered a heart attack. René told them he could never live without stress. "That's what keeps me alive," he laughed. "If there's no stress, no thrill, no passion, then I might as well be dead." Céline feels the same way:

I like stress and fear. They've been part of my life so long that I don't see how I could do without them. But there's good and bad stress. The feeling I get before I go onstage is good stress. I know I can master it. But when the airplane hits an air pocket or I get a call saying my mother is sick, that's bad stress because I can't do anything about it. It all has to do with power and control. My husband needs stress because he loves power. The only way I can fight bad stress is by staying in good shape, and watching what I eat, and protecting myself, resting, saving my strength and praying … because there are some things that even René Angélil can have no power over.

Chapter Fifteen
The Dove Takes Flight

Every time she sang "Mon ami m'a quittée ("My Friend Left Me"), Céline felt like crying. Where did she find the pain that filled her voice and brought tears to her eyes? No one had ever left her. When she thought about breaking up with Sylvain that summer, it made her feel sad because love hadn't come her way, even though she was ready and waiting for it. Though he'd done very little, Sylvain had left Céline a precious gift that all singers must have: a painful memory.

She immersed herself in that suffering. As she used to do in her diary, she made up sad and moving stories that awoke emotions in her, feelings she simulated and manipulated.

When she sang "Mon Ami Geh Nicht Fort" to the tune of "Mon ami m'a quittée," she cried. She didn't understand the words, even though she'd taken German lessons at Berlitz. The German record market is the biggest in Europe. In Germany, Austria and Switzerland, there are more than 100 million German speakers, and Angélil hoped to conquer that market now that things were going well in France. He didn't think it was logical for the time being, to take on the immense, English-language market. He considered the Americans protectionists, and he realized that the competition in the United States was fierce. In his opinion, Americans were too busy listening to their music, reading their literature, watching their television and movies to get interested in anyone foreign.

The Germans, like other Europeans, are more receptive. They're open to outside influences, and their tastes are more cosmopolitan. Every year, French and Italian songs break through to their market just as easily as American or British hits. Thanks to Claude Pascal and Eddy Marnay, Angélil had made important contacts in the German recording industry. Versions of "Mon ami m'a quittée" and "D'amour et d'amitié" were released on the EMI label, and Céline was scheduled to make several television appearances there.

In the spring of 1984, René Angélil had some propitious opportunities and lots of work to do. As part of the celebrations for the 450th anniversary of Jacques Cartier's discovery of Canada, Céline was to perform in Quebec City's Old Port as part of a megashow featuring some thirty musicians and singers for an audience of some forty thousand people. If the weather cooperated, it would be a fantastic event. In the fall, she'd put in a five-week stint at the Olympia Theater in Paris with Patrick Sébastien. Radio-Canada would be filming a special on her as part of the package. But first, Céline would record a new album in Paris, her sixth (counting the two Christmas albums) in less than three years. That was Angélil's plan of attack. But he hadn't factored in luck and chance, and that card that every gambler likes to have in his hand: the wild card.

They were in Paris in early summer 1984 to cut the demos for the new album when Angélil got a call from a woman named Sylvie Lalande. She's currently the first vice-president of Bell Canada, but at the time, she was running a communications firm with accounts such as the Montreal daily paper *La Presse*, which was organizing a centennial celebration. She and Angélil met for lunch in a little Lebanese restaurant near Place Clichy, and she mentioned that Pope John Paul II would be visiting Montreal that September. The Catholic church was preparing welcoming ceremonies for the pontiff, including a large celebration at Olympic Stadium. At first, a young, inexperienced priest had been given the task of organizing the events. In June, Father Lalonde from Saint Joseph's Oratory, who was responsible for the visit, asked composer Paul Baillargeon, Sylvie's fiancé, writer Marcel Lefebvre and choreographer Hugo de Po to look after the organization of the celebration.

Baillargeon and Lefebvre had written a musical about Brother André, a humble college porter who received divine inspiration and founded Saint Joseph's Oratory, a giant shrine in Montreal. Forty years after his death, Brother André remains an important figure in French-Canadian spiritual life. He was a popular figure whose reputation as a miracle worker had spread far and wide and attracted great crowds from around the world to the cathedral on the slopes of Mount Royal. Father Lalonde enjoyed the work Lefebvre and Baillargeon had produced, and he knew they were serious artists. He decided to give them his trust.

The church wanted to use the celebrations to stress the importance of young people, and their concerns, visions and expectations of today's world. For several weeks, the organizers worked on the central themes of the celebration and its stage show: love, suicide, divorce, racism, violence, world hunger. The budget was enormous, and an army of volunteers was ready to get to work. The stage would hold two thousand people. Religious songs would be sung. Under Hugo de Po's direction, actors carrying white banners would create the figure of an enormous dove spreading its wings.

Baillargeon and Lefebvre decided to write a song to bring the whole theme together. Naturally, their song was entitled "A Dove." They went looking for a young voice to sing it, and they chose Céline Dion. She was young, and she was a top-selling artist. No musician could help but be thrilled by her voice. And Baillargeon knew enough about René Angélil. With him, things would be simple, clear and quickly decided. It would be yes or no. If it was yes, everything would go smoothly.

As Sylvie Lalande talked to him in the small, crowded Lebanese restaurant, Angélil could hardly contain himself. The Pope! The Stadium! Sixty thousand people! Radio and TV from around the world! But he waited until he'd had a chance to hear the demo that Paul had made of "A Dove." He had a warm, bluesy voice reminiscent of Joe Cocker. The melody was very pretty. It flowed like a river and featured a lot of relief, the kind of melody Céline liked.

> Une colombe est partie en voyage.
> Autour du monde elle porte son message
> De paix d'amour et d'amitié.
>
> (A dove set out around the world.
> It had a message in its heart
> Of peace and love and joy.)

"He seemed truly moved," Sylvie Lalonde described the moment. "He put the Walkman down on the table and told me that he liked the song, but that he wanted to think about it all the same. But I was sure he was convinced, and that he'd convince Céline. He called me at my hotel a few hours later and said — I remember his exact words — that he and Céline "would be honored to perform this song before the Pope."

That same evening, Sylvie met Céline and her parents at their hotel near the Porte Mailhot in Paris. Angélil made everyone laugh when he described how Mrs. Dion had reacted. She simply couldn't believe that her daughter would sing for the Pope. She was sure someone was playing a joke on her.

René wanted Sylvie to accompany him and Céline everywhere they went: to the recording sessions, the meetings at Pathé-Marconi, the television interviews. Every time they met someone, René announced that Céline would be singing for the Pope the following September, and he introduced Sylvie as the program director for Montreal's biggest radio station.

"But I left CKAC more than two years ago," she said quietly.

"That doesn't matter," René answered. "Program director is the kind of title that impresses people."

Two days later, after a heated telephone conversation with his wife, René Angélil suddenly returned to Montreal. He was more and more obsessed by Céline's career. It took all of his time and energy — and all of his money. He was often on the road, especially in France. But even when he was back home in Montreal, he saw his children rarely, and only at the end of the day when they returned from school. Then he would rush off to meet songwriters and composers. He spent entire nights in the studio and evenings with the Dion family. He was like a man possessed. He knew himself well enough: he wouldn't change. He might soothe his angry wife this time, but he'd never give up on his dream. He couldn't. He returned to Montreal a tormented man, for he had the feeling that something that had been very important to him was gone forever.

That previous summer, he declared to the cameras that one day Céline Dion would be "the world's greatest singer." Those were his exact words. "The world's greatest singer." He hadn't really planned to say it, but when the words came out, he realized he really believed them. Everything seemed to be on his side. At sixteen, Céline had exceptional talent, she knew how to use it and she was gifted with steely determination. There was no stopping her.

On the plane that carried him back to Montreal, he was torn between despair and euphoria. He couldn't stop himself from thinking about Céline's next album, whose songs would be mixed over the next few days. He would ask Baillargeon and Lefebvre to add "Une colombe" ("A Dove") to the nine songs that Marnay had written with different composers. All the songs, in one way or another were about love. The title song, "Mélanie," spoke to children who were stricken with incurable diseases.

> Mélanie tu n'es pas seule si je chante pour toi.
> Tu n'es pas seule si l'on entend ma voix.
>
> "Mélanie,"
> Eddy Marnay and Diane Juster

> (Melanie you're not alone if I'm singing for you
> You're not alone if they can hear my voice.)

On the back of the record jacket, Marnay wrote, "Céline, these are the songs of your adolescence. They don't make you much older, and they make us feel a lot younger. With you, we reach out for life. We smile as we move toward the new millennium."

Thanks to Angélil, Céline developed an insatiable desire for everything in the show business world. She listened to all the music she could get her hands on and grew with every new singer. She memorized songs, entire albums by Stevie Wonder, Barbra Streisand, Robert Charlebois, Aretha Franklin, Leonard Cohen and Georges Brassens.

Everyone watched her grow and bloom. Everyone offered her music and lyrics, song ideas, warmth and love. Marnay was so excited that sometimes he would call her at eight o'clock in the morning, forgetting how she hated talking before noon. He would tell her how, that night, he'd come up with two or three lines, then suggested she sing them to a particular melody.

Angélil was also living in a state of euphoria. Every day, his artist surprised him. In less than a year, Céline had grown four inches. Her voice was firmer, fuller and rounder. Her onstage movements had improved immensely. She was taking dance lessons with Peter George. She was learning and assimilating and making new discoveries with a kind of energy that was contagious.

During the summer, Angélil kept tabs on the preparations for the Los Angeles Olympic Games. He would compare Céline to the Olympic athletes when he talked to journalists. That autumn, Céline was seen several times with Olympic diver Sylvie Bernier, and the two young women became good friends.

Little by little, Céline Dion's image was being molded. Family-oriented, well-behaved, always on the moral high ground, playful but thoughtful. She was triumphant, but she could express compassion too. Céline posed with medal-winner Sylvie Bernier and her niece Karine, who was afflicted with cystic fibrosis.

These images — happiness and misfortune, triumph and defeat — were part of the first show Céline took on the road. In the pages of the program, the audience read about the "close friendship between Céline and the athletes who brought us joy and pride this past summer. Both share the winner's strength, skill and determination." Beyond these images, we can see the sad, pale smile of little Karine.

In the late afternoon on September 11, dressed all in white, her long hair cascading down her back, in front of the Pope and sixty thousand people waving white handkerchiefs, Céline Dion sang "Une colombe." The day had been windy and rainy; and an hour before the ceremonies were to begin, they were expecting the worst. But when Michel Jasmin, who was doing the introductions, stepped onstage, the sky suddenly changed. Strong winds chased away the remaining clouds, and bright sun filled the Stadium.

Often, critics blame artists for not having enough soul. This time, they smirked because Céline cried as she sang the song. But her tears didn't alter her voice. It remained strong and firm.

By the next day, her song had become a smash hit all across Quebec, and the *Mélanie* album, which was released the month before, really took off. Before the Stadium event, the record sold less than twenty thousand copies since early summer. Those were respectable figures, but nothing out of the ordinary considering how popular Céline was becoming. Perhaps the subject matter was difficult for people to warm up to. Some songs are like that. They don't unleash their true meaning and impact until they're sung in the setting for which they were designed. When the song was combined with the Stadium show, everyone realized what it was really about.

After that appearance, Céline Dion's career took a giant step forward. On the very next Sunday — September 16, 1984 — the first show of Radio-Canada's "Superstar" series was dedicated entirely to her. The following day, at the Sainte Justine's children's hospital, a special issue album of her greatest hits was released.

On October 15, Céline accepted two more Félix awards (Top-Selling Album and Female Singer of the Year) in a teary ceremony. Then she jetted off to Paris to promote the *Mélanie* album and prepare for the show at the Olympia concert hall — a sacred, almost mythical place where, for over a century, the world's greatest singers have performed. From November 6 to December 9, Céline Dion would be performing there as part of Patrick Sébastien's show.

Once again, René invited the Dion parents to come and see their daughter in Paris. For days on end, Adhémar scoured the streets and subways in search of the giant posters of his daughter, featuring her radiant smile and triumphant gaze. A Radio-Canada camera followed Céline everywhere. She spoke honestly about her stage fright and fear of performing, and about her friendships, her fame and her family. Never before had she spoken with so much openness and pleasure.

The Olympia show was successful — but nothing more. The public had come to see French singing star Patrick Sébastien. His material was heavy and dramatic, an amazing contrast with the enchanting sentimentality of this fresh-faced young woman. But at sixteen years old, to have sung at this world-class venue for over a month was a remarkable feat. It helped Céline diversify her audience. "That's," as Angélil would say, "the whole point."

During this long European sojourn, they traveled to Rome to meet the Pope, who granted them a private audience. René was very impressed, and asked His Holiness to bless his family and Céline's. Two days later, they were in Castel Gandolfo, where Céline milked the Pope's cows. Then, as the journalists and photographers who'd come along for the trip watched, she drank a glass of the fresh milk. Journalist Louis-Bernard Robitaille, who had been living in Paris for more than a dozen years, wrote an ironic description of the whole scene, and his readers were treated to some sidesplitting humor. Céline Dion's visit to Rome became something of a running gag in her hometown, and it was satirized on television during the year-end review. The visit was a little ridiculous and easily parodied. Because Céline had had so much success lately with her singing engagements and her record sales, people wanted to laugh at her a little.

That's the way people are in Quebec and throughout Canada. They like to put down anyone who becomes famous overseas, or who dares to stand out from the crowd. There are plenty of examples of that. Writer Antonine Maillet was vilified after she'd won France's highest literary award, the Goncourt prize. Media personality Denise Bombardier received the Legion of Honor from the president of France and appears regularly on the highest profile TV shows in France, but she's mocked every time she wins some new award.

Consider Céline Dion. At sixteen years of age, she'd sung for the

Pope, on French television and at the famous Olympia concert hall. In French-speaking Canada and Europe, she'd sold over a million albums. Yet she was openly and harshly denigrated by some, especially by the intellectual "snobs." The gap between them and the ordinary people was wider than ever. It was as though the highbrows were ashamed to have Céline as their representative in France and Europe.

She never had the approval of the culture vultures. She wasn't very sophisticated or educated, and her speech would have driven a grammar teacher crazy. The intellectuals in her country would have preferred a more refined image abroad. But the image wasn't up to them. It was up to her to make!

The *Falling Into You* Tour
London, November 29, 1996

In the Dressing Room

London's Wembley Arena was built for the 1948 Olympic Games. It's no great marvel when it comes to architecture. The seats rise up at a gentle angle, which means that the seats in the rear are far away from the stage and the main floor. The sound rattles around the metal rafters, making it hard to control. But there are some impressive ghosts in the house. All the greats of American and British show business have played here — the Beatles, Oasis, Frank Sinatra, Tina Turner. Each performer occupied the tiny dressing room that Céline will be occupying tonight. It's like a cave dug out of a massive concrete block. In the distance, she can hear the impatient rumble of the throng in the stands.

Right after the sound check, Loulou escorts Céline to the dressing room. There, with the help of some technicians, she arranges the decor. She sets out large bouquets of freshly cut flowers and plugs in humidifiers and space heaters. (All artists like a warm dressing room.) She opens up the portable wardrobe and the closet where the performing clothes are hung. She sets up the makeup table with its brightly lit mirror. She opens the bottles of face creams and places them on the table, along with thick white towels, powder, eyeliner, brushes and lipstick. Here and there, she scatters her good-luck charms: stuffed frogs and amulets. Céline and her crew are like nomads who pitch their tent in a different spot every night, but who always find what they need to make them feel at home. The dressing room is her private cocoon where a moth becomes a butterfly, where the singer becomes a star. All alone, without anyone watching, she'll put on the costume that helps her face the world, and focus all her energy before stepping onstage.

Seeing a star in her dressing room is like surprising an exotic bird in its nest. In big cities, going backstage is a much-coveted honor. In Paris, London or New York, there are always people who insist they're VIPs, and who show up at the dressing room door, flapping their arms, wanting to see Céline. Tonight, Eric shifts his weight from one foot to the other, keeping an eye on this particular self-professed VIP, then tells him that Céline is busy putting on her makeup, or changing, or fixing her hair.

This evening at Wembley, the dressing room door is wide open, and Eric stands a bit to one side to let in the fresh air. By now, the show is a well-oiled machine. There's less stress and less stage fright. But the dressing room is overflowing. A retired magician named Reveen comes in and starts passing out business cards. Céline stands up; she seems feverish. "I'm thirsty," she says. Suzanne asked if she wants a sip of Coca Cola. She doesn't. It's too filling. And besides, it's better not to drink anything before going onstage.

"If it makes you want to fart, then fart!"

The loud and clear voice belongs to French stage and screen star Gérard Depardieu.

He immediately takes center stage in the dressing room. In a barrage of detail, he describes an incident in an intimate dinner theater in Paris: "I had a Coke before I went onstage. Suddenly I had to pass gas. I wanted to fart silently, but it came out noisily. The first few rows heard it. So I opened my eyes wide and stared at my partner, and everyone thought it was him."

Céline just melts every time she hears the musical quality of Depardieu's voice. She marveled at his performance as Cyrano. She first saw it with her sisters Denise and Manon in Sainte-Anne-des-Lacs, a resort north of Montreal. The three girls ended up in tears. Céline knows several of Cyrano's long speeches by heart. She and Gérard have a little fun in the dressing room, reenacting the play, she as Roxane, he as Cyrano.

Two weeks ago in Paris, Depardieu came into Céline's dressing room after her show. The place was packed with writers, fashion people, movie stars, politicians. In Paris, more than anywhere else in the world, people love stars and heroes. They respect and almost worship them. Céline felt like a prisoner in her own dressing room. Suddenly, Depardieu cut through the mass of people, strode up to her, took her face between his hands as if they were old friends, alone, with no one else around. He whispered into her ear that he had a project for her, and that he'd visit again in a few days or a few weeks, in Berlin or Milan or London, whenever he could. "I absolutely must speak with you!" Bernard Tapie was there too. Tapie had been a minister in the French government, and he was tremendously rich and very popular. Caught up in one scandal after another, he ended up in prison. He's not so rich anymore, but just as popular because he knows how to talk to the common man.

Céline sometimes is uncomfortable with people in her dressing room.

I put on two shows. One onstage and one in the dressing room. It's pure bliss onstage. In my dressing room, I have to make an extra effort. I sometimes feel like I'm empty. It's true that I could keep my mouth shut and ignore them, but I just can't. People come up to me, often they're intimidated, and I help them. I can't stop myself. I don't know how to be any other way: I want to please people. I reach out to them, I charm them, I act like the easiest person in the world to get along with. Sometimes I wonder why. Some of them aren't even very nice. But I want them to love me. I smile and make them laugh. That's part of my job, and I do it the best way I know how.

In the big cities, that's where you find the most important and the most demanding people. Céline prefers to have guests before the show. That way, she knows it won't go on too long. After the show, she'd rather be alone with her friends.

Céline is a true singer. She's not one of those iconoclastic, egomaniacal artists who attract all kinds of attention to themselves by doing outrageous things, who like to shock instead of move their audiences. She's not controversial like Madonna, whose main claim to fame is her wild personality. Neither is Céline a spokesperson for a cause like k.d. Lang or Sinéad O'Connor.

A few minutes before Céline goes onstage in front of the fifteen thousand people who are stamping their feet and shouting her name, Gérard Depardieu talks about the show he has attended at the Bercy concert hall outside Paris. "Your voice fascinates me. It goes right to the heart, I'm telling you." He takes her head in his hands again. "You sing with your soul. You know, some people study for years and years in conservatories and theater schools to reach that point — to make their soul visible, just a little piece of their soul — but they don't make it happen the way you do. Your soul is visible, your whole soul, and that's your beauty. Those American singers have no soul. Everyone can see that. They're machines, they're robots — that's all they are!"

It's five minutes before nine when René comes and tells Depardieu kindly but firmly that it is time for him to leave. Céline has to prepare for the terrible isolation of being onstage on her own.

As Depardieu leaves her dressing room, Céline calls after him, "Bye-bye, Gérard, sweetie, and be careful. Don't fart too loud!"

Chapter Sixteen
The First Fan

In 1981, René Angélil promised Mrs. Dion that, in five years, her daughter Céline would be a big star in France and Quebec. He had kept his promise — in less than three years. Céline had not yet beaten Ginette Reno's record for album sales. "Je ne suis qu'une chanson," which had gone platinum three times, was still the biggest seller in the history of Quebec music. But already, in Quebec, Céline had greater radio play, and she gave the largest number of concerts, which made her the most talked-about artist.

In France, she had topped the hit parade for several weeks in the summer and fall of 1984. Then, strangely, things started going sour. Despite her success at the Olympia, sales fell sharply. Soon the French forgot all about Céline Dion; they were simply indifferent. The same thing occurred in Germany, where her song "Was bedeute Ich Dir" had never really taken off. Angélil wasn't too worried. He had plenty of work on his side of the Atlantic, and he believed that all he needed was another hit record and everything would get back on track again. But Eddy Marnay was dismayed. He was still trying to understand what had gone wrong in France.

A song like "Tellement j'ai d'amour pour toi," which had been released on the previous album, must have seemed strange to the French.

Unlike people in Canada, they couldn't understand the very strong bond between Céline and her mother. And because they were not aware of Céline's involvement in the fight against cystic fibrosis and her closeness to her niece Karine, they couldn't comprehend that a song like "Mélanie" was really about a child suffering from an incurable disease.

However, the cooling off in France didn't really affect her. No one mentioned it, and she asked no questions. She was too busy with the positive side of her career. She was still playing the Olympia when René and pianist Alain Noreau, who was to act as orchestrator and conductor, began planning the winter 1985 tour of Quebec.

Rehearsals began right after the Christmas holiday. But very quickly, René realized that Noreau was not up to the job. He was messy and disorganized. Just a few days before the start of the tour, the orchestrations weren't even finished. Worse still, he didn't have the personality a band leader needed. A conductor must be able to lead musicians and work with them to find the right sound that will make the singer's voice stand out. Noreau might have been too kind. He let his musicians play the way they wanted to, each one going off on his own.

Angélil could feel that Noreau really wasn't happy with the job. He made up his mind. He would have to ask Noreau to step down. But that wouldn't be easy. He liked Noreau, and besides, he'd written some wonderful music for Céline to go along with Marnay's words — songs such as "Chante-moi" and "Le Vieux Monsieur de la rue Royale," Mr. Dion's favorite piece. Ever since he'd worked on the Christmas album, Noreau had become a close friend of the Dion clan. The decision tormented Angélil. But he knew he could not take any chances; Céline's career was his top priority. This first tour in Quebec would be the most important one in every way. It would establish Céline as a true professional. If the show was shoddy, she'd be labeled as a good studio artist, and nothing more. It would be a disaster. A true artist must succeed onstage.

One Thursday evening not long after Christmas, five days before the tour was to begin, Angélil called Paul Baillargeon, who'd written the music for "Une colombe," and asked him to replace Noreau. Baillargeon agreed to put aside the musical he was writing. That very evening, he went to Noreau's house. Noreau handed him a big box of documents, scores and arrangements, all in complete disarray. Baillargeon spent a good part of the night putting it in order.

The next afternoon, he met Céline and her musicians in a rehearsal room at the Place-des-Arts, Montreal's main concert hall. He sat down at the piano and played the melody from "D'amour ou d'amitié." Very calm and very sure of herself, Céline gave the song its perfect tone and rhythm. "It wasn't exactly on key," he recalled, "but it was perfectly solid. She had great projection, even when she wasn't singing very loud."

They took it from the top, this time with the bass guitar. "You're playing too loud," Paul said to the bass player. "Céline's voice has to come through. Your job is to complement her voice." Then he went through the same routine with the guitarist, who said that he didn't know how to play any other way.

"Then pack up your instrument and go home," Paul told him bluntly. "You're here to accompany her, not bury her." The guitarist turned down the volume and stayed in the band. Baillargeon saw the music as a kind of showcase for Céline's voice.

At that point, the band was made up of six musicians and two backup singers, directed by Baillargeon. Their show was diverse in the extreme. Of course, there were several Eddy Marnay songs. "Une colombe," naturally. Giraud's "Mamy Blue," always one of Céline's favorites. And Félix Leclerc's "Le Train du Nord." They threw in a few classics like "Over the Rainbow." With her take on "What a Feeling," Céline showed she could handle contemporary American songs. She even sang an aria from Bizet's opera *Carmen*. And she got together with Baillargeon to sing the famous duet that Joe Cocker had popularized, "Up Where We Belong." Then she launched into a medley of songs by Frenchman Michel Legrand, one of Marnay's old friends. This was her first real tour, and it was designed to show the world what she could do.

Meanwhile, Angélil had recovered from his bankruptcy. He paid off his debts and bought a house with Anne-Renée in suburban Laval. He also got "back in the game," as he called it, occasionally going on junkets to Las Vegas with Marc Verreault or Paul Sara. Some of these trips were fruitful; some were disastrous. As well, he tried to patch up his marriage. He saw his children more frequently that fall and spent more time with his wife. They went to the movies and restaurants together. But Céline's career still dominated his thoughts. He took care of every aspect of it: the staging, the arrangements, the lighting, her wardrobe, the between-song patter, the content of her interviews, the image she would project for the photographers. He spent hours with her, telling her about the history of show business, giving her advice and encouragement.

In January, he went on tour with her. The tour kicked off in La Sarre in the Abitibi region of northern Quebec, in the middle of nowhere.

In February, Anne-Renée had news for him: she was leaving. Had he been a more attentive and better husband, he might have been able to avert the catastrophe. Their marriage had lost all sense of harmony. He hadn't always been the most faithful and concerned husband in the world, even if he had slowed down quite a bit over the past years. Still, he was ashamed by the breakdown of his marriage. He hadn't even noticed what was going on under his own roof. He would keep the kids: Jean-Pierre, soon to be eleven, and Anne-Marie, eight and a half. And, of course, the management of Céline Dion, which he would now do all by himself.

After a few weeks off, the tour got back on track in another small city called Amos. The show was changed slightly. Some songs had been added, others, which had fallen flat, were eliminated. The overall image was younger and funkier. Baillargeon had put together a hot new backup band. He kept the two backup singers — Simon Leclerc and Catherine Léveillée — and hired Florent Richard on bass. Gilles Valiquette, a singer-composer-songwriter who'd had his hour of glory in the 1970s, would take care of the guitars, synthesizers and sequencers. His job was to store various sequences of prefabricated music (violins, for example) which had been programmed. Then computers would work the sequences into the music played by the musicians onstage. With Paul's keyboards, drums and the strings and woodwinds added by the sequencers, the sound was smooth, rich and modern.

Céline celebrated her seventeenth birthday on the stage of Le Carrefour college in the northern Quebec city of Val d'Or. In a little over two months, she gave thirty-six performances in twenty-five cities in Quebec, Ontario and New Brunswick. The show grew as she traveled. Her name was on everyone's lips. She traveled in a minibus, while the equipment followed in a truck. One day, as they rolled into Tracadie in the province of New Brunswick, they noticed giant banners reading, "Welcome, Céline." Wherever they went, they played to sold-out halls.

The shows were still fairly small-scale operations. Angélil invested everything he could in them, but he didn't have the means to build breathtaking sets or sophisticated lighting effects. Besides, they would have created a distraction. Everything had to be centered on Céline's voice. To ensure that the focus remained on her, Angélil often acted as stage manager or lighting man in some of the larger halls they played.

One evening in Quebec City, Eddy Marnay, who knew the show by heart, noticed a mistake in the lighting. Maurice Giraud had orchestrated ballet movements for the spotlights, which were supposed to dance with the melody. But they had remained completely motionless. Marnay turned to the lighting board. Angélil was watching Céline sing, totally transfixed, an ecstatic look on his face. He had forgotten all about the lighting and the effect it was supposed to have, and had become a member of the audience. After the show, when Céline asked him what had gone wrong, he had to confess that he hadn't been paying attention. "I was dreaming," he admitted.

"You dream while I sing?"

"I was listening too hard," he said.

The truth is that he was obsessed. Carried away. He had never been so fascinated by an artist before. He finally understood what Marnay had told him. In Céline, there was a strength that went far beyond them.

He was sure that many people had had the same experience that night. He told Céline and her mother what he'd felt while he was under that spell. He began coming into their room after every show and describing his reaction to the performances. Then he would kiss both mother and child on both cheeks and go to meet Florent Richard and Paul Baillargeon, to whom he was teaching the finer points of gambling. He tried to instill in them his passion for blackjack, which, for him, had become a metaphor in life. To succeed, in blackjack and in life, you have to know the rules of the game. "That's 90 percent of winning," he would say. "You have to learn how to play. Lots of people play blackjack just the way they go through life — like spectators. They don't know the game. They're on the outside looking in."

And he would launch into his philosophy of gambling. "Blackjack is a game of patience. When things are going bad, when the dealer always gets twenty-one, you bet less and you wait. Sooner or later, your luck is going to change. You have to be ready and know how to take advantage of it. You have to bet big when luck's on your side. Just like in life, when things are going bad, and when you don't even know why, you should never make any big decisions. Wait till the storm passes."

When he went on tour or on a gambling junket to Las Vegas, Angélil would leave the children with his mother. They called her Tété, and they adored her. When he wasn't on the road, he usually stayed home. Alone, or with his cousin Paul Sara and his friend Jacques Des Marais, he would play cards, working on and polishing a system he'd dreamed up during one of the tours. Paul Sara had been a bank manager for eleven years, and Jacques was a lawyer and a chartered accountant. They both knew how to count. Through the spring of 1985, for weeks at a time, night after night, they perfected their system.

René bought the green felt with the markings of blackjack table, chips and a slipper (the box from which the dealer deals the cards). He tried to find the most profitable way to play blackjack. When he got together with Paul Baillargeon and Florient Richard on tour, he would describe what he'd learned with Sara and Des Marais.

"We figured out that if we learned how to play right, we could win. We know that the bank wins 52 percent of the time. Most people always bet the same amount — $10, let's say. So they always lose 52 percent of the time. After a hundred tries, they've lost $20. But look at it this way: in life, everyone gets lucky. And when that happens, it doesn't rain, it usually pours. And that goes for good and bad luck alike. You just have to take advantage of your lucky streak when it begins. That means betting the most that you can when you're on a hot streak, and holding back when your luck cools off. The trick is figuring out when your luck is on the upswing and when it's cooling off."

That was Angélil's mission: getting to know Lady Luck inside out, following her tricky path, tracking her down and winning her over.

After months of research with Sara and Des Marais, using their sequence theory, he managed to build a system that seemed practically foolproof. But there was one problem. Applying the system was very boring. The gambler got used to winning little by little, always playing it safe, being patient, never taking needless chances — gambling with the calculator, not the heart. Paul Baillargeon objected, and not without good reason. In real life, seated in front of a real blackjack table, with real money, any gambler would have tremendous difficulty containing himself and keeping a cool head on his shoulders. If you strayed the slightest bit from the system, the whole thing would fall apart. Angélil knew his friend was right. He had spent years trying to find a way to eliminate risk and random chance. But he now realized that the whole point of gambling — the whole point of life — was, above all, the pleasure of taking chances.

That spring, René and Céline founded their own company. They called it Feeling Productions Inc. He asked Paul Baillargeon to become an associate for the production of the tour. Baillargeon refused, because he knew the company would never produce any profit, even if all the tickets were sold. He had observed Angélil's way of doing business. He would reinvest almost all the profits, enhancing the lighting effects, the sound, the promotion effort.

"He always wanted top-notch quality," Baillargeon said, "more than other producers. He was proud of having the highest-paid backup singers, musicians and technicians. He had the most expensive programs — sixteen full-color pages on glossy paper — and the most attractive tickets. The better the shows worked, the more they cost and the less profit they made. Their success only added to Angélil's ambition."

The only other show that had similar success in Quebec at that time was that of Alain Morisod and the Sweet People. Morisod was a Swiss pianist who was so romantic he was gooey. He attracted an older audience who enjoyed his type of melodrama.

Compared to the Sweet People, Céline was a young rocker. Her show was more eclectic too. There was a little bit of everything: funk, rock and roll, ballads, even lullabies. Céline naturally liked fast, hard rhythms, but René slowed her down. During rehearsal, she and her guitarist and keyboard player would launch into cover versions of songs by Stevie Wonder, Aretha Franklin and Janis Joplin. The musicians were always ready to keep that beat. But according to Angélil, to reach the widest possible audience, you had to start slowly. And Céline believed him. In her eyes, he was wisdom itself — experience and intelligence, strength and security all rolled into one. He took care of everything. He made sure she had whatever she wanted. Whenever she and her mother were on tour, they ate in the best restaurants and slept in the best hotels.

Mrs. Dion loved being on tour. She liked driving, seeing the countryside, watching the roads unfold, comparing the cities and towns and people. Just before the tour began, her husband lost his job. Adhémar Dion was sixty-two years old. He knew he probably wouldn't be able to find another decent job, so he decided it was time to retire. He'd go fishing and play golf with his pals. Join the tour? No thanks, he answered.

"I've knocked about enough in this life of mine," he added.

He couldn't imagine what he would do on a tour. When Céline sang in Montreal, he would go and see her. And cheer at the top of his lungs. When the show ended, he'd leap to his feet and shout out his admiration. People around him would stare. "That's my daughter," he'd explain. But that was good enough for him. He was her greatest fan, and that's all he wanted to be.

Mrs. Dion, however, had plenty to do on the tour. She helped her daughter choose her wardrobe, her makeup and her hairstyle. She was an excellent critic too. Every night, she watched the show from somewhere in the hall, and jotted down her observations. Sometimes she would criticize one of Céline's movements, or a problem with her dress, or a missed cue or a wrong expression in the song presentations.

Since the first show in the Abitibi region, Céline had become much more self-confident. When the tour hit Montreal at the end of May, people were eagerly awaiting it. Despite her youth, Céline Dion already had a show business past and an aura that fascinated, charmed and intrigued the press. A few days before the Montreal show, Radio-Canada television ran the special that had been filmed the previous fall when she'd sung at the Olympia in Paris.

On May 31, and June 1 and 2, Céline performed at the Place-des-Arts, Montreal's most prestigious concert hall. The critics loved her. They compared her to the world's greatest singers. She had a way of touching people, the press proclaimed. She reminded the music journalists of Edith Piaf and the great female jazz voices.

The press helped solve the thorny question of how to classify Céline Dion. Should she be placed in a middle-of-the-road category, as a singer for people who don't want to think too much about their music? Or should she be thought of as an interpreter of songs, doing the standards in her own way? Or was she above classification, up there with the best who defy all categories? That status hadn't been achieved yet. While the "artsy" audiences turned up their noses at her and criticized her for being too commercial, some commentators came closer to the truth. They wondered why she had to be so absolutely nice all the time. They characterized her as a girl who had a terrible need to please other people. Whenever she spoke, it was to praise everyone and everything to high heaven. One critic wrote, "She ought to get rid of that Pollyana side of her personality. She doesn't need it to succeed. The audience is already eating out of her hand."

At the 1985 ADISQ awards, Céline was a bigger winner than ever. She won for Best-Selling Song, Best-Selling Album, Best Female Singer, Best Pop Song, Best Pop Album. As usual, the happy winner shed plenty of tears of joy for the successful year. The summer before, she had triumphed wherever she sang. And right now, she was in the spotlight, her Best Female Singer award in her hand, while the adoring crowd looked on. She thanked René Angélil ... and burst into tears again.

In the coming year, she would enter a phase in her life that would fill her with dread. Soon she would take leave of her public, and that wouldn't be easy. Her audiences had been the only thing in her life that could fill the emptiness that came from not being able to love the only man she really wanted. A man who didn't love her — or so she thought — and who was as unhappy as he could be.

A few weeks earlier, Anne-Renée had returned to the family home. They'd reconciled and tried to go back to living as a couple, but it was too late.

Finally, Anne-Renée decided she wanted a divorce. On his lawyer's advice, Angélil left the family home and moved into the Sheraton hotel in suburban Laval. Every other day, he would go to visit the children. By now, Anne-Renée had custody of them.

René felt completely lost. His life had been shattered to its very foundations, and he had no control over what was happening to him.

He'd always been the decision maker. Suddenly, his wife took it upon herself to turn his life upside-down.

True to his sequence theory, he decided to put everything on hold at the end of the tour, and that included the album they'd worked on through the summer called *C'est pour toi.* He was heartbroken and without resources, and afraid of making the wrong decisions. The producers, director, composers and songwriters who had offers for him found that they could no longer get ahold of him. He was in Las Vegas, at Caesar's Palace, registered under an assumed name.

Céline kept busy while he was away. She was in the mood for a change. She wanted to be someone else, physically. An orthodontist was called in. She'd have to wear braces for several months. She learned English and went back to work with choreographer Peter George. She'd transform herself into a seductive young woman, and the man she loved would have to take notice of her.

Céline Dion was seventeen years old and madly in love with René. Judging from the songs he wrote for the new album, *C'est pour toi* (*It's for You*), Eddy Marnay must have guessed her feelings for her impresario. It was like listening to the voice of Galatea, the statue into whom Aphrodite, the goddess of love, had breathed life, and who'd fallen hopelessly in love with Pygmalion, the man who sculpted her. Through the songs, Céline spoke to the man she desired, but who didn't see her in the same light.

Non je ne suis pas
La Princesse en bleu de ton Bois dormant.
Tu le vois je suis bien réelle
Et je veux de toi pour amant.

Non je ne suis pas
La Sagesse même et mes sentiments,
Ne sont pas faits que d'innocence.
Ils sont faits de chair et de sang.
Mais je t'aime trop pour te perdre un jour,
Alors je te dis
Que si toi tu veux rester sage,
Je serai sage moi aussi

"Avec toi,"
Eddy Marnay, Thierry Geoffroy, and
Christian Loigerot

(No I'm not
the sleeping beauty all in blue.
See how real I am
And I want you for my lover.

No I'm not
a good little girl,
My feelings aren't made of innocence.
They're made of flesh and blood.

I love you too much to lose you,
so if you want me to stay
a good little girl,
then that's what I'll have to be.)

If you didn't know what was going on in Céline's life, if you knew nothing about her love for a man two and a half times her age, the song might seem strange. In these modern times, why would a man want a woman to "stay a good little girl" and refuse her love? And why would the woman singing the song have to be a "good little girl" to keep from losing him?

Eddy Marnay was writing the story of the beginnings of a love that couldn't be denied, yet could never flourish. This was the love that a young girl feels for a mature man who sees her only as a wonderfully gifted child, and who can't understand the feelings he's awakened in her. With songs like "Avec toi" and "C'est pour toi," Marnay was writing a running account of this love affair.

Ne m'oblige pas à tout te dire,
Puisque tu le sais déjà.
Tout ce que je fais aujourd'hui c'est pour toi.

(Don't make me say it out loud,
You should know it by now.
Everything I do I do for you.)

But Angélil was blind to this, or pretending to be blind. He didn't even seem to be interested in the fate of the album, the sales of which were rather weak, even in her home town. Instead, he'd gone back to being a full-time gambler.

He and Anne-Renée reached an out-of-court settlement. Meanwhile, he'd rekindled a friendship with his first wife Denise, the mother of his son Patrick, with whom he'd never really lost contact.

Lucky in business, unlucky in love, he would say to himself. He was spending half his time in Las Vegas. His friends kept him company, spelling each other: first Des Marais, then Verreault, then Paul Sara. He had little notebooks of graph paper, where he jotted down statistics and results. He noted down where he'd gambled, who with, how long, his winnings and losses. In January 1986, he won two blackjack tournaments. In eighteen months, using his system, he won $140,000.

But one day, he discovered just how right Paul Baillargeon had been. Winning with the system they'd perfected no longer brought him thrills and pleasure. "We're playing like pencil pushers," he said. "All we're doing is following our own orders." Little by little, because he was a natural-born gambler, he dropped blackjack and started playing craps, a dice game with much greater risk. He lay in wait for Lady Luck — he summoned her, teased her, waiting for his chance. He knew she returns to every man's life. You have to be ready to welcome her when she comes. Sometimes, he knew, even if you're not looking for her, she'll show up and bestow her favors on you. That's real luck. In the casinos of Las Vegas, Angélil kept his mind on his young artist and began preparing his plans.

René had known the pleasures of being onstage. He knew what it was like to hear the applause, and wondered how Céline would get along without that thrill during the year-long break they'd decided to take. A singer would need both steely determination and strength of character to disappear at the height of her popularity. But it wasn't that big a risk because Céline had demonstrated that she was here to stay. Not only could she sing and make records, she could perform onstage and on TV, and she knew how to talk to crowds and journalists. She was going to get prettier, she was going to grow up. Then she'd come back with a vengeance.

He promised to cut an English record with her. He'd wanted to do the same thing with Ginette Reno. "Singing in English isn't good enough," he told Céline. "You have to speak it too." Whether a record sinks or swims depends on several factors: on the music and lyrics, and whether they hook the listener; on the singer's image; and on the slant she gives the song. Then there's all the work that has to be done with record industry people and the media. Without them, a singer will never get anywhere. They need to know the artists they're working with, what their thoughts are, what they want from their careers. To make it in show business on an international scale, you have to be able to talk to PR agents, producers, artistic directors and the media in Hollywood, New York and London.

So Céline went to Berlitz to learn English. Nine hours a day, five days a week, for six months. Usually, musicians and singers have a good ear for languages. That makes sense, since language *is* music. But sometimes, the beginnings can be very tough. Céline felt as though she were drowning. She couldn't understand anything, she stuttered and stammered, and her ideas got mixed up. Then, little by little, very slowly, everything became clear, and she found herself speaking English.

She spent a lot of time at the movies and listened to the widest possible variety of music. She got a new hairstyle and a new look. The playful teenager was about to turn into a sensuous young woman. Her new image first appeared in a video she made for the song "Fais ce que tu voudras" ("Do What You Want"), directed by François Girard, a talented, young Quebec filmmaker.

Girard wanted to get rid of Céline's old image too. The first thing to go were her baggy pants and her turtleneck sweaters.

During Céline's absence, outlandish rumors about her were circulating in Canada and France. "Céline has entered a convent," some said. "Céline's pregnant," others said, "and she's having the baby in a secret location. Then she'll give it up for adoption to some woman in Switzerland." Then, when she emerged again, with her new womanly image, tongues wagged even more. "Céline and René Angélil have gotten engaged. They're getting married in Las Vegas." Soon, everyone in Canada was sure she had found the love of her life.

Indeed, there was some truth to that. "Life imitates art," Oscar Wilde said. Life can imitate the media too. And the media noticed, long before René did, that Céline was madly in love with him.

The *Falling Into You* Tour
Sheffield, November 13, 1996

Stage Fright

When it's time to step out onstage, every artist suffers from stage fright. Sometimes it can be hell. They get nauseous, suffer from the shakes and cold sweats. They forget where they are and what they're supposed to do. They think of the show they're about to begin and realize with fear and trepidation that they can't remember a thing: the song order, the words, the names of their band members. They'll be booed offstage. Deep down, they hope for an earthquake or a bomb to go off, anything as long as the show is postponed. They consider just running away, out the back door and into the street. They tell themselves that this will be their last night, that they're going to quit this crazy business that kills them every night. Some actually do. Jacques Brel said good-bye to performing before he hit the age of forty.

Céline generally keeps her cool. A few days ago, five minutes before going onstage, she videotaped a complimentary thank-you message for the people at 550, the American branch of Sony for whom she records. She was sitting at her makeup table, her hair all done, her make-up on, dressed in her show outfit. She looked straight into the camera and told the promotion people at 550 that she owed her success in the US to them. "I'm singing here at Wembley tonight, and it's all because of the work you've done," she said. They were all a big family, and she was proud to be a part of it. If she could have, she added, she would have attended their Christmas party. She wished them a happy and healthy new year. She blew them a kiss. It was perfect. Exactly one and a half minutes. One take.

She thanked the cameraman and the soundman, then went to her mirror. "I look terrible, Manon!" she exclaimed. Manon laughed, wiped the beads of sweat off her forehead and nose and fixed a few stray locks of hair. The cameraman and the soundman didn't move. Céline caught their anxious look. She turned to René. "There isn't anything else, is there?" she asked, hopefully.

Of course there was something else. She had to improvise another sixty-second spot for the annual meeting of the presidents of her American fan clubs. She meditated for a minute, more to get back into a better mood than to find the right words, because improvising is no problem with her. Then she gave warm thanks to her American fan clubs as the cameras whirred. Everyone applauded in the dressing room. But she wasn't happy.

"I just know they'll realize I did it at the last minute. As if like I was just getting it out of the way, don't you think?"

Everyone contradicted her. Then René herded them out of the room. The show was set to start in five minutes. There was no looking back. It was on to the next thing.

Tonight, in Sheffield, a thin, pale, pensive yet delighted nine-year-old girl named Leanne Oliver from nearby Grantham comes to meet Céline, accompanied by her parents and her nurse. Leanne, too, has cystic fibrosis. They are all dressed in their slickers and are carrying their umbrellas. Céline greets them in the little parlor off her dressing room a few minutes before going onstage. She kneels by Leanne's wheelchair, by the heavy oxygen bottles that are attached to its back. She thinks back to Karine, her niece, that laughing ghost child who has never left her, not even for a moment. A few days before Karine died, she came to see Céline sing at the Montreal Forum. That was in the spring of 1993, and like Leanne tonight, Karine was confined to a wheelchair and dependent on oxygen, without which she would have suffocated. The disease is still incurable, though thanks to research, enormous progress has been made. Now, the life expectancy of a person stricken with cystic fibrosis is thirty years, twice as long as it used to be.

Céline speaks to Leanne like a friend. She makes her laugh by taking off the girl's cap and replacing it with one with her name on it. She seems to have forgotten all the people and the cameras that filled the small room. Yet she knows that when the time comes, five minutes before the show, René or Dave or Barry will politely ask the visitors to leave. And even when she's with the people closest to her — René and Eric, Manon and Loulou — she'll still have to cross that river of darkness — the one that separates her from the brightly lit stage — by herself. Her friends will move aside, one by one. She'll experience stage fright, and it will fill her mind. But she will have to confront it straight on before stepping onto the stage and facing her fans.

Chapter Seventeen
A Beautiful Stranger

In Montreal, in the middle of the 1970s, any disc jockey who wanted to get ahead had to deal with Vito Luprano. Vito had direct connections to the disco world in New York, and he would go there two or three times a month. He never stopped searching for the newest sounds, for the latest rhythm and the hottest vibrations. He would go to the most "in" clubs, not to drink and dance, but to see what other people were dancing to. His specialty was buying dance music and reselling it to Montreal DJs.

Born in 1956 in southern Italy, he came to Montreal at the age of eleven with his parents and five siblings. The Luprano family had relatives in the Montreal area, but no one could speak either English or French. The first years after they immigrated were difficult; they had to struggle, but they hung on.

Vito loved everything about the New World. At sixteen, he left school to play drums for a group of musicians who played weddings and bar mitzvahs in the Italian and Jewish communities. Soon, Vito had become the man in Montreal who knew the most about dance music.

In the early 1980s, Bill Rotari, the boss of CBS Records in Quebec, hired him to do promotion. It wasn't long before people in the Toronto head office found out who Vito was.

Around the same time, Bill Rotari asked Mario Lefebvre to promote CBS Records in his sector. Mario had been the DJ at the Lorelei, an enormous disco club in downtown Montreal that could fit eight thousand people in downtown Montreal, back in the days when Vito had been the king of dance music in the city. He'd gone on to work as editor-in-chief of *Pop Rock* magazine. Mario liked being in the know when it came to show business. He wanted to know who was doing what and with whom in the music and recording industry. He wrote a kind of gossip column for *Pop Rock.*

He'd worked in promotion for Warner from 1977 to 1980 and met Luc Plamondon and Michel Berger around the time of the *Starmania* rock opera. By the time he began working for CBS at the beginning of the 1980s, he knew all about the music world — what worked and what didn't.

Rotari had put together quite a team. Vito knew what made young people tap their feet. He had an ear and a nose for music. He liked disco nights and days in the studio. More diplomatic, Mario knew how to make chemistry work between people. He could put together a team, conduct brainstorming sessions, convince and negotiate. Vito chose the songs and Mario promoted them, and thanks to the two men, CBS was the hottest record company in French Canada.

In 1985, Vito was offered the job of artistic director, what's called A & R (for artists and repertory) in the business. The artistic director works closely with singers. He finds them the right music, words, arrangers and producers, then herds them all into the studio, listens to the results, gives advice, signs up albums.

At the time, Vito was married to Lise Richard, who was working with Denys Bergeron at Trans-Canada Productions, part of the Quebecor group that distributed Céline Dion's records under the TBS label. Lise Richard spoke enthusiastically to Vito about Céline — about the tremendous success she was having in Quebec and France and about her manager René Angélil, a brilliant and visionary producer.

But Vito didn't care for Céline's style. It was too soft, too middle of the road, too adult. He liked the rock that was coming out of the States. But he listened to her latest songs and watched her "Fais ce que tu voudras" video. She did have an extraordinary voice, he admitted, and her presence was irresistible. But still, he wasn't impressed. He liked the artist, but didn't care for the material.

Fate would intervene to change his mind.

Not only were things moving at CBS, but big changes were about to take place in Céline's life and career. Angélil had shaken off his lethargy, and Céline had completed her metamorphosis from moth to butterfly. They were both ready for new adventures. They wanted to change everything: the look, the sound, the material, the music. With that in mind, and back from Las Vegas, Angélil went looking for financing for Céline Dion's next record.

Trans-Canada had initially guaranteed him sales of 100,000 copies of the last two records he'd produced: *C'est pour toi* and *Céline Dion en concert* (recorded at Place-des-Arts). TBS had paid all the production costs of the two albums, including the recording, manufacturing and promotion. In return, they received $4.70 for every copy sold. Trans-Canada, which was expecting net profits in the order of $300,000 to $400,000, had paid $470,000 in advance to Angélil. But when everything was added up, only some 75,000 copies of *C'est pour toi* and *Céline Dion en concert* had been sold. In Canada and in France, in the record business, people were speculating in hushed voices that Céline Dion's career was over.

Angélil had thought long and hard about the last albums. Perhaps they had been produced too quickly. Perhaps they were too similar to each other. When he listened to them again, he decided that the music and arrangements were old-fashioned. Céline had grown up enormously since *Mélanie*, but her material hadn't grown up with her. The songs were well constructed and straightforward, but there was nothing really new and catchy about them. And her career, recently, hadn't produced any highlights, unlike the exciting first two years — winning the Yamaha prize in Tokyo, singing "Une colombe" for the Pope, the show at the Olympia in Paris.

When he thought about it, Angélil realized that it hadn't been Céline's fault. Her singing was better than ever. But something was missing. He had boxed her into too small a space. He had given her songs that offered no new vocal challenges. She'd made *C'est pour toi* with a lot less pleasure than the earlier albums because she wasn't being pushed farther, because no one was making new musical demands on her. Outside the studio, she was interested in all kinds of music. She had to be given greater freedom. He made up his mind to find musicians more in tune with the latest trends. Yet he dreaded the day when he'd have to tell Eddy Marnay, his first and best ally, that he'd no longer be the sole writer for Céline.

In the spring of 1986, between two Las Vegas junkets, Angélil met with the bosses of Trans-Canada to renegotiate terms. He told them he had big changes in mind. Over the past year, Céline had made great progress with her singing, dancing and her English. He expected to be producing great things with her in the near future.

Angélil wasn't in a position to ask for a large advance. Instead, he requested a smaller, repayable amount of $50,000. The figure was equivalent to royalties on sales of only twelve thousand copies. He met the Trans-Canada brass, unveiled his plan and made what he thought was a reasonable offer. Everything seemed to be in the bag.

Three days later, he received a letter from André Gourd, the big boss at Trans-Canada. Quebecor had decided to stop giving advances to producers. Angélil was furious. Céline Dion had sold hundreds of thousands of copies of her first five records, and Trans-Canada, which had made a fortune off her, refused to grant her a $50,000 advance! Besides, it was unthinkable for a company not to respect what its executive had already promised, to force them to go back on their word. Worse still, they had no confidence in Céline Dion. They refused to give her the $50,000 advance because they didn't believe she'd sell twelve thousand copies of her next record.

The very next day, very calmly, very politely and at great length, he explained to Lise Richard, Vito Luprano's wife, why he'd never work with Trans-Canada again, even if the company changed its mind. "In five years, Céline Dion is going to be a big star in the big leagues. I can't work with people who don't believe in her the same way. In five years, André Gourd will be begging for us to come back. But it'll be too late. It's already too late."

Yet deep down, he was worried. He knew that some record industry people laughed at his dream and called him a lunatic. But you have to aim high if you want to get anywhere in this business.

The break with Trans-Canada turned out to be a tonic. The record company's refusal to give them the advance, the failure of the negotiations and the doubts that so many people had about Céline stimulated René and even brought him comfort. When it came to Céline Dion, every time René Angélil lost a round, he ended up winning bigger. Every time he was turned down, he ended up with a better offer elsewhere.

> When I think back at everything that's happened in my life, I have to admit that I've been a very lucky girl. It's incredible. The further René and I went, the better things got, the more doors opened for us. I guess I was born under a lucky star.

A few days after that bitter conversation with Trans-Canada, Angélil went into Decannes', a hamburger joint in the east end of Montreal. He spotted Bill Rotari, the boss of CBS Records in Montreal, whom he had known for some time. Bill had had his own singing group back in the days when the Baronnets were big.

Angélil sat down next to him at the long counter and ordered two hamburgers, fries and a Coke. He told Bill that he'd left Trans-Canada and had made up his mind not to produce Céline's records on the TBS label. As always, he twisted the truth a little. He didn't admit to Bill that Trans-Canada had refused his request for an advance. He said only that he wanted to work with a major label like CBS — if CBS would have him. He wanted Céline to be on the same label as the greats like Barbra Streisand, Michael Jackson, Julio Iglesias and Bruce Springsteen, and to work with people who had the know-how and the resources. "If I want to make my breakthrough," he said to Rotari, "I'll need the technical support and the money that only a multinational like yours can provide."

That same afternoon, Bill Rotari talked to Vito Luprano, his A & R man. He convinced Luprano to go see Céline, who was giving a private show the following weekend in a big Montreal hotel.

It was a French-speaking milieu, and Vito Luprano didn't exactly feel at home, even if he did speak a little French. Céline's rendition of Eddy Marnay's subtle and sensitive songs were so delicate that they frightened him. But Céline did feature a few English songs, like "What a Feeling," and that night, she sang it so well that she knocked Vito's socks off.

Her material was so diverse — that's what impressed him the most. She could sing everything, from ballads to rock to soul. "That's what really got me that first time," Vito remembered. "She could do it all." And over the next few years, people continued to be amazed by Céline the chameleon, always changing her look and her sound.

A few days later, Vito and Angélil met in Vito's office. He was interested in working with Céline, Luprano said, but only if the change in her sound was radical, profound and definitive.

"We want the same things," Angélil told him, "and so does Céline."

He was looking for more popular material. Soon he'd be meeting Luc Plamondon, the most sought-after songwriter in Quebec at the time. But he didn't want to lose the audience they already had. The next album would be a turning point in Céline's career. The challenge was to expand the audience without losing the fans she already had.

Angélil had his demands too. He wanted the record company to put its heavy machinery behind this album. And he insisted that CBS add a clause to the contract, promising to produce an English record next time. "That's a good idea," Vito agreed.

They got together with Rotari and agreed on an option for the production of an English record as long as the French one sold 100,000 copies. CBS promised to spend $30,000 to produce English versions for the music already recorded for the French album.

"Both of us knew it was impossible," Vito would say later. "Everybody knew it, even the bosses in Toronto who signed the agreement. Records didn't cost as much back then to make as they do today, but it still would have been more than $30,000. And translating the songs was hardly a brilliant idea. It had never been done for a complete album. But Angélil insisted on that option. For him it was a way of getting a foot in the door. Once he got that foot in, I knew he wouldn't pull it back."

Ben Kaye had gotten the same kind of agreement for one of his artists, a rock musician by the name of Michel Pagliaro, who had won two Juno Awards in Canada. But the company never honored the contract, and for years Pagliaro had been waiting in vain for the chance to make an English record.

"You see where that kind of option gets you — nowhere!" Ben Kaye told Angélil. René shrugged his shoulders. He liked Pagliaro. He was Quebec's best rock musician, but musicians like him grew on trees in the States. But Céline, *his* Céline, she was something else again. Couldn't Ben Kaye see that? She could open doors no one else could. She was unique. Angélil said even he didn't know how far her talent could go, and just where she might end up.

His plan of attack was very simple. He had to produce a French record that had strength and power and would sound absolutely new, that would knock the CBS guys in Toronto off their stools. "If they could just hear her sing, if they could only see her sing. I've got to work on that."

He came back from Paris with some very sophisticated and sexy photos of Céline. Vito introduced her to his friend Aldo Nova, a rock composer who'd worked with Bon Jovi. They had nothing in common with the French musicians who played with Eddy Marnay. Everything was going to change.

During the summer of 1986, Angélil finally managed to catch up with the fast-moving Luc Plamondon, the hottest songwriter in the French-speaking world. He had penned a long string of hit songs over the past ten years. Two of them, "Nuit magique" and "Coeur de rocker," were at the top of the hit parade that summer. Plamondon was a cultured man who could make the French language dance to rock and roll rhythms like no other. With Michel Berger, he'd written a rock opera called *Starmania*, which had been playing non-stop in Paris and Montreal for six years. He supplied songs for any number of French and Canadian singers. Celebrated for his extremely personal writing, he always managed to reflect contemporary society in his lyrics, sometimes in surprising ways.

Plamondon knew virtually everybody in Quebec and France: musicians, producers, singers, journalists and important people in the record and television world. He owned a magnificent apartment in Paris, another on Lake Memphremagog, just north of Vermont, and yet another in the exclusive Montreal district called Outremont, in front of a park four city blocks wide. Angélil met Plamondon in that house, which contained a jukebox, beautiful paintings and rare, expensive knickknacks. A few days before, he went to see *Starmania* with Céline. They both adored it. The show told a dark and gloomy story of wayward, directionless youth lost in a world of senseless violence, a world where love struggles to survive and where rebellion is the only way out.

After the show, they went backstage to congratulate the artists. Angélil told Plamondon that Céline wanted to play the leading role in a musical some day. "We'll take it to Paris and Broadway and London." Céline listened, shy but charming. In the rowdy backstage atmosphere, Plamondon hardly had time to speak to them.

A few days later, in his Outremont house, Angélil told him, "Forget everything you know about Céline Dion. She's a woman now. She wants to sing pop and rock, with words that mean something. She wants to get rid of her old look."

It wasn't the first time Plamondon had changed someone's image. A singer named Diane Dufresne had earned some fame for her cover versions of French singers like Jacques Brel and Léo Ferré. But in 1972, she turned into a completely different singer. Plamondon had engineered the turnaround.

Plamondon had received the same request shortly before he met with Angélil. Johnny Stark asked him to redo Mireille Mathieu's image. "I want you to do the same thing for Mireille that you did for Julien Clerc," Stark told him. "She needs new songs." Next, Orlando, brother of French singer Dalida, called Plamondon and made the same request.

"I didn't think either of those women should change," Plamondon said. "They were mature women, not like Céline, who was just eighteen, the ideal age to make radical changes. I couldn't turn them into rockers — that would have been artificial. It was completely different with Céline."

The big meeting between him and Céline took place in the fall of 1986, in Paris. Plamondon's apartment was luxurious, with a view of the Eiffel Tower and the Seine. He had invited some movers and shakers from the show business world in Paris: Bernard de Bosson and Gilbert Coullier.

"Céline didn't even have to open her mouth," Coullier remembered. "We saw how determined and sure of her talent she was. She was a completely modern young woman in dress and appearance, and she even seemed happy."

For once, she did nearly all the talking. She sang lines from songs popularized by Michael Jackson, Barbra Streisand and Janis Joplin. Plamondon was totally impressed. Then she sang some of the numbers from *Starmania*, imitating and parodying the singers who had played Marie-Jeanne and Cristal, the two female characters in the opera.

"I'd never heard anyone sing French that way," Plamondon would say later. "Her phrases were remarkably articulate. You could feel the influence of Eddy Marnay, his experience and respect for the French language."

Plamondon knew he was encroaching on Marnay's territory. That could create conflict and ill feelings. When he wrote "Coeur de rocker" for Julien Clerc, Etienne Roda-Gill, Clerc's official songwriter, had taken great umbrage. The same thing happened with Catherine Lara (who was working with Boubelil, the writer for *Les Misérables*) when she turned to Plamondon and his rock image.

He knew Marnay's work very well. "Marnay taught Céline how to sing and express herself in French," he said. "By the time I got there, most of the work had been done, and done well. Not only had Marnay written her first hit songs, he'd been a spiritual father to her, a mentor. He'd taught her the art of singing. Her diction is impeccable. She has a great sense of phrasing. And she learned it young enough that it really stuck."

In Quebec, at the beginning of the 1980s, when Céline began singing, audiences had stopped listening to music from France. The big-name singer-songwriters were in a slow period. She was lucky to have met a songwriter with Marnay's class and prestige. If it weren't for him, she could have ended up with meaningless, soulless words. Plamondon realized that, and credited it to Marnay.

Music, especially songwriting, took off in Quebec in the 1960s, with names like Gilles Vigneault, Jean-Pierre Ferland, Claude Léveillée and first-rate singers like Monique Leyrac, Pauline Julien and Renée Claude.

The 1970s were Robert Charlebois's decade. He took traditional tunes and totally transformed them, adding rock influences, using both French-Canadian dialect and the classic poets of France, as well as all the resources available in Montreal — including Luc Plamondon.

Angélil knew that Marnay would feel hurt. He also knew he'd understand and never advertise his disappointment. He'd written a half dozen songs for the next album. René would keep some of them, all of them — who knows? But he wanted fresh material from Plamondon, too. He'd do a quick transition from one writer to the other.

"He gave me total freedom," Plamondon recalled. "Use whatever music you like, he said. Write whatever you want. And the faster, the better — that's René."

Plamondon had some music written by Daniel Lavoie on hand, and he composed the song "Lolita" to it. The words were directly inspired by Céline. After seeing her that summer day in Paris, he imagined the girl becoming a woman, learning about passion and desire. The words are suggestive and explicit. There's no mistaking the intention: the girl wants to try her hand at love. The song is a long way from Marnay's precious imagery or "Une colombe," performed for the Pope. This time, passion isn't just platonic. It's physical. Love is definitely in the air.

Tu dis que je suis trop jeune
Pour vivre avec un homme.
Moi je te dis
Je m'en fous, je m'en fous.
I love you.

Lolita n'est pas trop jeune pour aimer,
N'est pas trop jeune pour se donner
Quand le désir dévore son corps
Jusqu'au bout des doigts.

Si tu ne viens pas, ce s'ra un autre.
Si ce n'est pas toi, ce s'ra ta faute
Si je regrette toute ma vie
Ma première nuit d'amour.

"Lolita,"
Luc Plamondon and Daniel Lavoie

(You say I'm too young
To be with a man.
I'm telling you
I don't give a damn.
I love you.

Lolita's not too young to love,
Not too young to surrender
When desire devours her body
To her very fingertips.

If it's not you, it'll be someone else.
If it's not you, it'll be your fault
If I ruin
My first night of love.)

Plamondon was afraid that Angélil would be shocked and ask him to change the words. He showed him the lyrics before giving them to Céline. Angélil read them carefully. "He was sitting across from me," Plamondon remembered. "He put the pages on the table and read them two or three times. Then he looked up and said, 'That's exactly what I was hoping for.' I've admired René Angélil ever since. He's courteous and respectful toward his writers, and gives them all the freedom they need. That's part of his success. He trusts people who create things. There are never any limits with him."

With Jean-Alain Roussel, Plamondon wrote "La fille aux bas nylon," which was a big hit for Julien Clerc in France. Roussel had worked as producer and composer with The Police, the Rolling Stones and Cat Stevens. He had an expert sense of rhythm. Like any composer, he was overjoyed at the prospect of writing for an instrument as remarkable as Céline Dion's voice.

Céline moved into the pop music world with a voice the likes of which very few people had ever heard. She could hit higher notes than any other singer Plamondon knew, and without falsetto or straining her voice. "Her natural register, the notes she can reach using her full voice," Plamondon explained, "is broader than any I'd ever heard. There's something spectacular and very touching about singing very high. You get a stronger emotional impact out of the performance. High notes stir emotions. The same song sung at a lower register won't have the same effect."

Céline sang "Incognito" very high, using a register practically unknown by female rock singers. This song revealed her as a true pop star. To make the French language really swing, you have to put the tonic accents in the right places. "Lolita" was a natural. The subject meant something to her, and she liked the arrangements. And it was much easier to sing than "Incognito."

In his little studio in the country outside Montreal, Jean-Alain Roussel asked her to improvise to prerecorded tracks. "I was just experimenting," he said. "Leaving her on her own. If she didn't know what to do, we'd try something else." But she knew exactly what to do. She improvised, staying on key, redesigning the music that Roussel had begun to develop, and to which Plamondon later set his words.

The eight songs that make up the *Incognito* album were recorded in February 1987. This was the first original material she'd recorded in two years. Three producers worked on it: Jean-Alain Roussel, Aldo Nova and Pierre Bazinet. Eddy Marnay had written five of the songs, Plamondon two and Isa Minoke one ("On traverse un miroir"), each one with its own special significance.

Incognito was launched on April 2. It revealed an entirely new side of Céline. She was becoming a fully formed woman. Soon she would spread her wings.

The *Falling Into You* Tour
Milan, October 30, 1996

Backstage Games

The impatient crowd is putting on a little show of its own, doing the wave. You can hear them shouting and chanting all the way back to the dressing room and the offices. Céline loves hearing the crowds. Every one has its own voice, rhythm and tone. Japanese crowds, especially in Tokyo, are so well-behaved that once Céline asked her brother Michel to go sneak a peek inside the Budokan hall to see if there was anyone there. In Nîmes or Nuremburg or Marseille, everywhere in Europe, the audiences are completely different. They chant her name and seem so impatient that she wonders whether they're going to tear the place apart.

Whether they are well-behaved or unruly, you should never keep a crowd waiting. Fifteen minutes before show time, there will be no one around Céline but her trusted friends. Manon and Loulou and Eric, and sometimes Michel and Suzanne. Patrick has already escorted Dave, Barry and their guests to their seats.

Using fluorescent tape, the technicians have traced a path for Céline among the machinery and the heavy coils of wire and cable. In the darkness, you can see the flashing, shimmering, luminous computer screens. Just before she crosses into that zone of darkness, Céline stops and turns back toward Loulou and Manon. Over her dress, she's wearing a long, hooded cape that protects her throat. Loulou holds out a cracker and a glass of warm water. The cracker cleans her throat and vocal cords, and the warm water helps the cracker go down. Manon pushes back the hood and fixes a few strands of her hair.

More laughter. She still has cracker crumbs in her mouth. She blows them out. They laugh some more. In the minute or two before going onstage, she has an instinctive need to laugh. Often, she'll say the first thing that pops into her head.

At Wembley, a representative from Sony in Turkey showed up to give her a gold record a few minutes before the show. As she posed with him, holding up the trophy so everyone could see, she blurted out, "You know, my husband loves Turkey with mashed potatoes."

There was a moment of stunned silence. Then everyone burst out laughing. Michel was still giggling as he escorted Céline to the foot of the little stairway leading to the stage. "That's nothing," she added, "I almost told him that posing with him made me hungry."

At the opening ceremonies for the Atlanta Olympic Games, where she was to sing "The Power of the Dream," she displayed her talents as a comedian. She and Manon were sitting with Eric and René in the tiny little dressing room, just below the stage. Much to Céline's delight, it was very hot. Heat, especially the damp heat of the South, is always good for the voice. Manon had to keep sponging off her cheeks, forehead, throat and shoulders. They started talking about the outdoor show Céline gave in 1984 in Quebec City, in the Old Port. Millions of tiny mayflies, driven mad by the lights, fluttered around the stage. Céline had them in her hair, on her dress, up her nose, in her ears and mouth. "There were even mayflies under my dress," she confided to Manon. "They were like hundreds of little fingers tickling me." As she sang "Une colombe," which hadn't yet become a hit, she must have swallowed a half-dozen of them. Her sister Claudette, sitting in the first row, very clearly saw her spit them out, then continue singing, a compassionate, look on her face, never once forgetting the words to the song or missing a boat. Twelve years later, in a tiny dressing room in Atlanta, five minutes and fifteen steps from the most important stage she had sung on to date, in front of 85,000 people and four billion more watching on television, the Dion sisters were overcome with the giggles as they pictured Céline spitting out mayflies onstage.

René was too nervous to play along with them, though he knew laughter was a source of relaxation for Céline. He stepped out of the dressing room and went to look at the throngs, the banners and the cameras. He came back three minutes before she was to go on. When they saw him, Céline and Manon became serious and silent. Céline spent a quiet moment alone, going through the song, word by word, in her mind.

Tonight, she doesn't feel the same enormous pressure she did in Atlanta. Milan's Forum doesn't hold more than eight thousand people. But this is Céline's first contact with the city, and first meetings can be stressful. Only laughter can dissipate fear and stage fright. Michel knows that, and he fools around to help his sister relax. He finds an old brush in one of the corridors, and now he's pretending to sweep the floor in front of Céline, like a curling player, while she bends down and acts as though she's sliding the rock down the surface.

A giant cheer goes up in the concert hall. The house lights have just been turned off. Claude Plante takes Céline by the hand and leads her along the narrow pathway studded with arrows of fluorescent tape, all the way to the steep stairs that she'll climb alone.

She stands very straight at the back of the stage, inside the protective cocoon formed by the curtains. In the shadows, the musicians turn to look her way. It's her last moment alone.

Like many artists, professional athletes and politicians who perform before large crowds, Céline loves ritual. She has a large number of superstitions and private ceremonies. Her lucky number is five, which came to her early in her career. For years, every time she saw a nickel on the ground, she'd bend down and pick it up.

In a little clear plastic envelope at the bottom of her Vuitton bag, she carries a coin she found on a stage in Trois-Rivières, Quebec. As she always does after her first two songs, she talked to the crowd that night, thanking them for coming, telling them how much she loved them and how she hoped they'd have a good time. Suddenly, she spotted a shiny coin with a beaver on it, tail-side up, right at the edge of the stage.

Angélil has a passionate relation with numbers as well. He likes coincidences and unusual events; he's deeply superstitious. Once he told her never to pick up a coin if it was tail-side up. "If it's tails, let it lie. It'll bring bad luck." But at intermission in Trois-Rivières, after the curtain fell, she leaned over and turned the coin so the heads side showed, then picked it up. It's been her good luck charm ever since.

These days, she doesn't find many coins lying around. She doesn't have much chance to walk freely in places where people might drop a coin. She can't go by herself down the street anymore, or linger on the avenues or in shopping malls.

During the Incognito *tour, before the curtain rose, she would perform a complex ritual, a kind of childish game that was both serious and reassuring. Just before the show, when everything was ready, she would do a funny little dance with Mégo, the band leader. She would go with him to his keyboards and pretend to hit the button that sets off the lighting, lifts the curtain and starts the music. Mégo would act shocked and angry, and would pretend to hit her. Then she would dance across the set and touch her right thumb to the musicians' and backup singers' right thumbs.*

As she stood in the shadows that enveloped the stage, Suzanne Gingue, her tour director, would hand her the microphone. Before taking it, Céline would press Suzanne's bare arm three times. Then she'd turn to Angélil who, at the time, attended every show. He would kiss her on both cheeks, her left cheek first. Then he'd put both hands on her shoulders and shake her very gently and gaze into her eyes with a serious look. Then he would turn her around toward the stage and give her a gentle push. "Okay, go ahead, you're ready. Go!"

The ritual has changed over time, but it's still as necessary as ever. It's not a game. For Céline, every movement has magical powers. She needs them, especially when she's on tour, far from her familiar surroundings, when every night the dressing room, the hotel, the stage and the crowds are different. These little games give her a sense of stability, familiarity and intimacy.

Before René leaves the backstage to slip into the concert hall, two or three minutes before its time for her to go onstage, she walks up to him. He holds out his left hand, palm open like an offering. She takes his palm and places the fingers of her right hand in it. Then with her other hand, she closes René's hand over her fingers. The ritual means everything to her because of its symbolism. René's palm is the bowl, the cradle, the vessel, the nest. She places her hand, her life, her future in it.

If ever René seems unfocused during this ceremony, if he doesn't keep his hand open the right way, she'll reprimand him. "René Angélil, look at me!"

Then, everyone who's part of the show — the musicians, backup singers and the dozens of technicians — will participate in the right-thumb ceremony. In the seconds before the curtain goes up, Céline will turn to each of her musicians and singers, look them in the eye and throw out her arms, thumbs up. They smile and raise their thumbs too. Then she'll go through the same ritual with Daniel Baron on her right, Jeff and Loulou at the foot of the stairway behind her, then her brother Michel, her sister Manon and Suzanne.

In Birmingham one night, Michel got tangled in the curtains and couldn't find his way out. His panicked sisters went looking for him in the darkness. Finally, he had to slip under the curtain and run to the foot of the stairway to raise his thumbs in his sister's direction. Only then did the stage manager give the signal.

And Céline stepped onstage, totally in character. A strong woman with strong feelings, a star, completely herself.

Chapter Eighteen
The Sound Barrier

To launch an album, you usually start by releasing the song you think will work best. If the public likes the song, it will carry the entire album, provided key radio stations cooperate. Once the song has done its job, a second one will be released, which will attract a different audience and keep sales going. To really work, an album must have at least three hit singles. Four is excellent. Five, gigantic. Anything more is a miracle.

The promotion departments at record companies carry out preliminary research with record librarians and programmers at radio stations. Each station has a well-defined sound, market share, and selected audience. The idea is to have several types of singles getting airtime on different radio stations. That is why it's a good idea to have several producers for the same album, as was the case with *Incognito*. Such an approach gives you greater variety in the color of the music. *Incognito* featured Nova's heavy, urban, chrome-plated funk, Bazinet's more careful arrangements and Roussel's sophisticated structures.

Mario Lefebvre, promotion man at CBS, had to convince local radio stations to play Céline's records — something none of them had done till then. Rock stations turned up their noses at her. They considered her middle of the road. Young audiences, the eighteen-to-twenty-five bracket, didn't know who she was. The rock stations they listen to didn't even have her records. Every time Mia Dumont would meet Guy Brouillard of CKOI, a dance music station, and try to convince him to add Céline to his playlist, he would tell her, "Sure, it's good music, but it's not our sound." Mia would tell him, "One day, you'll *have* to play her."

They tried to work with the rock stations without losing the "easy listening" or "adult" stations. Mario Lefebvre met the programmers one by one. He played "Incognito" and "Délivre-moi" for them. Meanwhile, Mia was preparing a launch for the record, which turned out to be the event of the season in the entertainment business. It took place at a very snobbish and very chic discotheque (which had once been a funeral home) in downtown Montreal. Everybody was there — the hip and the not so hip.

"We had a lot of visibility and credibility," Mario Lefebvre recalled. "CBS was very hot at the time. And we got a lot of people wondering who Céline was — the new Céline. We knew she'd win everybody over, even people who swore they'd never listen to her. She showcased 'Incognito,' 'Lolita,' 'On traverse un miroir' and 'Délivre-moi.' The reaction was fabulous. We knew that very night that the battle was won. All the stations would jump on the bandwagon."

The next day, *Incognito* was launched in Quebec City at the Hotel Concorde discotheque. It took some arm-twisting to get certain radio stations to show up. The rock station guys hung out at the back of the room, pretending they weren't really there, acting skeptical and blasé. While Céline sang, Mario and René watched them carefully. An expression of complete surprise came over their faces from the moment she sang her first song. After the second song, they too had been convinced. The media, the distributors, the critics — everyone was wild about her.

Céline's team played up the rock angle to the rock stations: Plamondon's words, Daniel Lavoie's music, Aldo Nova's production. These men were heroes of the rock and pop world. But Angélil & Co. didn't want to lose the fans who loved Eddy Marnay's style. Rather than bring out "Incognito" and "Lolita" as singles right away, they released a quieter song, "On traverse un miroir," written by Isa Minoke and Robert Lafond. They hoped to build a bridge between the two Célines and between her two audiences. That way, the switch over to a harder rock sound wouldn't alienate her traditional fans.

A few days after the album release, the rock stations told Mario they wanted to play "Incognito" as a single because it was making waves, musically and vocally. In the end, that song was issued as a single much earlier than planned.

Very quickly, carried by its five hit singles, the album went gold, then platinum. It sold 175,000 copies in Quebec alone. It was obvious that Céline was conquering new markets. She was being talked about by journalists from the mainstream media, the tabloid press and everything in between, including television and radio. Now, CBS had to honor the clause that Angélil had added to the contract and produce a record in English.

"When *Incognito* was released," Mario Lefebvre says, "Céline Dion's second career truly began." With "Lolita," "Incognito" and "Jours de fièvre," she moved onto the playlist of rock stations in English and French for the first time. And thanks to Eddy Marnay's new songs, the radio stations that used to play her, and whose interest had been dampened by the rather gloomy *C'est pour toi*, started spinning her disks again. She'd become a pop singer. And she became one of the first to cross over and be heard everywhere, from stations that played soothing music for overworked executives to the rough-and-ready rock stations.

Of course, some people would never give in. When she had Luc Plamondon on her talk show, a certain Radio-Canada TV host expressed her surprise that a songwriter of his stature would stoop so low as to pen words for that "little commercial singer."

"You're writing for everybody now, I see," the host said, "even Céline Dion!"

Plamondon has always been respected as an artist and a man, and he told the TV host that Céline Dion wasn't just anybody. Not only did she have an incomparable voice, she gave songs remarkably intelligent interpretations and was, despite her young age, "one of the world's great singers."

In her interviews, Céline never hid her hunger for success. Her naked ambition bothered some people and they considered it vulgar. Great artists, like politicians, who yearn for success should at least give the appearance of having high principles. What Céline was after — to be the greatest female singer in the world — shocked a few puritanical souls.

Mia Dumont, Céline's first press agent, moved to Paris to live with Eddy Marnay. During the first five years, especially since Anne-Renée's departure, she had been a mentor to Céline when it came to clothes, fashion and taste. She had taught the young woman about beauty, and Céline could listen to Mia for hours on end. Sometimes, they would go shopping together. Their aim was to learn about fashion. Buying clothes was secondary. But Mia never thought of herself as a teacher. She loved to watch Céline take pleasure in recognizing a certain designer's style, or a fragrance, or a well-made piece of jewelry.

"Céline is like a sponge," Mia said. "She soaks up knowledge quickly. She can learn anything because she knows how to ask questions. She's curious about everything. She has a passion for what's beautiful, whether it's clothes, bodies, places, objects or languages. She's always so eager to learn."

When Mia and Céline went their separate ways, both knew that they wouldn't be seeing much of each other anymore, and when they did, it would be only briefly. "Céline had taken off," Mia recalled. "Everyone knew she'd go far, and that whatever she did, you'd hear about no matter where you were in the world. I promised her I'd follow her from afar."

Thanks to the fax machine, they were able to have a long-distance relationship. They discussed Céline's image, her look, the way she carried herself during interviews, the artwork on her posters and album covers.

> It might sound strange, but my real friendship with Mia didn't get going until we stopped having a professional relationship. For several years, she represented authority in my life, although it was never anything that was forced on me. It was the authority that comes from knowledge and good taste. She intimidated me a lot because she spoke so beautifully and knew so many things. When she left, I discovered everything we had in common. And I realize how much she'd taught me.

On Mia's urging, René Angélil asked Francine Chaloult to look after Céline's promotion and press relations in French Canada. Angélil, Céline, Chaloult and Murielle, her assistant, met for lunch in an Italian restaurant in downtown Montreal. Angélil knew who Chaloult was by reputation. She could move heaven and earth to get what she wanted for her artists. She was adored, loved and feared, and had a way of getting people to do her bidding. Her assistant Murielle had worked at the Saint Charles studio in Longueuil where Céline had recorded most of the songs for her first album. Angélil didn't have much money at the time, and Murielle let him have the studio at a very affordable price, letting him work at night and not counting the hours. Angélil had never forgotten her help.

In Céline, Murielle found a changed woman. A very adult eighteen year old, knowledgeable about fashion, who talked clothes while René laid out his plans and described his dreams. He told Francine Chaloult that one day Céline would reach the highest levels of stardom. He didn't seem to understand the word "doubt." But Chaloult had seen her share of dreamers and doers. For the last twenty years, she'd worked with the greatest artists in France and Quebec, from Charles Aznavour to Gilles Vigneault. She knew them all. When they played Montreal, they always visited her at her home. She had become true friends with them, despite her intimidating personality.

She listened to Angélil rave about his artist. In the business, many people said he was a megalomaniac, or just plain naive. He compared Céline to Barbra Streisand and Edith Piaf — nothing but the best. But his calm composure caught Chaloult's attention. She realized that René was asking her to believe. To have faith. Because of him, she decided to believe that one day Céline *would* be the number one singer in the world. Even if she was going through a slow period, especially in France, where her last album was not doing very well.

In the summer of 1987, Patrick Sabatier, who had a popular variety show on French television, came to Montreal to record a special with Daniel Lavoie, Robert Charlebois and Céline Dion. Featured was a selection of songs from *Starmania*, which was still playing in Paris.

Since Céline's latest album was to be launched in France that fall, it was only natural for Plamondon to expect her to sing "Incognito" and "Lolita" on the special. When he got to the Spectrum concert hall that afternoon, Céline was there, rehearsing a song he'd never heard. A few minutes later, he ran into Angélil, who was obviously uncomfortable. Before Plamondon could say anything, René told him that the song was one Marnay had written before the *Incognito* album had been recorded. He reminded Plamondon that France, where the special would air, was producer Claude Pascal's property, and Pascal had the decision-making power when it came to marketing. He was afraid of offending Céline's traditional audience with songs like "Incognito" and "Lolita." That's why he decided to use the Marnay song. What Plamondon didn't know at the time was that not only would his two songs not be released as singles, they wouldn't even make it on the French album.

He found that out a few weeks later, in France. His colleague, Italian composer Musumara, told him the replacement song hadn't been written earlier. It had been written after the recording, with the express purpose of replacing "Lolita." "René Angélil didn't dare tell me the truth," Plamondon concluded.

The two Plamondon songs that launched Céline's pop career were never released in France. Perhaps Angélil felt guilty about having replaced Marnay. Perhaps he let himself be convinced that, rightly or wrongly, these two songs would hurt Céline's career in France. Both Marnay and

Pascal believed that French audiences would consider "Lolita" shocking, and incompatible with Céline's image. The French are very slow to accept change, and they still pictured Céline as an innocent little girl. Marnay also thought that the entire point of "Incognito" wouldn't be understood in France. In Quebec, everyone knew that Céline had made some big changes in her life, and that she'd gone from girl to woman. That wasn't common knowledge in France yet.

At the time, Plamondon was angry, but he kept his anger to himself. "Since then, I've realized that Eddy Marnay was sincere," he says now. "Maybe he was even right. Maybe the French wouldn't have accepted Céline singing 'Lolita.' Marnay saw Céline as the next Nana Mouskouri. He placed her in the tradition of sweet, harmless French songs, not as a pop singer, let alone a rock artist. He had worked with Barbra Streisand, but he'd never ventured into pop or rock. When you see Céline singing a Jacques Brel song like 'Quand on n'a que l'amour,' you can understand the image Marnay had of her."

But there were other reasons too, reasons that had to do with taste. Back then, the French didn't like big-voiced female singers. Fluty voices were in at the time; big voices were considered too brassy. Besides Edith Piaf, who was an untouchable national monument, the fashion ran towards little-girl voices singing little-girl songs.

"In France, people are true to their stars," Plamondon explained. "And they want their stars to be true to them. They're not supposed to change their ways. It would be very hard for any of them to do that. The poet Baudelaire claimed he had the right to make mistakes and change his mind, but he was one against many. Mireille Mathieu hasn't changed her look in thirty years. Neither has Dalida or Hallyday. You're not allowed to sing one style one day and another style the next."

Around the same time, Plamondon wrote a song for Marie-Carmen that was a hit in Quebec, and that Céline would later record. It was called "Piaf chanterait du rock" — Piaf would have been a rock singer. No one wanted to release the song in France. They were afraid the French would see it as an insult to Piaf.

So when Musumara went into the studio with Céline to record Marnay's replacement song, he told her she was singing too much, and suggested she put less voice into her song. Céline was angry and disappointed. In Europe, they wouldn't accept that she'd become a new singer. They wanted her to remain the sweet, innocent little girl — the dreamy virginal singer.

In Quebec, per capita sales of *Incognito* were ten times better than in

France. The album had a powerful effect on her international career and led to events that gave her greater visibility in English Canada. There were the Juno Awards in 1987, Eurovision in 1988 and, more importantly, the CBS national convention in Estérel, in the Laurentian mountains north of Montreal.

Every year in June, the CBS staff gets together somewhere in Canada, usually in a resort with mountains, a lake and a golf course. They talk about their past year's successes and their plans for the future. On June 22, 1987, they held their convention in the Laurentians.

The president of CBS Canada, Bernie DiMatteo, a number cruncher originally from New York, told René Angélil to bring Céline. The record company was giving her the chance to showcase her songs. That night, she sang two songs in French from the *Incognito* album: a rocker and a ballad. The audience applauded just a little more enthusiastically than what politeness demanded. They were professionals who knew how to recognize true talent. But what was a promotion person from Vancouver or Toronto supposed to do with a French song? Outside of Quebec, there was practically no demand for that kind of music.

Dan Hill was the featured star at the convention. He was a CBS singer-composer-songwriter who'd had great success with "Can We Try," a duet with Vonda Shepard. That night in Estérel, at the end of the presentation, when Dan Hill burst into song, the audience was surprised to see Céline Dion walk onstage and sing with him. It seemed as though the song had been written for her alone. She sang so well that the room exploded in applause. Everyone rose to their feet. This time, the audience of professionals wasn't just being polite. All 150 of them, from across Canada and the United States, gave this young unknown a standing ovation.

Afterwards Mario, Céline, Vito and René lingered in the deserted hall, unable to tear themselves away from this place where a historic event (for them, anyway) had just occurred. Like athletes after a superhuman effort, they didn't talk much. Except for Céline. Whenever she steps offstage, after a period of intense stress, she's always wound up and bouncing off the walls. She continued to sing, by herself, in a very high voice.

Ever since diMatteo had suggested that Céline sing the duet with Dan Hill, she and René had been in a kind of trance. They both realized the strategic importance of the performance. The slightest weakness in her singing, or even just a moderately good performance, and they were back to square one. René and Mario had wondered how they should act around Céline, given the circumstances. Should they hide their nervousness? Or, knowing how she fed off stage fright and pressure, should they remind her of just how crucial the opportunity was? But they needn't have worried. Céline stole the show from Dan Hill. The greater the pressure, the better she sang.

That same evening, Angélil met Paul Farberman, then vice-president of CBS Canada. Farberman was a young lawyer from Toronto who knew North American show business. He had the kind of qualities Angélil appreciated: he acted fast, he took the initiative — and he loved Céline. René reminded him that the *Incognito* album had gone platinum, that two singles were playing on English radio, even in Toronto, and that it was time for Sony to honor its promise to produce an English album. But with $30,000 — the sum that had been agreed on — no one could produce a decent product. Farberman, who had attended Céline's performance, told René he'd find him up to $100,000.

The *Falling Into You* Tour
West Palm Beach, March 12, 1997

The Show

At first you hear the words, barely audible, scattered by the wind through the darkness, high above the Coral Sky Amphitheater. The air crackles with electricity as crowd murmurs with anticipation. You can catch a few phrases, a whispered "I love you," soft but potent. Then suddenly, a voice rises above the chaos — clear and strong. The audience and the wind fall silent, and every heart is captured:

> The whispers in the morning
> Of lovers sleeping tight,
> Are rolling like thunder now
> As I look in your eyes.
>
> "The Power of Love,"
> Gunther Mende, Candy DeRouge, Jennifer Rush,
> and Mary Susan Applegate

Erratic lightning flashes split the darkness and throw furtive shadows across the clouds of smoke rising from the stage. The throng searches for the spot from where the voice is coming. Finally they see Céline at the top of the runway that divides the stage in two.

I hold on to your body
And feel each move you make.
Your voice is warm and tender,
A love that I could not forsake.

"The Power of Love" is an erotic song, the story of a torrid love scene. The twenty songs that make up the Falling Into You *show all speak of love — simple, classic, eternal love. A man and a woman.*

Just as Céline launches into the chorus, the stage is bathed in bright light, and her face appears on the giant screens on both sides of the stage. The audience leaps to its feet. For the rest of the show, Céline will be enveloped in light, exposed to every eye, singing of love.

Cause I'm your lady,
And you are my man.
Whenever you reach for me
I'll do all that I can.

For Céline and René, Palm Beach has all the advantages of a big city in Europe or America without any of the drawbacks — the noise or the crowds or the threat of violence. On Worth Avenue, you can find the best fashion houses, the highest-quality jewelers and the world's most famous restaurants. All around are beautiful golf courses, well-maintained beaches and nature that has been tamed and manicured.

Céline ends the song. She lets the applause wash over her, then tells the people, "I feel so wonderful being home with you tonight." Her voice is like velvet. Her words and the texture of her voice are like a lover fulfilled. The Coral Sky Amphitheater goes crazy. An electric charge rushes between Céline and the crowd. The show is going to be fabulous — pure pleasure. But there's always a danger that if an audience is conquered too soon, it can feel disappointed or neglected. But when it starts off cold, like the other night in Buffalo, Céline mobilizes all her energy and intelligence and charm to seduce the crowd. She'll do whatever she has to. She'll get down on her knees. She'll work her voice harder, she'll heighten the emotion. And when the audience rises to its feet, when they've been conquered, when they give her an ovation, only then will she savor sweet victory. But tonight, there's no need to dig deep into her energy reserve. The Coral Sky audience gets to its feet again when she sings "River Deep, Mountain High." She rides their ovations with natural grace. "I see a lot of my neighbors tonight," she says, smiling.

Bryon Rivers, a writer with the Palm Beach Post, scribbles in his notebook, "Dion doesn't have stage presence; she is *stage presence."*

It's been said many times that her presence is her greatest asset. She has more of it than her rivals, Whitney Houston and Mariah Carey. Even more than Barbra Streisand, who is often too stiff and tense. Céline knows how to communicate with the audience. And her communication is always honest, simple and filled with infinite warmth.

She's been touring almost nonstop for two years. She's seen Canada, the United States, Europe, the Pacific Rim, Asia. At the end of March 1996, back from Australia and New Zealand, she and her team decided to shake up the show a little, so they changed the songs, costumes and sets. Some of the songs from the old show had become a little tired. Others, from the Falling Into You *album, needed to be featured. With an eye to promoting the album, Céline and René gave the whole show a makeover. She asked for a month to rehearse the new version.*

But she got so busy with promotion, making videos and appearing on television that Mégo, her band leader, started getting worried. René originally promised him a week of rehearsals, then four days, then two. Mégo rehearsed with the musicians, but without Céline. The musicians were ready: they knew the music and were in control of their part of the show. Mégo was confident that Céline would learn fast, but Lapin was worried. He had designed the lighting and chosen color motifs for every song, but since he didn't know how Céline would move onstage, he couldn't place the spotlights. In the end, they had only three measly hours of rehearsals in the old Montreal Forum, which had closed its doors three weeks earlier. In that three hours, they made a quick inventory of the worst mistakes, but there was no time to correct them, except in each performer's mind. Everybody was terribly nervous.

The new show premiered in Vancouver on May 18, 1996. Things got off to a rough start. Everyone was so busy trying not to make a mistake that there was no harmony between the parts. And very little pleasure either, for the musicians or the audience. The critics were unanimously harsh. Ironically, they hadn't noticed the technical mistakes, the confusion or the disjointed lighting design, and instead attacked the songs themselves. They were too syrupy, they claimed, and they pointed to "The Power of Love" and "Because You Loved Me" as being out-of-date and totally politically incorrect. They wondered how, in 1996, a twenty-eight-year-old woman could tell a man that she lived only through him, and for him? How could she tell him "I am your lady, and you are my man, I am what I am only because you loved me?" The critics hammered away at that theme on every stop of the tour, especially in America. But no one failed to mention Céline's powerful voice, the quality of her stage presence, how she could charm the audience, how spontaneous and direct and natural she was. And no one failed to mention that the audience begged for more.

Angélil rarely finds anything useful in what the critics say, but he reads the reviews anyway. Sometimes he'll call a journalist to ask for clarification or point out a mistake. It's a game for him, not a way to actually learn anything new. When you've sold dozens of millions of albums, it's hard to always believe what your critics are saying. They listen to Angélil's point of view. Sometimes they're intimidated, sometimes they're polite. They might try to temper or soften their comments. They remind him that they also wrote about her extraordinary voice, electrifying presence, and how the crowd was eating out of her hand. But they still don't like the songs. They feel they're too syrupy and sentimental, assembly-line songs, stereotyped and springing from the same hit factory. The critics prefer Alanis Morissette and Annie Lennox. Their music is more original, and their words more significant and heavy with meaning. Those critics prefer singers who want to change the world (or who pretend they do) to those who sing about it as it is, or as they wish it could be.

Chapter Nineteen
A Rising Star

During the summer and fall of 1987, René began working on a new show and preparing the tour. He had to start from scratch: find a band, a leader, a stage manager, a sound recordist, a tour director. He approached one of the most powerful show producers in Quebec, Jean-Claude L'Espérance, a very serious man. He was no artist himself, but he was trustworthy and competent.

L'Espérance was known as the producer of Jean-Guy Moreau, a very caustic impersonator and comedian. Angélil also contacted Claude Lemay, (Mégo), Moreau's experienced band leader. L'Espérance caught up to Mégo in early September at the Granby Song Festival and made him an offer. Did he want to tour with Céline Dion next season?

Céline wasn't exactly Mégo's type. A few years earlier, he had put together an avant-garde, experimental rock group called Pollen that was more concerned with the formal structure of music than with charming the masses. As orchestrator in charge of the Granby Song Festival that was famous for breaking out new talent, he worked with the most dynamic musicians on the Quebec rock scene. As far as he was concerned, Céline represented everything that was commercial and middle of the road, well-manufactured and respectable, but not very creative. Jean-Claude L'Espérance told him to watch the TV special that would air three weeks later on Radio-Canada and call him if he changed his mind.

The TV special, also called *Incognito*, ran on September 27. It was directed by Jacques Payette and a group of researchers who'd worked very closely with Céline. They asked her what she wanted to do and who she wanted to be. "I want something theatrical," she told the crew. "I want disguise, I want to dance, and sing, of course — all kinds of things, even opera."

They began by creating an entire array of characters: a hot-blooded Lolita, a Garbo-style vamp, a hell-bent rock queen, a little girl who'd grown up too fast, an arrogantly beautiful model. They added two American standards to the list of songs: "My Heart Belongs to Daddy" and "Chattanooga Choo Choo."

Mégo watched the TV show. He couldn't believe his ears or eyes. He had a vague memory of a little singer named Céline Dion who had a very good voice, crooked teeth and a big nose. He'd heard and liked the summer's big hits: "Incognito" and "D'abord, c'est quoi l'amour?" But he hadn't really made the connection. He was too busy with the Moreau tour and the music and orchestrations he had to prepare for the Granby festival.

That September evening on his television set, he discovered a sexy young woman of nineteen who could move onstage and knew how to dance. Who could charm the pants off an audience with her extraordinarily powerful, supple and sensual voice. When the show was over, he called L'Espérance and told him he'd gladly put together a band and go on tour with Céline Dion. He knew musicians who would do her justice. He put Martin Daviault on saxophones, Marc Alie on drums, Pierre Dumont-Gauthier on guitars and Paul Morin on keyboards. He hired her sister Ghislaine as a backup singer. On bass, he got Breen Leboeuf, quite a surprising choice. Leboeuf played with the hard-rock group Offenbach, the Rolling Stones of the Quebec scene. He represented everything that was down and dirty about rock and roll.

To see Leboeuf sing a duo with that fresh-faced, innocent little girl in her spangled dress would be downright surrealistic. They planned on singing a Pierre Huet tune, "Mes blues passent p'us dans 'porte" ("My Blues Won't Fit Through the Door No More"), full of the profane dialect of Montreal French at its crudest. In rehearsal, Leboeuf would burst out in his incorrigible mixture of French and English, "Cette fille-là, elle est right on, man, elle est vraiment rock 'n' roll!" By drafting Breen Leboeuf, that monument of solid rock, Angélil would expand Céline's audience.

He would position her as a bona fide rock and pop singer. But she wouldn't neglect the material Marnay had created for her, nor the image she had projected ever since "D'amour ou d'amitié," the picture of a level-headed girl slowly awakening to the realities of life and love. She was all those things and more, and the fall TV special illustrated that fact. She was vamp and virgin, dove and tigress.

Mégo spent several days reading the scores of the songs and preparing the arrangements. One October day, he went to a small rehearsal room at Place-des-Arts to meet Céline and determine the keys she'd use to sing the Garland and Streisand songs she planned to do. Everyone knew the songs: "Somewhere over the Rainbow," "The Way We Were," Summertime," "Memories." It would be very difficult to give them a new slant, since they'd already been sung and mastered by all the big show business voices in America. Mégo smiled when he thought of a nineteen-year-old girl taking on those big stars.

At the Granby festival, he had accompanied dozens of young female and male singers. Most of them could hardly sing on key, let alone project their voice. Céline Dion did that with disconcerting ease, with as much strength in the high range as in the low. Mégo felt reassured. He knew he was going to have some fun.

Jean Bissonnette, who'd produced a lot of variety shows for Radio-Canada, had recommended Mégo to L'Espérance, not only because he was a good musician with the leadership qualities to put together and lead a band, but because of his theatrical side. Every time master impersonator Jean-Guy Moreau stepped offstage to change his costume or makeup, Mégo would announce to the audience that he could do impersonators too — which he did so badly that the audience would howl for more. He had a great sense of timing, he understood crowds and he showed a lot of empathy.

Jean-Pierre Plante, who had written Céline's between-song patter, asked Mégo to help out with some of the comic routines he'd composed. Plante had contributed material to quite a few comedians and comics. He developed made-to-measure skits that suited them astonishingly well, using their offstage lives, their look and their manners. With their consent, he enjoyed parodying them with his savage wit.

Plante listened to Céline's songs, read her press clippings, studied her career and its highlights. He wrote humorous material that let her poke fun at her own image. During one rehearsal, she did her own expert impersonations of Ginette Reno and Michael Jackson. Then and there, Plante decided that she should do them onstage. For additional help with the patter, he called upon Pierre Huet, the songwriter. At the time, Huet was working as editor-in-chief of *Croc*, a kind of Quebec *Mad* magazine, with an accent on the vulgar, the political and the risqué.

That year, the Juno Awards ceremony (the Canadian version of the Grammys) was to be held in November, while Mégo, Plante and Huet, under Angélil's direction, would be preparing the *Incognito* tour. The album had been a mega-success in Quebec. Through a small item accidentally "leaked" to the Canadian media by Angélil and Chaloult, *Billboard* magazine, the Bible of American show business, had begun to notice what they called "the Céline Dione [sic] phenomenon" that was breaking all sales records, even though she was still totally unknown on the English side of Canada.

The Juno organizers were impressed by the sales figures, though they knew nothing about the album. Yet they wanted Céline to perform a French song from her *Incognito* album. René was ecstatic. English Canada was a necessary step in Céline's career.

The year before at that same awards ceremony, Quebec singer Martine St.-Clair sang a song in French. Canadian record industry executives were moved by it, and they all agreed it had been sung wonderfully. But nothing more had happened, because nothing could happen. The movers and shakers of the Canadian industry had no interests there. They knew nothing about the business in France, or even about the French-language scene in Quebec where, in general, they had no contacts. They had asked Martine St-Clair to sing the year before for, essentially, political reasons. They wanted to show everyone that they were striving to bring the two language groups in Canada closer together.

Angélil accepted the Juno invitation, as long as Céline could sing in English. He tried to think of an appropriate song. It would have to be something well-known that everyone could relate to, a song popularized by Judy Garland or Barbra Streisand, a classic ballad that wouldn't offend anyone, and would act as a showcase for Céline's voice.

He discussed the dilemma with Céline, Mario and Vito. They decided she should sing something original instead of a classic from the past. After all, the first time Eddy Marnay had heard her, he was impressed because she'd chosen something new. Original material would let her display not only the strength of her voice, but how she could use it in a totally personal way.

There was a song on the *Incognito* album called "Partout je te vois," with music by Aldo Nova and English words by Nova and Billy Steinberg, who'd worked in the past with Madonna. The song would let

Céline show off the strength of her voice and give industry people — and the television audience — a better idea of her talent, since she'd actually be creating the song. She'd be its first singer, the one to set the standard.

Angélil asked Aldo Nova to go back into the studio. After forty-eight straight hours of rearranging, Nova came up with the music for "Have a Heart" in a key that was right for Céline.

Then they all set off for Toronto — Céline, René, Mario and Vito — all terribly nervous. Everyone would be there. It would be a who's who of Canadian show business. The big boss of CBS, Bernie DiMatteo, would be there too. The people who'd attended the Estérel convention the previous June knew who Céline Dion was. They knew about her voice, her strength, her warmth. They still remembered the incredible duet she'd sung with Dan Hill. But the general public and the media had no idea who she was.

Once she was onstage with the audience and the cameras, all nervousness disappeared. She performed "Have a Heart" with pleasure, passion and confidence. In return, she received thunderous applause. René wept openly. He realized that Céline had just opened another door. The next day, the record company scouts and decision makers would be chasing after him. One critic wrote, "She blew everybody away." Céline Dion had stolen the show from the other artists on the Juno Awards.

The next afternoon, René and Vito showed up in diMatteo's office and found him involved in a high-level telephone conversation. With one hand over the receiver, the big boss of CBS motioned to them to sit down. Once he'd hung up, he described how the president of another record company had called to tell him that Céline Dion was a regular gold mine. DiMatteo must have been pretty excited to talk that way in front of René and Vito. After all, the two men had come to negotiate money and contracts, and normally a record company executive has to appear coolheaded.

CBS agreed to increase the amount of money set aside to produce the English record. In June, in Estérel, thanks to Farberman's work, they'd increased the amount from $30,000 to $100,000. Less than six months later, the budget tripled — from $100,000 to $300,000. Angélil was in seventh heaven. But he had one more condition. "I want David Foster to be the producer," he insisted.

At the time, Foster was the boy wonder of the American record industry. A songwriter, composer, arranger, producer and band leader all rolled into one, he originally came from Victoria, the capital of British Columbia. He'd worked with the group Chicago, Barbra Streisand, Nathalie Cole, Frank Sinatra and Neil Diamond. He had established himself in Los Angeles, where many people thought of him as the best record producer going.

Bernie DiMatteo didn't promise anything. He didn't close any doors, but he didn't open any either. "If you want him to work with you," he advised Angélil, "you'll have to convince him yourself."

The rehearsals for the *Incognito* show continued in an atmosphere of total euphoria. Sponsors, who'd been reluctant up till then, hurried to climb on the bandwagon — everyone from Kentucky Fried Chicken to radio stations and newspapers. Two sound technicians joined the crew: Denis Savage and Daniel Baron. Savage would be in charge of miking the halls, while Baron would take care of the stage sound. As the Christmas holidays drew near, the show was in perfect running order. But one part was missing: a stage manager and tour director.

Jean Bissonnette suggested Suzanne Gingue, Mégo's girlfriend, who'd also worked on the Moreau tour. She managed Moreau's schedule, coordinated the stage setup, managed the actual performances, helped Moreau with his makeup, costumes and other details. The *Incognito* tour, with its fifteen musicians and technicians, would present greater demands. Suzanne didn't have much experience, but she was a fighter and had loads of determination. In January, she contacted the local producers. She filled her tourbook, reserved hotel rooms, and printed and distributed the programs and posters.

The *Incognito* show was designed like a giant menu that featured Céline's astonishing vocal variety. Every kind of song was included: from sentimental ballads to hard rock, with one stop on Broadway and another in Paris. Céline sang some material from the rock opera *Starmania* and hits that had been established by other female artists. She gave a new and profoundly moving interpretation of Jean-Pierre Ferland's "Ton visage." She imitated the most famous voices of our time, from Michael Jackson to Mireille Mathieu to Ginette Reno to Diane Dufresne. She was out to prove that she could do anything. She could sing any material in any style and in any key. She could even turn to comedy and parody if she wanted. She was a far cry from that teary-eyed little girl she used to be.

In Jean-Pierre Plante's comedic routines, she made fun of how she "tasted of the Papal milk" (alluding to the cows she milked when visiting the Pope). She described how she had joined a chapter of "Weepers Anonymous" (based on Alcoholics Anonymous), where people learned to choke back their tears. "Next week," she would tell the audiences, "will be one year since I last wept. And just to prove that I've really recovered, and learned to control myself, I'm going to sing a sad song without shedding a single tear."

But Céline was running a risk with that kind of diverse routine. She seemed to be unsure of who she was. She swung wildly between Broadway show tunes and garage rock. But all that mattered now was impressing the audiences, and she was caught up in the general euphoria. And she was happy and self-confident to boot.

On Sunday, January 10, Céline joined "Juste pour vivre," a show produced by the Quebec Heart Foundation. She sang "Comme un coeur froid," a Marnay and Roussel song. The next day, her *Incognito* tour began. This time, her mother didn't go with her since Céline was mature enough to be on her own. She'd soon turn twenty — and she was in love.

The tour kicked off on January 11, 1988 at the Théâtre du Cuivre in Rouyn, a city on Quebec's northern frontier. Céline gave seven performances in that region and two in Laval, a suburban city near Montreal. The shows were extremely successful, made even more so by the spin René Angélil and Francine Chaloult put on them in Montreal. That was Angélil's policy: keep hitting the media in the bigger centers. Keep building on Céline's success through radio, TV and newspapers of all kinds.

By the time Céline was ready to play Montreal at the end of January, her show had already become an event. The Dion express was moving at full speed, and nothing could stop it. On one TV talk show, Céline positively exuded self-confidence. "Maybe I shouldn't exactly say it this way," she admitted, "but I really think my show is great."

After the Montreal premiere on February 10, 1988 at the Théâtre Saint-Denis, everyone got together at the Jardin de Paris, Dodo and Guy Morali's restaurant that had moved to the New World. Céline arrived at thirty minutes past midnight. Star hockey player Guy Lafleur was there, along with Luc Plamondon, artist Jean-Pierre Ferland, several members of the Dion family (including Michel, her father and mother), Francine Chaloult and Ben Kaye. The appetizer was a smoked salmon mousse. The main dish was boneless breast of chicken, followed by a desert of orange truffle cake. No wine for Céline. She drank a Coke.

Mia and Eddy came from Paris to attend the premier. They hadn't seen Céline for several months. When she spotted them as they walked into the Jardin de Paris, she rose to embrace them. She stood in front of Mia so her friend could see the woman she had become, and their eyes met. Céline smiled and Mia could see her straight, white teeth. "She had been transformed. She was as beautiful as a princess from a fairy tale," Mia remembered. "I realized then and there that she was in love."

Angélil awoke at dawn to read the papers. The critics had fallen in love with Céline. Everyone was comparing her to Barbra Streisand. On the popular morning radio shows, the music critics spoke about how moved they'd been, almost to the point of tears. "Céline can hold her own against any singer," they declared. "She's generous and direct onstage. And besides, she's got great legs!"

But the culture vultures continued to wonder out loud in their newspapers. Céline was entering unknown territory. She was becoming an idol, an object of debate. Céline, a star? Come now! "Let's not lose our sense of proportion," Paul Cauchon wrote in the very prestigious and somewhat stuffy daily paper *Le Devoir*. He admitted she had "an exceptional, even fabulous voice," and that she'd learned to move onstage, and dance, and actually feel what she sang, and that her "vocal talent" held "great promise." But he criticized her pronunciation, which he called "terrible, most of the time," noting that she talked through her nose, which kept her from reaching true star status. "The way Céline Dion is being presented is an attempt to condition the public into accepting her automatically as a star. That's far from being the case. True stars personify myths. Stars lives create their own imagery. They are frail beings who are reborn onstage. For now, Céline Dion has no personal universe."

In some circles, people felt that Céline Dion had a long way to go before reaching star status. Out of false modesty — or perhaps she was fishing for compliments? — she herself would refuse to make that claim. "I'm not a star," she would say. "I'm just as regular girl."

She was also criticized for not representing an original, identifiable ideology, like k.d. Lang or Tracy Chapman. "Céline Dion is nothing more than an imitator," Montreal's biggest daily *La Presse* declared. "She has nothing to say," the intellectuals at *Le Devoir* announce. "She can boast of a voice that has its share of special effects, yet it communicates no life experience."

Yet she did represent a very well-defined character in society: a girl from the boondocks who wants to succeed, who has a dream inside her, and who lives for that dream. Hollywood has made countless films with that character and those themes. Great novels have been written about just that subject. But in Quebec, more than anywhere else, ambition is frowned upon.

Over a year and a half, at the Saint-Denis alone, the *Incognito* show was performed forty-two times. Before the tour, Céline wasn't thought of as a great performer. Many strong-voiced singers, such as Whitney Houston and Mariah Carey, have built a career offstage. With *Incognito*, Céline learned an enormous amount about being onstage.

But, in addition to becoming a course in Show Business 101, the show was to become her prison cell. Bissonnette, the old professional, directed her with a firm hand. Everything had been written down ahead of time, not just the music and the words, but the dance steps and conversation between songs. Céline thought of the heroine in *Flashdance* who'd gotten rid of all that needless teaching and swore that no one would ever tell her what to do and say again.

Yet *Incognito* had taught her how to master the stage. She understood that being onstage meant taking power. She learned how to react to the crowd and control her emotions — and the crowd's emotions too. She learned where to pause, how to elicit applause, how to cut short an ovation. What she lost in spontaneity, she made up in stage mastery. She learned how to work the media too. She expressed herself without hesitation. Instead of trying to project an image of perfection, she took pleasure in admitting her ignorance.

"I never hung around school much. I was a lousy student. I never thought school was very important. I've learned my geography by traveling. I don't need to know about math. I trust the people who look after my career. I've got other things to learn. Everybody has to make their own choices. I need to learn more languages, and I need to sing even better."

France remembered her again. She was offered TV specials and the chance to cut more albums. But, like Marnay said, America was awaiting her, and Céline began looking in that direction. It was inevitable. She and René had never dared to dream about conquering America. They thought it was impossible or, at the very least, premature. Now that dream was within reach.

René knew she would win over anyone who heard her. But she needed new opportunities. Her success at the Juno ceremonies was a beginning, and the *Incognito* sales were good. But the United States and English Canada had to discover her. It was time to make the record in English.

In February, with the *Incognito* tour going like gangbusters, Angélil announced that an agreement had been signed with CBS Records which had promised to invest "up to one million dollars," or so he said. The album would be cut that fall. Several of the songwriters and composers who'd been contacted were known for their work with Whitney Houston and Madonna.

Actually, nothing was in the bag yet. But Angélil was sure that nothing would stop Céline's rise to stardom. The road was still long, but she could overcome every obstacle. No setback seemed to discourage her. Her blind, absolute faith illuminated every aspect of her life. Convinced that Lady Luck was with him, Angélil threw himself into the task at hand.

He was gambling a great deal. He'd get on a plane with Ben, Jacques or Paul in the evening, after business hours. They'd be at the casinos in Naussau by the time the sun set, gamble most of the night, then return to Montreal on the first flight in the morning.

In the spring of 1988, in Atlantic City, Paul Sara and René lost $65,000 in one night. On the flight back, Paul was completely devastated. He'd just gotten divorced. He still owed $36,000 on the mortgage on his house. René was disappointed too. But he kept telling his cousin to stop worrying.

"You'll see," he promised. "In a couple of weeks, we'll be laughing."

The *Falling Into You* Tour
Nîmes, October 4, 1996

The Concert Hall

There's always a way to put on a good show, even in a concert hall with no soul and without a past. It all depends on the crowd — and the artist. But no matter what people say, it's much tougher to breathe life into a place with a mythical past like la Fenice in Venice or Madison Square Garden. It takes more than moxie to sing in the ruins of Pompeii, Carthage or Baalbek, or in the ancient Roman arenas that surround the Mediterranean, like Verona, Arles or Nîmes. Some of them are more than two thousand years old, and they're still used for classical theater productions, operas and other top-of-the-line shows. They're marvelous, inspiring places. But if you're a mediocre performer, there's nowhere to hide. In these arenas, if you're not great, you can fall. Hard.

Nîmes is one of the most brilliant cities of the Roman Empire. For an instant, Céline held her breath as she drank in the beauty of the place. It was so quiet you could hear a pin drop. And the aura it emanated was almost frightening. She insisted on working her way down alone to the stage level through the steep rows of seats.

The youthful crowd that fills the venerable amphitheater at sunset seems almost too well-behaved. Céline is worried. She can't imagine how people can ever let loose, jump to their feet and start dancing in a place like this. Somehow, it seems more appropriate to meditate here.

In France, Belgium and French-speaking Switzerland, the show always kicks off with "Je sais pas." Her opening number everywhere else, "The Power of Love," sounds like rolling thunder heading straight for the audience. But "Je sais pas" is a song that works its way under the skin.

> Défier les machines, narguer des lois.
> Les foudres divines, ça m'effraie pas
> "Je sais pas" — Jean-Jacques Goldman
>
> (Defy the machines, thumb my nose at the law.
> God's thunder and lightning don't scare me.)

Anyway you looked at it, the show is extraordinary. The sound, the lighting, the crowd, that dominating voice, the perfect communion. The Nîmes arena leaves its mark on Céline. From that day on, she pays closer attention to the architecture of the theaters where she sings, to their spirit and their soul. For several months now, the invitations have been flowing in from around the world. The finest stages are hers for the asking.

A few weeks before, Canada's ambassador in Tunis, Michel Roy, let Barry Garber know that a group of Tunisian promoters wanted Céline to sing at Carthage. But she was on tour in the western United States on the only available date. In fact, she was booked for the entire year. But she was enchanted by the invitation. Angélil even more so. Carthage was built nine centuries before Christ by the Phoenicians, ancestors of today's Lebanese. René still dreams of returning to Beirut, the city his father has described as "the world's greatest showplace." Since that nasty war, the country hasn't been able to get back on its feet. Maybe one day....

Céline Dion is one of the select handful of artists who can step beyond the everyday boundaries of show business, leave the established commercial circuits behind and open up new, unexplored territories. Invitations come flooding in from every corner of the earth. From the former USSR, from Israel, from South Africa, from countries she's never even heard of.

In Nîmes that October of 1996, it is clear that D'eux, *with words and music by Jean-Jacques Goldman, would be the all-time best-selling album in France, and that* Falling Into You *would break the twenty million barrier by year's end. For the next few months, wherever she will travel — Asia, Europe, North and South America, the Pacific — Céline will be singing to sellout crowds.*

What can you see when you're at the top? The unknown, as far as you can see.

Chapter Twenty
First Stirrings

Television producer Laurent Larouche, who'd moved to Toronto not long before, had an idea. His friend René Angélil should invite Carol Reynolds, then head of variety programs at the Canadian Broadcasting Corporation, to catch Céline's show at the Théâtre Saint-Denis, in the heart of Montreal's Latin Quarter. According to Larouche, Reynolds was impressed by her performance at the Juno Awards gala, and was looking for ways of presenting Céline to television viewers in English Canada.

Angélil called Carol. She accepted the invitation immediately. She was bowled over, not only by the performance, but by the fans' response. After the show, Céline, René and Carol met in a restaurant just across the street from the theater. Céline, whose English was improving rapidly, talked to her about her dream album, the one she wanted to record with David Foster. The problem was that Foster wasn't returning their calls. He was too busy with Neil Diamond, Barbra Streisand, Paul McCartney and all the other stars who used his services as arranger and producer.

As luck would have it, Carol Reynolds was leaving in a few days for Los Angeles, Foster's hometown, and she just happened to know him. She promised to show him the Juno Awards video.

One afternoon less than a week later, Angélil, liked to be there as often as he could, was on his way to the Saint-Denis. The musicians would be there for the sound check at around four o'clock, and Céline would come a bit later. As he was driving his Chrysler into the parking lot behind the theater, he got a call from Carol Reynolds. "I've got someone on the line who'd like to talk to you," she said. It was David Foster. Carol had shown him the Juno video and played *Incognito*. He found Céline "outstanding," and he was convinced she had what it took to break into the US. She could sing like no one else, he said. She had "that little something extra" that people were looking for ever since *A Star is Born*. Her voice was under complete control, yet he could sense its original colors. It was the voice of a white woman who had sung a lot of black music.

What deal had Angélil signed with CBS? he asked. When Angélil told him $300,000 (and not the million he liked to tease journalists with), Foster replied that it wasn't enough to produce a world-class album. "I'll handle the president of CBS in the US; you look after the Canadian side. We'll get this show on the road right now."

Angélil met Bernie DiMatteo to tell him they'd need at least twice the $300,000 he'd agreed to invest. Angélil, diMatteo and Foster held a conference call. Foster repeated what he'd told René. He was convinced Céline would be a hit in the States. And he promised diMatteo that he would work with her, even though he was up to his neck in work and didn't have a minute to spare.

Now it was up to Bernie DiMatteo to convince the top man, but he had plenty of ammunition. The support of a top international producer like Foster was the kind of opportunity you couldn't let slip by.

Céline's cross-Quebec tour was going full blast. Whenever she had a day or two to spare, she'd rush back home to her family in Montreal. One March evening, in Duvernay, she found her father in a deep funk. "Your mom isn't feeling well." He couldn't make any decisions about what to do, or even reason with that headstrong, hyperactive woman who kept on insisting that it was only fatigue, that she'd be fine in no time. But her face was drawn, her skin pale. Céline could barely imagine what it would be like to lose the person she loved most in the world. She would often picture herself at her dying mother's bedside, on the verge of a breakdown, paralyzed with grief. But now, she responded in a completely different way — so calm and collected that it astonished her.

She called Dr. Choquette, whom René had told her about. She set up an appointment for her mother at two o'clock the next day, in his office just around the corner from the Cardiology Institute. Mama Dion was irritated. "I'm sixty years old, child. You're not about to tell me what to do." Mrs. Dion was scheduled to baby-sit her daughter Linda's children. Ten minutes later, Céline had arranged for a substitute. And she asked René to postpone their departure for Chicoutimi, a town in northern Quebec, where she was scheduled to sing two days later. She knew that if she handled things well, she could leave with a clear conscience, and that everything would work out for the best.

She accompanied her mother to the doctor's office. His diagnosis was firm: she had to be admitted the hospital immediately. But Mrs. Dion refused to use the ambulance, and she walked to the Cardiology Institute where, later that day, she underwent a quadruple coronary bypass. When Céline sang in Chicoutimi the next night, she knew that her mother was out of danger. She also knew that in life, you had to make decisions, leap into new situations, act. Her father couldn't, so now it was up to her to look after her mother and father. Maybe even her whole family. It was her duty.

A month later, Céline was invited to participate in an event that would change her life again — and her career. It was the Eurovision competition, and she would represent Switzerland. The competition draws more than twenty participating countries every year, and it gives European artists the kind of visibility they dream about. It ends with a televised special that reaches 600 million viewers, one hundred times the population of the province of Quebec.

As soon as he heard that his protégé would be participating, Angélil began to spread the word that this was the world's most popular show, after the Academy Awards and the opening ceremony of the Olympic Games. The world's top performers (who weren't always the winners) had taken part: the Swedish group ABBA in 1974 with "Waterloo," the Spanish crooner with the velvet voice Julio Iglesias, the Greek songstress Nana Mouskouri, French vocalist France Gall, who represented Luxembourg in 1965 with a song by Serge Gainsbourg entitled "Poupée de cire, poupée de son," and Australia's Olivia Newton-John.

Each participating country selects the song that will represent it at the televised gala, held every year in a different city. Dublin's turn came in 1988.

Switzerland had only won the Eurovisions once, back in 1956, at the first-ever competition held in Lugano. The winner was called "Refrain," a song with words by Émile Gardaz and Géo Voumard, sung by Lys Assia. The composer, a native Swiss named Nella Martinelli from the Canton of Tessin, had tried her luck several times since. She finished fourth at

Dublin in 1981, fifteenth at Munich in 1984 and second at Bergen, Norway in 1986. The following year, she won another international competition with a song in Italian called "Bella Musica," which went on to sell more than a million records. And Martinelli herself became a star in Germany, Austria and Switzerland. So, in 1987, the same German producers whom René Angélil had approached a few years earlier played Céline's latest album for Martinelli, and she loved Céline's voice immediately. Along with her friend Attila Serestug, she composed a song that the rising Canadian star could perform at the Eurovisions. It was called "Ne partez pas sans moi."

Vous qui cherchez l'étoile,
Vous qui vivez un rêve,
Vous héros de l'espace,
Au coeur plus grand que la terre,
Vous, donnez-moi la chance.
Emmenez-moi loin d'ici.

(You who seek your lucky star,
You whose life's a dream,
You, the hero of outer space,
With a heart as big as the world,
Give me a chance.
Carry me far, far away.)

More than 250 songs were in the competition, but only nine made the cut for the national elimination round to be staged on February 9 and televised throughout Switzerland from the Beausobre theater in the town of Morges. One of them was the song written by Attila and Nella and sung by Céline Dion, who suddenly found herself in the middle of a lively controversy. How could a song interpreted by a Canadian, with words by an Italian-Swiss and music by a Turkish composer, possibly represent Switzerland?

Céline wasn't wild about the song; neither was René. The melody was careless and unfocused, and the words were pretentious and trite. But it was the kind of song that often worked in this kind of competition.

Céline finished with forty-eight points; her nearest rival with twenty-three. Her victory was so overwhelming that all the muttering stopped. Hers would be the honor of representing Switzerland at the Eurovisions on April 30. Ecstatic, the press concluded that "intelligence and professionalism" had won the day, that for once, the country had a hope of winning the Eurovisions again. After all, what was the point of arguing about the singer's nationality?

One month later, a team of Swiss technicians flew to Montreal to record Nella and Attila's song in French and German. The plan was to release the single in early May in the French- and German-speaking countries. And on April 28, Céline and René jetted off to Dublin where singers, producers, songwriters and composers from a full thirty countries were gathering.

The Irish are compulsive gamblers. In Dublin, in the days before the Eurovision finals, open legal betting was in full swing. Over the preceding week, Céline had established herself as one of the three favorites. After she appeared on a local television show, she vaulted into top spot. When rehearsals got under way in the immense Simmonscourt studios, she was a 7–4 favorite. Angélil held off before betting on his protégé. Down deep, he was a superstitious man. He believed that a man should never bet on questions of the heart, or on the outcome of events where his friends or loved ones were involved. Still, he bet 200 Irish pounds (roughly $350). He came within an inch of regretting it.

The night of April 30 gave a new meaning to the word suspense. Céline sang with passion, even if her song wasn't a masterpiece of inspiration. Her long wavy hair cascaded down over an impeccably tailored suit in hues of turquoise and dark berry. After the twenty-one finalists — whose order had been determined by a draw — had sung, they withdrew to the Simmonscourt green room where they awaited the verdict. The jury, made up of eight men and eight woman of all age groups from several countries, deliberated long and hard.

When one-third of the national ballots had been counted, Céline held an eighteen-point lead. But for political reasons, Denmark and Austria did not give Switzerland a single point. England, represented by Scott Fitzgerald, who had sung a song entitled "Go," leaped into the lead with 143 points to Switzerland's 119. That was when Angélil began to regret making his bet. Céline told him that she was upset by the title of Fitzgerald's song. She remembered that "go" means "five" in Japanese. "It's my lucky number, but I didn't get it."

They looked on as the television producers coached the young Brit on how to step onstage where the award ceremony would take place. He was sure that he would win. His face was beaming as the cameras were turned on him. René was beside himself. But Céline is not the kind of girl to carry a grudge: She just moves on, which is what she was prepared to do.

But everybody had forgotten about Portugal and Yugoslavia. The last two countries to vote each gave Céline nine points, and only two to Fitzgerald. The final score was Switzerland 137, England 136!

Céline already had a strong hometown reputation as a weeper. Victories and ovations brought tears to her eyes faster than any defeat. There, before the public at Simmonscourt and the 600 million television viewers watching the Eurovision gala, she broke into tears. Her message of thanks was an incoherent babble.

As he did after every performance, René joined Céline in her room and told her his take on the evening. He told her everything he saw, heard and felt. She sat there at the head of the bed, her legs crossed under the blankets, happy to be alone with the man she loved. She could listen to him talk all night, the next day, and forever. Her mother, her brothers and her sisters — they all knew she was madly in love with him, and they had known it for a long time. But did he know?

After he finished telling Céline about his impressions of the gala, René remained seated at the foot of the bed, not saying a word. Céline looked at him. Then he got up slowly, wished her good night and walked toward the door.

Every night, ever since their first tour together in the winter of 1985, when they stayed in cheap hotels and motels in small Quebec towns like Rimouski, Trois-Rivières or Amos, the routine was the same. He would give her a little kiss on the cheek and wish her good night. Nothing had changed when they went to Paris for a recording session or to Toronto for the Juno Awards ceremony.

And now, on this night of triumph and victory, he was about to leave without even a good-night kiss. He had already opened the door. He smiled. She came up to him and pressed herself tightly against him. "You didn't kiss me, René Angélil." Her head was bent, eyes downcast.

He didn't realize what was happening, even though he'd imagined this very scene a thousand times over the past few weeks. He leaned toward her and kissed her on the lips, the neck, and wrapped his arms around her in a powerful embrace. Then he dropped his arms and rushed off to his room. For a moment, she stood there, speechless.

Then she called out to him, "If you don't come back, I'll be knocking on your door."

The next day, Sunday, May 1, 1988, Céline returned in triumph to Montreal. Alerted by her new press agent Francine Chaloult, more than one hundred reporters, photographers, TV cameramen and other industry people were there to meet her. Angélil had a folder full of clippings from the British and Irish papers, featuring Céline on page one. They praised the "vibrant personality," the "irresistible charm" and the "spontaneity of the young Quebec vocalist." Angélil reminded the journalists that the Eurovisions were the world's most-watched television show after the Oscars and the Olympic Games. He couldn't stop himself from describing Céline's crying fit when she found out she'd won. Everybody burst into laughter. Then he added,"It's been a year and a half since she's had a good cry."

He went on to describe the Dublin press conference attended by seven hundred journalists from around the world and Céline's impact when she told them that she was the youngest child of a family of fourteen, and that she was from Quebec. He told them about the autograph sessions in Dublin airport and how, on the British Airways flight from Dublin to London, the captain mentioned that a star was on board and that the passengers all broke into applause.

When a journalist asked him about his own career, he answered in astonishment, "But Céline is my career! With her, my dreams have come true. I wouldn't change a thing, even if you gave me $10 million."

Céline broke in, "We've been together for seven years and he's never once made a mistake. I trust him. I tell him everything, all my secrets. His dream and my dream are the same."

After all, they were also sharing the same bed!

And yet, a few days later, on Montreal radio station CFGL FM, she told the host she was prepared to live a solitary life if that's what it took to succeed, that she saw her career as a kind of religious vocation.

In answer to another question, she said that one day, she wanted to make a childhood dream come true. "I'd like to go to Ethiopia and look after the children. When I was a little girl, I imagined what poverty would be like. It was awful. I couldn't stand living that way, but I had to imagine."

All around her, the rumors were flying. At the University of Montreal where Angélil's son Patrick was enrolled in cinema courses, he had to field frequent questions about his father and Céline. "I became a master of double-talk," he said. "My father told me he was in love with Céline, but for the time being, the two of them wanted it kept secret."

At the April 30 press conference in Dublin, just a few minutes after Céline won the Eurovision finals, a reporter asked if the winning song

"Ne partez pas sans moi" would be translated into English. No, answered Angélil. But they would soon be doing an album in English with CBS.

Actually, all he had was a promise. No budgets had been approved. But he knew that it was a done deal. He knew that the album would be produced by David Foster. What he didn't know was that in the audience, there were several CBS representatives who would be sure to contact headquarters. Sure enough, the next day, reps from CBS-Portugal and CBS-England called New York asking when the Céline Dion album would be ready.

On May 8, bursting with confidence, Angélil turned up at the CBS head offices in New York. Vito Luprano and Richard Zuckerman, artistic director for CBS-International, had already begun looking for songs for the album. After listening to hundreds they picked out some fifty possibilities. They wanted up-tempo, catchy tunes.

René briefed the CBS people. When the matter of money came up, the top man told him not to worry about it. "Find good songs, do the album and we'll look after it." CBS-Canada would inject whatever funds were necessary, and CBS-USA would handle the logistics. If it took off, CBS-USA would repay CBS-Canada in whole or in part.

"The key to success when dealing with people outside Quebec is to leave your ego behind, at home, under cover," René says. "When you're playing in that league, you'll never get anywhere if you try to play the big shot. You've got to know the rules of the game."

"I was just trying to let people know who Céline was. That was my job, first and foremost. As far as the rest was concerned, I made sure those people knew how to draw up marketing and promotion plans, how to launch an album, how to plan and think for the long term."

Keep it modest, but keep it firm.

"Céline's lucky, when you get right down to it. I made my mistakes with other people, before I met her."

The manager's desk is where the buck stops. He has to be a good listener and recruit top-notch people. Systematically, Angélil set out to build a network of friends throughout the show business world. He made allies in the media, with producers, in French and English Canada, in France, in the United States.

Céline's victory at the Eurovisions did more than just put the executives at CBS in a receptive mood. It also had a tremendous impact throughout Europe. Céline's latest album began to rack up record sales. Before the beginning of summer, more than 300,000 copies of her single "Ne partez pas sans moi" were sold.

On Monday, May 9, Céline left Montreal and flew back to Europe for a blockbuster promotional tour of a dozen European cities in ten days.

Tuesday, May 10: Zurich. Press conference. A huge, triple-decker cake. On the first layer the words "Céline Dion." On the second, "Eurovision." On the third, "Ne partez pas sans moi."

Wednesday, May 11: Paris. Taping for *Sacrée soirée*, a top French television variety show.

Thursday, May 12: Copenhagen. Television appearances, interviews.

Friday, May 13: Paris. *Intercontinental* with Guy Lux.

Saturday, May 14: Munich. Taping of *Wetten Dass*, Germany's most popular TV program, seen by thirty-five million viewers. With Elton John, who congratulated her long and loud, and promised to write her a song.

Sunday, May 15: Helsinki. *Juke Box Jury*, a popular TV show.

Monday, May 16: Montreux. The Rose d'Or Festival, broadcast to thirteen French-speaking countries (including French Canada, where it was carried live by both Télé-Métropole, the private network, and Radio-Canada, that rebroadcast Céline's *Incognito* show the same night).

Tuesday, May 17: Rest and recreation.

Wednesday, May 18: Cannes. The film festival. A big show, with Julia Migenes-Johnson and Michel Legrand.

Thursday, May 19: Paris. Television. *Lahaye d'honneur*, emceed by Jean-Luc Lahaye.

Friday, May 20: Paris. Rest. Shopping.

Saturday, May 21: Rome. Taping of *Domenica*, Italy's top-rated variety show.

Had Angélil accepted every invitation, Céline would have been busy for six months straight. He had no choice but to drop Spain and Portugal. What counted now was not the money, but the number of viewers, the size of the markets.

On May 29, Céline returned to Montreal to record a commercial for a local department store, a $325,000 contract.

People began describing her as the youngest, most promising millionaire in Quebec show business.

Finally, in early June, David Foster called to say he'd soon be ready to go to work with Céline, but that first he wanted to see her perform on stage. He would be in Montreal on the weekend of June 11. Mario Lefebvre checked Céline's date book. Damn! That night she was scheduled to sing in Sainte-Agathe, a resort town in the Laurentian mountains, in a tent. Why not the next week, from June 14 to 19? Céline would be performing at the Saint-Denis, a comfortable, well-equipped hall right in the heart of the city. But Foster couldn't make it any other time. "No matter," said René. "As soon as he hears Céline sing, no matter where, it'll be in the bag." They booked Foster a flight to Montreal's Mirabel airport. A limousine would be waiting to drive him to Sainte-Agathe, about an hour north.

With him was his wife Linda Thompson, Elvis Presley's former girlfriend. The two made a striking couple. When they reached Sainte-Agathe, the heavens opened. In the tent, the atmosphere was oppressive; the place reeked of dampness. The sound was appalling. But Vito and René knew Céline was always at her best under pressure. They reminded her just how important this show was for her career, and she gave it everything she had.

After four songs, she introduced David Foster to the audience, praising him in her halting English. He was the man of the hour in the recording business, the man who worked with Sinatra, Streisand and company. She laid it on so thick that the audience gave Foster an ovation, even though nobody in the tent in Sainte-Agathe knew him from Adam.

Foster couldn't help but be flattered. And flat-out impressed by Céline's voice, her presence, her charisma, her self-assurance. "As soon as you've picked your songs," he told them, "I'll get to work."

Foster had both authority and credibility. He would be an important ally inside the stronghold of American show business, which had to get to know Céline Dion's name and voice. But that June, René would discover that her career didn't belong entirely to him. In the shadows, her fans — more and more of them — were watching her every career move, and they were determined to have their say.

Toronto's French-speaking community invited Céline to sing at the city's Saint-Jean Baptiste Day celebrations, to be held June 24, 1988, at

Harbourfront. The open-air stage overlooked Lake Ontario. A few days before the show, the organizers and Radio-Canada producer Gabriel Dubé were astonished to learn that René Angélil was insisting that she sing a few songs in English. They tried to tell him that it might not be well received; Saint-Jean Baptiste Day is a very patriotic French-Canadian celebration. But René wouldn't back down. Come show night, they understood why. He'd invited big shots from Sony-Canada and Sony-USA and reserved first-row seats especially for them.

French-speaking Ontarians and visiting Quebeckers were offended. When Céline sang in English, they started to boo. Most French-speaking people in Toronto speak English at work and on the street. But the Saint-Jean Baptiste celebration is sacred, a time for French Canadians to rally together. Céline (wearing a sexy red leather dress) was visibly disconcerted. Claude Deschêsnes, the MC, was beside himself. Luckily, it started to rain, and the show stopped.

Angélil realized he'd made a mistake. He'd have to live with this particular political reality. A few years before, hockey star Guy Lafleur spoke out about his opposition to the Quebec nationalist movement. No one batted an eyelash. Everybody loved him just as they always had. But in Céline's case it was different. It was a much touchier situation. First of all, she belonged to the world of culture, not sports. Céline had become an idol, a symbol of French Canada, and French Canada would never let her abandon it. What happened in Toronto was a valuable lesson. Angélil understood that he had to win over Céline's Quebec fans. From then on, he kept them up-to-date on everything she did outside her native province, and made sure they understood the reasons.

That fall, CBS suggested that Angélil hire three producers for the album to improve their chances for a hit. That way, they could satisfy several audiences. The proposal pleased René. Yet it worried him at the same time. How could Foster, with whom he'd been in touch for months now, agree to share the work with anyone else? Meanwhile, CBS-International came up with two other producers: Andy Goldmark, an American, and Christopher Neil, an Englishman whose big success at the time was Mike and the Mechanics. Neil had also produced Sheena Easton and a few songs by Julien Clerc. Richard Zuckerman, artistic director at CBS-International in New York, put Angélil and Luprano in touch with the two producers.

But progress was slow. Zuckerman and Vito were always on the lookout for good songs. But they had to weed out the weaker tunes, and pick only the ones that would make people prick up their ears, that would sound new, that would show off Céline's voice.

While she waited, Céline had more than enough to keep her busy in Quebec. Between February and December 1988, she would be giving seventy-five performances of *Incognito* from one end of the province to the other. Mark Lepage, the Montreal *Gazette*'s hard-to-please pop music critic, attended the final show of the tour at the Saint-Denis. At twenty, he wrote, she was right up there with Ginette Reno, and even Barbra Streisand. Even though she was impatient to get into the recording studio, she was getting more pleasure out of her live appearances than ever before. She'd won four Felix awards at the ADISQ gala, including one for Best Stage Performance. Now Céline was recognized as a complete artist. And, at last, the money was coming in. Angélil would soon be needing it more than ever. In case CBS wouldn't put up the funds, he would have to get it out of his own pocket. Céline agreed. They weren't going to cut corners on their first English album. If they had to, they would borrow.

In September, they signed a lucrative contract with Chrysler. "In the high six figures" was how René put it. At the ad campaign launch, Céline declared that her artistic philosophy matched that of the automobile manufacturer. "Chrysler and I, we're looking for the same thing," she said. "Above all, we want to satisfy our customers."

The *Falling Into You* Tour
Zurich, June 26, 1997

The Ovation

"Zurich is something else," Céline and her musicians are telling the members of her entourage who weren't with her in November 1996. "Wait and see." It is the last stop on a tour that's already lasted nearly three years. A succession of tours, one after the other, to be exact.

The last shows on a tour are always special. "But Zurich is different," they say. "You've never seen a crowd anywhere else do what they do." And she leaves it at that. After all, you never know. Maybe last November's glorious ovation won't happen again.

But it does. More than once. More powerfully than anyone could have imagined. And sooner than anyone expects. On the last chords of "River Deep, Mountain High," the music seems to shatter into a million tiny fragments just as the lights go out. There's an instant of darkness, and a fraction of a second of silence. Then comes the applause.

Usually, every night, everywhere else, the same thing happens. It never fails. In the middle of the tumult that follows the explosive finale of "River Deep, Mountain High," you can hear a tiny laugh, the faintest snicker, the laugh of a happy little girl. You probably wouldn't have heard unless you knew about it. Céline herself may not even realize that every time people get to their feet to applaud her, she bursts out with that tiny peal of laughter.

In Zurich it is different. When the lights come back on, the triumph is

The Magic Years

Paris, 1994

With Luc Plamondon, Céline Dion explores a new idea, that of a young woman pushing herself to the limits to make "Le Blues du Businessman" her own.

With *Incognito*, she makes love her central theme, and it takes off from there.

Céline was very close to her niece Karine, who was afflicted with cystic fibrosis. She works constantly to support the Canadian Association for Cystic Fibrosis on an international basis.

Below: Céline and René at a fundraiser for Cystic Fibrosis in Montreal.

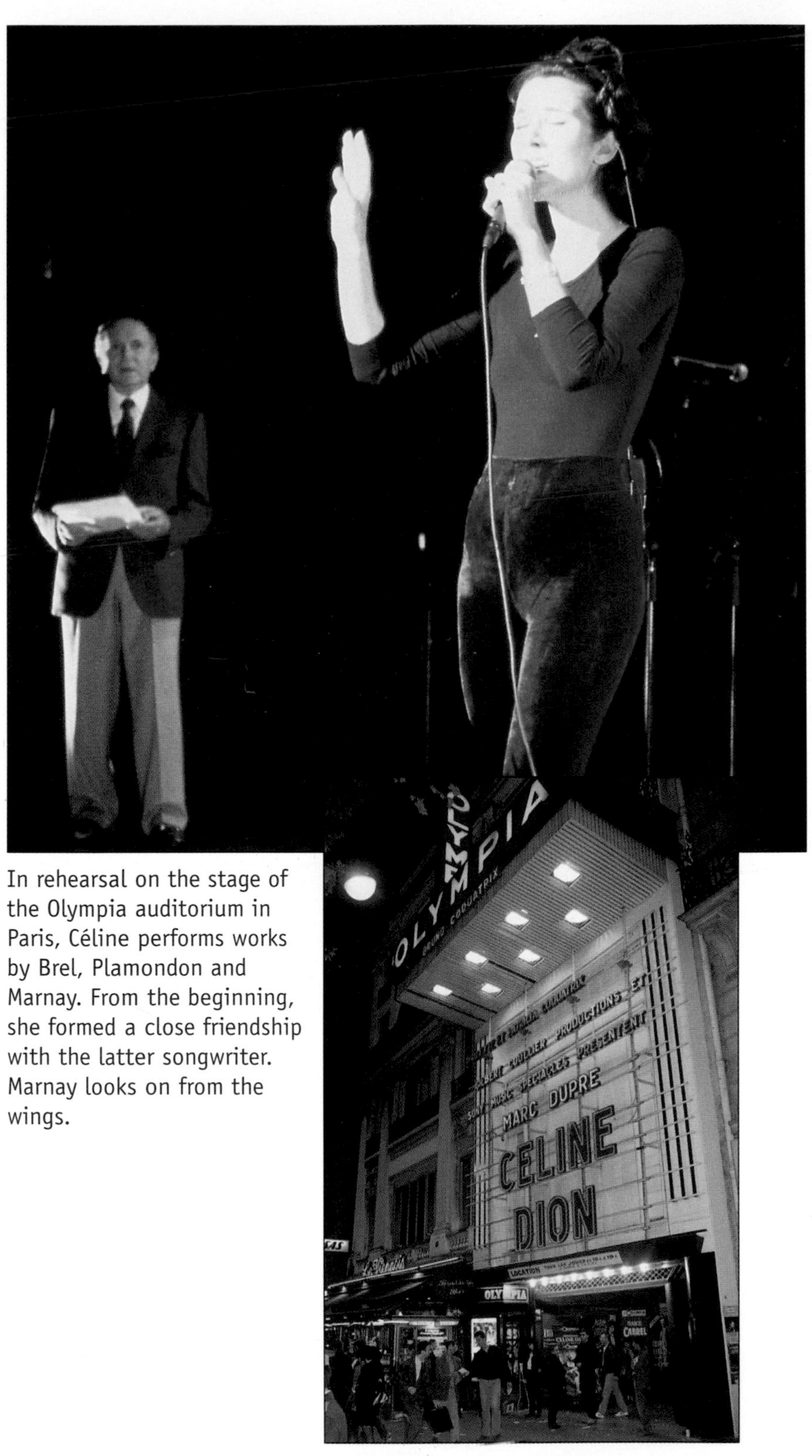

In rehearsal on the stage of the Olympia auditorium in Paris, Céline performs works by Brel, Plamondon and Marnay. From the beginning, she formed a close friendship with the latter songwriter. Marnay looks on from the wings.

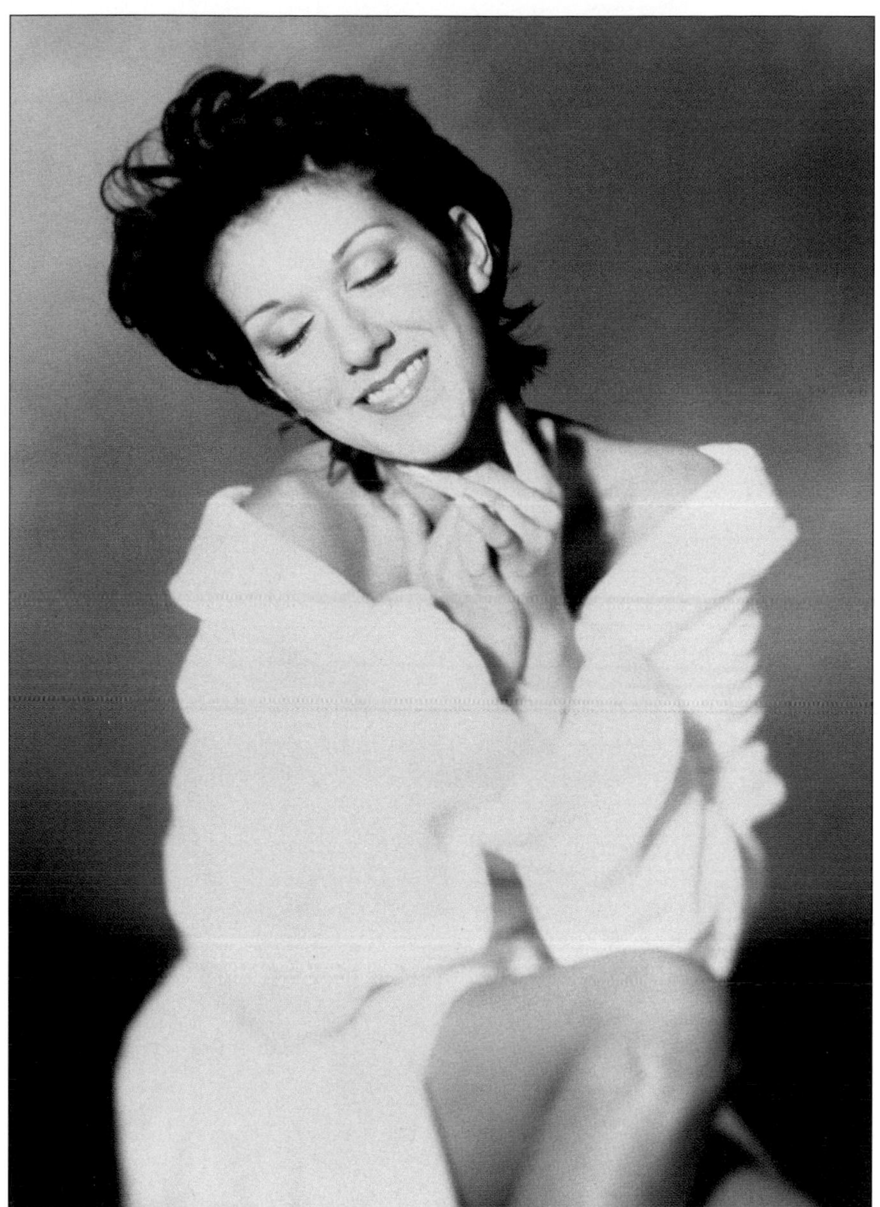

Céline quickly masters promotional tools such as videos and other media.

Vito Luprano, artistic director of Sony Canada, along with René Angélil and John Doelp, is responsible for the selection of songs for Céline's albums. The Sony team announces that *The Colour of My Love*, already a million-seller in the US and six times platinum in Canada, will go into distribution in Europe and the rest of the world.

Performing at home in Montreal is always important for Céline. Before walking out onstage at the Montreal Forum, she confides in the man she loves and performs her ritualistic gestures.

"Beauty and the Beast," recorded with Peabo Bryson, captures the American public.

Left to right: René, Richard Zuckerman (Sony), Céline, Paul Burger (Sony)

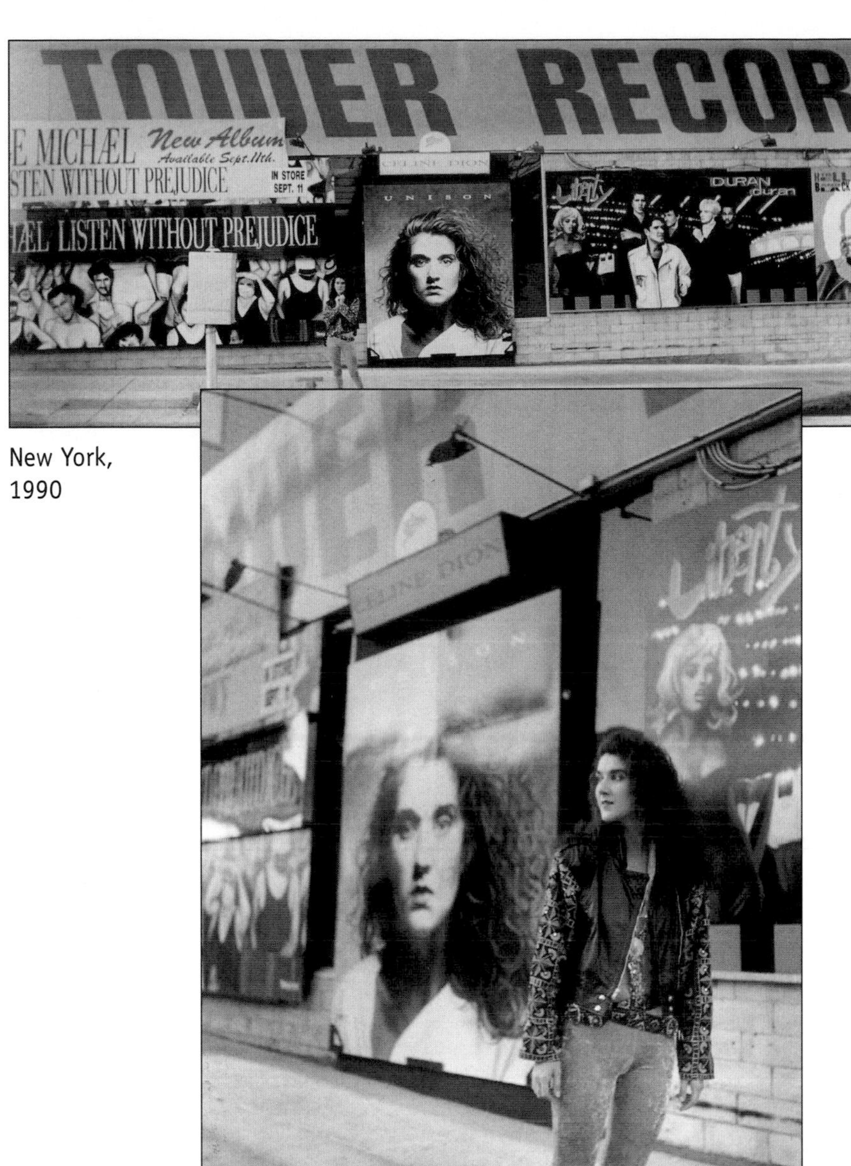

New York, 1990

With her album *Unison*, Céline takes the English market by storm. The Hollywood dream is knocking at her door.

Two songs from *Dion Chante Plamondon* reach the top of the charts in Quebec at the same time.

In France, the song "Ziggy" dominates the charts for weeks, and Céline becomes a regular on talk shows.

Already a superstar in North America and Asia, Céline overwhelms the United Kingdom with "Think Twice."

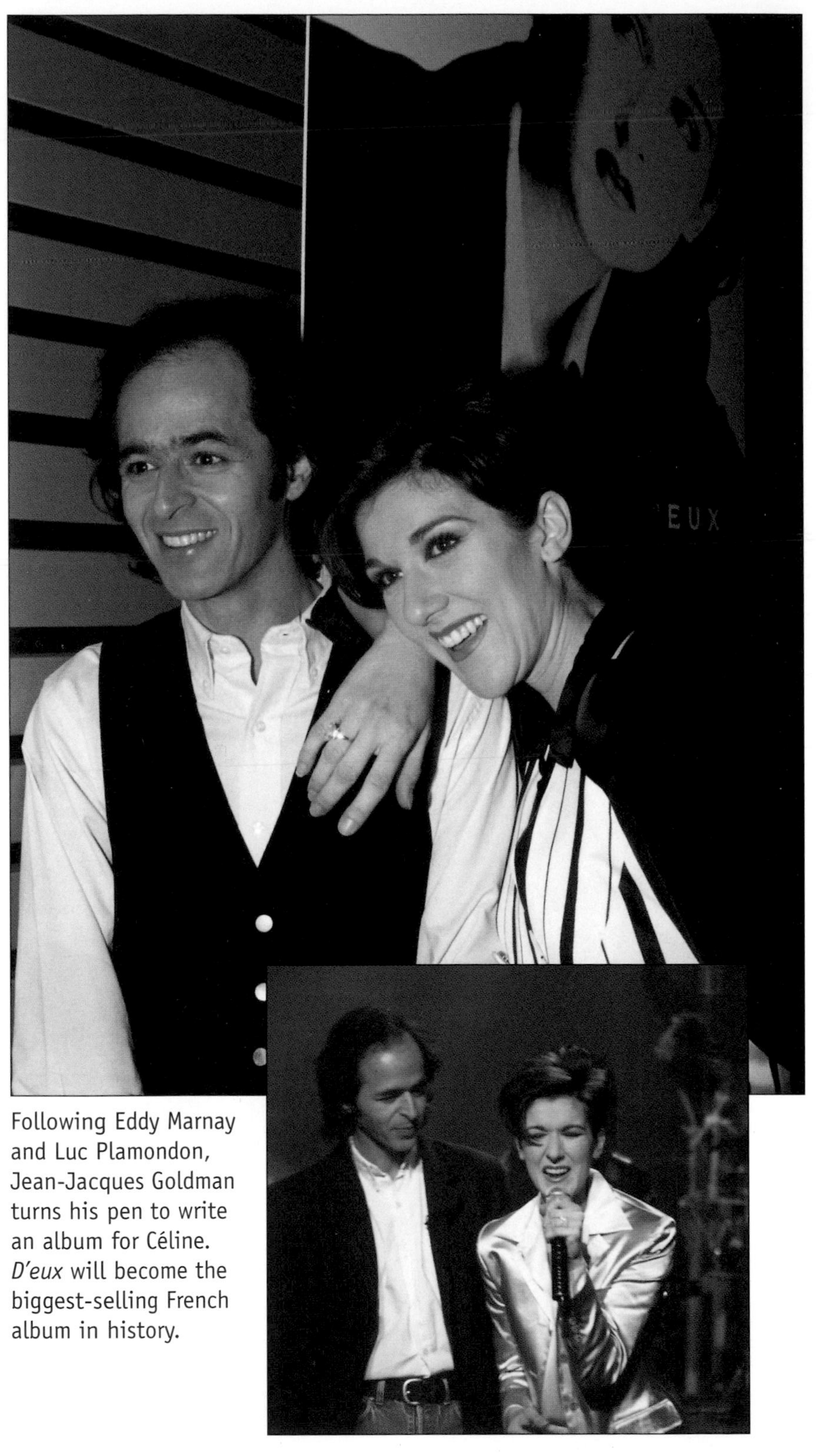

Following Eddy Marnay and Luc Plamondon, Jean-Jacques Goldman turns his pen to write an album for Céline. *D'eux* will become the biggest-selling French album in history.

Dave Platel and Paul Burger are far more than partners; they are friends of the Dion-Angélil family.

No stranger to awards, Céline knows successes with the Grammys, the Junos, the Felix and the Order of Arts and Letters.

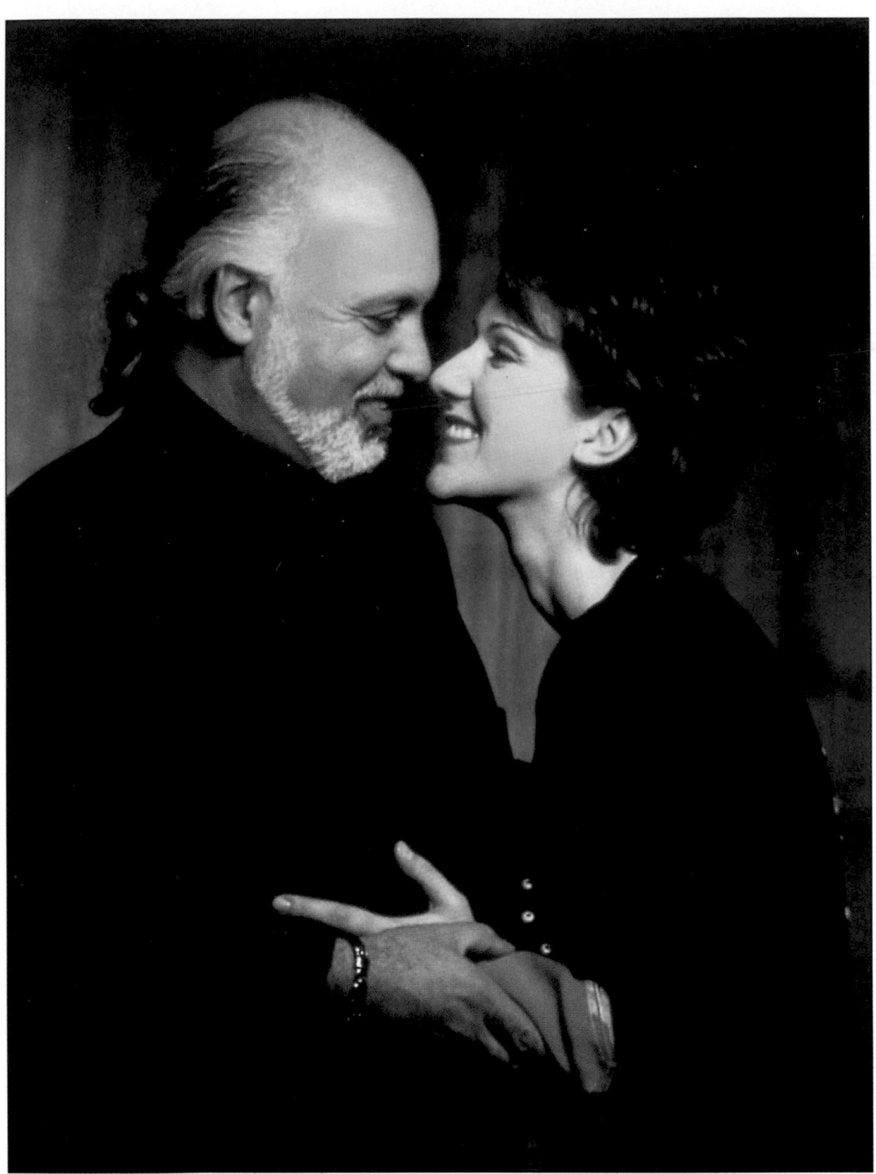

At last, Céline can live openly the life which she kept secret and sang about for so long.

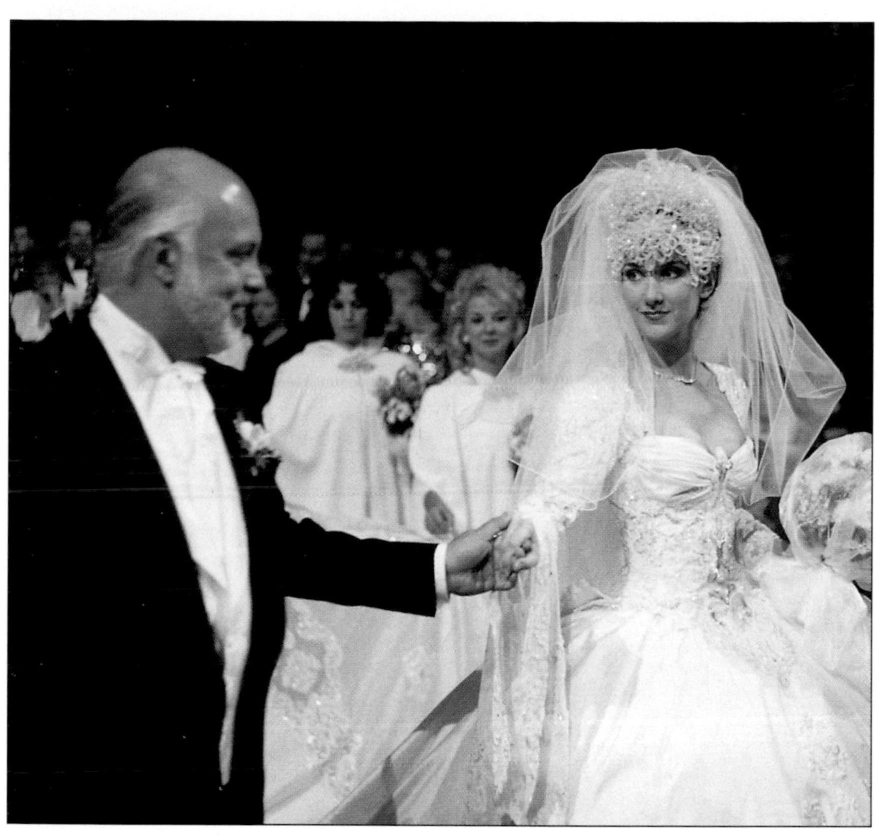

Notre Dame Basilica, Montreal, December 17, 1994. The star lives out her fairy tale.

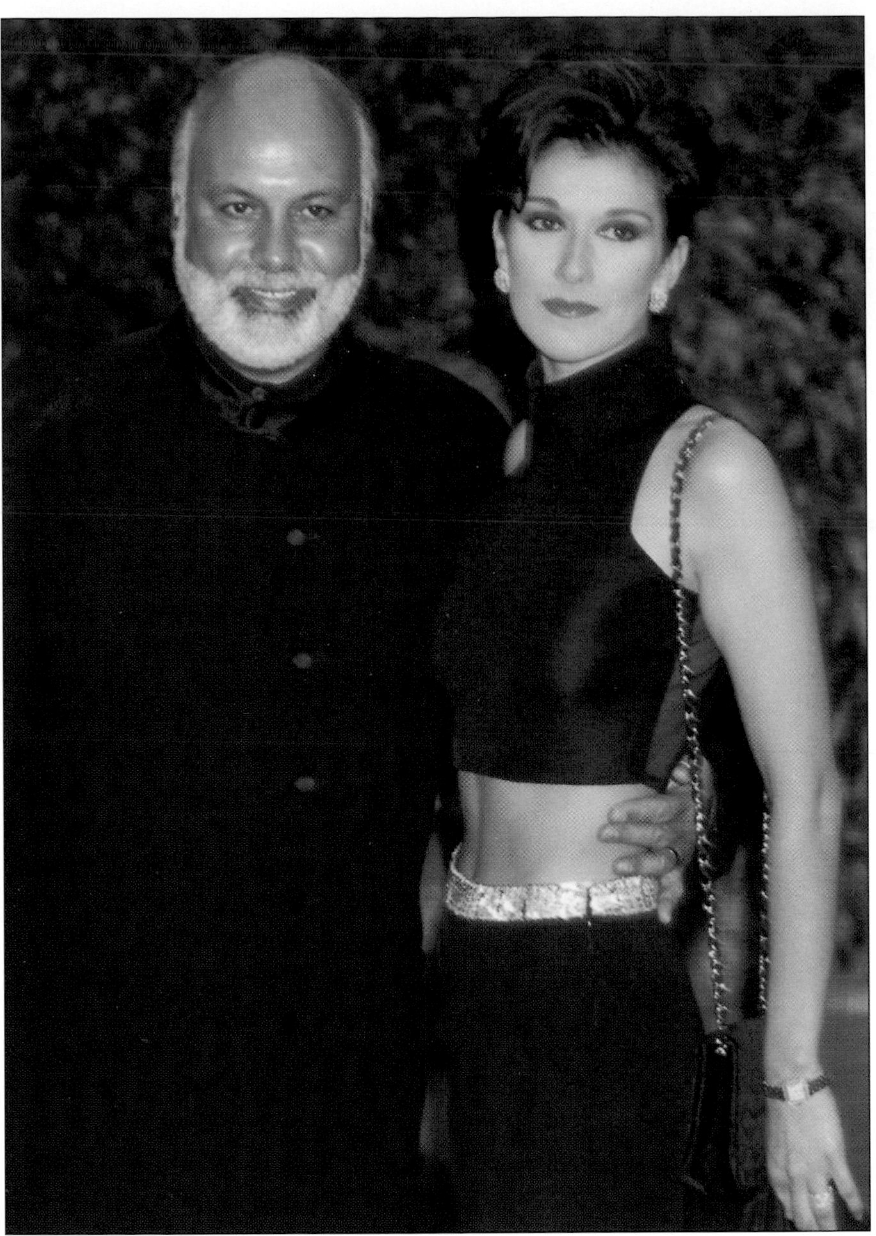

Love, always the theme of her songs, is now the theme of her life.

already assured. People are waving their outstretched hands at Céline. All you can see in the huge Leitzegrund Stadion is 100,000 pulsating hands, fingers spread wide, hiding faces and forming a windswept field of flowers. From that field sounds a long, drawn-out "Ahhh," soft at first, then swelling until it fills the stadium.

That's what made such an impression on Céline and her musicians in November 1996. But it came too late, almost at the end of a show that had never really gotten off the ground. At first the crowd reacted slowly, as if it had other things on its mind, as if it were melancholy. Céline did everything she could to reach the audience. Then, slowly but surely, the electricity began to build. After the last song, the crowd began that strange cry and waved its arms. It was beautiful, strange, frightening. When the British stamp their feet to create an ear-splitting din, when the Scandinavians shout "ohey, ohey," when the Americans start clapping in unison, when the French cry "un autre! un autre!" it's always impressive. But the Zurich fans show their approval in a different way altogether. Céline has the presence of mind to ask them to do it again "because what you do is so beautiful, and so rare." Lapin turns his spotlights on the audience. And Céline motions to one of the cameramen onstage to record the incredible crowdscape.

Tonight, the Zurich fans don't wait for an encore. As soon as Céline gets them in the mood, they start the wave — but with their own particular twist. The audience is on its feet for two or three seconds, arms waving back and forth, like light shimmering on a gently rolling sea.

After "River Deep, Mountain High" comes a short welcoming speech. The things Céline says in her shows give people a close-up, personal insight into her character, into the way she feels about show business. Her monologues are little gems of charm and persuasion. Each one starts out with a lengthy compliment for the cheering crowd. Then she tells people what's going on in her life. "We," she begins, "we've been on tour for nearly three years now. Tonight is our last show. We're going to take a one year break to work on some new songs and record an album in English and another one in French." Then she turns more personal: "At last, I can sleep in my own bed. And cook my husband's meals. And stow everything I bought on tour in my drawers. I just love shopping, don't you?" Speaking to the women in the audience, she says, "I bet you think I'm crazy for wanting to sleep in my own bed, do the cooking, clean house and put things away! But that's what I like."

These monologues of mine just grew, nothing was ever planned. I never felt like I had to talk about anything in particular. It just came, spontaneously. In fact, I did them with the help of the audience. I noticed that whenever I mentioned shopping, the girls laughed or shouted. Or when I said I liked straightening up my drawers and my clothes closets. It didn't take me long to figure out that people like it when I talk about the little things in life. I tell people about what I do in my life. They like to hear about it, and I like to talk about it. Sure, I could tell them that I fly in a private jet, and that I live in luxury hotels. And it would be true! But I'm just not interested in talking about those things, and I don't think I ever will be. I'd rather talk about the things we share. I think that's much more interesting than a star's life. And I think that's what people like.

In her interviews, she speaks much more freely about life's everyday details than she does about her career or her plans for the future. Onstage, she presents herself as a married woman, a housewife. A star who tells the girls and women who've turned out to cheer her that the life she leads is not that much different from theirs. That her desires and needs are similar.

"There's a rule, you know. It's not only my show." She points to the musicians and the back up singers. "It's not only our show, here on the stage." With a broad sweep of her hand, she embraces the whole stadium, from the far grandstands to the front-row seats. "Tonight, it's everybody's show." If you want to sing and dance, she tells them, go right ahead. And she reminds them one last time that she's just an ordinary girl. "I know what it's like to sit on a hard-backed chair for an hour and a half and listen to someone else sing." She pretends to be bored, yawns, glances at her watch, lets out a sigh. The crowd laughs. Everyone can see her face close up on the giant screens.

"Before you end up looking like that," she says, "get up, dance, sing along with us."

Eric, her bodyguard, is seated at her feet, facing the crowd. You can see his shiny bald head, then his face on the screens. Sometimes they do it just to irritate him. Don't be afraid of him, Céline tells the crowd. He's not dangerous. In fact, he's very nice and very polite. After the show, Eric says she shouldn't undermine his authority, and that he doesn't want people to think her bodyguard is nice and polite.

"But you are nice and polite," she says.

"Not when I'm on the job."

When he told me that, I realized that for me, it was just the opposite. For me, being nice and polite *is* part of my job, my trade. Sure, I could do things differently. Some guys, and girls too, make a career out of provoking people. But it never even crossed my mind to do that. I'm not out to change the world.

Pop music is often ruled by angry prophets, rebels and maniacs — desperate people with no illusions. When you look at today's world, you can't blame them for being that way. Wars are continually breaking out, deep-rooted racism and deplorable injustice still exist, as do deadly famines, and the widening gap between the rich and the poor. They want to change the world. Change also has and will take place. One day the world will surely be transformed. But in other ways. Anger and frustration are sometimes understandable and justified, but they don't bring peace, they don't heal wounds, and they've never brought anyone comfort.

Most of the great stars of the nineties have taken a completely different approach. They don't make a systematic effort to reject traditional values and overthrow the established order. Céline Dion, one of the most prominent, has chosen to fight not against power but against evil itself, against incurable diseases and, most of all, against illnesses that attack children.

Over the past few years, she's become deeply involved, along with Muhammad Ali, the Brazilian soccer star Pelé, and former president Jimmy Carter, in the peaceful struggle to protect the world's children. She knows they can hear her voice, wherever they may be. And her voice sings of love and peace. She lets them know people are thinking of them, trying to help them, to bring them food, happiness, hope.

During the Second World War in occupied France, Charles Trenet sang "Y'a d'la joie" ("There's Joy out There"). It was an act of faith. In spite of the grief and fear, he insisted that deep down in peoples' hearts, there was happiness. His song was an invitation to sing of love, to reach out to one another.

You had to have some kind of unshakable optimism to talk about joy in that dire world. You have to have a unfaltering faith to sing of love in today's world. You've got to realize that it's useless to hope that science and technology alone can avert the dangers that hang over us, useless to hope that some great change will take place, as if by magic, when the clock strikes one in the year 2000. All you can do is hope that the joy of living, smiling and loving won't pass you by. And that love songs will keep on being played and heard around the world.

"Plenty of things make me happy," Céline says. "Not only good reviews or the cheers of the crowd. What I really love is when people come up to me and tell me that one of my songs has helped them face life, to kiss and make up, to feel good about themselves or even, like 'Vole,' to accept the inevitable. That's why I sing. Singing for me is reaching out to people."

Chapter Twenty-One
Little White Lies

Early in 1988, Céline and René moved into the Malibu Inn, a small motel separated from the ocean by the Pacific Coast Highway. "Aside from me, they didn't know a soul in Los Angeles," says David Foster. "They came over to my place a lot to play basketball. They loved ball games back then. I'd even come across them playing catch in the motel parking lot with Mégo and Suzanne, who'd come down from Montreal to join them. They weren't rich, but they had plenty of spare time, and lots of fun. I'm sure that for them, life was beautiful and terribly exciting."

They were in love. They were hard at work on the songs for Céline's first album in English. Every song was about love, nothing but love. They were songs that would touch everybody who's in love, who wants to be loved, who's looking for love.

Artistically speaking, Céline was discovering another world. Another way of singing. Every song on *Incognito* was about love as well, like the new batch David Foster was preparing. But this time, the tone was different. Céline was walking on air. All of a sudden, everything was different. The words, and even her voice, seemed less familiar because it had taken on new texture, new color.

David Foster was Mr. Nice Guy. Attentive and very polite in everyday life. But once he's in the studio, nothing got by him. If Céline's pitch was off, if she missed an intonation, he had her start again from the beginning. He never told her she'd gotten it just right. He was always finding something wrong — too flat, too soft, too shrill.

In spite of it all, Céline was happy. She was working with top-notch people, the best musicians in the business in the top studios. And she was learning, which has always given her great pleasure. A new language new music, and a new way of singing. There's no doubt about it. English and French don't have the same rhythm. In French, the words flow into one another, and they're longer, so you often have to cut.

In March, they began working with "Love by Another Name," a song David Foster wrote with Cliff Magnes and Glen Ballard (who worked with Michael Jackson on "Man in the Mirror"). Then they recorded Aldo Nova's "Have a Heart" ("Our Lucky Star," as Vito Luprano called it), the song that became Céline's calling card when she went knocking on industry doors. They worked slowly. Three more songs followed: "I'm Loving Every Moment With You," "I Feel Too Much," "If We Could Start Over."

These first songs in English were critical. They would determine just where and how Céline would land in the world of international show business. If she missed the first time, there might not be a second chance. She had to make her mark with her first songs.

Back then, Céline was a total unknown in Los Angeles. But she was working with major-league musicians and technicians—people like Foster, arranger and pianist Tom Keane, guitarist Michael Landau, and engineers like Humberto Gattica, and Jeffrey "Woody" Woodruff. Gradually, word started getting out in the music scene. Time is always scarce in the big LA. studios, and there's always a lineup at the door. Producers and artists have to wait for an invitation. At Chartmaker Studios, Céline was often singing in front of people who had never heard of her, industry people or musicians who wanted to hear the voice that more and more people were talking about. It was an audience of insiders, professionals. She loved singing for them. And it paid off. Twice she was asked to sing duets: with Billy Newton Davis in "Can't Live Without You," and with Dan Hill in "Wishful Thinking" on his album *Real Love.*

Céline and René made the odd trip to Las Vegas, where they stayed at Caesar's Palace. While Céline would sleep in, René, who would have spent most of the night at the gaming tables, would call his friends — Vito, Foster, Marc Verreault and Guy Cloutier — to talk about the album they were working on and describe the most recent recording sessions, right down to the people who were there and who took part.

Céline had never sung better. In the afternoons, they would sunbathe. At night, the shows.

At the Sahara, they watched Liza Minelli's show from front-row seats. For Céline, it was a revelation. Liza sang with so much intensity, so much power, so much presence that she seemed to put her life on the line with every song. Céline was moved to tears. René, too, not only because he was delighted with the show, but because he could see how sensitive Céline really was. After Liza belted out "New York, New York," Céline handed her a rose. They stayed on for the next show.

A few days later, Céline found herself in the stifling heat of New York with producer Andy Goldmark. It was May. People there lived at a totally different pace — more rushed, but just as exciting.

> I adore New York. Here, people aren't laid-back like they are in LA., but they're straight shooters. If a guy looks like a killer, he is a killer. The guy who looks like a saint is a saint. In New York, the killers and the saints hang out on the same streets, in the same bars. There are no social barriers, like in Paris. No class distinction. A millionaire will step outside the St. Regis Hotel for a smoke and make small talk with the doorman. The society matron loaded down with jewelry will look at photos of her hairdresser's baby and tell her all about her hot flashes. When I'm in New York I always feel like I'm right in the thick of things. I can hear people's heartbeats, I'm in touch with humanity.

The song "Unison" was written for Céline by Goldmark and Bruce. Goldmark did the arrangements, produced it, played the keyboards and programmed the drums. It was designed and put together by engineers and technicians and fine-tuned to the nth degree in three Los Angeles and two New York studios. It's a dance tune through and through. Goldmark's style is fundamentally different from that of Foster. It's from another culture, with different rhythms. But Céline loves the changes, the new worlds she discovers. And she learns as she discovers.

Céline is confident of her talent, and she feels right at home in a studio. Music is her life. A talent like hers comes with being strong, and René is right behind her, urging her along, guiding and protecting her. The technicians — the best in the world, as he keeps repeating — respect her and treat her like one of them, like a pro.

Early summer found the two in London. They were scheduled to record two songs at West Side Studios under the direction of Christopher Neil. When they were looking for songs for the English album, Vito sent

Neil (as well as Foster and Goldmark) Céline's French recordings and the demo tape of "Have a Heart." He asked the three to send him their song suggestions. Neil's choice was a demo tape of "Where Does My Heart Beat Now." It was a loud rock number, with screaming guitars. René like the words and the tune, but he wasn't convinced it suited Céline. To put his doubts to rest he played the devil's advocate with Vito. Vito took the bait and played Neil's demo over and over again for him.

Earlier that spring Céline and René traveled to London where they met Neil and his arranger Wix for key selection. Angélil was more impressed than Céline. Wix had played keyboards with Paul McCartney. He'd also been a sideman with Eric Clapton, Elton John, George Martin, all the big names of British pop.

Unlike Foster and Goldmark, Neil didn't try to convince them that his tempos or ideas were best. Instead, he asked Céline how she liked to work. She hardly knew what to say. She liked to work when everything was going right. It was as simple as that. When she can feel that everybody around her is thinking, listening and doing their best. René warned Neil that she didn't like to sing, or even speak, before three or four o'clock in the afternoon, and that she didn't really light up until after dark. So Neil booked the studios and the engineers from four to midnight.

When they returned to London that summer for the session, he played them the new tapes of "Where Does My Heart Beat Now" that he'd recorded with Wix on keyboard, synthesizer and bass guitar. The only thing missing was Céline's voice. On recording night, she showed up at the studio an hour early. She was beside herself with excitement and impatience, already in the grip of her song. She'd rehearsed it a thousand times in her head, and she knew it by heart, right down to the tiniest detail. She'd worked hard on every note, every voice shading, the exact color of every sound, the texture, the volume of every breath.

There's always something very intimate in the moment of creation when a song is born, when all of the elements are brought together and given a soul, a breath, a voice. In all the great recording studios, when the time comes, the lights are turned down. You don't know whether you're in Los Angeles, New York or London — it's all the same. It doesn't matter whether it's midnight or noon, you're in another world. That's because a song is about to be born

Céline never liked rehearsing in full voice in front of other people, even technicians and musicians. It destroyed the mystery, the spiritual part. She liked it when she could bring something unexpected to a song, something that surprised even her. She paced up and down the cavernous recording studio while Wix finished setting up his control panel.

Every studio has a rest area, with a fully equipped kitchen, maybe an exercise room, a reading room, or a game room. Neil wanted to work one-on-one with Céline for a while. So at his request, René led Vito off to the game room where they shot some pool.

Both men played well. As usual, René insisted on betting. René always had to bet, even a tiny symbolic amount, or the game was meaningless. It was just a technical exercise. For him, betting was communicating, playing against someone, testing his moxie and pride. Less than a half hour later, Neil came bursting through the door with Wix behind him, laughing, and looked at them with a combination of delight and pity on his face, like they had just missed something.

"It's done," he said.

And he added, behind their backs, as if to excuse himself for wrapping up so quickly, "How was I supposed to know she's such a fast worker?" He even thought twice about a second take. The first was perfect. Still, they recorded it again because he never heard of recording a song on the first take, not counting garage bands or free jazz, of course.

The trick is knowing which take is the right one—knowing that when you've got it, you've got it, and there's no point in looking any farther. Messing around with a good thing is as risky as rushing through a job.

Angélil and Vito dropped their cues and rushed out to hear "Where Does My Heart Beat Now." Angélil burst into tears. He and Vito jumped around the studio shouting "We did it! We did it!" Céline, who kept her feelings under wraps at times like these, just wanted to record the next song, "The Last to Know." But the tapes weren't ready yet.

It was seven o'clock, London time. Christopher Neil phoned Zuckerman in his New York office to tell him he just recorded "the greatest song in the world" and that he was ready to record another one.

When they stepped out of the studio they were walking on air. All except Céline, who stayed as cool and collected as usual. But deep in her heart, she was jubilant.

When they got back to the Sheraton, René set up shop by the phone. For the next two hours, he was on the phone to Montreal, filling in Marc Verreault and Francine Chaloult on the details. He described West Side Studio, his game of pool with Vito, the look on Christopher's face when he came to tell them the song was done, his and Vito's reaction and Céline's.

Around midnight, he and Vito decided to go to the casino at the Sports Club. They sat side by side at a blackjack table. Without a word, they played and won, each man lost in thought, a smile on his face. Then Angélil turned to Vito and said, "Just think when she sings that on *The Tonight Show*. People will stop in their tracks."

The next day, an hour after arriving at the studio, Céline recorded "The Last to Know." The same scenario. Vito and René were playing pool. Christopher came barging into the room to tell them, "She did it again." That same night, Angélil and Vito played blackjack again, and won. They came to the Sports Club in a taxi, but were driven home in the winners' limousine.

Angélil couldn't stop thinking about his sequence theory. There are times in life when you just can't lose. When luck follows you every step of the way. The trick is knowing how to take advantage of it.

It was like a song. Everything was in perfect harmony. On May 6 in Lugano, Céline attended the 1989 Eurovision awards and sang "Have a Heart" in English before an audience for the first time in her life. The next day, she told a reporter who asked her about her international hits that she often "felt like she's been there before. Maybe in another life. But not as lucky as this one. Sometimes, it's like I've seen and done exactly the same thing before."

But she still had sacrifices to make, she added. She had to work out every day to keep her voice in shape. "Every day, I do my twenty minutes of vocal exercises, I sleep a lot, I never go to clubs. Singers are just like athletes; they have to work out every day to keep their vocal cords in shape."

She kept telling herself that she wasn't in love. So much the better. That way she could concentrate on her career, as if love was a barrier to success. It was one of Angélil's little white lies. The truth was, they were head over heels in love.

The *Falling Into You* Tour
Chicago, August 11, 1996

Her Song

As she sings "Seduces Me," the fans come and lay gifts at Céline's feet — everything from stuffed frogs and teddy bears to flowers, nickels, cakes and cookies, fruits, jars of jam and letters.

Some of them talk about their lives. Some talk about their dreams. When you get right down to it, we're all the same. We all have our dreams. I hope they help us to live. That's why we have them. They're like our organs, our stomachs, our muscles. They're there for a reason.

Sometimes I wonder if you stop dreaming when you get old, just like you stop wanting to make love. I guess it depends on the person. At fifty-five, René is still a dreamer. He's full of plans and ideas. He wants me to sing in Moscow, in Capetown, in Rio, in Beirut, in Bombay. I tell him he's thinking like an conqueror. The way things are going, what'll happen when I've sung just about everywhere in the world? Is he going to send me to Mars, maybe?

After they leave their offerings at the edge of the stage, most of the fans hurry back to their seats, but some stay on at Céline's feet with heads high, often with arms extended. They're waiting for her to look their way, to touch them. Sometimes she does. She bends over and touches their fingertips. Often they're little girls held up by their parents. Céline calls them "cutie-pie" or "sweetheart."

She always introduces "Seduces Me" as one of her favorite songs. It's like a quiet garden after the thundering storm of "River Deep, Mountain High." When André Coutu plucks a few notes on his guitar, a completely different atmosphere takes over. That's the magic of music, with all its extraordinary pull on the emotions. Céline changes her voice like she changes her gowns. Like a workman changes tools. Like a painter his paints or brushes. Now she brings out her bluesy voice, her subtle, soft voice that contrasts so strongly with the hard, brassy, piercing voice she uses when she sings the big, powerful ballads like "River Deep, Mountain High" or "The Power of Love." The crowd settles down. And so does Eric.

She always ends "Seduces Me" sitting down, in front of the backup singers, at the foot of the lamppost, wrapped up in emotion. As the applause increases, she keeps her head down, her hands folded. Then, on the guitar's final notes, she stands up and strides toward the audience. In Chicago, she knelt at the edge of the stage and planted a kiss on the cheek of a little girl. When Céline got to her feet, Mégo began playing "All By Myself," and the mesmerized crowd quickly shook itself awake.

What makes a song like "All By Myself" so touching? Of course, there's Céline's skill as a vocalist. David Foster rearranged the melody to make the most of her voice. But the song is the heartrending story of someone who doesn't want to go on living — a story everybody knows. It's the story of intolerable loneliness and rejection.

When I was young
I never needed anyone,
And making love was just for fun.
These days are gone.

"All By Myself,"
Eric Carmen and Sergei Rachmaninoff

During the musical transition (with Mégo's face in close-up on the big screens) Céline walks back up the ramp toward center stage and belts out the last refrain, straight from the heart. It's the show's highest note, and she holds it until the audience is on its feet.

Chapter Twenty-Two
A Key Man

In July 1989, René was on vacation in Daytona Beach with his children, Céline and her family. Ever since they got back from London, he'd been walking on air. What they had was as good as gold or diamonds. He was sure of it. When the CBS brass heard Céline's new album, they would want to release it as quickly as they could, maybe even in the fall. Late one afternoon when he came back from the golf course, there was a message from Vito. René was sure that it was the call he was waiting for, that the people at CBS wanted to meet him to draw up their marketing strategy.

But there was a hitch, Vito told him. He had played the songs Céline had recorded — six directed by Foster, two with Neil and two with Goldmark. CBS's head office in New York was pleased, but at the same time, they felt something was lacking. They weren't prepared to go ahead immediately.

René's shock soon turned to anger. He told Vito that he would buy back the album and sell it to Atlantic Records. Christopher Neil had some good friends at Atlantic. He'd played "Where Does My Heart Beat Now" for them, and the president was so impressed that he wanted to know if Céline had already signed on with CBS. With songs like that, she would be a big star in the USA, he said.

What really bothered René was that his longtime ally, Vito Luprano, seemed to agree with the CBS-USA people. Vito did his best to make him understand that CBS was taking that approach because they believed in Céline. They wanted her to score more than just a hit or two; they wanted her to climb to the top and stay there for a long, long time.

To make matters worse, Bernie DiMatteo, one of Céline's strongest supporters and René's best allies, returned to New York that summer of 1989. A new president took over CBS-Canada, a thirty-seven-year-old named Paul Burger who may not even have known who Céline Dion was. In fact, Burger had a vague idea of who Céline was, but he wasn't exactly sympathetic to her at first.

The New York-born Burger, who held a degree in administration, had produced the greatest hit ever produced in Israel when he headed the CBS subsidiary in that country. The single, by David Broza, sold 160,000 copies in a country that could boast only 1.5 million households. In 1984, he was promoted to head up CBS's European special marketing division with responsibility for catalog sales and all marketing except new releases. He was also given the job of introducing the compact disc to European markets. The following year, when CBS transferred its operations to London, he was named vice-president, sales and marketing, for Europe.

He was still holding that job on the morning of May 1, 1988, when he learned that a CBS artist, a certain Céline Dion, had just won the Eurovision grand prize in Dublin. "Good! Now, where's the record?" he said. He was astonished to learn that Céline Dion didn't even have a record in English. CBS-Canada had produced an album in French the previous year, and an English album was in the works. For Burger, the Eurovision award was so much wasted effort, a golden chance that slipped through their fingers. CBS-Canada had promised that the album would be ready for release before the end of the summer. Fall had come, then winter, and still no album. When Céline finally appeared in the West Side Studios in the spring to record, Paul Burger had almost forgotten her name. He didn't even make an attempt to contact Christopher Neil to find out how the session had gone.

Suddenly, he was being offered the top job at CBS-Canada, in Toronto, replacing Bernie DiMatteo. He began by drawing up an inventory of the company's properties, which included the songs Céline Dion had recorded in Los Angeles, New York and London. "Then and there she became my priority," he said. "I called Vito Luprano to set up a meeting."

Vito took him to Sainte-Anne-des-Lacs, the picturesque village in the Laurentian Mountains where Céline was living at the time. On the expressway heading north, Burger, a denizen of the big city, expressed surprise that such a supposedly prominent artist could live so far away from the bright lights, in such sparsely populated countryside. But the house was a magnificent specimen of modern architecture built high on a hillside and bathed with light; its floors, walls and ceilings were pure white.

The year before, Céline rented a country place in Sainte-Anne-des-Lacs for her mother, who was still recovering from her coronary bypass. That's how she came to know the house that had been owned by Dominique Michel, one of Quebec's most popular entertainers. In fact, if she hadn't been a star in the local musical hall scene for more than forty years, Michel could have been a real estate agent. She was constantly buying, renovating and reselling her houses, old and new, from one end of Quebec to the other. Céline bought her place in Sainte-Anne-des-Lacs. She owes much of her passion for houses to Dominique.

When Burger arrived, the house was full to the rafters. Céline's parents were there, many of her brothers and sisters, and René Angélil. "I liked that," he said. "I'm a family man. That's why I like Israel."

Céline wasn't fully comfortable with her English back then, so she spoke to him in French, as, of course, did Mrs. Dion.

One thing was really bothering him. It was something he didn't know quite how to bring up. For him, Céline's wardrobe wasn't right. She dressed like an older woman. He knew she was fashion conscious. But by then, they were relaxed enough that he could raise the subject.

"Do I like clothes? You should see what I've got in my room!"

He couldn't have hoped for more. They spent an hour going through her wardrobe. He told her he didn't understand why she dressed like a much older woman. He had enough experience to know that look and sound go together, that you can't market the one without the other.

"You're not an old woman, you're a girl. You should take advantage of it. Dress like a girl!"

She listened attentively and curiously. He found her energetic and lively. René, whom he was meeting for the first time, was reserved.

On the expressway back to Montreal, he told Vito Luprano, "This girl has something." And Vito answered, "Just wait. You ain't seen nothin' yet. Wait till you see her onstage."

Burger had seen the light in her eyes, the intensity and power. He knew that onstage, she could be exceptional. Angélil also made a good impression. He didn't talk much, but he was composed, and he was in charge.

"I said to myself, 'That man René Angélil is more than her manager. There's something between the two of them. Something that gives them a real power.' The two of them convinced me."

Of course, they talked recordings. Burger said that Céline's work was "timeless, not trendy," and she shouldn't try to keep up with fashion, but to stay ahead of it. He also told Angélil and Céline that he agreed with the top brass at CBS-International. The new album still needed one or two more songs. But he'd listened to it very closely. Céline had a magnificent voice, and the songs had to match it. Then and there, he decided to invest more money to record two more songs. And René quickly realized that he had an ally.

Since everyone liked the songs produced by Christopher Neil, it was decided that they would return to London at the end of the summer of 1989 to record two more titles: "(If There Was) Any Other Way" and "If Love Is Out of the Question." Once everybody was happy, the album went into production.

In Burger's opinion, Céline had enormous talent, and even greater potential, because of her voice, of course, but also because of her presence. He knew she could win over the people she met, men or women. Those were the days when the people at CBS were saying, "Well, she's not exactly my style, but I've got to admit she has an extraordinary voice." Once you met her, it was hard not to be captivated by her. Burger set to work to exploit Céline's charisma. He would make sure the right people heard her, and everything else would follow.

In Toronto, even in the corridors of CBS, people were laughing at Burger. After all, he was a new arrival. And now, after being on the job for just a couple of weeks, he decided to stake everything on an artist from Quebec who'd never sung a word in English. Besides, never in Canada did a French-speaking singer ever achieve a real career in English. But Burger liked the project too much to give up on it. This time, it was a real challenge. But when you got right down to it, Céline was only twenty, younger than many English-speaking singers just starting out. Sure, she wasn't yet comfortable with the language, but she had years of experience onstage, in recording studios, with the media, and in the world of pop music. This gave her a definite advantage over many English-speaking singers, an advantage Burger was fully aware of.

The *Falling Into You* Tour
Perth, March 18, 1996

The Monologue

The more than two million people in the Americas, Europe and Asia who saw Céline Dion's '96–97 tour must have a pretty good idea of who she is, where she comes from and the life she leads.

After "All By Myself," she asks Mégo, the band leader, to wait a few minutes. "I want to talk," she says. Then, turning to the crowd that packs the Entertainment Center in Perth, Australia, she adds, "You all know how I love to sing. But did you know I love to talk too?"

And the crowd, realizing that she's going to take them into her confidence, coos contentedly. In less than five minutes, Céline paints her own self-portrait, a little masterpiece of brevity and a storehouse of information about herself touching on the subjects that put people at ease: the family, childhood, school days.

She speaks in questions, and it isn't long before the crowd is on her side. "Did you know I grew up speaking French?"

There are shouts of acknowledgement from here and there in the Entertainment Center.

"Maybe you didn't know that I'm the youngest of fourteen children."

The audience screams, louder still. They know all that. Céline pretends to be discouraged. "You know everything. I'm wasting my time."

Then, in a confidential tone, she adds: "When there were sixteen of us at the dinner table, we had to keep our mouths shut. So today, I talk whenever I get the chance."

She tells how her parents didn't want children when they married. "Poor Dad!" And her face, in close-up, has a disappointed look. Then, shaking her head, she says, "I mean, poor Mom!" And with her hand she outlines a pregnant belly.

Then she recalls how she began singing when she was little, how her brothers and sisters stood her up on the kitchen table and stuck crayons in her hands.

In a stage whisper, she says, "I knew it wasn't a microphone. I'm not crazy, you know." It's her way of reminding people in a roundabout way that she's always known her trade is a matter of illusion, that show business is a suckers' game.

She tells the crowd that she was all the rage in her native Quebec long before she could speak English. And that she was always fascinated by American culture, by songs, movies and TV shows made in the USA.

"Have you seen Flashdance*? You remember the scene when the girl dances in the shower? Remember the song "What a Feeling?" I was twelve years old when I had my first real show, with music, lighting, my own production crew. That's the song I sang."*

After a pause she adds, "Well, believe it or not, I didn't understand a single word I was singing."

And the crowd bursts into laughter.

Throughout the tour, and not only in Perth, Céline introduces herself as the girl from far away, from a different culture, from a place that's not exactly American. Then she explains how she took English lessons. From nine in the morning until five in the afternoon, five days a week. It was long, hard, but marvelous. "What a pleasure it is to learn."

After that, she talks about teachers. "I love teachers," she tells the people of Perth, which never fails to produce guffaws, hisses, and good-humored booing. "Are there any teachers in the audience?" A few raise their hands timidly. Céline tells them she likes them because they're perfectionists. "Real teachers want to teach us something, and they want us to learn it well.

"We French speakers have a hard time making some of the sounds that are common in English. So, every morning, my teacher would start me out on them."

The crowd bursts out laughing. She's got a remarkable sense of timing. Angélil believes she could have been a great stand-up comedian.

"Life is funny, you know," she says, "Lots of times, it's the hard things that give us the most satisfaction. I worked hard to learn English. Today, I'm glad I did, because I can sing everywhere in the world, and get real close to you. I

can sing for you here, tonight, in Perth. It's such a lovely town, so clean and green, so close to nature. You know, we were all impressed by your toilet bowls. Those two little keys, one for pee pee, and the other...."

Céline Dion is a born charmer, a master in the art of friendly persuasion, a champion at making people feel she's on their side.

At the end of the world, Perth isn't the only place where Céline stresses her difference. Even in France, in all her presentations and her interviews, she's careful to remind people that she comes from somewhere else. One night, on the Parisian variety show Taratata, she performed with Kevin Parent, a singer from the Gaspé region of Quebec. As a joke on the host, she and Parent began to speak so quickly, with such a thick Quebec accent, that they were the only two people who knew what they were talking about. Then she said, "Whether I speak in French or English, I'll always have an accent. But when I sing, I don't have any at all."

It's a funny world. The sharpest criticism of her Paris shows came from Quebec, from French-Canadian journalists based in Paris. They know how touchy the French are about their accent, and they were worried (with good reason) that Céline's accent would get her in hot water. The French had criticized her accent, her twisted sentences. "Poor girl. Instead of talking, she should just sing." Americans aren't heavy consumers of foreign cultural products, but accents have never bothered them. But the French, even in the media, are still not comfortable with the slightest foreign accent. But even in this area, Céline has broken new ground. At the Olympia, the Zénith, at Bercy, in every big French hall she's performed in, she has spoken effortlessly, directly, simply. And she has touched people. That's her power. Like the Americans say, "she connects." Even if her sentences are a bit off, Céline communicates very well with people.

She ends her monologue by saying how happy she is to sing in English today, but that doesn't mean she's forgotten her roots.

And she sings "Pour que tu m'aimes encore." In French, in Perth, at the other end of the world.

Chapter Twenty-Three
The Rumor Mill

While the most powerful professionals of the recording world were fine-tuning and packaging Céline's songs in their Montreal, New York, London, Los Angeles and Toronto offices, while they were hard at work on promotion plans for her first album in English, Céline Dion was spending a few days with her parents in the big white house in Sainte-Anne-des-Lacs. It was fall, and the weather was pleasant and warm. Céline was completely happy. Almost.

She was twenty-one. She had an accountant, a notary, an agent and millions of fans. She was famous in Quebec and France. The toughest honchos, the top pros of American show business were fascinated by her voice and talent. As a spokeswoman for Chrysler, she was driving — what a pleasure that was — the latest Laser Turbo. She owned two houses. She was rich. She traveled. She loved shopping in the world's most expensive shops. She owned more than two hundred pairs of shoes, more than one hundred dresses, three fur coats, scads of the finest lingerie, whatever she wanted. Almost.

For the past three days, she'd been raking and gathering up the fallen leaves around her house. She stuffed them into orange garbage bags and lined them up along the driveway. She was humming to herself, composing a tune, a melodic phrase she would toy with for hours on end, softening it, breaking it down, starting over again. Sometimes, the following day, she tried to remember that tune, but all she could come up with were bits and pieces. She regretted that she hadn't recorded it. Then another tune popped into her head, and she would play with it, but refuse to record it. Those little melodies were her secret, hers alone. Everything else belonged to the public.

Journalists want to know everything about stars, right down to their most intimate thoughts and desires. And if you try to hide things from them, they'll just invent a story — sometimes even the truth that the stars were trying to conceal. It's always better to come clean.

But Céline just couldn't. She couldn't open her heart about one particular issue. And the lie she was forced to tell cast a shadow over her happiness, a shadow that eclipsed and confused her life. René didn't want people talking about their love affair. He was afraid people would feel scandalized. After all, he was more than twice her age, twice married, with three children.

But there was no way to stop the rumor mill. Plenty of people talked about how they knew someone who'd seen them on the street in Montreal or in Paris, arm in arm. Or in the first-class area on Air France or Air Canada, kissing or holding hands.

Some people were convinced that Céline Dion was already René Angélil's wife. Others were sure she was some kind of showbiz mystic, chaste and pure, someone who'd put love aside for the good of her career. In fact, that was her line. Because that's what René wanted to hear. For months, she'd been fending off the journalists who kept prying into her love life by telling them that she'd given up on love.

She'd just completed her very first album in English. It consisted of twelve songs, and each of them was about love—about burning, all-consuming passion. She was about to fly off to Nassau to tape a video that would reveal her as a sexy young woman with plenty of experience in the ways of love. The press photos for the launch of her *Unison* album showed her as an enticer, with tight jeans and a form-fitting top that exposed her shoulders and sun-tanned tummy.

It was all a game, of course. Nothing but showbiz and hype. In real life, she had to pretend she was a girl with no interest in love. But on the screen and in her songs, she was all woman, and then some.

The world of show business is all appearance and illusion, where anything goes. But curiously, her songs, videos and photos actually let Céline tell the truth. She wanted to be as frank and honest as she could be in real life. She wanted the whole world to know that she loved René Angélil and that he loved her.

She was just about finished raking up the dead leaves. As a perfectionist, she liked to have things in order. Straightening up the place where she lived was a way of putting her emotions, her feelings, her life itself in order. Then her fears would evaporate. That was certainly the reason that she loved to arrange things, file things away, and sort things in her closets and drawers. Especially when she was in one of her moods. She would feel a sense of certainty as everything fell into place, and that gave her a lift and put her mind at ease.

"One day I'll tell them the name of the man I love. I'll shout it from the rooftops. I'll make him tell the whole world he's nuts about me. He told me so. He tells me every day."

Nothing is harder to hide than when you're in love. It lights up your face and changes the way the whole world looks to you. How could Céline conceal the light that glowed in her eyes? How could she not talk about the man she loved? How could she not turn a radiant face toward him when he walked into the room, when he came up to her, when he smiled?

She never lied to her mother. Her mother knew before anyone else that her daughter was in love. But she wasn't overly concerned. She was sure her daughter would meet a young man her age, and forget all about him. She was convinced René wasn't even aware of the situation and that a handsome man more than forty years old couldn't possibly be interested in a teenager.

But Céline was no ordinary teenager. By the age of twelve she'd already invested all her intelligence, talent, energy—her entire life—in her one great goal. At fifteen, she was already a rising star, driven by ambition and a dream. At eighteen, she was already a star in France and Quebec.

She fell in love with René early on. For a long time, even she didn't even realize it. She only knew that she was happy. Marnay spotted the love affair and used it in the songs he wrote for her. Mia noticed it too, and Anne-Renée most certainly did. But everybody believed she'd get over it.

By then, René Angélil did realize that Céline was in love with him. She was entranced by everything he said. Not an hour went by without her inventing some excuse to talk to him on the telephone or see him. Yet she didn't believe he could really love her. She saw herself as awkward and plain. So when she changed her appearance, it was only for him.

In 1986, they hadn't seen much of each other. He was away in Las Vegas or Nassau much of the time. She was hard at work learning to dance, keeping up with her English lessons, having her teeth straightened. But she thought of him every moment.

One day, after they'd been apart for several weeks, he came to pick her up at her home in Duvernay to introduce her to some CBS people from Toronto and New York. She answered the door. It was summer. She was tanned, and she was wearing a miniskirt and a tank top. Her sister Manon had just done her hair, which tumbled in light curls over her bare shoulders. For a moment, he just stood there gaping, at a loss for words.

She saw how she'd affected him. That day, she realized that anything was possible.

The following year, during the *Incognito* tour, the kiss he planted every night on her cheek edged closer and closer to her lips. Mrs. Dion was far away. They spent more and more time together in long, quiet conversations, in restaurants, in René's car, in Céline's dressing room. Sometimes even when the room was full of people, it felt like the two of them were the only ones in the room. He talked, she listened and learned.

Angélil is a born storyteller. He told her the story of show business as if it were a Homeric epic. Its heroes were Elvis Presley, Edith Piaf, Barbra Streisand, Frank Sinatra, but also the people who managed them, who set up the powerful machinery around them and guided their careers, people like Colonel Parker or Brian Epstein. Thanks to him, with him, she was already part of that world. There were many electrifying moments, the triumphs they experienced together that brought them closer to each other, and set them apart from the rest.

After they'd declared their love to each other, René spent hours reminding her, with a thousand details, just how and why it had happened — how he admired her, how sexy, beautiful, and brilliant she was. And Céline discovered that their love had deep, deep roots. It was a story full of twists and turns, of special moments, of confessions that they pretended not to see or hear. Twice, a hundred times over, they rehashed the same story, just for the pleasure of hearing it again. "The time you came onto the airplane with your navy blue suit," or "the time you came to pick me up in Duvernay," or "the time you fell asleep on my shoulder," "the time I pretended to fall asleep on your shoulder."

Angélil had resisted for the longest time. He'd even told Eddy Marnay. It was at the Hotel de l'Étoile in Paris, near Place Maillot. After they'd taken Céline and her mother to their rooms, the two men sat down on the hotel stairs. René told the man he looked up to like a father how confused and torn he was. He was afraid of ruining Céline's life, of ruining her career too — both their careers. Marnay told him, "If you really love her, and I think you do, there's no danger. Love never hurt anyone." Then he added, "Céline is your future. And anyway, you can't hide your love. Not from the people who love you."

A few weeks later, René got a call from Mrs. Dion. From her tone of voice, he realized that she knew everything, and that she was angry and hurt. "I want to talk to you," she said coldly. She came over to tell him how disappointed she was, that she thought he'd betrayed her. "I trusted you. Céline is my little princess. I wanted a prince charming for her." And instead of a prince charming, she'd fallen for a man twenty-six years older and twice divorced. She walked out in tears, convinced that he'd destroyed Céline's life, and hers at the same time.

But Mrs. Dion realized she had no choice. Céline and René lived alone in their own world. They could no longer live without each other. They shared the same soul. Their destinies were joined forever. They were kindred spirits.

Everyone in Céline and René's entourage understood. René was worried how the public would react. But the embargo he'd laid on their affair would soon be a source of dissension between the two of them. But she would fight back, and she would win. She would challenge the man she loved so that their love would win out, so that the whole world would know that he was her lover, her man.

There wasn't a single leaf left on the lawn or in the flower beds. Even though her father had told her to leave a few because they made good fertilizer, she raked up every last one. When she tied up the last bag she felt dejected, like the way she felt when a show ended, or when she finished a recording into which she focused all her energy, her heart, her soul.

The *Falling Into You* Tour
Manchester, November 14, 1996

The Bodyguard

From Stockholm to Melbourne and from Cleveland to Lyon, one song never fails to bring the crowd to its feet: "J'irai où tu iras." It's a hard-driving, catchy rock-and-roll number featuring bass guitarist Marc Langis and Céline. From the first chords, the same people who have just sat quietly through the torchy "All By Myself" are up and dancing in the aisles. They are mostly young people, singing and dancing along with Céline. That means plenty of work for Eric, her bodyguard. Fans like to throw teddy bears and bunches of flowers in her direction.

This night in Manchester, René uses the commotion to win and bring an end to a little game he and Eric started earlier at Bercy, in Paris. The idea is to catch each other off guard by sneaking up from behind and tapping him on the shoulder. If the tappee turns toward his tapped shoulder, the tapper scores a point. They bet 50 francs — about $10 dollars.

René loves games, any kind of game. He just can't resist them, whatever it is. The business with Eric went on for days. There was nothing else on his mind. It didn't matter how many problems he had to sort out. That's when he was lining up the South American campaign, the Asian tour, and the New Year's Eve show in France.

At Bercy, Eric scored a point. René was eating a piece of cake in the canteen. His mother was with him, so was Mrs. Dion, Jean-Jacques Goldman, Francine Chaloult. Gilles walked up to René on the right and René grinned at the camera. When Eric tapped his left shoulder, René turned toward him. And the whole thing was on tape. You could hear René cursing and Eric's voice saying, "twenty-one points for me."

In Liévin, in France, Angélil scored a point when Eric let his guard down. Michel Drucker, one of René's closest friends, was with them working on his show, French TV's top variety program. Angélil evened the score at 2-2. Later, in the plane back to Paris, Céline, René and Drucker were lost in a long, involved conversation about Edith Piaf and Brigitte Bardot. In her autobiography, which had just come out, Bardot described the birth of her son as a painful, disgusting experience. René was shocked. That's when Eric snuck up and tapped him on the shoulder. Score: 3-2.

When they were traveling to England a couple days later, the two agreed to up the ante to 10 pounds sterling, or about $20. René evened the score in Cardiff. In Sheffield, after the show, René was waiting for Eric in the dark, right beneath the stage. Eric was on high alert, and walked all the way around the stage. René was caught in his own trap. That made it 4-3 for Eric.

Since that night, René has been on the lookout for a chance to score. He'd tried sneaking up on Eric at least twenty times. But like any bodyguard worth his salt, Eric caught on to him and foiled his schemes. When René tapped his left shoulder, he looked to the right. When René tapped his right shoulder, he looked to the left. The two men crept along the corridors with their backs to the wall, trusting no one, looking behind them, trying to recruit accomplices from among the musicians in the band or the technical crew.

Nobody likes to lose, even the smallest amount. High in the air over England, on the way from London to Manchester on the Lear Jet, René came up with a winner.

Here, in Manchester, the moment Céline breaks into "J'irai où tu iras," he slips beneath the stage. Directly overhead, the ear-splitting din of Marc Langis hammers out the beat.

Prends tes clic et tes clac et tes rêves et ta vie,
Tes mots, tes tabernacles et ta langue d'ici.
"J'irai où tu iras,"
Jean-Jacques Goldman

(Take your stuff, your dreams and your life,
Your cussing and your down-home twang.)

René creeps stealthily over the electrical wires, the cables, the conduits. Eric is standing right in front of him, facing the crowd. In front of him, young people are dancing and jumping up and down. René taps his right shoulder. Eric jumps and snaps his head to the right. Then René taps his left shoulder. Same reaction. He whispers into Eric's left ear, "5-4, game over." Then he turns back the way he came, a happy winner.

Eric pays up. Gentlemen always pay their debts.

Chapter Twenty-Four
The Battle of Quebec

Heavy snow was falling as Céline pulled up at the Chanteclerc Inn in Sainte-Adèle, a resort in the Laurentian Mountains an hour's drive north of Montreal. She was alone behind the wheel of her Chrysler. The man she loved would be arriving in an hour or two, and they would spend the evening together. She would be looking her best. He would be nervous. She had a table brought up to the room. They'd eat dinner by candlelight, just the two of them. He would tell her magical stories about the biggest stars, and she would drink in his every word. They'd be all alone, just the two of them in the whole world, alone with their dreams, their plans for tomorrow, their love. He'd talk about the things they'd done, the English album that would introduce her to English Canada and the United States, then to the rest of the world. She'd be a great star. And he'd always be beside her.

From her room, she watched the skiers gliding down the floodlit slopes. Outside their professional activities, they tried to avoid being seen together. Wherever they went, they booked separate rooms. At first, their little game of hide-and-seek was amusing. Sometimes she'd even wear a disguise, just for the fun of it. One night in Quebec City she'd gone out with René wearing a blond wig and dark glasses. No one recognized her, not even René's old pal Guy Cloutier. René Angélil had a new flame, people would whisper. And Céline would be jealous of the young woman she'd impersonated. But ever since then, the urge to tell the whole world about their love was growing stronger, until it almost overpowered her. Now it was causing arguments between her and René.

In a few days she'd be twenty-two years old. Most girls her age were free to say and do what they pleased, to appear in public with the men they loved. Many of them were already married, with children. Why should she hide?

René had his reasons. The difference in their ages was the main one. She'd counted the days, including leap years. From January 16, 1942 to March 30, 1968, there were 9,570 days. René had lived all those days without her. But he'd spent so many hours telling her what he'd seen and heard, what he'd done and learned during all those years that she often had the feeling that they belonged to the same generation. He'd given her everything, told her everything. His spirit was in her.

But René was afraid that people would laugh and accuse him of wielding too much power over her. Nothing made him angrier than when people said she was a robot, doing exactly what he told her to do. In his opinion, she was extremely intelligent. In ten years, she'd gained extraordinary experience. She did what she wanted to, and made her own choices. That was what had attracted him to her in the first place. And her ambition. At age fifteen, she told him, "I want to be the greatest singer in the world." He burst out laughing. But he knew she had it in her.

More than fifty journalists, disc jockeys, critics and promoters from the all across Canada were scheduled to meet her at the Chanteclerc that weekend. They represented the biggest radio stations, the top-selling record stores, the big dailies from Toronto and Western Canada: Winnipeg, Edmonton, Calgary, Vancouver.

René played the songs from Céline's *Unison* album which was due for release in a few days, on April 2, 1990. Already a catchy slogan was circulating: "Remember the name, because you'll never forget the voice." The following night, Saturday, after the banquet in the main dining room, she sang four songs, including "Where Does My Heart Beat Now" and "Any Other Way," which were about to be released as singles. Then she met everyone in the room. For two days running, they asked her questions, photographed her, recorded her words, talked to her about her family, her career plans and about Quebec nationalism (always a big issue for journalists from English Canada). She had no answer for many of the questions. But she was charming and generous with her time. She had to be. The fate of her next album was in their hands.

Unison was launched on Monday, April 2, 1990, three years to the day after *Incognito*, which had now gone platinum three times over. The launch took place at the Métropolis, a huge discotheque on St. Catherine Street in Montreal. It was televised live by MusiquePlus, the Quebec equivalent of MTV. Céline sang six songs from the new album. Earlier that afternoon, fans began to congregate on St. Catherine Street, and their limos had to inch through the crowd with blaring horns. Inside the Métropolis, the atmosphere was charged with electricity thick enough to cut with a knife. The Chrysler company colors were flying, and huge posters of Céline hung everywhere. It showed a close-up of her face in a serious pose, in black and white. The shot was taken by Dimo Safari, from the new album cover.

Paul Burger, president of CBS Records, explained the strategy to the crowd. Céline had decided to record an album in English because English was the international language of success. Everybody broke into applause.

"The most important thing is to win over English Canada first," he said. "If everything goes well, we'll try our luck in Europe and in the USA. Right now, our promotion people are meeting radio station record librarians and record store owners. So far, the response has been more than positive. France, the USA, England and Germany have already shown lots of interest in *Unison.*"

Céline was reaching the same level as Madonna and Whitney Houston, the world's most popular female vocalists. "It's the biggest challenge of my life," she told the journalists. "It's scary, and wonderfully exciting at the same time." She was working hard, she said, but she still had a lot to learn. Questions came from all directions. They focused on her life, on the eternal themes of love, loneliness and happiness. Some of the journalists noticed that René looked tired and thin.

The next day, the album was launched in Quebec City, complete with seventeen interviews, photo and autograph sessions. By midnight they were in Toronto. The next day, Céline was lined up for four interviews on TV, six on radio, and a big press conference. Then on to Vancouver on the ninth, Edmonton the tenth, Calgary the eleventh, and Winnipeg the twelfth. In ten days, she had met hundreds of journalists and disc jockeys.

> I'm not happy when I'm caught in that kind of grind. It's not like singing. When I'm singing, I'm in control two hundred percent. I do what I want. I'm totally free. I don't have that same freedom anywhere else. Sometimes I wonder what I should do in real life. Turn right or turn left, smile, talk to this person or that. I'm not sure. Onstage, I always know.

> When I'm doing record launches or promotional tours, I don't belong to myself. I don't even have time to enjoy life. You've got to smile all the time, have something intelligent to say. And you have to answer the same questions politely, over and over.

She remembers the advice Anne-Renée and Mia gave her: "Don't let them push you around. Only answer the questions you want to." But it's not always that easy. Some journalists like to set traps. Sometimes she senses that people are jealous of her success, or think it's tainted, as if she hadn't gained it honestly. And there's no end to it. Day and night, they're always after her.

Even so, the launch was a smashing success, and the sky was the limit. *Billboard* called Céline Dion the Canadian artist most likely to make it big in 1990, ahead of Alannah Myles and Blue Rodeo. Toronto superstation CHUM-FM, with its 1.2 million listeners, promised to play "Any Other Way" twice a day. It wouldn't be long before Céline topped the charts in Canada, right up there with Heart, Sinéad O'Connor, and Laura Branigan. But it would go no further. For mysterious reasons, despite all expectations, despite Operation Chanteclerc and the standing-room-only launches, the album was just not taking off in English Canada.

Even in Quebec, it began to level off after only a few weeks, totaling 120,000 copies. It was okay, but only just. Barely a third of the sales of *Je ne suis qu'une chanson* twelve years before.

At the time, Canadian radio stations were required by the Canadian Radio and Television Commission (CRTC) to carry between twenty and thirty percent Canadian content (Cancon). The problem was that the first two songs of *Unison*, which CBS had launched as singles, weren't considered Canadian. The singer was Canadian, but the music, words and production were foreign. For the CRTC to consider a song Canadian, at least two of the three had to be Canadian. Things would change when the David Foster songs came out. But for the time being, Céline was going up against the Americans and the British, up against Billy Joel and Madonna, and not against Alannah Myles or Burton Cummings. But deep down, René Angélil wasn't upset. The way he saw it, Céline would improve by comparing herself with the greatest. He kept right on believing that one day, Céline would be a great singer. He worked hard on his belief, he nurtured it, he made others believe. Only true believers would ever work with Céline. If you're halfhearted, stay away.

"Angélil's strength," said his old friend Mario Lefebvre, "is that he knows the trade inside out. He's done live performance and recording. He's had hits and flops. He's gone bankrupt. He knows marketing, promotion, the works. When he has to make a decision, he weighs all aspects down to the ounce. Plus, he really believes in Céline. He'll never waver. He's a believer. Working with René and Céline, even back then when they were practically unknown outside Quebec, you had to believe that nothing was impossible, that everything would turn out just like in their wildest dreams. Even when things were moving slowly, when nothing was happening. Like with *Unison* after the launch."

Meanwhile, René Angélil had made up his mind to put all his eggs in one basket: a monster promotional campaign. He was sure, like Burger, that there was no better way of convincing people than having them see Céline live, onstage. The idea was to produce a show in English and take it on the road across Canada. But he didn't have the money. And producer Jean-Claude L'Espérance wasn't anxious to sink a lot of money into the venture. In fact, Angélil had to twist his arm to get him to agree to stage a show in English at the Spectrum, a downtown Montreal pop-music venue. They decided to invite the English-language press to the event.

More than a few industry insiders, as well as the media, thought it was a risky move. So did the English-language media, which like to play up Quebeckers' sensitivity to language. The Spectrum show took the place at the same time as the Meech Lake Accord (the latest in a long line of attempts to reconcile English- and French-speaking Canada) was being defeated in provincial legislature. It was only a few days before Saint-Jean Baptiste Day, the national holiday of the French Canadians, and the province of Quebec was more alone, more bitter and angrier than ever before.

A Toronto journalist visited Pauline Julien, a Quebec singer who made no secret of her support for Quebec's independence, in an attempt to get her to turn against Céline. But Julien answered calmly that Céline Dion, like any other singer on earth, had a perfect right to sing in English if she wished. It had nothing whatsoever to do with the conflict between Quebec and Canada.

In late May, Jean-Claude L'Esperance told René that he didn't believe Céline could ever make it in English, and that he intended to pull out.

The final break between Angélil and L'Esperance came at the Diamond Club in Toronto. Burger bought 175 of the three hundred tickets, which he distributed to journalists, DJs, musicians and other influential people in the industry. He bought radio time as well. The show created a sensation in Toronto.

But it was too late. Angélil seemed to delight in telling L'Esperance that they couldn't work together any longer. René believed that L'Esperance was short on vision and on faith. In the meantime, he'd contacted Donald K. Donald Productions, who produced all the big out-of-town shows at the Montreal Forum and the Olympic Stadium—acts like Madonna, Pink Floyd and the Rolling Stones. Together, they began to plan a tour for the fall, first in Quebec. And then they'd see.

But Canada still wasn't won over. That became an obsession with Angélil. In the USA, in spite of CBS's interest, things were dragging. Burger was telling people that Don Grierson, the boss at Epic, CBS's American subsidiary, was interested, and that he loved the album. He kept feeding his American colleagues reports showing how popular Céline was in Canada. "*Unison* is going gold in Canada." "*Unison* is going platinum in Canada." The truth was that ninety-nine percent of sales were in Quebec. By the summer of 1990, *Unison* still hadn't made it out of the province. And in France, where she hadn't had a hit for several years, people were forgetting who Céline Dion was.

In July, Angélil was in Las Vegas. The heat was scorching. But he still managed to get his golf in early in the morning. In the afternoon, he and Paul Burger would meet by the pool at Caesar's Palace. Burger had just found out from Shirley Brooks, Julio Iglesias's impresario, that CBS-International would be holding its annual meeting in Quebec City on July 18 at the Chateau Frontenac. It would be the perfect occasion to introduce Céline. All the CBS bigwigs from America and Europe would be in one spot. And a heap of media people too. What a great opportunity for exposure!

"Céline's got to sing for them!" Angélil said.

On July 17, they were in Quebec City. The weather was warm and sunny. That evening, René had a small stage set up in the conference room, along with a powerful sound system.

The next morning, the lobby of the stately hotel overlooking the St. Lawrence River was buzzing as people from the four corners of the world headed for the conference room. At meetings like this, each country presents its hopefuls— the album or the artist they're counting on for a hit. When Paul Burger's turn came, he presented twenty-two-year-old Céline Dion, "an established star in Quebec and in France, who's going to conquer the world." To be in good voice, Céline had gotten up at six o'clock that morning for her voice and breathing exercises. Right after the delegates finished breakfast, at about ten o'clock, she sang. When she finished "Where Does My Heart Beat Now" and "No Other Way" there was a moment of silence, of disbelief. Then the audience was on its feet in a thunderous ovation. She laughed, spoke to them for a while, thanked them all.

That night when Burger, his wife Ossi, Céline and René were leaving for a restaurant, the courtyard of the Chateau was packed with people. Chance, that crafty stage manager, saw to it that singer George Michael and Walter Yetnikoff, the head of CBS-USA, were arriving at the hotel at that very instant. They saw the crowd cheering and clapping. George Michael quickly realized that the applause was not for him, but for Céline Dion. Yetnikoff had heard her sing that morning, but he couldn't believe what he was now witnessing. So it was true. That young girl *was* quite a star in her own country.

They'd won the battle of Quebec City. Now the invasion of Canada could begin. Better still, the Americans decided to move up the release date of *Unison* in the US.

Céline was at the top of her form. Her voice had never been better, although it still sounded a bit nasal to her, as she told anyone who cared to listen.

The fairy tale had just begun for her. But that same summer, she made up her mind to try a bit of acting and step into the shoes of a pathetic, battered and abused young woman.

When she read the script on the plane to Los Angeles, she cried. It was a sad, sad story that reminded her of the things she used to imagine. It was a dramatic miniseries for Quebec television called *Des fleurs sur la neige (Flowers on the Snow)*. She would play the part of Elisa Trudel, a young woman who'd been beaten and abused by an alcoholic father and a cruel mother, an abusive father-in-law and a brutal, nasty husband. But Elisa takes control of her fate and, because she has faith, courage, and a little bit of luck, she turns her life around.

The producers and the director of the miniseries offered her the role after she sang "Ton Visage" ("Your Face") by Quebec singer Jean-Pierre Ferland in a TV special on the world of show business. What struck the director was her intensity when she sang. They sent her the script, and she was sold. But not Angélil. It wasn't a suitable role for the modern, self-assured young woman Céline had become since *Incognito.* Elisa's whole life was a series of beatings and abuse. Céline's life was one of love, tenderness and admiration.

That four-hour miniseries had a strange, backward-looking impact on Céline's career. It was closer to the Céline at the time of "Une colombe" than the hard-driving, sexy songstress she had become. CBS was pushing *Unison* as hard as they could. Sooner or later, the doors to the world stage were bound to swing open. What was the point of filming a miniseries that no one outside Quebec would ever see?

The filming wasn't easy. Céline, who always walked ramrod straight, had to learn to walk bent over, with tiny steps. From the start, her fellow actors didn't want anything to do with her. The girl didn't have any acting experience, no skills. She hadn't been to theater school or the Conservatory. She should have auditioned just like everybody else. It was clear that she'd been chosen because she was so well-known.

She had to struggle twice as hard. Against the actors who looked down on her with contempt and suspicion. Against the fear of portraying a troubled, tormented character. Against fatigue. Her days were long and she had many things on her mind — her secret love, the album that wasn't taking off in English Canada and the US. She was learning how to live with success, with glory, and with criticism. She was studying English. That summer, whenever they had a chance, Mario Lefebvre, Vito Luprano and René spoke to her in English. And she had to cope working in English with some people, in French with others, flying to Los Angeles or Paris, meeting new people every day.

Every day, she learned something new. In her Louis Vuitton bag, along with the five-cent piece she'd found on the stage in Tokyo, her hairbrush and all the other things women carry with them, was a book the producer had talked to her about: *An Actor Prepares*, by Konstantin Stanislavsky, the Russian actor and director who died in 1938. Stanislavsky was a great theoretician of the theater, a complex and tormented man, and a serious, demanding author.

In her spare time, she studied the book. When she didn't understand what he meant, she began over again. She was certain that even when the filming of the miniseries was over, the theater would still interest her. But she didn't really like the tight little world of actors.

> Generally, they're cold people. Physically or emotionally, they don't really touch you. They've got their technique, their tricks. They know how to cry fake tears. When I cry, I cry for real. When I touch, it's because I want to feel, because I need it or because I want to give somebody pleasure.

When they filmed the violent scenes involving her character, she ended up with real bruises. She cried real tears, because she was truly worn out, miserable, beaten, battered. She had a technique of her own. She imagined that she was really experiencing her heroine's unhappiness. And so, she'd gotten caught up in the game, like she used to when she kept her diary.

One evening, she and Mario Lefebvre took in Elton John's show at the Montreal Forum. Two years earlier, a few days after she'd won the Eurovision grand prize, she and John shared the stage on the big German variety show "Wetten Dass." After her number, she waited in the wings until the end of the show. Elton John came over to her, and she made as if to stand up. With a firm gesture, he told her to stay where put, and he knelt down beside her. Then, in halting French, he told her that he saw her on the Eurovisions, that she had a remarkable voice, and that he wanted to write a song for her. For days, weeks, months after that, she dreamed and waited. To protect her, Angélil told her not to get her hopes up. She had to realize that an artist like Elton John was a busy man. There was no doubt about his sincerity, but he was caught up in the same grind.

When Mario suggested they take in Elton John's show that summer day, she accepted immediately, and added that she would like to meet him. She secretly hoped he would remember her. Plus, she wanted to get a close-up look at the man she considered to be one of the world's top singers and finest composers. There was something mysterious about the big stars that totally fascinated her.

Just before the show, she went backstage. She and Mario lined up just like everybody else — the fans, the winners of a contest organized by the record company and a rock radio station, and two journalists who'd been promised a couple of minutes in the star's presence. There they waited, outside his dressing room door. People were surprised to see Céline Dion. Some came over and asked her for an autograph. When Elton appeared, all smiles, at the dressing room door, people stopped talking. No one dared to step forward, not even Céline. Not because she was intimidated by Elton John, but because she didn't want to step out of line.

He took a step forward, shook hands with the first fan in line, said a few words, and moved on to the next. Each fan had a compliment or a pitch. He signed album covers, T-shirts, programs. He shook Céline's hand as she told him how much she liked his songs. He smiled, thanked her and turned to the next fan. Disappointed, Céline was about to leave when Elton stopped short as he was extending his hand to someone else, turned around and said to Céline, "Hey, I know you." Curious, he walked back to her. She reminded him: Germany, the Eurovisions, spring, 1988. She wanted to say, "You promised me a song, Elton dear."

That night, she understood that what had been an important event for her was just part of everyday life for Elton John. She saw what it meant to be an international star. That's what she wanted to be one day: fascinating, radiant, somebody whom everybody looked on with respect and passion.

The morning after, she stepped back into the shoes of poor Elisa.

One Friday afternoon, after a long day of shooting, she was heading back to Sainte-Anne-des-Lacs in her Chrysler. Just before the first service center on the highway, she passed a car she recognized. It was her cousin Christian driving Karine to her mother's. Céline waved at them. A fraction of a second later, Céline lost control, and her car spun to a stop on the median.

Céline never could figure out what had happened. It was hot, she was exhausted, the setting sun was reflecting off the hood of the car, maybe she fell asleep. She was shaken, but uninjured. She got into her cousin's car. Back home, Mrs. Dion drew a bath for her daughter who promptly fell asleep in the tub. She was still dreaming when her mother opened the bathroom door to check on her.

René was in Las Vegas. He called, as he did every evening, to find out what Céline had done that day. As soon as he heard the news, he decided to fly back to Montreal. Céline was delighted. She wanted to be close to him. He would comfort her, console her, love her. He promised that he'd never again leave her alone when she was working. Because she loved him so much, Céline didn't want him tied down by a promise of that magnitude, and she let him know it. "Just as long as I know where to reach you...." But René persisted. "I'll always be close to you whenever you're working." She knew it was a promise he couldn't keep. They were no ordinary couple. They were experiencing the same adventure, but they couldn't always be physically close. There were always people to see, and they had some different interests. René had his passions: Las Vegas, gambling, golf, his friends. And the two of them believed that you can't stop someone from living the life they want. "I know you mean it, and I believe you," she said. "But I won't hold it against you if you can't keep your promise. I swear it."

She was a woman fulfilled. So determined that nothing could frighten her. Neither the car accident, nor her solitude.

In August, they signed a coproduction agreement with Donald K. Donald Productions, and they began in earnest getting another show ready. But there were many people, even at CBS, who refused to believe that it would succeed.

In her previous shows, Céline had been told exactly what to do and when to do it. With script written by Jean-Pierre Plante and stage direction by Jean Bissonnette, she'd learned an enormous amount. "It was like going to show business university," as she put it. She'd learned and grown. But now, she didn't want to speak someone else's words; she didn't want to use body movements designed and scripted by another stage director. She wanted to have a say, and she wanted more latitude and freedom. She asked René-Richard Cyr — an actor, author and director, and one of Montreal's outstanding theater personalities — for his opinion. He told her that the show should have more rock and roll, more dancing. It should be younger.

But once again, a totally unexpected event was to turn Céline's career and life upside down. She was to emerge from it even more mature, with an aura of splendor, just in time to kick off her fall tour of Quebec with a brand new show.

The *Falling Into You* Tour
Los Angeles, March 25, 1997

The Duet

For Céline Dion, Hollywood is the capital of show business, a place of almost mythical proportions. This is where the people who have created the most extraordinary legend in the history of the showbiz world live.

You'd think that people in Hollywood have seen it all. That they're blasé and hard to please. Well, it's just not so. The people who are crowded into the Universal Amphitheater are happy and carefree, and they leap to their feet when Terry Bradford steps onstage, mike in hand, to sing "Beauty and the Beast" with Céline.

Singing in Los Angeles is quite an experience. For me, it's got a kind of echo, a kind of amplification you don't find in any other city. There's likely to be someone in the audience listening to you, watching you, who'll come up to you with a proposal that will change your life. A film, or a song. In Hollywood, on *The Tonight Show*, I first made it into the world of international show business. In Hollywood, I sang at the Oscars two years later. In Hollywood, the man who used to call himself Prince heard me sing and had the urge to write a song for me, "With this Tear." In Los Angeles, an artist gets more exposure than anywhere else.

Terry Bradford was a backup singer in Los Angeles when a girlfriend told him that Céline Dion was looking for a singer who could record "Beauty and the Beast" with her, the same tune she'd recorded with Peabo Bryson. He turned up for the audition slightly nervous. This was normal enough, even if you've had plenty of stage and studio experience.

Born in Alabama, Terry grew up in Orlando, Florida. His father, who was a member of the rhythm-and-blues group Hank Ballard & the Midnighters, and had written "The Twist," popularized by Chubby Checker. At age ten, Terry sang in the choir that traveled with the televangelist Jim Bakker. He could move, sing, and play all kinds of instruments with mind-boggling ease. He'd sung on the sound track of The Lion King, *and with Tina Turner, on "What's Love Got to Do With It."*

Just before the audition for "Beauty and the Beast," he went down to the underground parking lot to warm up and calm his frazzled nerves. The sound was always exceptional in places like these. It was at the end of the day, and people were just leaving their offices and heading for their cars, when they heard his striking voice. Terry hardly blinked; he sings everywhere: in elevators, on the street.

When his turn came to audition, he stepped forward all alone on the stage and began to sing. The full spotlight was leveled on him. Some people can't take that pressure. In a studio, there's always a certain degree of intimacy — the lights are low, and you can even hide behind a screen.

His nervousness evaporated after a couple of measures, and he began to sing with real pleasure, forgetting everything and letting his voice soar — until he saw a woman emerge from the shadows and walk toward him. It was Céline Dion singing the duet with him.

He'd never seen anything like it. In every audition he'd ever been to, the hopefuls were always alone onstage. It was terrifying, but those were the rules of the game. Everyone did his or her number, thanked the darkness and left. And most of the time, nobody said a word. Then they'd go home and wait for the phone to ring.

But here was Céline Dion herself, walking right up to him and singing a duet with him. He was so astonished that he forgot the words; she had to whisper the refrain. But she knew — both of them knew from that moment on — that they would be working together. Their voices blended gloriously.

Céline was delighted. And Terry was bowled over by Céline's skill, her technique. From that moment on, they've sung together on every continent.

Chapter Twenty-Five
Born in the USA

On September 6, 1990, Francine Chaloult called a press conference to announce that *Unison* would be issued in eighteen countries. The strategists at CBS-International were organizing a gigantic promotional campaign. In the United States, radio stations were finally starting to play "Where Does My Heart Beat Now," the song that was scheduled to come out as a single on September 11. The PR job for the American campaign had been awarded to Rogers & Cowan, the firm that handled the Rolling Stones and New Kids on the Block, who were very hot at the time.

Fifteen minutes before the doors to the press conference room were thrown open, Francine rushed up to René to tell him that Glenn Brumann, who handled public relations for Epic Records, had just called from New York and he wanted Angélil to call him back as soon as possible. He had good news for him. Brumann had played Céline's latest album and the video of "Where Does My Heart Beat Now" for the researchers at *The Tonight Show*. They wanted her to appear on the show. In fact, they had a specific date in mind: Friday, September 21. That evening, the show would be hosted by Jay Leno, and one of the guests would be Phil Collins. It was the kind of offer you couldn't refuse. *The Tonight Show*, even with Leno at the helm sitting in for Johnny Carson, was a must, an institution in its own right.

Angélil announced the good news at the press conference. And he explained to the journalists that *The Tonight Show* producers usually wait until artists have proven themselves, until a song is comfortably at the top of the *Billboard* charts before extending the invitation. Céline's song wasn't even on the market. "But *The Tonight Show* people like her album so much, they have so much faith in it, that they want Céline as soon as they can get her."

But there was a problem. Céline and her musicians needed work permits to play in the United States. Usually these permits took three weeks to get, and they had only two. The very next day, CBS's lawyers took up the matter with the federal authorities. Thanks to some friendly arm-twisting by Canadian cabinet minister Marcel Masse and Mila Mulroney, the wife of Canada's prime minister Brian Mulroney, who happened to be a friend of David Foster, they got their permits in the nick of time.

Angélil had a policy of keeping people in Quebec abreast of everything Céline did abroad. He invited several Quebec journalists to join them in Los Angeles to attend the rehearsal for *The Tonight Show.* They left on September 19. Céline was so excited she couldn't sit still, but she was worried at the same time. That same morning, her father had been admitted to the Sacré-Coeur hospital in Montreal where he was to undergo a prostate operation the same day as her appearance on *The Tonight Show* — and her debut on the world showbiz stage.

In the limo that took them from the airport to their hotel, Céline heard her voice on American radio for the very first time. Right after the opening notes, the disc jockey said her name. "Celeen Dion. Great voice." René was on the verge of tears. He motioned to the driver that he wanted to tell him something.

"Do you know this singer?"

"Never heard of her," said the driver.

Angélil repeated her name two or three times over. "Celeen Dion, you hear me? Remember the name, because you'll never forget the voice."

When they pulled up in front of their hotel, he asked the driver's name.

"Brian."

"Brian, I'd like to introduce you to Celeen Dion."

Céline laughed, shook hands with the chauffeur and called Angélil a big baby. She was embarrassed, but happy.

The next day, René took Céline down to Sunset Boulevard, to the world's most famous record store, Tower Records.

"Look!"

In the window, there were three huge displays: albums by George Michael, New Kids on the Block — and Céline Dion.

On the afternoon of September 21, Céline and her band arrived at the NBC studios. Angélil had gotten passes for the Quebec journalists who were going to watch the rehearsal. Usually, when Céline rehearses, she doesn't sing full out, like most artists. But Angélil found out that *The Tonight Show* researchers, and producers Peter Lassaly and Freddy De Cordova, always watched the rehearsals from the control room, because they wanted to know ahead of time what their guests were really made of. René told Céline to give it her best shot.

She sang as if all America was listening. No sooner did she finish her song than Debbie Vickers came rushing out of the control room and told René that the producers were extremely impressed. They wanted Céline back again, the sooner the better, with Johnny Carson. Angélil and Debbie locked themselves in a little office with their date books, looking for a suitable day.

Céline's schedule was very hectic. In the weeks to come, she would be putting on shows from one end of Quebec to the other. The tour would end on November 11, at the Saint-Denis Theater.

"Could she do it on November 12?" he asked.

"That's a Monday," Debbie said. "A good night."

"The best?"

She hesitated.

"Not the best. To be honest, the best night is Thursday because the *Cosby Show* airs right before, and it pulls in a lot of viewers."

So it was agreed, Céline would do *The Tonight Show* on Thursday, November 15. She would sing "Unison."

One hour later, Céline was singing "Where Does My Heart Beat Now" in front of Jay Leno, Phil Collins and millions of television viewers, the largest audience she'd faced to date. She looked slender in a black dress, looking almost like Piaf (or what the Americans liked to think Piaf looked like), hair curled like on the album cover of *Unison.* She did her own hair and makeup, and Suzanne Gingue helped her out, gave her advice. "Céline never asks for anything," Suzanne said. "Maybe that's why people are so happy to do things for her."

There was no interview after her song, but Jay Leno and Phil Collins were won over, and they said so, loud and clear, to the viewers. At the end, Jay Leno called her over, held her hand and showed the viewers the *Unison* album cover. That's when Phil Collins, who was at the top of the charts, came over and gave her a kiss.

"See you again," he said.

"You bet!" she answered.

Drummondville, a small town halfway between Montreal and Quebec City, was the place they chose to premiere Céline's new show in English and the *Unison* tour. Next they would take it on the road across the province, just like the two earlier shows. The *Unison* performed was a showcase of Céline's know-how, her multisided talents. It was also a transition, a turning point. She would be singing old and new songs, in French and in English. The opening number was "Love By Another Name," followed by "Delivre-moi," and the first ovation of the night. By now, Céline had nearly ten years of hits behind her. Now she added exciting new numbers to her repertoire, songs like "Calling You," the hit theme from the movie *Baghdad Cafe*. She heard it one day in her hotel room, and the melody stayed with her. Or songs like "Ce n'était qu'une aventure," a song by the late Quebec pop icon Gerry Boulet, who had made his name with the rock group Offenbach. Or songs like "Tôt ou tard" by a Montreal poet and composer named Sylvain Lelièvre, warning about the dangers of pollution.

She had four consecutive shows lined up. Two in Drummondville and two in Sherbrooke, a midsize city close to the Vermont border. But on the night of the thirteenth, in O'Bready Hall in Sherbrooke, disaster struck. Her voice broke severely, and she couldn't finish the show. She promised the fans she would be back, but as soon as she stepped backstage, she collapsed.

The Montreal premiere was slated for October 16, but it had to be postponed until the twenty-third. The wildest rumors began circulating about Céline's broken voice. People were saying she was exhausted, that her voice was ruined, and that it was beyond repair. For the fans who lined up for the show in Montreal, the atmosphere was tense. Some were murmuring that it would be the last show, the end of the dream for the singer who had had everything going for her. This hint of drama and uncertainty was added to the excitement of the Montreal premiere.

Two days before her premiere performance, on the stage of Place-des-Arts (Montreal's temple of culture) Céline initiated a whirlwind of controversy by refusing the Félix award for Best English-Language Female Singer, a trophy won in previous years by groups like The Box or singer Corey Hart.

"I'm not an English speaker," she declared. "Wherever I go, no matter what country I'm in, I tell people I'm a Quebecker."

There was a moment of stunned silence, a few boos, then thunderous applause. ADISQ president André Ménard rushed backstage, where a soap opera-style drama was brewing. Ginette Reno was lecturing Céline. "You're not making any sense. If you didn't intend to accept the award, you didn't have to accept the nomination. You made a bad mistake, girl." Céline was sobbing. René tried to get Ginette to listen to reason. When he saw Ménard, he turned toward him, thinking he was going to bawl Céline out. But Ménard's intentions were peaceable, and he just wanted to talk. He knew that Céline's rejection of the award would cause trouble, and sooner or later, someone would have some explaining to do.

Angélil knew Ménard. Despite their differences, they respected each other. But when it came to show business, they were worlds apart. Ménard was the artistic director of the Montreal Jazz Festival, an event he helped create. Two winters before at the Spectrum, which was owned by his production company Spectra-Scene, he saw Céline's hilarious impersonation of Cyndi Lauper singing "Girls Just Want to Have Fun" during a recording session for an episode of *Samedi de rire,* Quebec's equivalent of *Saturday Night Live.*

"She bowled us over," is how he remembered it.

He also remembered René Angélil's wide-eyed passion and that unshakable certainty of his that one day his artist would reach the top. At the 1990 ADISQ gala, she hadn't yet reached the peak. Far from it. But she was a good part of the way there.

Céline's refusal and her statement set off a hot controversy in a province where everything related to language is hypersensitive. Even Jacques Parizeau, the leader of the Parti Québecois and a die-hard supporter of independence, joined the debate by sending Céline his congratulations. So intense was media reaction that the award winners themselves were forgotten completely. In the industry, people were accusing Céline and Angélil of undermining the winners. ADISQ even claimed that Céline and Angélil had planned the whole thing. Mario Lefebvre, head of promotion at CBS records, had signed and returned the entry form approving the category Best English-Language Female Singer.

What Angélil did do, however, was bring before the public a debate that the ADISQ people would have preferred to conceal. He admitted to a reporter from the Montreal daily *La Presse* that they'd decided to act three weeks earlier. "I only hoped Céline would win so she could make her statement."

Since the summer before, he'd been criticizing ADISQ for adding categories so that all their young hopefuls would have a better shot at an award.

"At first, I didn't realize what was going on," he admitted. "Then, when I figured out what they were trying to do, I said to myself that it would serve them right to be shown up as fools. Either they're idiots and they can't realize how badly they're making Céline look in Quebeckers' eyes, or they're smart and they're doing it on purpose. It was a pernicious prize. Sure, Céline recorded an album in English, but that didn't make her an English-speaking artist. The ADISQ people were trying to put us in an impossible position. As far as I'm concerned, it was a setup."

During that same ADISQ gala, a local comedy group performed a cuttingly satirical song mocking Céline and her sister Claudette, who had just released an album produced by Angélil. It depicted Céline as a compulsive winner, and her sister as an envious, frustrated loser. For Angélil, it was proof positive that ADISQ, and particularly the hard-core pseudo-intellectuals who had taken it over, had nothing but contempt for his artist.

So it was that the day after the ADISQ gala, Céline sang at the Théâtre Saint-Denis. After her first song, "Love By Another Name," she spoke directly to the audience. "I feel much more at home here with you than at the ADISQ gala at Place-des-Arts." The applause was thunderous. Then people turned toward Angélil, who was seated in the orchestra next to Denis Savage at the control panel, and gave him the thumbs-up sign. Angélil grinned. The snobs at ADISQ had gotten more than they had bargained for.

But the following day, reaction came from the city's English-speaking community. They were not amused. In *The Gazette*, Montreal's only English-language daily, people wrote in to say how shocked they were that Céline would say she wasn't an English speaker but a Quebecker, as if the two were mutually exclusive or incompatible. "So, according to Ms. Dion, we're not really Quebeckers?"

Just like many great stars, Céline had become a barometer of public opinion. Through her radiated the attitudes, the dreams, the conflicts of the Quebec people. The whole controversy demonstrated one more time the ambiguity of being a French speaker in North America.

The category English-Speaking Artist or Group was replaced the following year by Quebec Artist with the Most Distinguished Achievement in a Language Other than French. The new category could accommodate Céline Dion, an old-time French speaker, Corey Hart, a Quebec-born English speaker, or Kashtin, a duo that sang in Montagnais, a Native language.

The Montreal premiere of the *Unison* show was a huge success in spite of (or because of) Céline's lost voice and the ADISQ controversy. But critical opinion was mixed. *La Presse*'s respected pop critic Alain Brunet still wasn't a Céline Dion fan. He didn't like her repertoire, even though he had to admit that he liked her voice. "Less nasal and really touching," was how he put it. Sylvain Cormier of *Le Devoir*, Montreal's intellectual daily, blasted the show. "Grade B stuff," he called it. Harking back to the Place-des-Arts incident, he wrote, "She couldn't have made a worse career move. She may be doing what her heart tells her, driven on by the utopian vision of her mentor, the ex-Baronnet René Angélil, but Céline Dion is leaving herself open to some heavy score settling."

Sylvain Lelièvre's ecological song didn't fare much better. "It's a wonderful song, but when Céline Dion sings it, it just sounds opportunistic and exploitative." First, she was criticized for singing only love ballads, and now she was being raked over the coals for taking on more socially sensitive issues. She was free to travel all across the map of the emotions, but there was no way she was going to deal with anything ideological. For her, that was strictly off limits.

She'd entered a field where they played hardball, where people were jealous and hypersensitive. There were pointed questions from the show business world and the media. Just how much were the Americans really interested in Céline Dion? Maybe all the buzz was mostly bluff, a huge PR campaign orchestrated by that master manipulator René Angélil and the all-powerful CBS company. Did they arrange for her appearance on *The Tonight Show* and the favorable coverage in the American press by using a little friendly persuasion?

The top executives from CBS-International were in the audience at the Saint-Denis to hear Céline sing. For them, she was serious business, someone worth watching. They wanted to find out what she could do, what kind of songs she could sing how available she was. After the show, René invited everybody to the Latini, Montreal's top Italian restaurant. Among the guests were Polly Anthony, artistic director Richard Griffith and people from 550 and Epic, CBS's two American subsidiaries. They hardly knew René.

"Without being arrogant, they were vaguely condescending and patronizing with us," recalls Mario Lefebvre. "It was understandable. Our plan was to make it in the big leagues, on their home turf, and nobody here had the know-how or the expertise required at that level." So there were the Americans showing the little Quebeckers what big business was all about.

Céline had to rest her voice that evening, since she still had a series of shows to sing, so she begged off. During the meal, René hardly opened his mouth. He listened calmly and politely and asked a few questions.

Mario and Vito recalled that during the dinner at the Latini, they saw the Americans' attitude changing. Just like the CBS-Canada people the year before, they were beginning to realize that there was someone in Quebec they could deal with, someone with enough experience, someone who was capable of learning and understanding the rules of the game. A few weeks later, Angélil was able to call up Tommy Mottola, the head honcho at CBS, in his car or at home, day or night.

"It was a stroke of genius," Mario recalled. "In the United States, thousands of agents and producers dream of talking to Mottola just once in their lives. Only a few ever succeed. Of those, more than a few live to regret it. They simply get bulldozed, blown away, or sent packing. Mottola is one of the most powerful people in the business. He liked Angélil. Why that was is hard to say. Angélil is a born diplomat who has a flare for singling out the movers and shakers and cutting a deal with them. That may be his greatest talent."

The *Falling Into You* Tour
Melbourne, March 23, 1996

A New Song

Everybody is on pins and needles in Melbourne. Everybody, that is, except Céline. It's been a full week since they arrived in Australia, enough time to recover from jet lag. But for people from the northern hemisphere, it's a difficult place to get accustomed to. At noon, the sun is in the north. At night, the southern sky is strangely devoid of stars. There's the Southern Cross constellation, of course, with its longest arm pointing seemingly toward the South Pole. But directly above it is a huge black hole that's hard to look at without shuddering. Back on earth, everybody's hard at work on the show, smoothing out the rough edges and adding new material. In fact, it's almost a completely new production.

A few days earlier, to Barry Garber's great surprise, René Angélil made the decision to drop "To Love You More," the song Céline recorded with the Japanese violinist Taro Hakase. Since the song wasn't part of any of her albums, it wouldn't really contribute much to the tour. René, who was back in Montreal, believed you couldn't force totally unknown songs down the public's throat. The show that was planned for Australia that spring of 1996 was made up almost entirely of songs from Céline's four English albums and from D'eux.

When Robby Wada, Taro Hakase's manager, heard the news, he was dismayed. He told Barry Garber that the move would be seen by the

Japanese recording industry and by the Japanese public as a humiliation. It wouldn't take them long to realize that they weren't getting what they had paid for. There'd been advance publicity, press releases, interviews for the upcoming Japanese performance, the Japanese media had shown interest. Taro would be heartbroken.

Garber discussed this with Angélil, who agreed to put "To Love You More" back into the show's line-up. In any case, there was nothing to lose. Besides, the song was already a major hit in Japan.

Take me, back into the arms of love.
Need me, like you did before.
Touch me once again.
"To Love You More,"
Junior Miles and David Foster

That first night in Melbourne, Céline was electrifying. When Taro Hakase stepped onstage with Céline for the first time with his electric violin under his arm and his long curly hair tumbling over his bright red jacket, people didn't know what to think. "Who's that guy?" But the song's broad rhythm, the violin solos and the beauty of the duet quickly won the audience over.

Right after the show, Barry called René to tell him about the extraordinary performance, the crowd's enthusiastic reaction, the ovation, the tears. Angélil couldn't believe it and asked him to set up a telephone link so he could hear the next day's show, and hear the crowd's reaction again in Melbourne. Suzanne Gingue hooked up a telephone to the sound console. It was five in the morning when he heard Céline, and the crowd breaking into cheers with the last words of the song.

I'll be waiting for you
Here inside my heart.
I'm the one who wants to love you more.

They'd used the same type of telephone hookup for Eddy Marnay when Céline sang at the Tokyo festival, and he'd wished someone had done it for him for the premier of her European tour in the fall of 1995. It was in October, in a city in the south of France: Marseille or Montpellier. That show was the predecessor of the one now wowing the Australians. It had had its dry run at the Capitole, in Quebec City, the theater their old friend Guy Cloutier had restored at his own expense.

March 2, 1996 was Adhémar Dion's seventy-fourth birthday. Céline was on tour in Australia. She called the family at the Nickels restaurant owned by her mother and her brother Paul in Repentigny, a Montreal suburb. She invited her parents, brothers and sisters to step outside to see René's birthday gift to her father: a superb, sable-colored Mercedes.

Chapter Twenty-Six
Conquering Canada

Ever since she lost her voice in Sherbrooke, rumors were buzzing about Céline's health. She was trying too hard, people were saying. Her manager was pushing her. There was talk of anorexia, burnout, depression.

René was feeling tired himself. He wasn't getting much sleep — maybe five or six hours a night, rarely more and often less. No matter where he was, he was always up at dawn, feeling rushed and under stress.

One morning, Céline woke up practically without a voice, feeling like she had a red-hot poker in her throat. René Angélil hurriedly set up an appointment with Dr. Marcel Belzile, an ear, nose and throat specialist. They hoped the doctor would prescribe Céline medication to let her sing that night at the Saint-Denis. Then she could take a few days off. It was the last show of the tour, and she didn't want to cancel it for anything in the world.

To reach the doctor's office, they had to fight their way across Montreal at rush hour and cross the perpetually congested Jacques Cartier Bridge. After an hour of twiddling their thumbs in the traffic, it became clear that they would never get there on time. The only way was by subway, and she was hardly in the mood for dealing with crowds. She was pale, worried and voiceless. But she was wearing a hooded coat, and with the hood pulled over her head, no one would recognize her.

> But I recognized the people. They were my people. The same faces I see every night in the halls where I sing. I look at those people and I tell myself that they're the ones I work for, they're the ones who cheer me, who love me. All of a sudden, the will to sing for them was so powerful that I knew the doctor just had to heal my voice. I knew that in a few hours, I'd be onstage at the Saint-Denis.

The doctor did heal her—temporarily. But he ordered her to take a long rest, beginning the next day. "Your vocal cords are tired and irritated. You've got to give them some rest."

The truth was that she never entirely recovered from that case of acute laryngitis she came down with at the start of the tour, and that had left her without a voice in Sherbrooke. Excess fatigue and a full schedule only complicated matters. "If you're not careful, we'll have to operate," said Dr. Belzile. "And an operation could alter your voice."

Vocal cords have two main enemies: fatigue and the nodules caused by misusing the voice. Singers can damage their vocal cords irreparably by singing outside their normal range. Nodules and polyps are caused by deficient technique, not by infection. You have to know when to force your voice, and learn how to position it.

Irritants such as cigarette smoke and pollution also have a negative effect. So can viral or bacterial infections, the flu or common colds. But a voice that's in good condition can resist these kinds of stresses. The main culprits are fatigue, overuse, anemia, pressure, stress and, most of all, improper use. You can eliminate cigarette smoke from your environment. But how can you live without stress when your ambition is to become the greatest singer in the world?

Some singers use cocaine therapeutically. The drug is a potent vasoconstrictor that, when applied topically along with cortisone, can have almost miraculous short-term effects. Singers who have lost their voices in the afternoon will be able to give their best that very same night. But they'll risk tearing their vocal cords, causing hematomas or bleeding, not to mention being unable to sing for weeks, perhaps months, after. Or face having their voices changed forever.

Céline and René were in it for the long haul. There was only one remedy: silence. Three weeks of absolute silence. It was an experience as amazing as it was tortuous.

After a few hours without speaking, everything seems to be moving in slow motion. The first times can be scary. You start thinking of stories. I dreamed up a gloomy, frightening novel, and it made me cry. But I stuck with it. I imagined I was totally mute for life. When I gave interviews, I had to use an interpreter.

"You stopped singing and they still wanted to interview you?"

Of course! I might be mute, but I still had things to say, and I wanted to keep on working. I became a great pianist, I wrote songs, novels, scripts, I had all kinds of ideas.... The things I have in my heart and that come out through my voice just took another path.

I've invested my whole life in my career. I've sacrificed a lot. But I'm not in it for the applause. I couldn't live any other way. They'd have to tie me down, and I wouldn't stand for it.

I always hated school, math most of all. But if I had to learn algebra or chemistry to sing better, I'd work on it every day. And I'd end up enjoying it, I'm sure. Everything that happens to me fits right in with my career, one way or another.

"Where Does My Heart Beat Now" was in eleventh place on the *Billboard* charts when Céline went silent, in mid-December, 1990. In the United States, three quarters of the 250-odd radio stations gave the tune airtime. As early as November, twenty-one stations were playing the song once every three hours. Seventy-seven were playing it three times a day, and twenty-three, once a day.

In January, when she started to talk again (in a low voice), the song had risen to tenth place on the "adult contemporary" chart, the new designation for what used to be called MOR (middle of the road). The industry and the media broke down popular music into several categories. The names of the categories changed gradually with time and custom. At the beginning of the nineties, the AC category grew in importance. That's where you found conservative, don't-rock-the-boat pop for the whole family, at the opposite end of the spectrum from the heavy metal that used to top the charts in the eighties.

As Céline Dion was entering the US market, a strange transformation was under way. It was an upheaval she had helped to create, one from which she benefited. The look, the sound, how the stars behaved and what they sang about — everything was changing rapidly. The heavy-metal groups, the rappers and the rockers were slipping gradually into the shadows, and polite, well-dressed performers were taking over. They were the champions of adult contemporary, and they would be the top stars of the nineties. Most of them were women. Madonna, of course, was the trailblazer. But those who followed didn't have her provocative, hard-headed style. Most of the top vocalists of the nineties were laid-back, trustworthy, reasonable women like Whitney Houston, Mariah Carey or Gloria Estefan. They didn't drink, smoke or take drugs. They weren't trying to shock anybody, or turn the world upside down. Their idea wasn't to change the world, but to celebrate it as it was, and help people enjoy themselves. More than any of them, Céline adopted these traditional, middle-of-the-road values. And made them her own.

Nickels, the restaurant concept Céline and René developed at the beginning of the nineties, was to be a visual expression of their world and their image. Paul Sara, René's cousin, would guide them with the business part of the venture.

When he left banking, Paul bought several Harvey's restaurant franchises. In 1990, he approached Céline and René about setting up a restaurant chain. He remembered that on one of their trips to California, they had an idea: to open a diner-type restaurant. Together, they developed the concept, and Céline designed the waitresses' uniforms. They hit on a name Nickels, as in Céline's lucky five-cent piece. The soft gleam of the coin would highlight the decor. The first restaurant opened its doors on December 5, 1990 in St. Laurent, a Montreal suburb.

Today, the Nickels chain is a permanent fixture throughout Quebec. The decor is stylized nostalgia. The walls are covered with old posters of the Hollywood greats of the fifties and earlier — stars like James Dean, Marilyn Monroe, Humphrey Bogart, Elvis Presley. There are pictures of Charlie Chaplin, Abbot and Costello, the Three Stooges, Dick Tracy, Superman, Tarzan, along with Hollywood's most prestigious trademarks — Rolls-Royce, Ferrari and Harley. On the walls of the Nickels restaurant in Repentigny, which is owned by Mrs. Dion and her son Paul, are Céline's platinum and gold albums, and photos of Céline with Michael J. Fox, Prince and Elton John. TV screens air nonstop baseball or hockey. Of course, an old period jukebox plays oldies and Céline's greatest hits. Over the door, you can't miss a blown-up check, the restaurant patrons' contribution of more than $10,500 to the Cystic Fibrosis campaign. A little collection box for the cause is situated next to the cash register.

On February 28, Radio-Canada set up a private screening for the whole Dion family of *Fleurs sur la neige*, the miniseries starring Céline. They even let Karine leave the hospital for a few hours. It was her fourteenth birthday. She was thin, pale, and so weak she could hardly stand up. Every breath was an effort. She knew, and everyone else knew, that she probably wouldn't live to see twenty. During the screening, Céline glanced at her. My God, she thought, life had been so good, so generous to her; but for her niece, it was hard — as hard as for Elisa T., the heroine of the series.

> For me, that's the one big mystery of life. They say "God helps those who help themselves." I really believe it. But there are people who do their best to help themselves, and they still can't make it. They're born to lose.

Fleurs sur la neige was aired on Thursday, March 7, 1991. It followed *Les filles de Caleb*, a historical drama that set an all-time Quebec Nielsen ratings record, reaching more than 50 percent of the potential audience. But Céline's new miniseries didn't fare as well. The story was a bit amateur and too melodramatic. Still, some people liked it. A lot of Quebeckers just eat up stories about poor, abused little girls — and mention their intense curiosity about Céline Dion.

Angélil made up his mind not to release the title song as interpreted by Céline. It was a pleasant enough tune, but it didn't fit in with Céline's new, up-to-date repertoire, with her new image as a dynamic young woman, nor with Angélil's hopes and dreams.

All winter long during 1991, René and CBS were working hard at improving Céline's visibility in Canada and the US. A major American tour was in the works. In February, she took part in "Voices That Care," organized by David Foster and Peter Cetera of Chicago. The project brought together a whole constellation of top stars — Little Richard, Al Jareau, Michael Bolton, Céline Dion, Wayne Gretzky, Cindy Crawford, Richard Gere, Chevy Chase, Kevin Costner, Michelle Pfeiffer, Sally Field, Whoopi Goldberg, Dudley Moore and many more. It was to be a message of encouragement to the American soldiers fighting in the Gulf War against Saddam Hussein, featuring a song and a video. People in the industry were starting to recognize her.

Barely two weeks after the end of the Gulf War, at the American Music Awards gala, Céline presented the award for the Best Heavy Metal Hard Rock Group. The winner was Slaughter. Just for fun, she translated cohost Will Smith's presentation remarks into French. (Smith was starring in the TV show *Fresh Prince of Belair* at the time.)

People in the United States didn't know her that well. They didn't recognize her face. But sometimes in an elevator, in a taxi, in a store, she would hear her voice. Each time it came as a surprise, a sheer delight. She had the feeling that her career was on the move.

Barry Garber, a newcomer with Donald K. Donald Productions, was given the job of organizing the first full-fledged Canadian tour. He quickly discovered that most of the producers in English Canada had no idea who Céline Dion was. More than once he had to pronounce and spell out her name. Céline might have been a top star in Quebec and in France, CBS might have been launching her album in the US, but in English Canada, they weren't convinced that she had what it took.

Garber's background wasn't the pop music world, but that of legitimate theater. He knew all there was to know about Canadian theater, and about performance spaces that seated 750 to 2500 people. The directors of these theaters were the people he called on to host the tour, not the usual pop and variety show producers of the music business. So Céline Dion owes her debut in English Canada to the world of the theater, where the audience was likely to be more curious, more interested in new faces and possibly even more demanding than in the traditional variety venues.

In early February, a month ahead of time, the tour was ready to roll. In Toronto, Calgary, Edmonton and Vancouver, they were waiting for Céline in small or medium-size theaters. Soon, a series of events would take place that would make the tour infinitely more popular than anyone could have imagined, and that would create an even more powerful demand for Céline.

That year, for the first time in twenty years, the Juno Awards gala was held in Vancouver, at the Queen Elizabeth Theater. It was raining heavily. A few weeks earlier, "Where Does My Heart Beat Now," the song Céline was to sing that night, jumped to fourth place on the *Billboard* charts. Céline became the most popular Canadian artist in the United States, ahead of her natural rivals, Whitney Houston and Mariah Carey. There wasn't a single representative of the Canadian recording and show business industries at the Junos who didn't know who she was. Excitement seemed to follow her wherever she went.

Céline walked away with the two top awards: Best Female Singer and Best Album.

Events like these are crucial for an artist on the way up. If you want to prove your prowess, if you want to be unforgettable, you've got to be seen and heard. Managers, composers and show business professionals are always in attendance. The New York TV researchers and Hollywood agents in the audience went on to give Céline more visibility than she'd ever had before.

One particular group of researchers was working for David Letterman's *Late Show*, on which Céline appeared one week later. It wasn't one of her best experiences. Letterman wasn't particularly warm. He introduced her as a great singer, but stretched out his monologues and interviews so much that he could spare Céline only a half minute at the end of the show to speak with her. It didn't matter. Tens of millions of Americans — late sleepers, young people, music fanatics and fans — heard and saw Céline sing. They certainly weren't going to forget her.

Mike Gorfaine and Sam Schwartz were in attendance at the Queen Elizabeth Theater, representing James Horner and Will Jennings, the songwriter-composer team that boasted ten Oscars for best film music. They were looking for a voice to interpret "Dreams to Dream," Horner and Jenning's theme song for *An American Tail: Fievel Goes West.* The film was produced by Steven Spielberg, and David Foster had agreed to do the song. They'd approached almost all the top female vocalists — Whitney Houston, Dolly Parton, Anita Baker, Debbie Gibson, Cyndi Lauper and Linda Ronstadt, who sang the theme song of the first film about the brave mouse Fievel that sets out to conquer America.

When they heard Céline sing at the Junos, Gorfaine and Schwartz knew their search was over. That night, they contacted Paul Farberman, vice-president for music at MCA/Universal's California studios, Spielberg's producer. Farberman, a CBS veteran, had developed close relations with Angélil and Céline back in the *Incognito* days, and he was more than happy to work with them again. He reached them by phone in Las Vegas, where they were getting a bit of rest before their first big Canadian tour. The idea of working with Spielberg made an enormous impact on Angélil. After he hung up, he sat for a long moment in silence, overwhelmed by the good news. Then he went out for a long walk on the Strip. It was warm, and the sunset was painting the desert a dusty rose. And Angélil laughed to himself. Thanks to the little mouse Fievel, the Hollywood big shots would find out exactly who Céline Dion was.

There was just one problem. Céline was under contract to Epic, CBS's American subsidiary. Universal had its own record label, MCA, which would naturally produce and distribute the film sound track. Record companies don't like to trade artists, and when they do, things can get terribly complicated. But Horner, Jennings and Foster, songwriter, composer and producer respectively, wanted Céline and nobody else. Farberman and Angélil were confident that everything would work out.

Meanwhile, the Canadian *Unison* tour that Barry Garber put together in January and February was getting under way. Spirits were high. with two Junos, appearances on *The Tonight Show* and *The Late Show* and a song in fourth place on the *Billboard* charts. And, of course, there was the wonderful film sound track project that Céline and René were keeping to themselves, out of superstition, and because Farberman insisted on it.

On Friday, March 8, 1991, Céline sang in an even smaller hall, the 520-seat St. Albert's Arden Theater in an outlying suburb of Edmonton with a French-Canadian population. Céline was even more excited than usual. This was only the second show she headlined in English Canada. The response was overwhelming, with three ovations. In the *Edmonton Sunday Sun* the next day, Peter North related how he'd been won over by her voice, beauty and elegance, her "gracious, charming and sincere personality. She moves like a moonbeam." To him, Céline represented "what this country needs right now ... some hope that communication will not give way to isolation or polarization." From her very first appearance in English Canada, Céline aroused national passions and was seen as the hope for reconciliation. She told audiences in English Canada, "I'm at home right here, onstage. And you're a guest in my home, our home."

In the *Toronto Saturday Sun*, Toronto journalist John Sakamoto, who attended the Winter Garden show, described Céline as a veritable magician. She could play the vamp and the ingenue alike, she could be confident one moment and delightfully awkward and timid the next.

Chris Dafoe, writing in the *Toronto Star*, Canada's largest daily newspaper, said, "She does more than sing songs. She experiences them, turns them into melodramas, tragedies, comedies where she plays the lead role brilliantly." She gave every appearance of believing in love, the timeless cliché she sang about in her songs. She sang those "little while lies about love" with such innocence and passion that Dafoe, and everybody else, wanted to believe them too. But, in an interview in Vancouver with a French journalist, she stated that she didn't have a boyfriend, that she couldn't have. Her career simply took up too much of time and energy.

Farberman sent her a demo tape of Horner and Jennings's "Dreams to Dream." It was a finely wrought, touching melody, and she couldn't get it out of her head. She planned to record it in Los Angeles as soon as she could.

In April, the conquest of Canada was complete. Céline threw herself into a new promotional campaign in the United States where there was still much to be done. In less than two weeks, she visited a dozen cities, including Kansas City, Philadelphia, Washington, New York, Los Angeles, Minneapolis and Chicago. She gave radio and television interviews, met journalists, promotion agents from CBS, record store owners and disc jockeys.

In May, she made a quick trip to Japan where the promotion schedule was just as busy. In five days, from May 6–11, along with René, Dave Platel and two journalists from the Montreal magazine *Sept Jours*, she visited four cities: Tokyo, Osaka, Nagoya and Fukuoka. More than in the USA, and far more than in the United Kingdom, where reaction was cool, the Japanese warmed immediately to *Unison*. The record promoters set up a tight promotion schedule. They'd even visited her home in Charlemagne to photograph Céline's birthplace. To exhibit her songs, they prepared a video montage of pictures representing Canada, its wheat fields, its snowy summits, its pristine forests, its caribou herds, its wild rivers.

No sooner had she returned to Quebec than Céline kicked off another tour that was to last most of the summer: twenty-five cities and towns and thirty-seven shows between May 19 and August 4.

That spring, the readers of *Chatelaine*, a popular women's magazine, selected her as one of the ten women they most admired. She finished third on the list, behind two authors — competitive television personalities whose combined age was three times hers. Céline was delighted that women had voted for her. She remembered earlier in her career René Angélil telling her that for her to be a superstar, women had to like her, not just men. "Think of Judy Garland, Barbra Streisand." Then she added that the woman she admired most was her mother, "because she's an intelligent person, a good person, a mother who brought up fourteen kids and cared for them. She's an extraordinary woman, a success in life."

Some of her detractors accused her of giving a performance that was more athletic than artistic, or of following a career plan where strategy was more important than art. They criticized her for being dazzled by the American dream, of forgetting her identity. But no one who heard her shows ever said she didn't have a wonderful voice, and virtually everybody was won over by her charm.

Angélil compared Céline's rise to a baseball player's career. By recording *Unison*, CBS was drafting her as a pinch hitter. One fine day,

Céline the rookie stepped up to the plate. "Where Does My Heart Beat Now" was a clean base hit. They would use her again, and it wouldn't be long before she hit her first home run — then belted her first grand slam.

CBS-USA handled some fifteen American artists who occupied the show business summit, including Michael Jackson and Bruce Springsteen. Now Céline was part of that winning team. Sure, she spent a lot of time on the bench, but it seemed as if she was getting all the breaks.

But as cruel fate would have it, Tommy Mottola, the top dog at CBS, wouldn't let Céline do the song for Spielberg's film. Angélil had expected objections from MCA, but never from CBS. Mottola argued that "Dreams to Dream" couldn't carry an album, and that it would hurt "Where Does My Heart Beat Now," which still had plenty of life left in it. Sooner or later, "Where Does My Heart Beat Now" would drop from the charts, and Mottola's argument would lose its validity.

Angélil and Donald K. Donald scheduled a tour-ending monster show for the Montreal Forum on June 19 to celebrate Céline's tenth anniversary in show business. It was ten years earlier, to the day, that she made her first public appearance on Michel Jasmin's show. Angélil was determined to commemorate the event with a blockbuster show that would involve all the media — television most of all.

For starters, he sought out Michel Chamberland, head of variety programming at Télé-Métropole, Quebec's largest private network. Chamberland was more than interested. But a few days later, he called Angélil back to let him know he couldn't afford it. So Angélil turned to Radio-Canada. Their first reaction was to stage a top-of-the-line production. They were ready to step in with a major investment if Céline would give them first broadcast rights to the album she was scheduled to release that fall.

But Angélil had already made a deal with MusiquePlus. The Montreal all-music station produced the extraordinary live coverage of the launch of her previous album that drew more than a million viewers. The show won a Gémeaux award for the year's Best Variety Production. Radio-Canada got the message. But they did agree with Angélil that immediately after the launch on MusiquePlus, Céline would kick off her promotional campaign on *Studio libre*, the publicly owned network's new talk show produced by their old friend Laurent Larouche. This was the same Larouche who had put them in touch with Carol Reynolds and David Foster two years earlier. Larouche was also Radio-Canada's coordinator for the taping of the June 19 show at the Forum.

On Monday, May 27, Céline guested on *Ad Lib*, a popular Télé-Métropole talk show hosted by Jean-Pierre Coallier. No one could have suspected that this would be the first clash in what was to become a cold war between Angélil and the private network.

On Wednesday, May 19, the Forum was bursting at the seams. At 23, Céline Dion was celebrating the first ten years of her career with her fans. The venerable hockey arena's sixteen thousand seats sold out in a matter of hours. One dollar of every ticket sold was to be donated to the Quebec Cystic Fibrosis Association. Radio-Canada, with Laurent Larouche at the controls, was taping the show, which was sponsored by Diet Coke and Stereo Plus, a Montreal audio and video equipment rental specialist. Montreal's Metropolitan Orchestra, under the direction of Richard Grégoire, accompanied Céline. Grégoire had rearranged all the original versions of her songs for a sixty-five-piece symphonic orchestra.

The first number was the "Voices That Care" video. The audience was already on its feet, lighters glowing in the dark. The second song, "Delivre-moi," drew an ovation. From then on, it was two hours of joyful pandemonium.

Céline was wearing one of her sexiest outfits. She thanked her songwriters, Eddy Marnay, Diane Juster, Luc Plamondon, Marcel Lefebvre and her mother. "In my book, she's the greatest, the one who began it all." When she sang "Ce n'était qu'un rêve," the whole Forum sang along with her. She followed it up with "Une colombe," "Incognito," "D'abord c'est quoi l'amour" and "Tellement j'ai l'amour," songs people knew by heart. Then came "I'm Calling You." With Breen Leboeuf, she sang "Mes blues passent p'us dans 'porte." But the songs from Plamondon's *Starmania* elicited off the loudest cheers.

For her first encore, she bounced back onto the stage wearing a Montreal Canadiens hockey jersey and carrying a Quebec flag. The Forum went wild. The audience started doing the wave, and singing a traditional ballad to Céline.

Onstage, behind Céline, was her sister and backup singer Ghislaine, who would be turning 23 in a month. Ghislaine looked on in awe, but also with despair. She knew it was too late for her. She had a magnificent voice, just as powerful and supple as Céline's, but with a rougher edge. What was she doing wrong? Perhaps she wasn't determined and disciplined enough. She knew she would always be known as Céline's sister. She looked on as her little sister, the sister she loved and envied, gathered up the bouquets and stuffed animals that came flying onstage.

After the show she'd go out for a drink, get a buzz on and forget. Was there any other way to brighten the shadow she was slipping deeper and deeper into, like her brothers Claudette and Michel? Hadn't their group, The Show, simply fallen apart for lack of engagements?

After the show, Céline held a press conference flanked by the CBS execs. She was their most precious treasure. She spoke of happy things and made the journalists laugh. "I've cried enough in my life," she said. "Now, when I'm feeling low, I hold back my tears and make the most of the moment. I savor every bit of happiness." In front of the assembled journalists, CBS-Canada president Paul Burger handed her a triple-platinum disc symbolizing the *Unison* album's 300,000 sales in Canada. Donald K. Donald boss Donald Tarlton handed her a gold ticket, attesting to the fact that every show of her Canadian tour was a sellout. Burger suggested that the press keep its eye on Céline. She would soon be doing great things in the United States and elsewhere in the world. When asked, he admitted that *Unison* was his biggest production to date, but that it hadn't really taken off in the United States, in spite of how well "Where Does My Heart Beat Now" was doing.

"We really believe in Céline Dion," he said. "And we've got plenty of projects for her." He was referring to an upcoming album and to the theme song from Spielberg's film which they still hoped to do, in spite of Mottola's opposition.

On June 29, Céline performed at the National Arts Center in Ottawa for Princess Diana and Prince Charles. After the show, she and René spent a few hours with the royal couple. Céline talked fashion with the princess, who was warm and in high spirits. But beneath her apparent cheerfulness, Céline noticed something disturbing. Boredom or weariness, perhaps.

Céline was overflowing with joy, but the rumor mill was working overtime. People were now talking openly about an affair between her and her manager. Pierre Brassard, who masquerades as a fake television reporter called Raymond Beaudoin, came up to Céline with his camera and microphone. "This is Raymond Beaudoin with Céline Dion. Céline, you English with America, you English with American Music Awards, you English with Johnny Carson.... Do you French with René Angélil?"

Céline was at a loss for words. René slowly lifted his arm and put his hand over the camera lens. Then, turning to Brassard, he said softly, in a tone that left no room for disagreement, "You're not going to broadcast that now, are you?" The item was never shown. Angélil had acquired the authority to match his success. Some people called him "the godfather" on account of his barely audible voice, his bulk and his power.

Two days later, the Quebec tour was back on the road, with quick forays into Ontario. After months of suspense, the *Fievel Goes West* affair was about to be resolved in a totally unexpected way.

When it was clear that Mottola was not going to back off, Farberman went calling on other vocalists including Linda Ronstadt and Anita Baker. David Foster repeated that he wanted to work with Céline at any price, and convinced Angélil to speak to Mottola again. MCA was ready to let Céline use the song in her next album. As she didn't have any other hits on the charts that "Dreams to Dream" might hurt, Mottola finally gave in. There were still some minor details to be ironed out between the two record companies, but it looked like everything would be worked out.

In late July, Céline and René traveled to Los Angeles for the recording session. In the limousine that picked them up at the airport, they found a stuffed Fievel with a huge bouquet of flowers and a note from Steven Spielberg thanking Céline for taking time out from her vacation to work on his movie. René was elated. For him, the theme song for a Hollywood film produced by a famous, rich and powerful director, was as powerful a vehicle as you could find.

Several days later, Farberman called René to tell him that everything was going great. Everyone, from Spielberg on down, was more than satisfied with Céline's performance. The movie would be coming out in the fall. Angélil contacted Suzanne Gauthier, a Montreal journalist, to break the news. The next day, it would be on the front page of Quebec's most popular morning paper, *Le Journal de Montréal*.

But a few days later, the wheels started to fall off. Around midday, René dropped by to see his cousin and friend Paul Sara at the new Nickels restaurant in Laval. While he was waiting for Paul at the counter, reading a paper, the cashier handed him the phone. It was Farberman, who'd just arrived at his office in Los Angeles. In a choked voice, he told René that Linda Ronstadt, who'd originally refused to sing "Dreams to Dream" had thought it over. She wanted to sing the theme song for Spielberg's film herself after all. As it turned out, she was Spielberg's first choice, and he was ready to sacrifice Céline's version.

"We can still try to work things out," said Farberman. "But I'm being honest with you. We don't stand a chance."

Thirty seconds later, Paul Sara stepped out of his office. René was no longer at the counter. "He just stepped out," said the waitress. Paul spotted René's car, with the driver's door open. René was seated behind the wheel, his head in his hands. Paul came up to him slowly and stood beside his friend. René was crying.

"It's the worst day of my life, Paul. You'll never believe what happened."

What made the pain and humiliation even worse was that the story had just come out on the front page of *Le Journal de Montréal*, and that all the Quebec media were talking about it. How was he going to tell Céline that the venture that had thrilled her so much had suddenly fallen through?

That very same day, Céline was singing at a festival at Saint-Perpétue, a tiny farming hamlet in the heart of rural Quebec. René rented a Winnebago. On board were Dave Platel, Céline, Suzanne Gingue and a representative of Sony-Japan.

He didn't have the heart to tell Céline she wouldn't be singing the Fievel song. Only Dave Platel knew the truth. On the way, Céline broke into "Dreams to Dream" a couple of times, telling their Japanese guest how much she liked the song. Angélil watched the bleak landscape rush past as he wondered how he would ever get himself out of this mess.

First of all, he had to find an "official and honorable" excuse to tell the media that it was Céline's decision not to record the song. On July 29, Angélil told *La Presse* journalist Alain Brunet that Epic was going to reject the offer from Spielberg and MCA/Universal Studios. The reasoning was that simultaneously launching two Céline Dion songs on the market would create confusion and put her in competition with herself. Angélil was convinced the public would accept his explanation. Of course, no one in the industry would believe a word of it. Everyone knew that *Unison* had gone as far as it was going to go, and that none of its ten songs was going any further on the charts.

But they were still hanging onto a glimmer of hope. Farberman let René know that Foster and Horner were doing everything they could to convince Spielberg to keep Céline's version since they weren't keen on working with Ronstadt, who'd originally turned her nose up at their song.

Two days after they returned from Saint-Perpétue, Céline and René left for a promotional tour in the United Kingdom, where *Unison* had never really gotten off the ground. René still hadn't told Céline that Linda Ronstadt was insisting on recording the song. He called Paul Farberman three times each day. One morning, he told René that James Horner, the composer, wasn't at all happy with the way Linda Ronstadt was treating his song. But later the same day, he called back to say that she'd agreed to return to the studio and rerecord it. At midnight, LA time, nine in the morning in London, he informed

Angélil that Ronstadt had rerecorded the song and that Horner was satisfied. "Sorry, René, it's all over."

René sat there in his armchair in the darkness of their hotel suite. He sat there for hours, until he heard Céline calling him, "Lover!" He went into her room and sat down on the edge of the bed without a word. He looked so crestfallen that she started to cry, fearing that something terrible had happened to her family. When she realized that nobody had died or was ill, she consoled René. But she was bitterly disappointed. She adored the song. She was proud of her version, and was already looking forward to singing "Dreams to Dream" onstage.

As it turned out, their misfortune turned out for the best. In Céline Dion and René Angélil's life, even losing was winning. Another project would soon come along, and it would be infinitely more rewarding. If Céline had sung the theme song for Spielberg's movie, this marvelous opportunity would never have happened.

The *Falling Into You* Tour
Hiroshima, February 10, 1997

The Video

As Céline sings "It's All Coming Back to Me Now," the screens set up along the sides of the hall show a video made in April 1996. It was shot in a Bohemian castle not far from Prague, in a part of the world and at moment of her life that she would always look back on with intense emotion.

At the airport, the Czech customs official, a tall, blond young woman, stared at her passport without daring to look up. Then she said in a low voice, without raising her eyes, in slightly broken English: "Céline Dion! You are my most favorite singer." Finally, pulling together, she looked up and added, in perfect French, that she adored D'eux, *particularly "Pour que tu m'aimes encore" and "Je sais pas." She liked "Ziggy" too, from* Starmania.

How many languages did she speak, Céline asked. Aside from Czech, French and English, the young lady was fluent in Italian, Russian and German, and could get by in Romanian and Spanish. Céline told her how envious she was, that she'd always dreamed of speaking more languages, that she wanted to learn Spanish as soon as she had the time. She'd start with cassettes, then she'd go and live for a few weeks in a town in Spain or perhaps Mexico.

Dave Platel was waiting behind her, watching with fascination. It must have been the hundredth time he'd seen Céline get involved in a conversation with people who rushed through her life — people like customs agents, elevator operators, chambermaids, chauffeurs, airline flight attendants.

"In a few seconds, she can create intimate familiar relations with people who seem intimidated at first. In Prague, she talked with that young lady as if the two of them were old friends, as if there were no one else in the world. I've seen plenty of artists who can face the crowds, but who are terrified at the idea of being alone with someone else. Not Céline. That's probably her main strength, the greatest gift she's been given — the ability to warm to individuals as well as to crowds."

When you live a nomadic life like I do, you get into the habit of making friends quickly. Some people are so timid that they try and hide and never speak to anyone. My timidity drives me toward people. I talk to perfect strangers, all the time. Maybe it's my way of protecting myself. I like to take the initiative.

Sometimes, the encounters are unforgettable. I'll probably never see the girl from the Prague airport customs again, but I'll never forget her, just like she'll never forget me. I'm sure of it. We shared an experience. I know she's there, somewhere in the world. Her presence comforts me and reassures me. I could see in her eyes, and hear in her voice that she was a good person.

The "It's All Coming Back to Me" video took more than a week to complete. It was shot in an ancient abandoned castle that the people of Prague claimed was haunted — just like in the video. It tells the story of a broken love affair. A young woman waits for the man of her life in a castle in Bohemia, but only his shadow, his phantom, his heartrending memory will ever reach the castle.

While the cameramen and the technicians were getting ready for the shoot, Céline and Manon visited every nook and cranny of the castle — which had been bombarded during the war — from the prison cells in the dungeon to the crypts, chapel and turrets. Cloves of garlic hung from the walls of every room. On the floor of one empty room they found a German newspaper dating from 1942. "The year René was born," Céline said to herself. It was wartime. There was a photograph of a warship on the front page and smiling soldiers. "They're Japanese," said Manon.

Céline was enchanted by Prague, by its breathtaking beauty and the calming, well-played music was heard everywhere. After a few days in that city, she felt as though she was transported to another time and place. The war and the communist occupation had horribly disfigured most of the cities of Eastern Europe, especially the capitals: Warsaw, Bratislava, Budapest, Bucharest. But Prague, located in the heart of Europe, between the Baltic, Adriatic, Black and North seas, escaped unscathed from the colossal struggle, as it did from the countless upheavals around it for more than one thousand years. Perhaps the city was spared because it was so beautiful. Its occupiers, the Germans and then the Russians, loved and protected it.

Prague has grown old gracefully. It's become a city of lovers, who are everywhere, kissing on the bridges and in the squares, embracing in the theaters and the museums and on the banks of the winding, majestic Moldau. "There's got to be a reason," said Céline. "There must be something in the air, something in the water." She began dreaming of a magic potion that she could pour into the water systems of all the great cities of the world, to transform all people into lovers.

"That wouldn't stop wars," said one of her cameramen. "There are people who would kill or die for love. It's not enough to be in love; you've got to be loved. And by the right person."

The well-behaved, young crowd in Hiroshima, like the fans in Fukuoka and Osaka, seem particularly fascinated by the images of the "It's All Coming Back to Me" video. The castle in Bohemia and the decimated landscapes of central Europe must seem alien to them. When Céline finishes her song, they sit there for a moment, gaping, staring at the silent screens.

In Japan, I've always had surprises — which really doesn't surprise me. A lot of times, I get a strong sense of déjà-vu. It's like I'm seeing the landscapes I used to imagine in my dreams. This morning, it was snowing in Hiroshima, big fluffy flakes that I watched fall on the garden. They were more like white feathers. Three days ago in Osaka, close to the amphitheater, the plum trees were in bloom.

It's not just a sense of déjà-vu that I get, but one of "must see again." I'll see these landscapes again, because when I look at them, I see myself as a lonely old woman.

Today, Hiroshima is a bustling city of almost two million. It's a brutally modern town, strictly business. Unlike Prague, there's nothing romantic about it. But like Prague, the streets are full of lovers. The Green Arena, where Céline is singing "It's All Coming Back to Me Now," is full of lovers as well.

Unlike Prague, Hiroshima was destroyed. On the morning of August 6, 1945, 145,000 people died instantly. Céline was expecting to find sadness, bitterness, feelings of horror.

Maybe it's just one of those ideas you get. You expect cities like Hiroshima that experienced horror and suffering, plenty of suffering, to have some kind of mark left on them. You expect them to be more serious, like children with incurable diseases. Like Karine, who was so serious in everything she said and thought.

"Céline has the gift of arousing the pure feelings in people," Dave Platel says. "Her voice goes straight to their hearts and sets off passionate emotions, emotions that are stronger if they've been hurt. When she sang in Belfast in November 1995, people broke down in tears. Wherever people have suffered, Céline makes them cry."

In Hiroshima, she has them laughing too. As her last song, after the encores, after "To Love You More," she sings a cappella with Terry, Rachelle, Elise and Mégo, the lovely little ditty Mia sent her:

Watashi watashi wa
totemo shiawasene
anata no ai ni
tsutsumare teirukara

(I am happy
because your love
is all around me.)

Chapter Twenty-Seven
Beauty and the Beast

Céline and René were still in London when Chris Montan, musical director at Walt Disney Productions, called them with an offer. Disney was working on a new animated film which was sure to be a hit, he said. They wanted Céline to sing the film's theme song. Montan was the producer of "Voices That Care," and he wasn't the kind of man to talk through his hat. He was efficient, and he knew how to get things done, and within twelve hours, a demo of the song was on its way to London. Still upset over "Dreams to Dream," Céline refused to listen it and it wasn't until they were winging their way home that she agreed to listen to the melody. She didn't like it.

But she did agree to go to Los Angeles the following week with René and Vito Luprano. At the Disney studios, she was polite, courteous, smiling. But René knew she was still smarting and in no mood to enjoy this particular adventure. They knew that the film they were about to see was unfinished. The editing wasn't complete, and the sound track wasn't properly synchronized. Still, they were dazzled. When the lights went on in the projection room, Céline leaped to her feet, applauding. And on her way out of the studio, she was singing "Beauty and the Beast."

They returned to Montreal contented and certainly relieved. In her heart, Céline still loved "Dreams to Dream," but the song didn't go very far. Neither had Spielberg's film. On the other hand, "Beauty and the Beast" would become Céline's signature song, and would establish her firmly at the top of the major leagues. With it, Céline would hit the home run Angélil had always predicted.

On Sunday, September 15 at 8:00 p.m., Radio-Canada broadcast the anniversary show they'd taped on June 19 at the Montreal Forum. Meanwhile, in Paris, where it was two o'clock in the morning, Céline Dion was leaving Michel Berger's studio, Face B, on Boulevard des Batignolles, where she was recording her new French-language album, *Dion chante Plamondon* (*Dion sings Plamondon*). The night air was mild. Angélil and Plamondon, both hearty eaters, suggested they go for a bite in the Halles district where Plamondon knew some good restaurants that stayed open late. Céline begged off. They would be talking business, marketing and strategy. She preferred to go back to the hotel and rest. She still had four songs to record. Angélil accompanied her back to the hotel on Place de la Concorde, and then went off to join Luc, Mario and Vito at the Pied-de-Cochon. Mario was telling Luc that the album they were working on would have a short, intense run. The following spring, Céline would be bringing out her second album in English. Ideally, Plamondon's songs would have run their course by then.

This album, *Dion chante Plamondon*, was Céline's eleventh but it was the first album she really got involved with. Usually, when she walked into the studio for the recording session, the music tracks were ready. All she had to do was lay her voice down over the accompaniment, which she was hearing for the first time. This time, she insisted on working on the production process itself. Serge Perathoer, the French coproducer and arranger, had come to Quebec to rehearse with her for a few days. Céline told him the kind of music she liked and the kind of sound she was looking for.

Plamondon was a prolific composer. But he'd narrowed down the choice to fifty songs. Céline chose eight: four from *Starmania* made popular by Quebec singers Fabienne Thibault and Claude Dubois, two other songs that Quebec diva Diane Dufresne had sung ("Oxygène" and "J'ai besoin d'un chum"), one written for Martine St-Clair ("Le Fils de Superman") and one recorded by Marie-Carmen ("Piaf chanterait du rock"). Plamondon also penned four originals: a heavy-rock piece called "Des mots qui sonnent" based on a tune by Aldo Nova and Marty Simon; "L'Amour existe encore," a haunting, romantic ballad with music by Richard Cocciante; a dance music item with Romano Musumara called "Je danse ma tête;" and finally, "Quelqu'un que j'aime, quelqu'un qui m'aime," that was to be the song of 1992 in both Quebec and France, based on a melody by Erown.

Recording new versions of eight hits was a challenge. To make the songs her own, Céline had to give them new color and shape. Michel Berger, a huge star in France, a great musician, sensitive songwriter and a restless soul, happily agreed to rework the arrangements of the four songs from *Starmania.*

The new songs, "Des mots qui sonnent" and "Je danse dans ma tête" in particular, were vocally demanding. Plamondon was venturing onto dangerous musical ground. "Je d-d-d-danse dans ma tête" was written for a trumpet, said Musumara. "There's no singer who can do that. Vocally, it's downright impossible." Of course, that kind of vocal fireworks was right up Céline's alley. The result was breathtaking.

Dion chante Plamondon would be the logical, natural extension of *Unison*, the show that Céline crisscrossed Canada with in 1990 and 1991. It featured several tunes from *Starmania* that never failed to bring the crowd to its feet. Vito Luprano's idea was to bring out all the songs together and add four original Plamondon numbers that would really drive the album.

For Plamondon, the prospect of an album in English wasn't the best of news. His songs wouldn't be on the hit parade for very long. Only four months later, CBS would start promoting its next album. He hit on a daring idea, which he explained to Mario, Vito and René that very night. It was crazy, it was risky: they could bring out two singles at the same time. The songs might cancel each other out, but they might both make it to the top of the charts. There was a moment of silence. René broke it, saying he thought it was a terrific idea. "I like it. It's daring. And it's never been done before."

Plamondon was rubbing his hands at the thought of having two songs in the top ten. At the same time "L'amour existe encore" was cutting a swath through the adult market, "Des mots qui sonnent" would be thrilling the younger crowd.

Then and there, in the Pied-au-Cochon, they decided to go ahead with the plan. There would be a huge launch, the biggest ever held in Quebec. In August, Angélil, Francine Chaloult, Vito Luprano and Mario Lefebvre drew up their promotional plans. The meetings took place in various Nickels restaurants in the Montreal region. They picked a date: November 4; a place: the Métropolis, at eight o'clock. The event, to be hosted by Sonia Benezra, would be televised live by MusiquePlus. Working closely with the record stores, Mario nailed down guaranteed

The International Years

New York, 1997

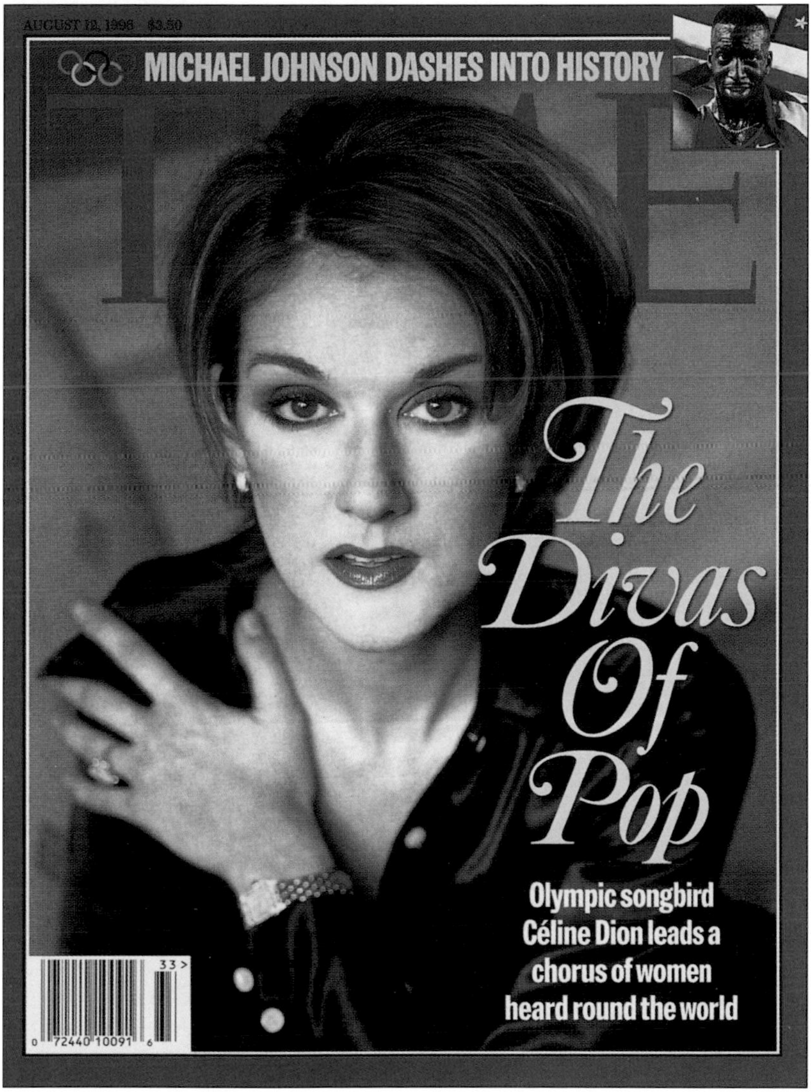

AUGUST 12, 1996 $3.50

MICHAEL JOHNSON DASHES INTO HISTORY

TIME

The Divas Of Pop

Olympic songbird Céline Dion leads a chorus of women heard round the world

After she sang at the Olympic Games in Atlanta before the biggest audience ever, *Time* magazine put her on the cover of its international edition.

During the *Falling Into You* tour, Céline wins two Grammys, for Song of the Year and Album of the Year. She is now a permanent fixture at the top of the hit parade.

Performing for hours onstage requires exceptional physical conditioning.

The backup singers. Top: Terry Bradford and Élise Duguay. Bottom: Rachelle Jeanty, who, during the *Falling Into You* tour in Memphis, was replaced by Julie Leblanc.

The musicians. Top (left to right), surrounding the conductor Claude "Mégo" Lemay at the piano, are bassist Marc Langis, guitarist André Coutu, percussionist Paul Picard, keyboardist Yves Frulla and drummer Dominique Messier.

Céline's sister Manon, her confidante and wardrobe consultant, is always beside her, just like her bodyguard, Eric Burrows.

Suzanne Gingue, tour director from the beginning, became a valued friend.

René is flanked by Barry Garber, Céline's agent since 1990, and author Georges-Hébert Germain.

At the end of the *Falling Into You* tour, Céline discovers a passion for golf. She "crosses swords" with the author.

Michel Drucker produced a major year-end show for French TV, with such stars as Alain Delon.

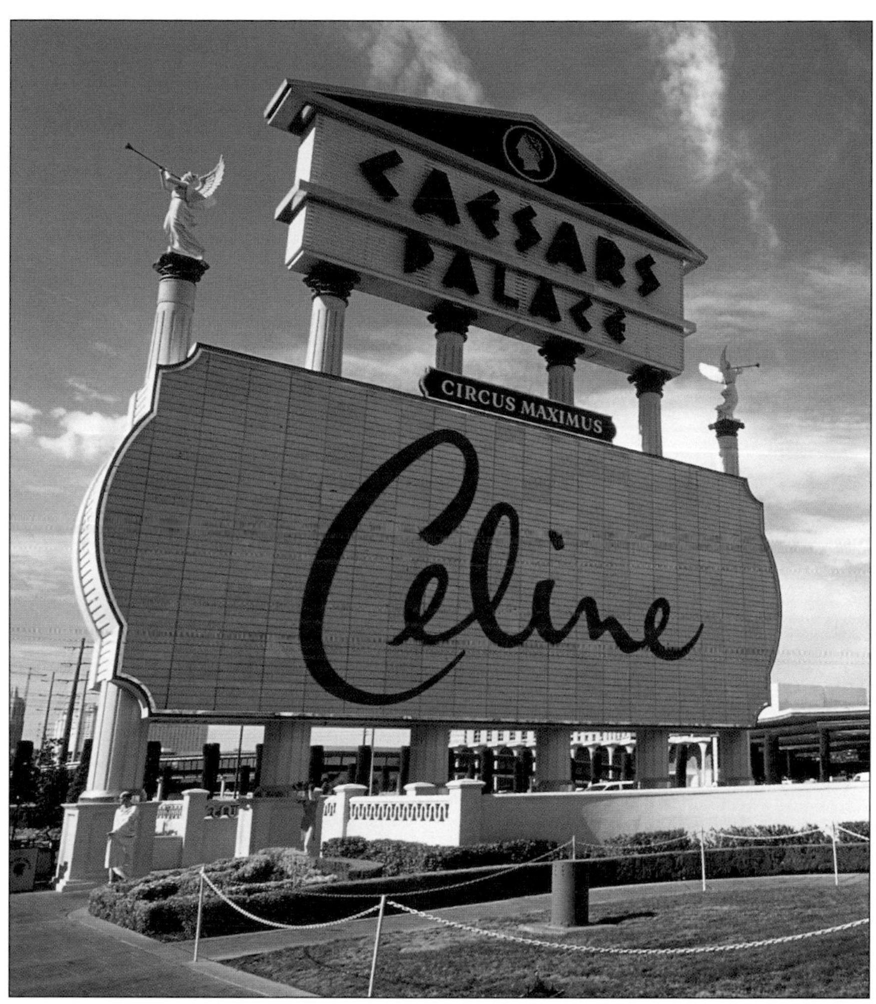

On The Strip in Las Vegas, the star needs only her first name.

Céline triumphs after making history by singing twice on the same night at the 1997 Academy Awards.

On Ophra Winfrey's talk show, every member of her family except Claudette, who was in Barbados, joined in with Céline and sang the song her mother wrote, "Ce n'etait qu'un reve." The American public begins to understand the star's roots.

In London

Backstage at Wembley

Sir George Martin, who was instrumental in creating the sound (and the legend) of the Beatles, wanted, before retiring, to work with "the most intelligent musical instrument that exists today," the voice of Céline Dion. Martin helped to record a song by Carole King, "The Reason."

At the Hit Factory in New York, the Bee Gees record "Immortality" with Céline, a song they wrote for her.

The duet "I Hate You, I Love You," a remake of a popular seventies' song by Tony Renis, brought the pop star together with Luciano Pavarotti.

Her long-time idol Barbra Streisand became a partner and friend, with whom she sings "Tell Him."

New York, 1997

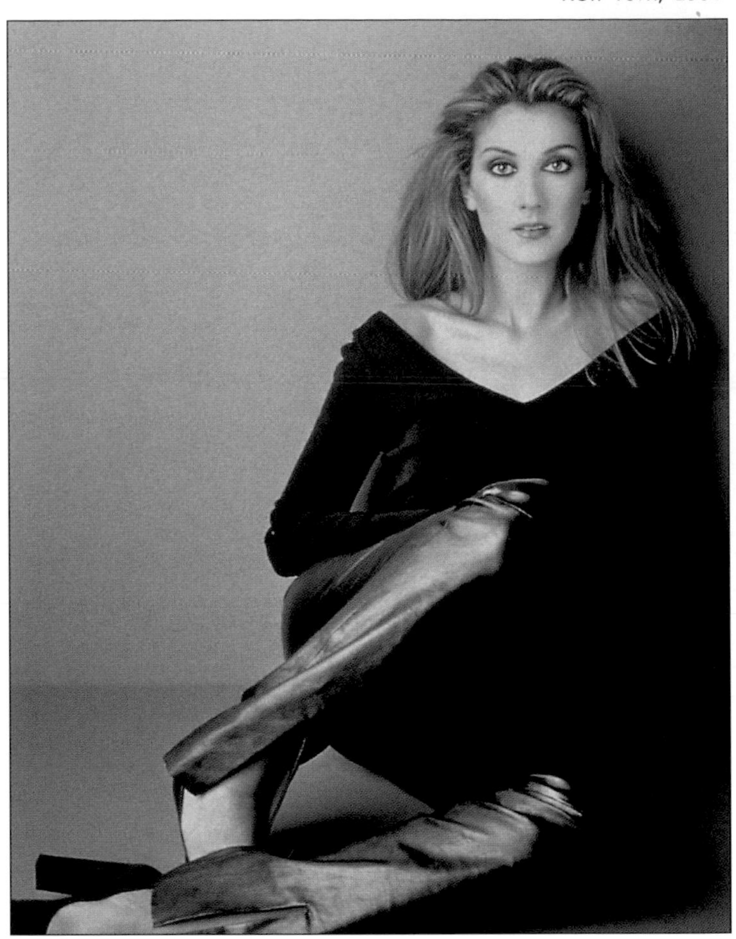

The simple theme of love drives the whole album *Let's Talk About Love*.

immediate sales of fifty thousand albums. The record would be certified solid gold the very night it was launched. Céline was doing ads for Diet Coke at the time, which naturally, would be part of the event too.

Two months before the album was scheduled to hit the stores, the promotional campaign was ready to go. As agreed when Radio-Canada taped the big anniversary show at the Forum, Céline and Luc would break the news on *Studio libre*, the public network's new talk show. The following Monday, November 11, would see an appearance on *Ad Lib*, on Télé-Métropole. Mario took pains explain to the *Ad Lib* researchers why Céline would be appearing first on *Studio libre*.

On September 30, Angélil was in Los Angeles, from where he called Diane Bonneau, head researcher for *Ad Lib* to talk about the show. Diane, a close friend of his, reminded him that her show was involved in an unrelenting struggle with *Studio libre*. Télé-Métropole's producers, and most of all its program director, were intent on getting the story first. She was confident that "because it's Céline," everything would work out.

Three days later, on October 3, she called Angélil to inform him that Jean Guimond, the show's producer, refused to have Céline on *Ad Lib* only a few days after her appearance on *Studio libre*. She would have to wait two or three weeks. But René made it clear to all concerned that Céline would be leaving Montreal on November 15 to record her second English-language album on the West Coast, and that Plamondon was expected in Paris no later than November 13.

He called Guimond. "We shouldn't be depriving *Ad Lib's* viewers of a performance by Céline," he said. "They'd be the losers." Then he talked with the show's host, Jean-Pierre Coallier, who claimed he was disappointed. Finally he chatted again with Michel Chamberland, the network's program director, to ask him not to involve Céline in the ratings war. Chamberland wouldn't listen.

"We'll be happy to have Céline before *Studio libre*, or two weeks after."

"In my books, two weeks later might just as well mean never," Angélil shot back.

Chamberland wouldn't budge. It didn't take long for Angélil to let it be known that as long as Chamberland was in charge of programming, Céline Dion wouldn't be appearing on Télé-Métropole. When Chamberland quit his job five years later, Angélil had kept his word all that time.

"I think you like a fight," Céline told him. It wasn't a criticism. She realized that he was at his best in a scrap.

In the fall of 1991, he was at war with the ADISQ board of directors again. The organization was refusing to let Céline's Quebec tour and anniversary show at the Forum be nominated for best show of the year.

The new rules (laid down by President André Ménard, who also convinced the CRTC to force radio stations to adopt stricter Quebec content standards) specified that shows nominated for the award had to be at least 50 percent in French, and almost two-thirds of the songs in Céline's show were in English. The two men engaged in an epic battle and yet emerged on friendly terms.

Angélil insisted that every song was introduced in French. As far as Ménard was concerned, these presentations meant nothing. "But they're monologues," Angélil shot back. Ménard accused him of acting in bad faith. ADISQ is the only organization of its kind to operate in French in North America. If Angélil wanted a prize for Céline's show, he could enter her in the Junos. But he couldn't do both at the same time. Angélil replied that Céline was a French-speaking artist above all, and that an album of songs by Luc Plamondon was in the mixing stage. In a few days it would be out, and it would be a red-hot seller in Quebec and in France.

Ménard was an intelligent, cultivated man and fair minded. He invited Angélil to make his case before the full ADISQ board, and Angélil, who had once dreamed of being a lawyer, prepared carefully. He knew that he had more than a few adversaries in the group, which he considered to be largely comprised of snobs and pseudo-intellectuals.

Angélil began by reminding the board that Céline was Quebec's greatest artist, that ADISQ was wrong in turning up its nose at her and that the attitude of the board's members would hurt the profession as a whole. In fact, their best bet was to make her their ally.

"Céline is going to open doors in France, in the United States, everywhere in the world," he concluded. "Give her your support. It's in your own best interest."

Then he withdrew to let the board deliberate. The board's members were almost unanimous in rejecting Angélil's demands. The industry could hardly afford to turn its back on the Quebec intelligentsia.

When René stepped back into the room, Ménard had the painful task of informing him that the board had rejected his request. Céline's show would not be nominated. René stood there for a moment. He looked around the room. He was sure that more than a few producers were jealous of his success with Céline. Then he spoke. "Guys, I wish you a happy life." It sounded a lot like a final good-bye.

Alerted by Angélil, the Quebec media were on the case. A few weeks later, when he saw the *Billboard* headline, "Céline Dion snubbed in her own country," Ménard called Angélil in the hope of stopping the fratricidal conflict. Angélil reminded him of ADISQ's rejection and said he was directly responsible.

The squabble was to last for months. To a certain extent, Angélil could understand why his rivals felt the way they did. Fair's fair. Everyone had the right to defend the artists they managed, even if it meant pushing Céline aside. But Angélil was still convinced that, under the circumstances, it would have been better for Quebec show business to rally behind Céline.

Dion chante Plamondon was launched on November 4, 1991. It was an electrifying occasion. In spite of the bitter cold that hung over Montreal, thousands of young people gathered on St. Catherine Street in front of the Métropolis and the MusiquePlus studios right next door.

After announcing that a new song called "Beauty and the Beast" was about to be launched in the United States, and that it looked like it would be the hit of the holiday season, Bill Rotari and Paul Burger gave Plamondon and Céline their gold records symbolizing preliminary sales of more than fifty thousand copies in Quebec record stores. Céline, her hair curly, wearing net stockings and a fringed skirt, performed a few songs and fielded questions from the journalists.

Dion chante Plamondon was Céline's first album in French since *Incognito* four and a half years earlier in 1987. It was a serious, hard-hitting work. Plamondon's songs explored a whole range of subjects, all resolutely modern and, for the most part, disturbing. They spoke of the difficulty of living, of existential torment, of the confusion of the modern world. "Le monde est stone," from *Starmania*, was the cry of a woman who wanted to escape the unbearable pressure of the today's world. "Le fils de Superman" told the story, inspired by a real event, of a little boy who was given his favorite superhero's costume as a gift. Confusing dreams and reality (a frequent theme in Plamondon's songs), the boy leapt — and crashed — from the fifth floor of a Manhattan apartment. Wounded and crazed by the mechanized life of the big city, the girl in "Je danse dans ma tête" sought refuge in music. "Oxygène" was a song about anguish and panic. "Le blues du businessman" was the sad song of a dissatisfied man who was successful in business, but unhappy and at his wits' end because he never knew what he wanted to be. Céline sang the song in its original version, not Nicole Croisille's feminist interpretation.

"Eddy Marnay was right. Céline is a new Judy Garland," said Plamondon that night. "She has an exceptional voice and a feel for French phrasing."

Six weeks later, 125,000 copies of *Dion chante Plamondon* had been sold. By the holidays, the two singles reached the top of the charts, one in the top twenty-five rock, the other in the top twenty-five adult. No other artist in the history of the Quebec recording industry had ever done anything comparable, nor had any other songwriter either.

The Plamondon album wasn't to be launched in France until January, so as not to compete with *Unison*, which was still doing well. The adult audience still remembered the little girl who sang songs like "D'amour ou d'amitié" and "Mon ami m'a quittée" back in the early eighties. But with "Where Does My Heart Beat Now," young people would discover a completely different Céline, a real woman in the grip of passion, a true musician. Now a kind of aura surrounded her. People were fascinated and intrigued. She had that extra something that the others didn't.

Angélil carefully kept track of what was said and written about Céline first and foremost in the media. Wherever he was, he made sure that he was kept up to date by fax or phone on whatever the Quebec media were saying about Céline.

In early January, the couple were vacationing in Aruba, a tiny island in the Dutch West Indies. They got a call from Montreal. Céline had topped a public opinion poll as Quebec's personality of the year for 1991. With 43.6 percent, she was far ahead of everybody else. Angélil liked nothing better than reading opinion poll results, and something about the new poll intrigued, disturbed, delighted and astonished him. English-speaking Quebeckers liked Céline even more (50 percent) than French speakers (42.4 percent)!

The *Falling Into You* Tour
Toronto, June 23, 1996

When a Song Fades

The song Céline sings most often in her shows is "Where Does My Heart Beat Now." Recorded in London in March 1989, it was her first to hit the Billboard *charts and has been featured in almost every one of her shows for the past seven years.*

It's a magnificent song; I really like it. But some nights, singing the same words is hard work. The challenge isn't to sing the song, to control my breathing, to push the notes, but to put my heart and soul into it. Some nights I feel distraught, my heart feels cold. I get energy by generating the heat it takes to really get into each of my songs, even the ones I've sung a hundred or three hundred times.

Eddy Marnay, who knew Jacques Brel, once told me why Brel decided to quit. He couldn't perform the same songs over and over again for months and years. But Brel wrote the words and music to his own songs. I'm a singer. I'm fortunate to have a huge repertoire, dozens of songwriters and composers who work for me. Which means I can change my shows regularly. But, at the same time, I have to give people what they want. And people still want "Where Does My Heart Beat Now" seven years later.

We can tell from sales and audience response. This is true everywhere but in France where the great success of *D'eux* overshadows the English songs.

In Toronto, on this night of June 23, as Mégo is rippling through the first chords, for a fraction of a second she almost hates the song coming at her for what seems like the umpteenth time. This time, she's afraid she won't be able to carry it off.

Where does my heart beat now
Where is the sound
That only echoes through the night

In London, she told the crowd at Wembley that it was the first song she recorded in English, "Right here in the West Side studios." She could picture herself, seven years before, in Christopher Neil's little studio. She remembered how delighted they were — René, Vito, Christopher, Neil and Wix — when the recording was over. That lifted her heart.

With any song, there's always a honeymoon. I discover it, and sometimes it's love at first sight (as with "Calling You," for example). Then, one fine day, I realize the magic is gone. It's like I've gotten everything I can out of the song, all its flavor, all its colors. It starts to sound dull and insipid, like a piece of gum you've been chewing too long. It's like love. Sometimes you've got to fight against the wear and tear and force of habit.

In Toronto, I felt like I was completely outside the song. No matter how much I told myself that I liked it, no matter that it had been my faithful companion for all these years, I just couldn't get into it. I just held my breath and dove into a piece of music that suddenly seemed dark and murky.

Then, all of a sudden, it occurred to me that the song described exactly what I was going through. Where does my own heart beat now? For whom? Why? Where is my voice, my breath?

That's how I got back into the song. That's how I fell in love with it all over again.

I feel my heart beat now
Now that I've found
The feeling lives inside.

Chapter Twenty-Eight
You Can Always Count on Love

On March 29, 1992 Céline was in rehearsal at Ocean Way studios in Los Angeles. "Beauty and the Beast," the song she would be singing with Peabo Bryson at the next day's Academy Awards gala, was a full-scale production number, with a ninety-piece orchestra under the direction of Bill Conti. It took hours to rehearse. The dance troupe is directed by Debbie Allen, who did the choreography for *Fame*. Céline was impressed by the hard work and the attitude of these professionals. It was the largest set she had ever seen.

Allen wanted Céline to wear a black dress by a leading designer for the occasion, and offers had already come in from Chanel, Versace and Armani. Céline could pick and choose. At age twenty-four, she already had a marvelous feel for fashion trends. She was still looking for her own style, but the fashion world fascinated her almost as much as music.

Bill Conti adored Céline. She made him laugh. Whenever she sang, he was always amazed by the clarity and maturity of her voice, her sense of rhythm. In a matter of days, he had become an ally and a friend. So had Gil Kates, who had produced the Oscar gala for the past several years.

Céline and Peabo Bryson had already sung "Beauty and the Beast" on January 27 at the American Music Awards. But the Oscars were infinitely more prestigious, with one billion television viewers world-wide. "The very biggest of the big times," as they said in Hollywood. That was why Céline was nervous. The *Beauty and the Beast* theme song was a huge hit all across North America, and it had been nominated for an Oscar. A slight case of tonsillitis added to the pressure. The doctor prescribed antibiotics and lots of rest after the ceremony.

Céline liked the fear. It excited her, almost reassured her. Singers were constantly worried about hitting a wrong note. Sometimes stage fright could alter your voice or make you lose your breath. Your voice could start wobbling, and if you lost control it would go off the tracks. But if you didn't have that crazy fear, you were worried that something else might go wrong.

The theme song from the Disney film, written by Alan Menken and the late Howard Ashman, quickly soared to the top of the AC and the famous Hot 100 lists, and sold more than 500,000 copies. It had become Céline's signature song, the one that finally gave her her big international breakthrough.

That same evening, March 29, after the rehearsals at Ocean Way studios, she participated in the Juno Awards ceremony in Toronto by remote TV hookup. For the second consecutive year, she won top female singer of the year.

The day after, Monday March 30, her twenty-fourth birthday, Céline sang at the Dorothy Chandler Pavilion to a full house of more than 2,400 motion picture industry professionals and stars. Unknown to her, René had flown her parents in from Montreal.

She knew that she was at a turning point in her life. There she was, on a Hollywood stage, in the spotlight, while the show business celebrities she'd always admired, the people she used to watch and dream of becoming, looked on. She was still young. Just yesterday, she could only dream of meeting Barbra Streisand, Liz Taylor and Paul Newman and all the other greats. Her whole life long she'd dreamed of meeting the stars and now, there they were as she sang, watching her, listening to her, standing up to applaud when she finished her song and when "Beauty and the Beast" won the Oscar for Song of the Year.

> After the ceremony, René and I walked through the hall. Famous people came over to greet me and congratulate me. They all seemed smaller than I imagined they would be. We chatted for a bit with Paul Newman, with Tom Cruise and Michael

> Douglas, with Elizabeth Taylor. It's true what they say about her eyes: they're extraordinary. We saw Barbra Streisand but didn't talk with her. And Liza Minelli. At one point, I knew there was someone behind me, a magnificent voice whispering in my ear, congratulating me. It was Anthony Hopkins. At the banquet, there I was, making small talk with Michael Jackson and Brooke Shields. We laughed a lot. Jackson is nice, but he doesn't talk much and when he does, you have to strain to hear him. I could see he and Brooke were very close friends. I had met her before, at a New York hairdresser's. That night, at the banquet, I told her I wanted to be in pictures. I was really just trying to start up a conversation, but when I said it, I realized it was true, that I really wanted to get into the movies. I was always busy doing something else, but I must have been thinking about it a lot. Now, here I was in the heart of Hollywood, with big stars all around me. And everybody was so nice and so happy. I felt right at home, like part of the family.

She'd stepped through the looking glass, just like Alice in Wonderland. She was astonished, still overwhelmed by the people who applauded her that evening.

René was looking every inch the fan himself. He was a born star gazer, a guy who loved keeping track of the big names of stage and screen. At the Dorothy Chandler Pavilion, his head was twisting right and left, as he pointed out to her in a loud voice that there was so-and-so or what's-his-name. When they got back to the hotel that night Céline, teased him and called him a groupie.

On the other side of the continent, Quebeckers watched her moment of triumph. They knew she wanted to sing in every language, everywhere in the world, on the great stages. She never hid her ambition for a minute. Now, finally, they could see that her dream was coming true. They could see that she was thinking of them. She whispered in their ear, in front of a billion viewers, a few words that they alone could understand, in that down-home accent of theirs. It was her way of telling the American public: "Of course you worship me, and I can never thank you enough, but I'm not 100 percent yours."

It was a critical moment in Céline's career, and for Quebeckers too. March 30, 1992, was the first time that their identity was mentioned on the world show business stage. How could Céline not have remembered them?

The Quebec media made much out of her performance. There was plenty of comment about a harmless incident that took place during the gala. When host Billy Crystal presented "Beauty and the Beast," CTV, the Montreal English-language network that was rebroadcasting the ceremony by cable from ABC, was still on commercial break. That meant that viewers in Montreal didn't hear Céline Dion's name. But in the Quebec City region, where the ABC signal was retransmitted by a Vermont station, the presentation came through loud and clear.

That same day, March 30, 1992, with the Juno and Oscar awards still echoing around her, she launched her second English-language album, *Celine Dion*, in Canada. Recorded in New York, Los Angeles, San Francisco and Morin-Heights in the Laurentians, the album featured fourteen songs, including "Beauty and the Beast." It also included five songs by Diane Warren and one by Prince, "With This Tear," that would be made into a video. Prince, the creator of *Purple Rain*, is an incomparable musician. Every single song on the album was about love.

The big CBS machine was less concerned by the content than by the form of the songs. The content was straightforward: love, love, love. *Celine Dion* was much more a producer's than a musician's album. *Dion chante Plamondon* (called *Des mots qui sonnent* in France) was a wordsmith's album. In English-language albums, the voice and the music counted far more than the words. Albums were created by arrangers, producers, technicians, engineers. In the seventies, Phil Spector convinced everybody that the producer of a song, the person who supervised the recording in a studio, was just as much a creator as the songwriter, the composer and the singer. Spector made his mark with female voices like Tina Turner, Ronnie Spector, and Darlene Love. Mixing brass, strings, percussion and voices, he completely rewrote the book on pop music. His motto was: express the feelings of the moment as if they were going to last forever.

The words to *Celine Dion* no longer explored her inner world. They had ceased to reveal her soul, her happiness, her hurt as they once had. The listener could no longer enter the singer's imagination the way Marnay did. Céline might never again experience that deep intimacy with a songwriter. From then on, she became an instrument. Songwriters were no longer exploring her soul or her dreams. She would vanish behind a character, someone enigmatic, close yet inaccessible.

René, like Céline, was becoming popular in his own right, especially in Quebec. The kind of person people went out of their way to greet, the kind of man people respected. Even when Céline was performing "Incognito" at the Saint-Denis, he would get requests for autographs. At first, it was because people recognized him from the Baronnet days, but slowly but surely, the Baronnets were forgotten and he was seen as a true creator in his own right. After all, he was responsible for much of their success.

The day after the Oscars, on March 31, Céline went on *The Tonight Show* for the fifth time. *Céline Dion* was released in the USA, where 350,000 albums were shipped. For the next two months, her job would be to promote *Dion chante Plamondon* and *Céline Dion*, back to back, in Europe, America and Japan.

On Wednesday, April 1, after the Oscar ceremonies and before kicking off the campaign, she flew back to Montreal with her parents, René, Vito Luprano and Bill Rotari, the president of Sony-Quebec. The Montreal press and a crowd of fans were waiting at the Airport Hilton in Dorval, shouting her name: "Céline! Céline! Céline!"

The only thing she told the journalists was how happy she was. René ran down the list of offers. And he dropped those little words, made famous by Al Jolson, that would be repeated hundreds of times over. They expressed Angélil's outlook at the time, "Just wait. You haven't seen anything yet."

During a short stopover in Montreal in April 1992, Céline confessed to Anne Richer of *La Presse* that she was in love. She had been talking more and more about it, without ever naming anyone. It quickly became the question everyone wanted to ask her. In the May 1 edition of *Le Journal de Montréal*, it was speculated that she would be getting married in Las Vegas. It wasn't until the end of the article that readers found out it was an April Fool's joke. Angélil didn't find it funny. He never did find rumors of his amorous relation with Céline particularly humorous.

Céline often said that she dreamed of having children who would follow her wherever she went, who would get used to traveling, to jet lag, to the bohemian life she lived. After all, she managed well enough herself. Many nights she had slept in restaurant booths in the Vieux Baril or the Bord-de-l'Eau.

But she could never surrender completely to her daydreams. She didn't even belong to herself anymore. She had too much to do. Every day, she had people to meet, people to convince, people to charm, everywhere, all the time. She had to give her heart, her energy, her every waking minute. In mid-April she set out on a particularly trying promotional tour. First stop, USA. She appeared on all the talk shows, including *Good Morning America* and *The Tonight Show*.

Everything was moving fast. Too fast, perhaps.

People are funny that way. When terrible things happen, we realize afterward that we were expecting them. René had his heart attack on April 29, 1992 in Los Angeles. Only then did I realize I'd been worried and upset. As if I'd had a premonition of what was going to happen.

They'd spent a few hours by the hotel pool. Both of them adored the sun. That night they were scheduled to leave for New York. René went up to his room complaining of a backache. When Céline called him a bit later, his voice was weak. She hurried up to the room and immediately realized he was in trouble. He was confused and out of breath. The hotel staff helped Céline bring René down to the entrance in a wheelchair where an ambulance picked him up. When they drove up to the emergency ward of the Cedars Sinai hospital, Céline (who was still wearing her swimsuit) used every bit of her energy and every bit of her charm to persuade them to look after René right away.

When she saw the look on the face of the young physician who ordered him admitted to intensive care, she knew his situation was critical. René was crying and telling her the names of the people he wanted around her to protect her career.

As soon as she could, Céline telephoned René's mother, who spent three weeks at his side, in Los Angeles. She brought along his children, too. Patrick, aged twenty-four, a curious, good-natured young man, talked about his travels. He wanted to see the whole world before starting a career. Jean-Pierre, at seventeen, was much more taciturn, secretive and distant and an excellent pianist. Anne-Marie, who would soon turn fifteen, was a pretty, timid girl who liked to laugh, and who also liked music and fashion. Without him, what would become of them? He'd often been away, but he was a loving father. He was sure of it. He deeply loved his children. But was that enough?

He spent hours with his mother talking about his childhood, his father and his children whom she probably knew better than he did. He rediscovered how close he felt to her. His friends began to arrive. Paul Sara, Marc Verreault, Pierre Lacroix. With their help, he put his life and his personal affairs in order. If, one day, the worst happened, they would be able to protect his loved ones.

His convalescence turned into a kind of open-eyed reflection on his life, his friendships, the love he felt for his mother, his brother André, his daughter and sons. And, of course, for Céline.

Two days later, Céline had to be in New York for more promotions. She had to do a photo shoot for a magazine on Times Square. René asked

Ben Kaye to fly from Montreal to New York and meet her at La Guardia. She was helpless. It was the first time she traveled alone.

"I was there to put his mind at rest," said Ben. "I took her for a walk. And, I remember, we saw a large poster of her in the window of a record shop on 6th Avenue. And I took a picture of her standing on a bench."

A few days later, when she returned to Montreal, journalist Michèle Coudé-Lord asked her, "You almost lost your second father, didn't you?" "Not at all," she replied. "My father is my father, and I've only got one. He protects me, encourages me, he loves me and I love him. René is my heart. He's the one who makes it beat." For the first time, almost explicitly, she was speaking of René as the man she loved. She added that she trusted people to respect her private life. "I've got a treasure that's mine alone. I'm ready to share everything else. But not that."

She also said she felt guilty. "If he'd died, I would have said to myself, 'Céline, you killed him.' If I'm Céline Dion today, admired and respected by millions of people, I owe it all to him."

Would she have kept on if the worst had happened? "Yes, I would have kept going. For him."

A few days earlier, the *Wall Street Journal* described Céline's as a "once-in-a-generation voice." The front page of *Billboard* headlined, "Dion's Language is Universal. Artist has Hits in French, English." It was proof that "a French-Canadian artist can carve out an international career without abandoning her culture or denying her roots."

But what good was all the glory if he wasn't there to see it?

René made a rapid recovery, but he'd gotten the scare of his life. "Lucky for you," his physicians told him. "In your case, fear can be a healthy thing." He would have to lose weight, exercise regularly and learn to live with stress. But René knew he couldn't avoid stress. He enjoyed living in the fast lane. He knew he wasn't about to change his life. Eat less? Maybe. Exercise? If he had the time. Stop struggling to push Céline toward greater glory? Never!

> The experience affected me tremendously and made me more mature. I never doubted the love I felt for René, but during those days, I realized just how strong it was.
>
> I know I'll waste away because I'm likely to witness the death of all the people I love. I'm the youngest. I could lose them all, one by one. I'll be like a daisy with its petals plucked. Those people are my petals.

She prevailed on him to drop his promise to be with her whenever she was working. She left for Europe with Suzanne Gingue. On May 14, in Monaco, at the World Music Awards, she received a prize for the Best-Selling Canadian Female Artist. In six weeks, sales of *Céline Dion* had overtaken *Unison.* During the summer it would produce five hit singles.

On June 4, Céline was in Orlando, Florida, at Sony South America's annual meeting. On the fifth, she appeared on a CBS television special. On the sixth, she returned to Montreal by private jet to make a video, "Nothing Broken But My Heart," directed by Line Charlebois. On the night of the seventh, still with Suzanne — her friend, protector and maid rolled into one — she left for Norway, the Netherlands, Germany, England, Sweden, Italy and France. On June 24 she was back in Montreal. Six days later, she was in Seville, which was hosting the 1992 World's Fair. This time, René was with her. On July 8 they returned to Montreal after a few days rest. Then, without warning, something happened so quickly that no one even noticed.

On July 1, 1992, Céline Dion's picture was featured on the front page of *Le Journal de Montréal,* the only daily newspaper published in Quebec on Canada's national holiday. She was looking her best, her hair sleek, her arm held above her head like a flamenco dancer's. Above her shoulder, in fat red letters flanked by quotation marks, were the words: "Separation would be awful." Below, in smaller type, in bright orange letters on a dark green background: "Céline defends Canada."

It happened at the World's Fair in Seville, while Céline was a guest performer at the Canadian pavilion. At a press conference, she'd blurted out an answer to a *Journal de Montréal* reporter. The reporter, Pierre Leroux, had asked for her opinion on the separation of Quebec from Canada. She replied that she was "obviously against any kind of separation." She repeated her devotion to Canada, and stated clearly that separation would be, as she put it, "awful."

She spoke of a place she knew, Switzerland, "where three cultures live in harmony." That country showed that people could get along even if they didn't share the same culture or speak the same language. She added that Canadians were lucky to have two cultures. She'd even talked the matter over with English-Canadian singer Bryan Adams, whose song "Everything" had shattered sales records a year before. The two of them were planning to record a song on the subject.

It was easy to imagine the uproar in Quebec where, at the time, 54 percent of Quebeckers were in favor of independence, according to public opinion polls taken following the failure of the Meech Lake

Accord. Lots of readers wrote in, most of them to express their disapproval. But others insisted that she had a right to her opinion.

The following Saturday, July 11, Céline made the front page of the *Journal* again. A large red headline read, "Céline Comes Clean," and in smaller black type, on a yellow background: "Even my mom was on my case." Now she was wearing a conservative hounds tooth check outfit, her open hand over heart, a look of contrition on her face. It was damage control all the way. She repeated how much she loved Quebec, and that she believed that "for the time being, we've got nothing to gain by separating, and if it was up to me, there would be no borders at all. I'm for Quebec and for a better world." A bit further on, she added, "There's no feelings in politics. My specialty is feelings."

Angélil figured that time would heal the wound, and that people would forget. In fact, he was delighted that Céline had spoken so freely on the subject. He knew that some people claimed he put words in her mouth and shaped her opinions. "No matter what people think, René is no control freak," said Suzanne Gingue, who'd been close to Céline for nearly ten years, especially at that time. "Sure, if he thinks he's right, no one in the world can make him change his mind. But he listens to other peoples' views. Céline's most of all. If I had to sum up Céline Dion's career in a nutshell, I'd say it was the story of her striving for independence and freedom. Céline is a free woman. And I know that René encouraged her and helped her to win those precious things. He doesn't like soft people, people without opinions. He wouldn't love Céline so much if she obeyed him blindly."

He wasn't at all concerned that she'd spoken her mind in Seville. "Be yourself," was his advice to her prior to her press conferences. And if she said things that had to be unsaid or toned down later, so be it. You can't make an omelet without breaking a few eggs. He was proud of her.

That same Saturday, July 11, as skeptical Quebeckers were reading her statements clarifying what she'd said in Seville, Céline was kicking off a tour of the United States at the Hollywood Bowl. She was the opening act for heartthrob Michael Bolton whose show was called "Time, Love and Tenderness." In the space of one month, they would perform the show twenty-five times.

Bolton was a different kind of person. His three teen-age daughters were often on tour with him. He'd given his name and a lot of his time to a foundation that raised funds for women and children in distress or victims of violence. He even had a softball team, the Bolton Bombers, that challenged local radio stations to fund-raising games for his charitable work.

He couldn't stand anyone seeing him going from the dressing room to the stage. After they'd finished their numbers, Céline's musicians had to wait in their dressing rooms behind closed doors when the stage manager announced that Bolton was coming. They heard his footsteps in the corridor, smiled and exchanged glances. As for Bolton, he hardly even looked at them. Unlike Céline, he didn't have warm relations with his entourage. Céline, however, would eat in the canteen and laugh and joke with the musicians and the technical crew.

An opening act has nowhere to hide. The public is there to hear the star they know and like and they can get impatient and show it. Her part of the show lasted only forty minutes, but every night Céline had to win the audience over and take charge. She still wasn't well-known in the United States, even if she'd had a few hits that she included in her program, like "Beauty and the Beast," "Where Does My Heart Beat Now" and "With This Tear."

As soon as the Bolton tour was over, Céline set out on another tour of Quebec, where people still hadn't entirely forgotten her unfortunate statements in Seville. She regretted ever getting involved in politics, but she didn't have any time to spare for self-pity or remorse.

On Saturday night, July 15, she sang at a gala show at the Parc des Îles, on an island in the St. Lawrence River facing Montreal called "Montréal au rythme des Ameriques." Among the other participants were Joe Cocker, Daniel Lavoie, the Neville Brothers, Buffy Sainte-Marie, Kashtin and Peabo Bryson. The fans hadn't forgotten what she'd said in Seville, and there was some booing, but it was quickly overwhelmed by cheers.

Céline came in for a trashing from Sylvain Cormier, pop music critic at *Le Devoir.* He called *Unison* so much "pasteurized disco pap," and her interpretation of Plamondon's "Blues du Businessman," a "bungy leap into the lower depths of cheap sentimentality." But the public couldn't get enough. By the fall, her Seville slip was forgotten. Quebec watched, fascinated, as Céline continued her climb to the top. It was almost impossible to keep track of her. She was in Japan, in Switzerland, in Australia. She was on *The Arsenio Hall Show*, then late-night TV's most popular talk show. She appeared on *The Tonight Show* for the seventh or eighth time. By this time, her international career was taking off, and back home, people were wondering about her love life.

On September 11, 1992, her famous *Tête-à-tête* appearance was taped for broadcast a month later. Host Lise Payette, a maternal-looking woman with an instinct for the jugular, had plenty of questions. She pushed Céline to within an inch of confessing and brought her to tears.

But before talking about love, Céline made a startling announcement about her relations with her family. She openly admitted that several of her brothers and sisters had asked her for money. A few hundred dollars at first, then money to buy a car, a house, a business. She had to put her foot down. She told them exactly what she thought. That she was hurt and angry to see them quarreling. Within the family there were cliques and intense rivalries. The beautiful harmony that Céline remembered from her childhood was shattered, once and for all. In Quebec, the Dion family had almost become an institution. People were fascinated by it, and the tabloids wrote about it.

In the final minutes of the interview, Lise Payette asked Céline if she was in love. She answered, with a torrent of tears, that she loved a man but couldn't reveal his name or her career would be in jeopardy. And she broke into sobs. Her host handed her a hanky.

Barely a year before, Céline was claiming she was prepared to face a life alone. Was it a lie? Probably, because she was in love at the time, though she may have thought her love for Angélil was platonic.

During the taping, René was in the control room. He was crying too. Céline and he had spent hours and hours talking of their love. She was twenty-four years old, and she loved René with all her heart. She believed it was her right to tell the whole world. If he insisted on keeping their relationship secret, she told him, it was because he didn't believe it would last. A true passion couldn't remain a secret, she said. Her song "With This Tear" was at the top of the charts in Quebec. The song described what she was going through, but what she was forced to deny.

Standing behind the producer, the script girl, the soundman and the technicians, René could see his own tear-stained face in the control room windows. He saw the woman he loved suffering on account of him. He wished with all his strength that she would admit everything, then and there. But he knew that she wouldn't. She would be strong, in spite of the tears and pain.

In November, when Céline inaugurated the newly rejuvenated Capitole theater in Quebec City with a fourteen-show sellout, she was never far from tears. She'd just heard the demo of "When I Fall in Love," the Nat King Cole hit she would sing with Clive Griffin. It was to be the theme song for *Sleepless in Seattle*.

When I fall in love
That will be forever
"When I Fall in Love,"
Edward Heyman and Victor Young

The only thing she believed in was love — absolute, unchanging love. In the past, she had to search out the pain that alone could give a song depth and life. Now it was hers in spades. She was singing better than ever. Her art was the cure for her ills, a soothing balm.

For the second year running, René invited the whole clan — his family and Mr. and Mrs. Dion — to Aruba for the Christmas holidays. He rented a luxury villa with a swimming pool, garden and a broad terrace overlooking the sea and the palms.

As he came back from the casino one day, the telephone rang. Five minutes later, he was sitting at the edge of the pool, telling Céline and her parents the news. She had been nominated for a Grammy in several categories. Female Pop Vocalist of the Year, along with Annie Lennox, Mariah Carey, Vanessa Williams and Canada's k.d. Lang. "Beauty and the Beast" was nominated for Theme Song of the Year, in the duet and pop group categories. *Unison* was in the running for Best Album of the Year.

The Grammy gala was held on February 24 at the Shrine Auditorium in Los Angeles. The hall was packed with stars who René, true to form, identified in a loud voice, overcome with awe. Since it was impossible to award eighty prizes during the televised gala, some had been handed out earlier in the day, including Céline's and Peabo Bryson's Grammy for Theme Song of the Year. They had been up against George Michael and Elton John, Prince and The New Power Generation, Patti Smith and Don Henley.

Céline was becoming better known in the United States. A few days before, she sang at President Bill Clinton's inaugural ball in Washington DC. At the end of January, she appeared on the American Music Awards. But she still didn't believe she could win in any other category. Neither did René. "Being nominated is an achievement in itself," was how he put it.

k.d. Lang won the Grammy for Best Female Singer, and got in a little plug for gays and lesbians. Eric Clapton took home the Best Song and Best Album award for his "Tears in Heaven" and "Unplugged" respectively.

At the end of the ceremony, when the artists who received their awards earlier in the day were asked to come onstage, host Gary Shandling forgot to mention Céline. René was upset and angry. "Let's just be happy with what we've got and forget everything else," said Céline. But they're not the same person. Angélil may not be more ambitious, but he's more easily dissatisfied. Still, he was happy about the Grammy they were taking home. Nothing helps sell a new album or show like an award. Indeed, one week later, on Monday, March 1, the seventy-five thousand tickets to her second Canadian tour (eleven cities, from Toronto to Vancouver) sold out in a few hours.

On March 15, looking worn out and suffering from a cold, Céline was a guest on one of Quebec's most popular television talk shows hosted by Claire Lamarche. For an hour, ninety fans selected at random from the hundreds who lined up outside the studio peppered her with questions: about the stars she'd met, her personal life, her training, the man she loved, her family, the sacrifices she had to make. Someone asked, "What would you have left if you lost your career and your family?" "The flu," she answered.

When the time came to reveal her lover's name, she would shout it from the rooftops. The question became more and more pointed. The lover was none other than René Angélil, people suggested.

For the past five months, ever since Céline's half confession on the Lise Payette show, rumors had been flying thick and fast in the press and on the radio.

When Claire Lamarche's show was broadcast on Thursday, March 18, Céline was in Toronto, barely over her bout of flu. She was rehearsing for the Juno Awards, of which she was to host in a few days.

The yearly ADISQ gala generated much more excitement than the Junos, which reached only 1.5 million viewers from one end of Canada to the other. More than two million watched the ADISQs in Quebec alone. Year in, year out, you could count on the clashes, conflicts and scandals that marked cultural spirit. In Quebec, the ADISQ gala was the most awaited and most controversial event of the year.

Dave Charles was president of the Canadian Academy of Recording Arts and Sciences (CARAS), the organization that staged the Junos. Charles wanted the ceremony, televised by the CBC, to be as successful and to create the same kind of buzz as the ADISQs. When the organizers asked Céline Dion to host the 1993 gala, they knew what they were doing. Only she, who was popular from sea to sea, could bring out a larger audience and bridge the gap between Canada's two cultures. With Céline Dion at the controls, a good many Quebeckers would be drawn to the show. As it was, most of them didn't even know what the Junos were.

Standing behind her glass lectern, she rehearsed her transitions, learned how and when to pick up the director's signals. Everything was stage managed down to the tiniest detail. After the opening song, she was to walk over to the microphone and say, "When I was asked to host the Juno Awards, I was delighted and honored." Then she would pause for an instant and add, "The shock came when they told me it would be all in English." Another pause to give the audience time to laugh.

The day before, rehearsals and a press conference were canceled because of her flu. She stayed in bed, reading and rereading her lines, and changing the words when she felt like it. She asked René to call up the script writers for additional details, or to offer suggestions. She didn't like memorizing a text. Her style was to say things her own way, to master the idea rather than the words.

On Friday, she was ready.

On Saturday afternoon at the O'Keefe Centre, her hair in curlers and a sweatshirt thrown over her shoulders, Céline Dion was still in rehearsal along with the other participants: Leonard Cohen, Barenaked Ladies, Rita MacNeil, Gordon Lightfoot, Anne Murray.

She was in the running in seven categories, an all-time record, twice for Best Song ("With This Tear" and "Beauty and the Beast"), for Best-Selling French-Language Album (*Dion chante Plamondon*), Best Single of the Year ("Beauty and the Beast"), Female Vocalist of the Year and Best Dance Music Recording for "Love Can Move Mountains."

She kicked off the ceremony with a rendition of "Love Can Move Mountains," backed by a high-powered choir, Kaleefah. As host, she quickly won everybody over. She was direct, relaxed, warm and quick to laugh. Her slight accent charmed English Canada. And when she won the Juno for Female Vocalist of the Year, she thanked Angélil and, in her native French, told her parents how much she loved them and thanked her loyal fans from Quebec.

You could see it coming. She'd barely slowed down before trouble reared its ugly head. "When I'm hard at work, what I want is peace and quiet," she told Lise Payette in her television interview. "But I just can't stand being alone and doing nothing. Maybe deep down, I'm afraid of myself." Every time she stopped, even for a day or two, she would start being apprehensive of the fear rising in her. At times like these, it never failed. She would come down with a cold or a sore throat.

On March 30, her twenty-fifth birthday, she traveled to New York with Suzanne Gingue. In three days, she would be singing at the Montreal Forum, and she still had a burning sensation in her throat. She went to see Dr. Riley, her voice coach. Everything was fine, he told her, and prescribed two days of the silent treatment. When she returned in the afternoon, René was waiting for her at Dorval Airport. In the limousine, Céline informed him that, on doctor's orders, she would be keeping quiet for the next two days. Her voice had to be in shape for April 2.

René convinced her to postpone switching off her voice a few hours. He'd reserved a suite at the Four Seasons Hotel and ordered a candlelight dinner for two, accompanied by baroque music. He was nervous and tense. During the meal, he pulled out a small box from his pocket and placed it on the table between them. He told Céline that he loved her deeply, like he'd never loved anyone in his whole life. She opened the box, saw the ring and broke into tears. She understood. At last, their love would be known.

In the coming weeks, René spread the word of their engagement among their closest friends. One spring evening, as he was showing Francine Chaloult the house they'd just bought from his friend Pierre Lacroix, he told her from the top of the broad, sweeping staircase, "This is Céline's and my room, here on the left." On the wall was a huge candid photo of the two of them, looking at each other with broad smiles. "When we saw that photo," René said, "Céline and I decided that we couldn't keep on hiding our love. It was bigger than both of us."

That night, they played four of the songs from the upcoming English-language album for their press attaché, including René's favorite, "The Colour of My Love," which would also be the album title. René was head over heels in love with the song. David Foster originally wrote the song for his wife, and had already turned down several leading singers, including Whitney Houston, Barbra Streisand and Natalie Cole. Angélil kept on insisting until Foster finally gave in, "because Céline is the future," was how he put it.

Céline inaugurated the Théâtre du Forum on April 2, 3 and 4 with songs from *Dion chante Plamondon* and her two English albums, *Unison* and *Céline Dion.* The new configuration had 5,500 seats, making it about the size of the Zénith in Paris. To create a more intimate atmosphere in the Forum, a huge black curtain was stretched across the hall, cutting the amphitheater in half. It had been two years since Céline last appeared on a Montreal stage. She was more eagerly awaited than ever. When tickets went on sale in mid-February, they sold out in less than five hours.

Every night, a different local artist would open the show. The crowd's response, from opening night on, was emotional. When Angélil walked down the center aisle with Barry Garber and Vito Luprano, people stood up and applauded.

Céline herself had worked hard planning and staging the show, which was to be simplicity itself. The introductions to each song would sound like they were improvised. She had her own ideas about the stage set and lighting. No special effects, no blinding lights, no explosions. Nothing but a voice and music. And soul.

"Slowly but surely, the vocal athlete is turning into a singer," wrote *La Presse* critic Alain Brunet. "Her style is much more personal. Céline doesn't have to show who's influenced her or prove how powerful and flexible her voice is."

After "L'Amour existe encore" the audience was on its feet, singing "Happy Birthday to You."

> Singing is what I love best, and the thing that scares me the most. When I'm feeling good, it's like nothing can touch me. But some nights, it's a struggle, against myself, against fear.

The show won praise even from her relentless detractor Sylvain Cormier. The *Le Devoir* writer could only tip his hat at her success. "A voice that carries, the dedication of a football team the night before the Super Bowl and the kind of simplicity that no one can resist for long." She even handled "(You Make Me Feel Like A) Natural Woman," the song the great Aretha Franklin created in 1968, the year of Céline's birth.

But Angélil disagreed with the critics. He didn't like the show. Céline seemed distracted and off balance. She hadn't really touched people deeply, he said. Of course, they applauded. But she hadn't moved them. "She's tired," he said. "I must be pushing her too hard." He was surprised at the good critical reaction, especially in *Le Devoir.*

Céline reassured him. No, she wasn't tired. Physically, she was in top shape, but she was worried. She could see that her niece Karine did not have long to live. The little girl was at the Forum to witness the triumph of her aunt, her friend, her idol. But she was critically weak. Céline sent a limousine to Sainte Justine hospital to pick her up. Karine came escorted by a physician and two nurses. They also carried the two oxygen bottles she was connected to.

A month later, on May 3, 1993, Karine died in Céline's arms. It was early afternoon, and she'd just arrived from London. She hurried to Sainte-Anne-des-Lacs for a shower and a change of clothes, then rushed to the hospital.

René was standing at the foot of the bed. I remember how touching he was — there was nothing he could do. René always knows what to do, but for one of the first times in our life, I saw him helpless and powerless.

Céline went up to Karine. The little girl seemed resigned to die. "I've been waiting for you," she said to Céline. They'd given her morphine. Then she asked to be changed into fresh pajamas. René hurried out, found a clothing store open on Sundays and bought three pairs.

At the hospital, Liette and Céline helped Karine change into her new pajamas. Then Céline took her in her arms, sang "Les Oiseaux du bonheur" and talked to her in a soft voice.

Karine started naming all the things she loved in life. Very specific things: the dinners my mother used to cook, two or three of my songs, the river, her favorite dresses. It was like an inventory, a kind of testament, a list of memories, as if she wanted to take the few beautiful things she'd known in life with her. Then she died. She was sixteen.

There are so many dangers in life, so much illness, so many accidents. We're all like tightrope walkers. Some of us are lucky, some aren't. The high wire snaps, and they fall. That's one of the great mysteries of life: what makes happy and unhappy people different. It's got nothing to do with the quality of a person. It's simply a matter of luck. Pure luck.

My life is a fairy tale, and I know it. I've heard it often enough, believe me. But I know I live in a frightening world where thousands of children die of hunger every day. I saw this program on television, a report by the BBC on Chinese orphanages. There was this little blind girl, and they'd left her to die all alone, behind closed doors. I'll never forget her face and her pain. I don't want to forget. We can't forget.

Every time my period is late, I hope I'll wake up with morning sickness. Then I'll go for a pregnancy test. I see myself telling René I'm pregnant. For the longest time, I was sure I would have a daughter. I could see it all clearly. She comes and sees me on stage as I'm singing. Then I bend down and she jumps into my arms.

But for the last little while, I pictured a boy. I'm older

than I am today; thirty-five, maybe a bit more. He doesn't come onstage. He waits quietly backstage. He's dressed like little boys in Europe, with knee socks and short pants. I go shopping with him, buy him clothing. But he's independent. And whenever he goes away, it breaks my heart.

The *Falling Into You* Tour
Memphis, March 15, 1997

Walking with the King

From atop a bluff, Memphis overlooks the Mississippi, the river that's inspired as many songs as the Seine or the Danube. The city is located on Route 66, the highway celebrated by generations of bluesmen and folksingers, rock and rollers, beatniks and hippies. For millions of men and women, Memphis, where Elvis Presley was born and now lies buried, is a place of myth and legend.

On March 14 and 15, 1997, Céline sang two nights at the Mid-South Coliseum in Memphis. She often thought of Elvis. She even had a gold costume made, like the outfits he wore at the end of his career. She wanted to sing one of his songs, but there wasn't enough time to rehearse it with the band. A new backup singer, Julie Leblanc, had just joined the team, and Céline wanted to spend a few hours working with her. As well, in Memphis, they would be taping a major network television special.

But she talked about Elvis. Or rather about her husband's passion for the King. "I feel like he's part of the family, that he's like a big brother I barely knew, but who inspires the people around me."

It is just before "Declaration of Love," the most spectacular, the most physical of the show's nineteen songs. Céline moves from one end of the stage to the other, pulls André Coutu and his guitar over to Mégo's piano, then sits down and finishes the song on her knees.

When I sing, I get an extraordinary physical pleasure. They say that once you've felt that pleasure and that power in your life, it's not easy to do without it. It hit me for the first time when I was so young I can barely remember. For me, singing is as simple as breathing. It's my whole life.

After the show, they visit Graceland. Overcome with emotion, Eric and René pause in front of the grave where the King was buried a few years before. But Céline isn't overly impressed by Presley. She knows his records, of course. She has seen the films, some of which were real turkeys. She's also seen his last Las Vegas shows on video three or four times. She likes his voice, his songs, the way he moves onstage. But she doesn't have René's gut feeling for him.

More than once, René has told her that Colonel Parker, whom he's met several times, compared her with Elvis for the way she could "get in touch" with people.

When I was in Graceland, I could only imagine how someone could be so totally unconnected with reality. And I wondered what had gone wrong. For all his money and glory, the King didn't know how to be happy. What about me? Will I be able to stay happy? Could I lose my sense of values, of friendship and love in this weird world I live in?

Elvis also loved his mother deeply. It was his mother's image that Céline searched for in the baroque castle they called home. What had Grace looked like? Was she happy, proud of her son, as proud as Thérèse and Adhémar are of their daughter?

Chapter Twenty-Nine
True Love Revealed

At twenty-five, Céline was in full bloom. Her talent was hers to wield. She knew the power and richness of her voice. She was rich, admired and wild about fashion. Her closet held four hundred pairs of shoes, from Clergerie to Kelian by way of Versace. Not to mention the high-fashion outfits from designers such as Dolce & Gabbana, Alaïa, Yamamoto. She loved working on her look almost as much as on her voice.

> My mouth is too small. My lips are too thin, my nose is too large. One of my eyebrows is thicker and lower than the other. I wish I had a squarer face, teeth like Chiclets and bigger breasts. I like my hair, my legs. I hear I've got a nice back.

Whenever she had a spare moment, she would drift away into her daydreams. In her mind's eye, she would picture all kinds of situations: her wedding, her funeral.

> I dream up costumes to match the event. Right down to the smallest detail. I want to look like a princess all dressed in white, with a crown. I'd like to have full control of my body, my face, my image, in every part of my life, right till the end.

> One day a journalist asked me what I would like God to say when I go to heaven. I told him that the only thing I wanted was for Him to look at me like my mother does, without a word. And for his eyes to tell me that everything's better than perfect. And for Him to tell me, "I'm proud of you, my child."
>
> She'd like the Lord to be her fan. Her number one fan.

Céline was in New York recording "The Colour of Love" when she got the urge to change her look. The urge was overpowering. Ever since she was a little girl, she'd worn her hair long. In 1987, when the great metamorphosis took place, she'd cut off only a few inches. Today, she was sick of that flowing mane that took two hours to prepare for every show, irritating sprays, new Velcro rollers every day and endless backcombing sessions.

Angélil's daughter knew the fashion world inside out, all the models, the hairdressers and the makeup artists. She tipped Céline off about Fréderic Fekkai, whose Fifth Avenue salon was one of the most stylish — and expensive — in the world. A simple haircut ran between $250 and $300.

Fekkai spent an hour casually exploring Céline's hair with his fingers. He looked her over, stepped back, turned away, came back, circled her. He talked to her about Paris, Key West and an off-Broadway show he'd attended a few days earlier. Finally, he suggested that she change the color of her hair slightly. And change her style radically.

When he came up to her, scissors in hand, it was all Céline could do not to pull back. For the first time in twenty years, as far back as she could remember, she was going to have short hair. She had a nasty case of the jitters. But no sooner did the first locks fall than she felt relief, and a strange sense of liberation. Immediately, she liked her new hairstyle for the sheer look of it and the surprise it would create, but also because she could adapt it more easily to her state of mind. And it would always be easy to handle, quick and comfortable.

How would the fans react? She tried to imagine herself through their eyes. What would they think, what would they say? René was always telling her not to try to satisfy everybody. There would always be people who would claim that short hair made her face harder, that with a chin like hers, she'd be better off with long, curly hair that would soften her features. Others would insist that with a long face like hers, she should never have worn her hair long in the first place.

> I'd be lying if I told you that René's opinion is the one that matters most to me when it comes to my hairstyle and my clothes. Of course, I want to be beautiful and desirable for him, but I know that sometimes, the things I want to wear surprise him, or even shock him. We've had plenty of arguments about my dresses or my hairstyles. I finally learned how to stand up to him. I know him. He'll end up liking what I've made up my mind to wear. And when René likes what I'm wearing, I'm happy.

Céline's first public appearance with her new look was at the Capitole in Quebec City. It was for the taping of a special show, directed by Tony Greco, that was to be broadcast in December by CTV and in February by Disney. The sets were pure Hollywood. Greco's cameras taped two full shows that included scenes from "Ce n'était qu'un rêve" and location shots in the streets of Quebec City's picturesque old town.

The program was a portrait of the artist and a show rolled into one. The whole thing had been worked out down the last detail by Angélil and the people from Sony, along with Disney. The show featured five songs from her upcoming album plus two already famous duets, "Beauty and the Beast" and "When I Fall in Love." And, to wind it up, Elvis Presley's "Can't Help Falling in Love." It was a song she'd always liked, a song that, months later, would be the cause of an astonishing encounter.

Since she'd stopped accompanying her daughter on her promotional campaigns and tours, Thérèse Dion was at a loss. She'd always been a busy, active woman. Now she was forced to rest, and it didn't agree with her. One day, her son Paul suggested she market her meat pies. In the seventies, Thérèse Dion's meat pies were famous in Charlemagne and Repentigny. The kids delivered them, hot or cold, to the employees of the community grocery store. They became so popular that Mrs. Dion couldn't meet the demand, even with the help of her daughters and sons. In 1981, she left the kitchen behind to travel with Céline. For the next five years, she spent most of her time with her daughter. But now she was bored silly.

Paul set up a company with links to Maple Leaf Foods, one of Canada's largest distributors, to market Mrs. Dion's meat pies.

On Thursday, November 4, in the magnificent Art Deco restaurant that occupied the top floor of Eaton's department store in downtown Montreal, Mama Dion launched her line of meat pies. All fourteen children were on hand, not to mention the press. An hour later, Céline flew off to Toronto, where she was to meet CBS to plan the launch of her upcoming album.

The following Monday, at the Métropolis, she launched her third album in English, *The Colour of My Love*. During the event, Jean Lamothe and Eric Burrows stepped into Céline Dion's life to stay. Lamothe took over record promotion from Mario Lefebvre. From then on, he would be handling requests from radio station record librarians, singles launches and keeping the record stores stocked. Eric Burrows was appointed Céline's full-time bodyguard. They met when Madonna sang a few days earlier at Montreal's Olympic Stadium. René reserved seats in the first row for Céline and himself and all their friends. His pal Donald Tarlton, who was producing Madonna's show, suggested that he ask Eric Burrows, who would be looking after stage security during the show, to do the same for Céline. In shows like theirs, a lot of jostling in the first few rows was the norm.

Eric knew Céline from way back, though he really hadn't paid much attention to her work. He preferred urban music, rhythm and blues and soul. As far as he was concerned, Céline Dion wasn't all that popular. But when she walked into the stadium, there was a huge ovation that lasted until she sat down. People got up from their seats and tried to get close to her, crowding in until she was surrounded. That's when Eric stepped in. Gently but firmly, he guided everyone back to their seats.

Two days later, René called and asked him to handle security for Céline's launch at the Métropolis. Eric accepted with pleasure. A few minutes later, René called back to ask, all peaches and cream, "Eric, do you have a suit?" He wanted his artist's bodyguard looking sharp. Madonna's bodyguards wore jeans, and nothing matched. René Angélil wanted a well-dressed man for Céline, with a tie if possible. Eric didn't give him a straight answer. He only laughed and said, "Don't worry, you'll like what you see."

It so happened that Eric loves fine clothes. When he was a teenager, he drove his mother crazy shopping at the most fashionable stores.

On November 8, at four o'clock in the afternoon when he joined Céline's entourage at the Four Seasons Hotel, Eric Burrows was wearing a custom-tailored suit, a perfectly pressed shirt and a tie. He sat down beside the chauffeur of the limousine as it drove east along St. Catherine Street to the Métropolis. Inside, people were in such a dither that they hardly noticed Céline's arrival. At seven o'clock, they opened the doors and let in the first two thousand who were waiting in line. The atmosphere was electrifying, even explosive.

The event, once again emceed by Sonia Benezra, was broadcast live on MusiquePlus and Télévision Quatre-Saisons, and on four Montreal radio stations. Télé-Métropole was out of the picture now. A handful of producers had made a behind-the-scenes reconciliation attempt, but ever since their quarrel two years earlier, René was determined that Céline wouldn't talk to the private network. The first questions came from Benezra, then Véronique Cloutier and Philippe Fehmiu, from TQS and MusiquePlus. Then she had a short, live conversation with David Foster, who was sitting in his living room in Los Angeles. He repeated his now-classic words: "Céline is the future."

A lot of people already had the album. Six of its fifteen titles featured the word "love." But what caught their attention wasn't the song titles or the credits. Céline had written a long list of acknowledgments, thanking all the people who had inspired her, supported her, helped her along. In French, she wrote, "To mom, to dad, to my sisters and brothers ... I love you with all my heart." They were followed by the words that finally revealed, in the most explicit way, that she was in love with René Angélil. "René, for so many years I've kept our special dream locked away inside my heart. But now, it's too powerful to keep inside me. So after all these years, let me 'paint the truth, show how I feel, try to make you completely real'... René, you're the colour of my love. L.V."

There was much speculation on what those two letters L.V. meant. Céline and René never said a word. Las Vegas? No. 55 in Roman numerals?

> It's our secret. Not that it's anything important. But it stands for something.

The night *The Colour of My Love* was launched, she announced that she was going to marry René Angélil. It had become an open secret, but her confession had an impact. People in the Métropolis were touched. At last, life and her songs were coming together.

She sang seven of the album's fifteen love songs, including "The Colour of My Love." The song ended with a thunderous ovation, with her in the arms of her man. With the final chords, Angélil stepped onto the stage and walked over to her. A tear slid down her cheek. She wiped it away. Then she took Angélil's chin in her left hand and kissed him on the mouth. Shouting and applause erupted, and the giant screen showed the kiss in close-up. It was almost as if they were married that night at the Métropolis in front of 2,500 guests and viewers from two television networks.

That same night, they left for Toronto. The next day, Céline kicked off an all-out promotion campaign that was to last through the Christmas holidays. The idea was to present her new album, but on *The Tonight Show*, on *Good Morning America* and on *The Arsenio Hall Show*, she seemed to prefer talking about the man in her life. "He made all my dreams come true, and now he's my lover." The conquest that had taken her so many years was the greatest of her life.

But her life was no longer her own. The territory she'd conquered was so huge that she had to keep traveling to keep it under control. That meant traveling to every corner of the world — from amphitheaters to television studios, from galas to movie sets — and at a pace most normal people couldn't match but that Céline Dion thrived on. Movement gave her that sensuous feeling of being fully, marvelously alive, deeply in love and in the thick of life.

In mid-November, Céline was in New York. She was there to tape "The Power of Love." The clip, set in a Victorian townhouse in the West Village, not far from SoHo, was to be directed by Randee St. Nicholas, who'd worked with Prince and Whitney Houston.

On November 21, direct from Eurodisney, near Paris, she cohosted a Disney special with Gloria Estefan in California and the Kriss Kross duo in Tokyo. On November 23, it was back to the Capitole in Quebec City. And on December 3, after an early morning appearance on *Canada AM*, she guested on the *Shirley Show* at one o'clock. At 11:30 that night she was at the other end of the continent, appearing for the ninth time on *The Tonight Show*, where she sang "The Power of Love."

The following week, in addition to taping the "Misled" video, she participated in the "David Foster Christmas Special" with Julio Iglesias, Natalie Cole and Johnny Mathis.

Less than two weeks after it hit the stores, *The Colour of My Love* had gone triple platinum in Canada and five times platinum in the USA. In France, "Ziggy" from *Dion chante Plamondon* topped the charts. The ballad (the romantic story of a naive young girl desperately in love with a boy "who isn't like other boys") was getting a far better reception than "Je danse dans ma tête," a heavy rock number with powerful words, one of Plamondon's favorites. *Dion chante Plamondon* was Céline's ticket back to the top of the hit parade in France after an absence of nearly ten years, dating back to "D'amour ou d'amitié."

On February 14, 1994, Sony announced that *The Colour of My Love*, which had already sold more than a million albums in the US and was a six-time platinum in Canada, would be distributed in Europe and the world. Her song "The Power of Love" had been on top of the charts for three weeks when, on the nineteenth, Céline sang it on *The Jackson Family Honors* special taped at the MGM Grand in Las Vegas and broadcast a few days later by NBC. Michael Jackson, Janet Jackson and the Jackson Five paid tribute to Elizabeth Taylor and Berry Gordy, president and founder of Motown records. The spectators had paid between $500 and $1,000 to watch the taping, with all profits going to the victims of the Los Angeles earthquake.

Céline Dion was in demand. In the US, France and Canada, there wasn't a gala she wasn't invited to. To finance his operations, Angélil no longer had to beat the bushes for sponsors. More and more, people wanted the names of their companies and products associated with Céline Dion. Her 1994 Canadian tour (thirty concerts in eighteen cities) was sponsored by Procter & Gamble. Sponsorship and marketing strategy now became an additional responsibility for Barry Garber.

Angélil also plunged into merchandising, a side of the show business industry he'd neglected. The idea was to have total control over the artist's name and image. Dave Platel took over this task and set up a company called Five Star to market Céline T-shirts, lighters, caps, jackets, signed photos, programs and other fan memorabilia.

In early March, Céline was singing to sold-out crowds at Toronto's O'Keefe Centre. Critics compared her to Ethel Merman for her drive, her "brash power and bravado," to Whitney Houston for her range and the strength of her voice, and to Michael Bolton for "the *faux* emotionalism." Once the show was under way, Céline would turn to the crowd and say, "You and me, we understand each other. We ought to go on tour together." It was her way of showing how at home she felt. She'd come a long way from the awkward, strangely attired girl who, only two and a half short years before, had been the opening act for Michael Bolton's show.

Now she had a way of moving onstage that was hers alone. She always held the mike in her left hand. During the musical transitions, she sometimes imitated a guitar or a saxophone player, beating time with broad movements. It was as if she were directing the music, the lighting, driving the whole machine. Before a tough passage, she would take up position on stage, spread her legs apart, strike her chest with her right hand, throw her head back, her body arched backward as far as it could go.

Her songs may have all revolved around one single theme, love, but musically, her repertoire was more diversified than ever. She sang inspirational songs like "The Power of Love," "Think Twice," "Refuse to

Dance" and "With This Tear" that could touch an older, more romantically inclined audience and at the same time, shake up the youngsters who weren't drawn to romanticism. Then she would swing into breathless dance numbers like "Misled" or "Everybody's Talking My Baby Down" that would have people up and dancing, even if they'd never set foot in a discotheque or at least not since the days of the BeeGees and *Saturday Night Fever*. CBS, which had just been taken over by Sony, was delighted. Céline's public was becoming broader and younger than it was two or three years before. Using her charisma, she brought together different audiences.

In Toronto, Halifax and all across English Canada in that spring 1994 *Colour of My Love* tour, she sang two Plamondon songs in French: "L'Amour existe encore" and "Je danse dans ma tête." Back in Montreal in late March and early April, she gave six sold-out concerts. Two thirds of her songs were in English. When she finished "Can't Help Falling in Love," the Forum crowd was on its feet, ecstatic, just like at the O'Keefe Centre in Toronto.

Particularly in Quebec, where she was now an icon, her shows were more like love-ins. She called her fans "my loves." At the Forum Theater, where everyone in the crowd (5,500 per show for six shows) knew all the details of her life, she opened her show with "Ce n'était qu'un rêve," the song written by her mother who was seated in the fifth row every night. Céline sat at the edge of the stage as she sang. For the love songs, she turned toward René. It wasn't a show anymore but an exhibition of love.

In Céline and René's entourage, there was more talk of marriage. The wedding would take place in late summer, or early fall. Now they could be frank and open about their love affair. It's rare, even in the world of show business, to see people wearing their hearts on their sleeves, to see lovers publicly discussing their passions. In Quebec more than anywhere else, people had been waiting, predicting, prognosticating. When the love that had been so painfully and carefully concealed was finally revealed, Céline's image rose to new heights. At last she could live her life on her own terms.

Angélil turned out to be wrong. He was concerned that people would think they were a mismatched couple. Quite the opposite happened. People quickly warmed to Céline and René. In music and in life, Céline Dion had made love fashionable again.

From April 21 to May 6, 1994, she traveled to Japan accompanied by René, Dave Platel and Barry Garber. There she sang in Tokyo and Osaka as part of a tribute to producer David Foster. It was a country she always adored. It was so clean, so polite, so orderly, with the rituals and the ceremonies she picked up intuitively, with their beauty and grandeur. She may not have been a religious person, but she believed in reincarnation. Every time she set foot in the land of the rising sun, she felt as if she'd lived another life there, in the age of the samurais and the geishas.

"The Japanese can't get enough of Céline," said Dave Platel. "There's a connection between the two, in her shows and in everyday life. They like her honesty and her simplicity. She makes them laugh when she blurts out the questions that pop into her head."

At a banquet one evening, she brought the conversation around to the traditional Japanese dress. Several women finally escorted her to the restroom to show her how the kimono was worn. She insisted on learning all the details, the undergarments, the ceremony, the preparations, everything. She even took the ritual hot bath. An hour later, she returned, her hair combed, her face powdered, wearing a magnificent kimono. For the rest of the evening, she did her best to imitate the other women.

Japan was in her pocket. Angélil's plan was to move forward, one country at a time, establishing solid contacts wherever they went, creating friendly ties with Sony, the media and the record and show business industry. When they finally conquered a new territory, worked hard to entrench themselves for the long haul.

The *Falling Into You* Tour
Las Vegas, August 23, 1996

Love Song

From satellites orbiting five hundred miles above the Earth, Las Vegas is the brightest city on the face of the planet. At night, it's like a radiant diamond glistening in the dark velvet setting of the Nevada desert. In the summer when the weather is too hot, people play baseball and softball at night. Parks are open until two or three o'clock in the morning. It's a town made for night owls, for gambling and show business — a perfect place for Angélil and Céline.

The dry desert air grates on the voice. Céline has installed humidifiers in each room of their immense apartment at the top floor of Caesar's Palace, "the most beautiful suite I've ever seen," Angélil says.

You'd swear it is a Venetian palazzo. Marble everywhere, colonnades, huge potted plants, a terrace with a pool and a putting green, an immense kitchen with a six-burner gas stove and a refrigerator with a transparent glass door.

It's after midnight. René's gone down to the casino where he'll spend most of the night at the gaming tables. He'll return dangerously exhausted. Céline and her mother are alone. They make tomato and lettuce sandwiches with mayonnaise. Mrs. Dion is telling her daughter stories about her childhood in Saint-Bernard-des-Lacs — the trout stream, blueberry picking time, the pine grove where her brothers would trap wild hare. Wrapped in a long white peignoir, Céline dreams of the countryside her mother is describing. How far it is from her world, how much farther from Angélil's. Laughing until tears come to their eyes, they imagine him fishing, tending the garden or setting traps.

How can the same man, René Angélil, gamble tens of thousands of dollars and still stoop to pick up small change, rubber bands and paper clips from the street? "I do the same thing," Mrs. Dion says. "I respect money. It means work, time, the effort that someone, somewhere, has put in. Finding money in the street is good luck. Anyway, I always pick up whatever I can. When my father saw two sticks of wood forming a cross, he would set them down respectfully in a safe place where their order would be protected. In today's world you don't see things lying around anymore, you never see things like that, two sticks making a cross."

Mother and daughter spend most of the night chitchatting in the kitchen. When they finish their snack, they put everything back where it belongs. There's a sumptuous living room in the suite and a wide balcony overlooking the great, scintillating lake of light that is Las Vegas. "But for talking," says Céline, "you can't beat a kitchen."

Manon leaves dozens of programs and photos that the fans bring after the show for Céline to sign. By now, her signature is famous: you see it on T-shirts, caps and other objects. They're the brain child of Manon Robillard, who handles merchandising when they're on tour, and coordinates sales to the fans in the halls and amphitheaters where Céline sings. The signature is also on the huge red, rear-lit poster that's visible at the far end of the strip advertising Céline's show at Caesar's Palace.

The Circus Maximus at Caesar's Palace, with its vivid red-and-gold-leaf decor, can accommodate nearly two thousand people. The audience is usually diverse and cosmopolitan, but tonight it's full of Quebeckers. There are journalists, winners of a trip to Las Vegas contest and personal friends of Angélil's, here on an all-expenses-paid few days in the world's gambling capital.

One of the photos is from a session in Paris last fall. Céline's hair was short, and her face rounder than it is today. "It's one of my favorites," she tells her mother. "Every time I look at this photo, I imagine I'm pregnant." There's something peaceful and reassuring in her languid look, the kind of serenity you often see in pregnant women.

She knows that when she's up against Las Vegas, she can't win. Every time they set foot here, René pushes himself to the limit. If he wins, he wants to win more. If he looses, he wants another shot. But he loves the life, the surroundings, this legendary place where the King lived, where Sinatra, Minelli and Streisand sang.

Angélil has a real passion for his job and great respect for people who do the same thing. He reveres two managers above all others: Brian Epstein, who discovered the Beatles, and the legendary Colonel Thomas A. Parker, who developed Elvis Presley's talent and guided his career. He's read everything he can about them. Another of his favorites is Mike Ovitz, the man once known as Hollywood's greatest agent. Ovitz was the founder of the Creative Artists Agency (CAA), representing people like Steven Spielberg, Robert de Niro, Robert Redford, Sylvester Stallone — and Céline Dion.

Angélil adores these tales of the titans — their meteoric rises, their crashing falls. He feels at home in their world. He's drawn by power, success and the people who create them. He likes well-planned careers, hard bargaining. He tracks negotiations with an eagle eye, like sporting events, pouncing on the hard hits, the errors, the dodges.

Brian Epstein had the manager's instinct. He died young, leaving behind him one of the century's greatest accomplishments: the Beatles. But, according to Angélil, he made mistakes. He sold their rights in the United States for peanuts because he didn't believe his artists would have such international success. Colonel Parker made Elvis the best-known artist of the century, but he also misdirected the King's career. He could have brought him to the top, but Elvis never reached his full potential because he was unable to leave his country. Colonel Parker did nothing to encourage him to grow. People say that Parker himself couldn't leave the United States. It's possible that he committed a crime in Holland, the country of his birth.

The challenge for any manager who's brought his artist to the top is to keep that artist there. Harder still is to keep him happy, to keep him from cracking, to make sure he doesn't turn into an antisocial monster.

Angélil knew he held a priceless treasure in his hands. "I knew it right away, from the first day I met Céline," he says. "I could tell she had an extraordinary voice. I found out that she was as determined as they come, that she had a desire, a need to sing. And heart. Lots of heart."

August 1987 marked the tenth anniversary of Elvis Presley's death. Colonel Parker set up guided tours of the singer's suite at the Las Vegas Hilton. He'd turned it into a museum of sorts, with a souvenir display, photographs, guitars and a selection of the King's costumes. A ticket cost $5.

Back then, Angélil was spending most of his free time in Las Vegas. With his pals Marc Verreault and Ben Kaye, who had a camera, he went over to the Hilton. Under heavy pressure from Kaye, the elderly Colonel finally agreed to have his picture taken with each of them. Once the ice was broken, Kaye told the old man that Angélil was also the manager of a great artist. "The next Barbra Streisand," he tacked on.

The Colonel cut him short. "Let me tell you something, son. Never compare your artist with anybody else. Don't ever say she's surpassed this one or that one, and don't ever claim that she'll take their place. There'll never be another Barbra Streisand. Your singer will be your singer and no one else. She won't even be the one you want her to be. Let her be herself. It's her best chance to succeed."

Angélil never forgot the lesson. He never again compared Céline with anyone. His job was to help her become what she wanted to be. He would do it by leaving her totally free. A few years later, he repaid Elvis's manager in kind.

Fast forward to spring 1994. Ben Kaye, who was now working closely with Angélil, got a call at the Feeling Productions office in Laval from someone who claimed to be the illustrious Colonel himself. The man said he wanted to talk to René Angélil. Thinking it was a practical joke at first, Kaye did some serious checking before even trying to reach René, who was out playing golf. Finally he was able to confirm that the Colonel had gotten the Feeling phone number from Mel Ilberman, who used to work at RCA, Elvis's record company. Ilberman now worked for Sony, Céline's producers. And just why did the great man want to speak to Angélil? "Because he saw the television special at the Capitole in Quebec City," Ilberman answered. Céline wound up the show with a song that Elvis had made famous, "Can't Help Falling in Love," with its sad melody and touching words. It was a great song that touched people's hearts, and Céline had sung it with shattering intensity.

It was after eight o'clock when Ben Kaye finally got in touch with Angélil, and midnight, Montreal time, when he made up his mind to call the colonel back.

The Colonel told him how fascinated he was by Céline's voice, her eyes, her movements, her stage presence, her charisma, and by the way she could communicate with the crowd.

"I'd like to meet her," he said to Angélil. "Are you ever in Las Vegas?"

Angélil probably felt more at home in Las Vegas than anywhere else in the world. Since 1970, he'd been there several times a year. He's spent thousands of hours playing blackjack, throwing the dice, at the roulette wheel, defying luck, trying to beat it.

They set up a meeting for the following week. Along with Marc Verreault and Ben Kaye, the same two who'd accompanied him on his pilgrimage to the King's suite at the Hilton a decade before, he showed up at the Colonel's house in a Las Vegas suburb. It was a sprawling ranch house surrounded by a cactus and yucca garden. He still remembers the long corridor with its walls covered with photos of Elvis. The Colonel had aged in seven years. He came up to them in a wheelchair, a plaid blanket on his lap. He didn't recognize them.

They followed him into a spacious living room where the spirit of Elvis seemed to be everywhere. There were photos, guitars, gold records.

He told them about his good and bad deals. About the money he'd demanded for one Elvis show or another. Cash, cash, cash. Angélil was disappointed, even a little shocked. When it came to money, he was close-mouthed and was a hard bargainer. That was his job; that was the game, the rules. But once the deal was closed, there was no more talk of money. It was vulgar, and it could bring bad luck. He wanted the Colonel to talk about Elvis, about the way he lived, what he ate for breakfast, and about his job, the manager's job.

Then the Colonel turned to Angélil. "I saw your Céline's show the other day. Let me tell you one thing, my boy: you've got yourself the future Barbra Streisand there." Angélil reminded him of the lesson he'd given them seven years before. Suddenly the Colonel remembered their meeting. Turning to Ben Kaye, whom he recognized as the man who wanted to take the photos, he said, "Did you bring me the pictures, at least?"

Kaye had the pictures. The Colonel took a long, hard look at the photo of him and Angélil taken in 1987. It showed the two men standing side by side, smiling. The Colonel was already an old man, a bit stooped. Angélil was at his prime, thinner than he was today. Then he raised his head with a grin and threw Angélil a salute. It was as if he was paying tribute to a brother.

Viva Las Vegas!

Chapter Thirty
Leave it to Chance

In the early nineties, three graduates of Tokyo's top music schools formed a jazz combo called Krysler & Company. It didn't take long for the group to catch on with the devoted jazz fans who hung out in Japan's big city clubs. But their manager Robi Wada was looking for a way to introduce them to the public at large.

In Japan, the best way to catch the public's eye is to appear on a television miniseries. Wada had excellent contacts at Fuji Television, one of the country's (if not the world's) largest multimedia consortiums. Prime time shows drew as many as 50 million viewers. In the spring of 1994, Fuji was putting the finishing touches to a TV series that told a heartbreaking love story. Everybody was predicting that *Koi Bitoyo* would smash all ratings records. Robby Wada made up his mind that the music of Krysler & Company would be a part of it.

Unfortunately for him and his trio, the producers didn't want a simple instrumental theme. They were looking for a song sung by a great voice that would bring the program alive. They wanted something flamboyant and romantic.

Wada wasn't the only one in the race. The cream of the Tokyo crop — producers, agents, musicians, songwriters, composers and interpreters — were scrambling for the perfect song, a glorious mix of words and music. And most of all, the voice that would carry it all. He thought of Mariah Carey, of course. But she was too big a star. It probably wouldn't work. She was too expensive, too busy. Ditto for Gloria Estefan. It could only be worse for people like Whitney Houston or Barbra Streisand.

Then Wada thought of Céline Dion, a rising star who just might be interested in hitching a ride on the *Koi Bitoyo* rocket ship. She had power, and the rich, smooth texture of her voice would blend in perfectly with the violin of Taro Hakase, one of the members of the trio. Someone had the idea of writing a duet for voice and violin. For a couple of days, Wada couldn't get the idea out of his mind.

He got in touch with Sony-Japan which forwarded his query to Sony-Canada. They in turn called René Angélil. But he had other irons in the fire, decisions to make, people to see, problems to solve. Céline Dion's career was taking off.

The Colour of My Love had topped the six-platinum plateau in Canada and passed the two million mark in the US. Now it was coming out in England, Holland and Germany. A new promotion campaign had to be orchestrated, show producers and television broadcasters had to be dealt with. In France too, people wanted Céline. *Des mots qui sonnent* was still so strong that Angélil made up his mind to hold off bringing out her new English album. "The Power of Love" was dominating the charts. Céline Dion's name had become magic. You could hear her voice everywhere. One night, you saw her on stage at the MGM Grand in Las Vegas with Michael and Janet Jackson, and two days later you could catch her in Paris or London.

How was Angélil supposed to evaluate all these proposals from television stations and producers? A manager's job consists of making choices. Just like any creative artist. The writer has more words than he can possibly use, the painter his paints, lines and forms. The manager can pick and choose the songs his artist will sing, the interviews he'll give, the shows he'll participate in, the causes he'll support. When he checked, Wada was told that Céline Dion's manager had gotten his proposal, but that he should be patient. Above all, don't be in a rush. He kept his hopes high.

One night, in the taxi carrying him home from the office, he read an article in *Time* about the divas of pop — one of whom was Céline Dion. He got a sinking feeling. A singer who gets talked about in one of the most influential international magazines wouldn't be interested in doing a song with an unknown, especially if the song didn't even exist.

"Too late," he said to himself. "She's in the big leagues now, like Houston, Streisand and their kind." The negotiations would be horribly complicated, probably impossible. But he kept on reading the article that spoke so positively of the young Canadian singer. He learned that she'd been born in 1968 in a small town in the Montreal suburbs, the last of fourteen children. She'd been a star in her own country since age thirteen. A few lines down, the article mentioned her manager and husband René Angélil. Wada closed the magazine, then opened it again.

"René Angélil! Why, I know that guy!" he said to himself.

There was a photo that showed Angélil beside the star. His cheeks were fuller, his hair a bit thinner. But it was the same man who'd accompanied the teenage Canadian singer who won the second Yamaha World Song Festival. Wada remembered everything. He was a young producer at the time, involved with the organization of the Tokyo festival. He met all the winners, and even shook hands with Frank Sinatra, the guest of honor.

But that meeting had taken place more than twenty years before. And even though Wada was in close touch with Western culture, as a businessman, he respected protocol and hierarchy. In Japan, companies do business, not individuals. It's not easy to call on friendship when you're negotiating a deal.

He made up his mind to let things take their course. He was told once more that his proposal had been passed on by Sony. But Angélil hadn't responded yet. Either he didn't like the trio's music, or he hadn't listened to it.

There was a surprise waiting for Wada a few days later. An advertisement in *Asahi Shimbun* revealed that Céline Dion was on her way to Japan. She would be at the Budokan theater on May 6, accompanied by a full orchestra directed by Canadian musician, David Foster.

That night, Wada was in the audience at the Budokan. After the show, he went backstage, met Angélil, reminded him who he was, and described how he had tried to get in touch.

"Why didn't you call me?" Angélil exclaimed.

"It just isn't done," said Wada. "Not in Japan, anyway."

Even though they hit it off wonderfully, the two men were poles apart, culturally speaking. Angélil thrived on direct, personal contact. Over the past fifteen years, he'd labored to set up a network of contacts. Unlike Wada and most of the people in Japanese show business, he knew the Sony reps in every country, from top to bottom. An album by Céline was never launched if he hadn't created ties with people in that particular country.

But that wasn't the last of Wada's surprises. David Foster, who directed the Tokyo Orchestra that accompanied Céline that evening, had been contacted by Fuji to write the *Koi Bitoyo* theme song. He'd already thought of a few melodies he could use for the duet.

A few hours later, in a suite at the Capitol Tokyu hotel, Céline, René and Wada listened to a cassette with the music of Krysler & Company. Céline really liked the sound and the rich harmonies of Taro Hakase's violin. The next day, René asked Foster to listen to the cassette. He immediately sat down and wrote the song in which voice and violin respond to one another.

Céline's voice and Taro's violin made a splendid combination. Ironically, the words were written by a competitor, a close friend of David Foster's, Montreal multimillionaire Edgar Bronfman Jr. Bronfman was the CEO of Universal, which owned MCA, Sony's rival in the record business. Under the name of Junior Miles, he wrote the words to "To Love You More," a song that became a colossal success in Japan, then around the world.

The *Falling Into You* Tour
Montreal, December 17, 1996

Her People

The cameramen who provide the pictures for the onstage screens know the show by heart. Every note of music, Céline's every move, every lighting effect. It's barely changed for months. At first they had trouble following her onstage. She wasn't sure of her steps, her movements and words. But as time passed, everything fell naturally into place. Now the show is a well-oiled machine, a piece of precision clockwork that never loses a second.

Just for fun, Lapin plays three different recordings on the monitors. The cameramen and the technical crew watch closely. In most of the songs, Céline's movements are perfectly synchronized. The same moves at the exact same moment.

But there are times when she departs from the norm, when she's tired or nervous, for instance. In Montreal, every show is different; you never know what's going to happen. It's as if Céline wants to rediscover the confusion, the innocence, the vulnerability of old times, to be herself, in this city more than anywhere else. It's like two people in love who meet after a long separation. There's always a sense of the unknown, the tantalizing shyness.

You could argue that, in purely technical terms, the show is not as good in Montreal as elsewhere. There are flubs and mistakes. Between songs, Céline sometimes struggles for words. But there's also a directness, a warmth, a sense of intimacy, a spirit you can't find anywhere else. In

Montreal, everyone is always on pins and needles, and rarely completely satisfied. There's always the feeling that things could have been better, more magical, without mistakes or foul-ups.

At the Molson Centre on the night of December 17, 1996, the cameramen are having trouble keeping up with Céline. Her moves aren't the same. They are more abrupt, less rounded. Denis Savage picks up a note of nervousness in her voice.

Before the show there'd been a tense press conference. For the first time, Céline had snapped back at journalists who asked her questions she didn't like, questions she'd answered time and time again. For years, Mia had been urging her on. "Too nice is not nice," she told her. "Don't try to make the journalists happy. Be yourself. Say what you think, what you feel and not what you think they want to hear. Don't let them put words in your mouth."

Too often, the interview game boiled down to putting the other guy in an untenable situation where he would reveal a hidden aspect of himself. Céline had played that little game often enough.

"You're on top," Mia added. "Your job is to make people dream. To give young people the urge to go further, try harder. Everybody knows you're all sugar and spice. So stay on top where you belong. If you think no, say no."

The first question she fielded was about the age difference between her and René. "Are you looking for your father through him?" She answered that she saw no reason to look for another father, that she already had one, that his name was Adhémar Dion, and she loved him dearly. And if she was René Angélil's wife, it was because she loved him. "I just listen to my heart, it's as simple as that. Through René, I'm looking for happiness. That's all."

The journalist was booed. Then a little girl not more than ten years old stepped up to the mike, and in front of the entire Montreal press corps, proclaimed that she wanted to be a great singer. Then she asked Céline, "Would you be jealous if I became a greater singer than you?" People applauded. Céline gave a long answer. She wasn't in competition with anyone but herself.

It's true. I don't believe in competition. Every singer has her own voice. Sure, there are things you can measure. The number of albums sold, for instance. But that doesn't mean that the singer who sells the largest number of albums is the best. I'm in competition with myself. Barbra Streisand hardly gives any shows. She sells fewer records than Mariah Carey, Alanis Morissette, Whitney Houston or me. But in my opinion, she's the greatest singer in the world. Because she's the one who can control her voice the best, who can use it to communicate emotions, not only her own but those that are in the music and the words she sings.

Then mementos were handed out, and a mass of people gathered in front of her dressing room. Just before going onstage, she asked to be left alone for a few moments. She and René strolled around the backstage area. The show promised to be difficult and complicated.

At 8:50, Céline is on live television as she sings "It's All Coming Back to Me Now," the show's fifteenth song. It is a part of a special benefit program for the amateur athletics foundation which was taped six days earlier at a Montreal indoor sports arena. Céline appears dressed in the Canadian Olympic uniform diving, running and jumping with Olympic champions Sylvie Bernier and Annie Pelletier. With them are a dozen athletes who leap onto the Molson Centre stage when she begins "The Power of the Dream," backed up by the Montreal Jubilation Choir.

Her job is going to be more than a little bit complicated. And that means pressure. Everyone in her entourage knows it is creative pressure, but it isn't always easy to put up with.

As soon as she steps on the stage, most of the tension evaporates. Throughout the show, which begins with "J'attendais," Céline talks and laughs a lot. She is eager to let Montrealers know that she is one of them, that she hasn't changed a bit, that she is nice and simple, just like them.

She tells how, when she came back to Montreal after being away for several months, she asked her driver to stop at a convenience store. René went in and bought some white bread, "You know, the kind that sticks to your teeth and the roof of your mouth" and mock chicken "that doesn't taste like anything." When they got back home, they made sandwiches. She talks of the pleasure of sleeping in her own bed. She wants Quebeckers to know she still has the same down-home tastes they do. That she hasn't changed.

As she sings "Love Can Move Mountains" a fan places a small paper bag at the edge of the stage. Usually gifts start arriving much earlier in the show, during "Seduces Me" or "All By Myself." When she finishes the song, everyone notices the bag at her feet. She bends down, picks it up, peeks inside and exclaims, "Good Lord in Heaven! Cookies!" She sits down on the edge of the stage in front of Marc Langis and tastes one.

Sure I knew René, Eric, everybody would be beside themselves. Who could tell what might be in those cookies? But I was so sure of myself, I knew nothing bad could happen to me. Sometimes I feel that way when I'm onstage. As if nothing can hurt me. It's an extraordinary feeling.

She calls to René, who is sitting in front with his mother and daughter Anne-Marie. "Here's one for you, my love." She lays down on the stage so that their heads are be at the same level and hands him the cookie, saying, "It's our night tonight. Forget the diet."

So it is their second anniversary. Sony has given her a five-karat diamond cut in the shape of a heart. René rents a room the Westin. It is the same room they'd had on their honeymoon night. He orders exactly the same menu. They will be alone together, a rare, intimate moment.

Chapter Thirty-One
Words that Sing

From June 8 to August 27, 1994, Céline toured the United States with Michael Bolton. They performed in twenty-thousand-seat arenas, and in the "sheds" that open onto natural amphitheaters. That summer alone, more than four million copies of *The Colour of My Love* were sold.

On Thursday, August 18, Céline Dion and René Angélil made it official. Their wedding would be celebrated in the coming months in Montreal's Notre Dame Basilica.

Less than two weeks later, Céline was back in Montreal. Assisted by René Angélil and Jean Lamothe, the thirteen restaurants of the Nickels chain were organizing a Cystic Fibrosis Day. One dollar would be donated for every sandwich sold. That day, Céline made appearances at five of the chain's outlets in the Montreal area. Covering her were MusiquePlus, four FM radio stations and reporters from the daily press. Each one got an interview. The subjects ranged from her upcoming wedding and her latest round of meetings in Hollywood to her future plans. These included a show at the Olympia the following month and a French-language album with Jean-Jacques Goldman. That news stunned the nay-sayers. Most of them were convinced that Céline and Goldman belonged to two absolutely incompatible worlds.

Jean-Jacques Goldman was a rarity in show business. In France, and to a lesser extent in Quebec, he was a cult figure among young people, students in particular. Without playing the PR game, keeping a low profile, he's managed to remain at the top of the show business hierarchy for more than fifteen years. Born in 1951 of a Polish Jewish father and a German Jewish mother, Goldman was the personification of the antistar who refused to talk about himself, who stayed far from the limelight, but who could still sell records by the millions. His music was brassy, faintly exotic, young and impulsive. Goldman himself was timid to the point of being reclusive. He was also a master.

When he heard Céline's voice for the first time, he was overwhelmed. "I could remember that voice from as far back as 'D'amour ou d'amitié' at the beginning of the eighties. We were on stage together at MIDEM in 1983. Her voice touched me. I tried my best to keep track of her. Sometimes I lost her, then she'd pop up singing a song by Plamondon or something in English, but every time, she touched me. At the risk of stating the obvious, there's something very special about Céline Dion. She sings, and people listen. That's not as easy as it sounds. You're in some public place, there's noise all around you, you're thinking of something and suddenly a voice comes looking for you and goes straight to your heart. That's Céline. That's what I find fascinating about her. Not only the power of her voice, not only its timbre, no matter how gorgeous it is, but the way she has of touching you to the heart."

For years, whenever he was asked whose voice he would like to write for, Jean-Jacques Goldman named Céline Dion. That irritated his purist fans to no end. "In the spring of 1994, I decided to treat myself. I called up Sony and told them I wanted to write an album for Céline."

A meeting was arranged at "Chez Pauline," a little restaurant near Place de l'Opéra in Paris. Goldman, dressed in jeans, a T-shirt and biker boots was waiting when Céline and René arrived. He outlined his idea for them. The three chatted for four hours about everything under the sun — except words and music. They talked about the people they liked, their families, their friends. Goldman told them how, for ten years, he'd kept track of Céline's voice, "whose quality and incomparable technique touched the musician in me." He wanted to write an album for Céline, a dozen songs in all, words and music. As they got up to leave, René handed him a cassette of *The Colour of My Love*, which had not yet been issued in France.

Before the meeting, René listened to Goldman's recordings, but he knew very little about him, so he did some homework. Céline didn't know much about his music, but Goldman's simplicity had won them over. He had an easy directness that reminded Angélil and Céline of Eddy Marnay.

It was destined to be a winning combination. Goldman was Sony's number one in France, and Céline was one of Sony-International's top assets. Together, they were bound to come up with a great success.

At the end of the summer of 1994, Céline was in New York for an appearance on the *Late Show* with David Letterman, where she was to give a spine-tingling interpretation of "River Deep, Mountain High," a song made famous by Tina Turner under the direction of the legendary Phil Spector.

René went along. Every morning, his Laval office faxed their hotel room the articles and sales figures for *The Colour of My Love*. The album was nudging the one million mark in Canada and two and a half million in the United States. It had gone platinum in Korea and Malaysia, gold in France, Japan, Indonesia, Hong Kong, New Zealand. A grand total of 13 million sold worldwide. Céline was a global star in that late summer of '94, even though there were still places where they would have to start from the ground up. It was extraordinary. From one month to the next, you could see Céline Dion's empire spreading over the face of the earth.

For Céline, all those numbers were terribly abstract. She was pleased, of course, but she had no desire to visit that cathedral of figures that René spent hours constructing. He was a man who adored numbers, the kind of man who spotted coincidences everywhere. He didn't keep a telephone book or a date book and could memorize automobile license plate numbers, telephone numbers, the most insignificant addresses, the birthdays of all his friends.

He read every single article written about Céline. Ofttimes, he would call up a writer in his calm, velvety voice to offer his thanks, or point out a factual error. Everything that was said or written about a star became part of the material used to build his or her image. René was in constant contact with Francine Chaloult's press office, which kept him abreast of everything that was spoken, written or thought about Céline in the Quebec and French media, and in the Montreal and Parisian show business world. In return, he fed Francine a constant stream of information on the comings and goings of his artist abroad.

Sometimes Céline's indifference exasperated him. She simply wasn't interested in figures. Months could go by without her reading a single review. If she got wind of negative opinions, she'd mull them over, then try to forget them, or even look for their positive side. "They say I sing through my nose, and they're right."

"You don't need anyone to tell you that," René answered. "You knew it already."

Of all the facts and figures the office had forwarded to their hotel room, two caught Angélil's attention. First, of all the countries where the album was being distributed, England had the slowest sales. Not even 100,000 copies had been sold since the launch of the album nine months earlier.

The other figure was a pleasant surprise, and totally unexpected. More than 100,000 copies of *Dion chante Plamondon* had been sold in the United States. This was unheard of for a French-speaking artist in an English-speaking country. In France, where it was known as *Des mots qui sonnent*, the album had already topped the 400,000 mark, and in Quebec, 200,000.

From New York, Angélil rang Jean-Jacques Goldman to tell him about the enormous success of *Dion chante Plamondon* and suggested that Luc Plamondon write the words to several of the songs on their upcoming album. Goldman seemed disappointed. He'd already started working, he said. He could agree to a compromise for Quebec, but for France, it would be harder. The songs he was writing would be a coherent unit, an impressionist portrait of the vocalist. Someone else's songs would sound out of place.

René later learned that Goldman had done his homework too. He'd ordered a file on Céline from Sony, including a folder of press clippings. He listened to all her recordings, familiarized himself with her story, her big family, Karine's death. He'd read the gossip sheets with their stories about her and René, their secret love affair, all the rumors and all the truths. He'd come to his own accurate conclusions about the woman she'd become — determined, ambitious, generous, "neither victim nor dove," a strong-willed woman. He read about her involvement in the Quebec Cystic Fibrosis Association.

"Because she was always talking about herself, and because the Quebec media had this remarkable curiosity about her, I thought I really knew her," Goldman was to say later. "Her pride in her origins and in the French language, her urge to leave her mark, her need to please people, all these things gave me a wealth of original material."

While Goldman was writing his songs (starting with the music), Céline was rehearsing for her show at the Olympia in Denis Savage's Economik studios not far from downtown Montreal. Angélil wanted Luc Plamondon to sit in on the rehearsals. He wanted Plamondon's advice on the show, which was to consist mostly of his songs. But he also wanted to break the news to him that even though he had scored a prodigious coup with *Dion chante Plamondon*, he wouldn't be writing the words for her next French album.

Angélil felt that something was missing from the Olympia show. He wanted surprise, a new interpretation of a classic, but not a Piaf song. In Luc's opinion, that would have seemed impolite and even irreverent to a majority of the French public. They looked around for a song everyone knew, a song Céline could interpret in a completely new way.

The first songs that came to mind were those of Jacques Brel. More than Aznavour or Bécaud, Brel touched René deeply, more with his voice than with his words. So he suggested to Céline that she sing "Ne me quitte pas" or "Quand on n'a que l'amour." She agreed to the second on the spot. It would be her first encore, Luc said.

One evening, in the Latini, an Italian restaurant in downtown Montreal, after a long work session, Angélil told Plamondon that Jean-Jacques Goldman was writing an entire album for Céline. Luc was surprised and very disappointed. He was familiar enough with the milieu to know that even if Goldman could be obscure and elusive at times, the album he produced would be well done, and would be a huge success in France and in Quebec.

Angélil's decisions are based on the needs of Céline of her career. Then he moves ahead. But the Goldman/Plamondon affair tormented him. It was like the time he fired pianist Alain Noireau, or gradually pushed Eddy Marnay aside. "That's my job," he says. "I try to make friends with the people who work with us. When the job is done, for whatever reason, it's always painful. But the only priority is Céline's career."

At their first meeting, Goldman promised that he would have a few songs ready by the end of September when Céline would be at the Olympia. He worked fast, turning out the words and music to a dozen songs in three months. "They were nothing like I'd imagined in the beginning," he said later. "At first I wanted it to be a classic album, something in between Barbra Streisand and Edith Piaf. But as I listened to Céline, I let her voice guide me, and I ended up with something closer to the blues, to soul."

A few days before the premier at the Olympia, they were eating in a Moroccan restaurant in Paris. Goldman was nervous and he wasn't confident about his songs. He'd read up on Céline; he'd done his best to get to know her and paint a portrait of the young lady she'd become, but now, he was assailed by cruel doubts. Maybe he was wrong; maybe he didn't understand, maybe they would be upset. Halfway through the meal, after much talk about this, that and the other thing, he pulled a few sheets of paper from his pocket. They were crumpled sheets of lined paper on which he'd jotted down the words to his songs. He handed them to Céline, then changed his mind and took them back. They should come to his studio the next day, he said. Then he would present his songs to them.

At the studio, he was much more at ease. He sat down at the keyboard, a guitar on his lap. Céline and René were standing close to him, at his right. He handed them the sheets he'd shown them the night before. Then he began to sing.

> J'ai compris tous les mots, j'ai bien compris merci
> Raisonnable et nouveau, c'est ainsi par ici
> Que les choses ont changé, que les fleurs ont fané
>
> (I understand what you say, to the very last word
> It all makes sense, that's how it goes
> When it's time for a change and the bloom's off the rose)
> "Pour que tu m'aimes encore,"
> Jean-Jacques Goldman

Three quarters of the way through the song, Angélil and Céline were in tears. Then Goldman sang "J'attendais." Seeing how moved they were, he took back the sheets of paper he'd given them and removed one. That evening, he played eight songs for them.

Next day, they were in the studio trying to find the right key for each song. Angélil told Goldman that the recording session would have to be scheduled for between November 1 and 19. Goldman was startled. He'd never produced an album in such a short time. Of course, all the tracks would be ready by November 1. It was simply a matter of dubbing Céline's voice over the music, but he wanted to direct her. There were certain things about her voice that irritated him, that bad habit she had of overdoing it, that peculiar way she rolled her "rs."

Like dreams, show business is a double life, another world. It's a world Ghislaine and Claudette Dion no longer inhabited. Michel left it only to return but this time not in the spotlight, but backstage, where he brings passion, love and fire to his humble tasks. After his own group The Show collapsed, he became a manual laborer for a couple of years. Then René offered him a job handling Céline's musicians. Michel rediscovered his little sister, for whom he'd once been a model and idol. That was back when he dreamed of a great international career.

Today, it's just the other way around. She's the one in the spotlight; he's hidden backstage. But they're as close as always. "She was a little girl when I last saw her," he says. "And now she's a grown woman, and a great star. But she's just as sweet and simple as she always was."

On opening day at the Olympia, he found himself at center stage as the band members were finishing their sound check. For a moment, he stood there facing the empty hall. He looked down at the seats, row upon row, and into the terrifying, overwhelming darkness. His dream had come true, but not as he'd expected. Still, there he was, standing on stage at the Olympia, an hour before his little sister was to triumph.

"I made up my mind never to dream again," he says. "Not everybody can make their dreams come true. Not everybody is so lucky. If you can't manage it, it's better forget it and get on with your life."

Jean Jacques Goldman was as surprised and stunned as everyone else by Céline's extraordinary presence and by her disturbing interpretation of Luc Plamondon's songs — and of Jacques Brel's "Quand on n'a que l'amour." But something bothered him. The feeling wasn't really getting through. "The introspection was missing. The vocal fireworks were hiding the real richness of her voice. The French can be a bit distant. Too much exuberance, too many special effects can put them off. But she still charmed them with her naturalness. People will forgive her thick accent and bad grammar because of it."

The day before the final show, he sent René the demo of a song entitled "Vole." When he heard it, René understood why Goldman had insisted on holding back the words to the song and not playing it for Céline until only a few hours before she took the stage at the Olympia. He knew she would have been deeply moved. In a way, "Vole" was a continuation of Eddy Marnay's "Mélanie," a song for her niece Karine who died the year before.

A few days later, Goldman sent them "Prière païenne," "Je sais pas" and "Regarde-moi." They were enchanted. When they left Paris, Angélil told Goldman that the recording session would be even briefer than they'd anticipated. As a matter of fact, on October 30, Céline would be appearing on a special show at the Ford's Theater in Washington, DC called *A Gala for a President*, honoring Bill and Hillary Clinton. The show, emceed by Whoopi Goldberg, was to be broadcast by ABC across the United States on Thanksgiving day, November 25.

It was six weeks to their marriage. Before then, Céline had to cut a record in France, launch the album based on her show at the Olympia in Montreal and in Paris, do a one-night stand at the Forum, fly to Japan to promote *The Colour of My Love*, make another appearance on Johnny Carson's *Tonight Show*, put up with innumerable fittings, shop for her wedding gown and prepare for the megaevent that was to be her wedding.

Recording got under way on November 3 at Méga Studios in Paris. Goldman and Céline had already talked things through, and he'd passed on a few tips. "Unsing" a little, he told her, use fewer ornaments and flourishes. Don't roll your "r's" so much, enunciate your "m's" better. "She understood right off the bat," he said. "I never had to tell her again. Céline's weaknesses are a sign of her qualities. She uses a lot of flowery figures because she's so creative. Too creative. But she's kept a capacity for coming up with new ideas. She can suggest changes or additions to a melody, she can breath life into it, transform a musical motif or phrase."

Céline would be recording two songs per session. Starting with "Pour que tu m'aimes encore." She got it in two takes. Goldman could hardly believe his ears. He was worried. Were they moving too fast? But Céline didn't want to rehearse too much. Her main concern was to keep the freshness and the feeling. She never did more than two or three takes.

Méga Studio, where they gathered every evening around six o'clock, boasted a Ping-Pong table, where Goldman would take on the sound engineer and the technicians. They played well, especially the songwriter, who was a fast, lively, aggressive player. Angélil watched him out of the corner of his eye. He himself hadn't played regularly for a good ten years when he spent most evenings at Guy Cloutier's place in Duvernay. Cloutier had a table in his garage. René was becoming obsessed by the idea of taking on Goldman. But the only way he could practice was in his head.

As he walked into the studio one evening, René challenged Goldman to a game. Goldman grinned with a touch of condescension. Angélil was fifty-two years old. He couldn't be a good Ping-Pong player. It was a game for people with quick reflexes. Goldman accepted the challenge to placate him. It wasn't long before he realized he was up against a top-flight player. They played three games that night, and Angélil won all three, and every other game on the following nights. He briefly considered letting Goldman win, but he had too much respect for the game and its rules. That would have been cheating, and Goldman would have known it.

"It's a fact; I lost every game I played against Angélil," admitted

Goldman. "But Ping-Pong brought us close together. I would never have figured out what was happening between us if I'd won every game. I don't think René likes to lose. But he was playing for pleasure, not the physical pleasure of the sport, but the pleasure of communicating with someone else. Culturally, we're at opposite ends of the spectrum. He likes Las Vegas and Hollywood, driving around in limousines. I prefer the country, and my motorcycle. In my dealings with him, I discovered that he's an artist at heart. Infinitely more than all the managers and producers I've met in my twenty-five years in the business. When you're talking with him, no matter the subject, emotion is always the important thing. Feelings are what make him work. Céline too. That's why their production company is called Feeling Inc."

The recording of a song is a ritual, a ceremony. It marks the transition from imagination to reality, from silence to life. It's like a dream coming true. It's always, as Goldman puts it, "A bit of a trial for a songwriter — except for these exceptional cases. There are a handful of rare voices who have the gift and the power to make the dream even more beautiful. Céline Dion is one of those voices. She was able to interpret my songs. She gave them breath, coherence, soul."

To preserve the intimate atmosphere that Goldman and arranger Roland Romanelli worked so hard to create, "Vole" was recorded at Haut de Gamme studios, in Boulogne. This time, musicians and singer recorded together.

"After Céline finished the song," Goldman related, "everybody, the technicians in the control room and the musicians in the studio just sat there motionless, without speaking, overwhelmed. Then they looked at each other like people who have just been through an overpowering experience, or who've just awakened from a kind of hypnotic spell. That's exactly what happened. Céline has that ability to wake you up. Her voice comes and orders you to wake up."

The *Falling Into You* Tour
New Orleans, March 16, 1997

The Band

It's bound to happen sooner or later during a show, and it almost always does. Most of the time, it's a subjective thing. Mégo, Picard and Messier may be delighted and say, "What a great show!" While Céline, Frulla and Langis are upset. Or the other way around. There are the shows that start off badly and wind up with a roar. Once in a blue moon, there's absolute consensus, catharsis, epiphany, total magic — everything clicks, everything floats, from beginning to end. That's when Céline and her musicians look each other in the eye and smile blissfully. They're happy, each in their own world, yet together. Dublin, Nîmes, Seoul, Lyons and Zurich were the unforgettable shows of the Falling Into You *tour.*

Often, the performance of the musicians is one of the highlights of the show. It comes, in the English version, just after "It's All Coming Back to Me," and in French, after "Je sais pas" or "J'irai où tu iras." Come along with us on a journey, it seems to say.

"Let's travel to a small town in the south of France. Let's use our imagination. We step into a tiny club where they're playing jazz or blues. It's late at night and we're together. You're clapping your hands and snapping your fingers to the beat."

The musicians lay down the rhythmic line for Goldman's "Ballet," a steady cadence people can snap their fingers to. That's when Céline calls out to the city where she's performing.

Nagoya, lemme hear you!
Berlin, keep it up!
C'mon Sydney, higher!
New Orleans, I wanna hear you!

In New Orleans, where people are still nostalgic for old French culture, it is a special moment. The fans keep the beat going loud and clear.

Ça t'arrive sans crier gare
Au milieu d'une heure incolore.

(It hits you without warning
Just when the sky's gone white.)
"Le Ballet"
Jean-Jacques Goldman

She sings a shortened version of "Le Ballet" which she interrupts sharply, with the words "Yup, that's life!" And for an instant all you can hear in the UNO Lakefront Arena is the crowd snapping its fingers. When the music starts up again, powerful and rousing, Céline strides over to André Coutu, singing the highest notes from his guitar at the same pitch. In a quick shift, she calls on Langis's bass in a deep, bluesy voice. Then she moves on to Frulla, mingling her voice with the keyboards, weaving with them light, ethereal patterns. All the while, the crowd is clapping, snapping its fingers. When Céline comes up to Messier's drums, the fans can feel the excitement. Soon she's trading spectacular riffs with him. It's the same with Picard, who can make his percussion sound like a heavenly game of marbles. The crowd just eats up those good-natured "duels" between the singer and her musicians.

Then she works her way down to the backup singers with high-pitched cries, her voice soaring above the riffs of the bass and the percussion and the snapping of fingers, until she's out of breath. She makes a face, sticks out her tongue and rolls her eyes, all shown in close-up on the screen. The crowd breaks into laughter, especially in Asia. Sometimes she'll pull three or four grimaces. "I can do it because I feel good up here in front of you. You're wonderful." The crowd goes wild.

After greeting the backup singers, she turns toward Mégo and throws him a little phrase which he repeats on the piano, throwing in a flourish or two. And then the duo takes off, to the far limits of cacophony. Céline is shaking Mégo by the shoulder as he rips up and down the keyboard in furious arpeggios, until finally Langis's bass and Frulla's keyboards bring him under control. As the crowd applauds, the band eases back into the theme from "Le Ballet."

The musicians like it here in New Orleans. That's important.

The city we're playing in has an effect on our show through its rhythms, its general feeling. It influences the music, predisposes it. Some towns make things difficult. There's one, which I won't name so as not to hurt its feelings, that we all hated the moment we set foot in it. It wasn't cold, the sky wasn't cloudy. There was a lake and nicely kept parkland all around it. But everybody we met seemed out of sorts. The food was bad, even in the most expensive restaurants. And while out on their evening constitutional, the guys almost got mugged two or three times. The show was difficult. It's a real job to try to entertain someone you don't like.

Here in New Orleans, it's quite the opposite. For all the rain and clouds, the stink of Lake Ponchartrain, there's something in the air, something in the way people look — everything you need for a great show. And a full moon never hurts.

Chapter Thirty-Two
Like a Fairy Tale

When Céline and René finally announced that they wanted a church wedding, tongues wagged ferociously in countless living rooms — and in the Quebec media. Could the twice-divorced Angélil even be married in a Catholic church? He married Denise Duquette in church in 1967, but divorced her in the civil courts. Then he married Anne-Renée, whom he later divorced, in a civil ceremony.

René had already taken steps to annul his first marriage, and religious tribunal approved his petition. That meant he could remarry in the Catholic church. But there was grumbling. He and Céline were getting special treatment, people complained, because they were rich and famous. Or because Céline was going to sing for the Pope.

Still, they weren't the first, either in show business or from other walks of life, to get an annulment. A few months earlier, the judges of the ecclesiastical court in Rome had annulled the marriage of Caroline of Monaco and Philippe Junot. And, in point of fact, an ecclesiastical divorce costs much less than a civil procedure.

Not only did Céline and René want a church wedding, they wanted a grand wedding, grander than anyone had ever seen. Mia Dumont and Coco Lacroix, Pierre's wife, would organize the event. They were given carte blanche.

That summer she went shopping with Céline for her bridal gown. They visited the chicest shops on Fifth Avenue in New York. But none of the gowns Céline tried on really clicked. Meanwhile, Angélil heard from Pierre Lacroix that Mirella Gentile, a seamstress in the Montreal suburb of St. Leonard, could produce marvels. Mia dropped into the workshop for a look and came away impressed. Soon she returned with Céline, who immediately loved what she saw.

She knew she would be opening herself up for criticism, but she'd made up her mind to wear what she liked. She wanted a gown with a long train, a bejeweled, spectacular gown with a wasp waist and frills and flounces aplenty. Mia showed her two films, Martin Scorcese's *The Age of Innocence* and *Dangerous Liaisons* by Milos Forman. Céline was fascinated by the gowns worn by Michelle Pfeiffer and Glenn Close. Later, when the two friends got down to serious planning for the wedding gown, they code-named it "The Age of Innocence." Her pumps were to be handmade by a Parisian craftsman. The corset, by a master corset maker in the French capital. The wedding band was to be created by Mauboussin, a jeweler in the Place Vendôme. Mia found a heavy tiara in Mirella's shop. It took all the ingenuity Louis Hechter, Céline's longtime hair stylist, could muster to find a way to keep it in place and adapt it to her hairpiece.

Before Céline's appearance there on Thursday, November 24, a press conference was held at the *Mise au Jeu*, the Forum restaurant, to launch *Céline Dion à l'Olympia*. The album went platinum that very same day. Rick Camilleri, the Sony Music Canada representative, handed Céline a diamond record commemorating more than a million sales of *The Colour of My Love* in Canada alone, not to mention trophies for *Unison* (six times platinum), *Céline Dion* (seven times) and *Dion chante Plamondon* (twice).

The room was packed to the rafters and was suffocatingly hot. The Sony people had covered an entire wall with a map of the world. On the map, they pinned flags on more than thirty countries in Europe, North America and Asia. "The empire that Céline Dion rules" was the way Camilleri put it in his presentation.

> That's what they call it, "The empire that Céline Dion rules." Sometimes I get the feeling the empire's ruling me. I never could understand what people meant when they said that they didn't belong to themselves any more. But there I was, my wedding was two weeks away and I was off to Japan on tour.

Osaka, Nagoya, Tokyo. I spent hours on the phone with René, with Mia, with Coco. They were hard at work on the final preparations.

Céline and René spent the evening of December 16 in the Carmelite convent in Montreal, praying. From the limousine that was driving him home, Angélil called Francine Chaloult. "Nothing can touch us now. Whatever may come, we're happy."

The day was cold. At dawn, light snow began falling on the city. It was a lovely sight, but one that made it impossible to lay carpets on the steps leading up to the church. A wooden passageway was hastily built to keep the route dry. The snow finally stopped less than an hour before the ceremony, which was to begin at three o'clock. The wooden ramp was in place, and over it lay a royal blue carpet with the letters "C" and "R" in gilt. Céline's feet would be dry as she entered the church.

Shortly before three o'clock, the convoy of limousines (some had to be imported from the United States) left the Westin Hotel with a police motorcycle escort. Place d'Armes and the area in front of the church were thick with people. Public figures like former Canadian prime minister Brian Mulroney and his wife Mila, David Foster and Luc Plamondon were cheered.

René was surrounded by his best man and ushers: his brother André, his cousin Paul Sara, his friends Marc Verreault, Vito Luprano, Pierre Lacroix, Guy Cloutier, Ben Kaye, Jacques Des Marais. A few moments later, when Céline swept in on her father's arm, followed by her maid of honor and bridesmaids, her eight sisters all in white, the church rang with ovations, shouts and sobs. The image of Céline making her entrance into Notre Dame Basilica with her sisters holding her bridal train, wearing her white mink bolero and her jewel-studded tiara, will long remain etched in the Quebec popular image.

The decor was as brilliant as it was magnificent. Then the Montreal Jubilation Gospel Choir broke into song.

The reception was held at the Westin, sumptuously decorated for the occasion. The program handed to the guests contained an eight-page gastronomic and musical menu.

Everything was true to their image as a couple. Flamboyant, larger than life, unique. The hotel's interior had been decorated to make the guests feel they were transported to a place beyond space and time. It was a dizzying, heady sensation. Some of the decorations were pure surrealism, like the section of floor covered with flower petals, or walls draped with the finest silks embroidered with gems, or the all-white gallery where pure-white doves fluttered in white cages. From a scene straight from the Arabian Nights, guests stepped into an English pub, from a western bar to a tiny Parisian bistro. On one counter was sushi, on another, tapas. Magicians pulled aces of hearts from the guests' sleeves, and the champagne flowed. There was music everywhere. A string quartet here, a rock band there. There was a casino, of course, complete with blackjack tables and roulette wheels. The money was fake, but not the winners. They were for real.

Nothing could have prepared the guests for the banquet. Bouquets of flowers came floating down from a starry sky to land softly in the center of each table. Crooner Warren Wiebe, flown in from Los Angeles for the occasion, sang "The Colour of My Love" accompanied by a thirty-piece orchestra directed by David Foster. The wedding cake consisted of 2,677 cream puffs in the shape of a Christmas tree. Emotions were close to the breaking point when Céline's thirteen brothers and sisters gathered around her to sing "Qu'elle est belle, la vie!"

Quebec had never seen another wedding ceremony like it. Before, during and after the event, people couldn't stop talking about it. There were the indignant detractors who saw it as a vulgar marketing gimmick or as the arrogant swagger of wealth at the expense of the little guy. Luc Plamondon came up with a snappy reply to the critics. "People are fascinated by the splendor of Hollywood, by the gilded legend of the princesses of Monaco or the British Royal Family," he said. "For once, we've got a real legend all our own, a true fairy tale made in Quebec. It would be stupid not to make the most of it."

Deep down, Céline Dion respected traditional values and was never one to latch onto the popular views of the day. There was something deliberately unfashionable about Céline, something that went against the grain. The power ballads that were her greatest successes were songs of women possessed, willing slaves overcome by single-minded, all-consuming love — about as far removed from feminist orthodoxy as you can get. Curiously, not a bit of it was designed to provoke. And none of it created controversy. Deep down, Céline touched the truth of the man and woman on the street, in all their contradictions and simplicity. For all the official talk with its big words and big ideas, people still liked to hear about the love of a woman for one man.

"Céline never tries to stir up controversy," said Dave Platel. "She never tries to get your attention by shocking you with far-out or disturbing ideas. She conquers you with her voice, her charm and by projecting a simple, balanced way of life."

Céline was the kind of woman who seemed to love life, who loved the man she married. She was a kind of lucky star. Just as she used to sing openly of the love she kept secret, now she enacts in her songs the submissive, dependent woman she is no longer.

The *Falling Into You* Tour
Detroit, August 8, 1996

The Chorus

Detroit is the Motor City — Motown — home to the automobile and to a very special sound: a blue-collar, funky, young black music. For years, Céline Dion has been exploring black music, singing hits made famous by Tina Turner, the Supremes and Aretha Franklin. "Love Can Move Mountains," the song she sings toward the end of her show, is pure Motown. The crowd never fails to get to its feet when the flurry of wilderness images (rushing rivers, fjords, glaciers) rushes by at dizzying speed on the screens, followed by the words Faith, Love, Trust.

Last year, a Detroit critic devoted a lot of space to an analysis of Céline Dion's voice. "She has accomplished the rarest of exploits, reconciling the great traditions of popular music." He went on to say that she sang black just as well as white, that she sang with her mind and with her heart. Her album The Color of My Love *was a collection of the most popular musical styles of the end of the century. "Ms. Dion's French roots may have a lot to do with it," he opined. "Also the fact that she comes from a working-class background. French Canadians make up less than a quarter of the population of Canada. They are poorer and not as well educated as their English-speaking counterparts. Some people have even compared them to lower class blacks in the United States."*

It's the singers' origins that determine the depth of their voice. None of the great pop singers were born into the moneyed classes. A pop singing career is an escape, a way to climb the social ladder.

Sylvain Cormier of Le Devoir, *an intelligent journalist and an excellent writer, does not see it that way. Writing about Whitney Houston's album* The Preacher's Wife, *he remarks about Céline Dion and Mariah Carey that "they make up for a deficit of soul with big sound effects." For him, Whitney Houston is the only one of the three singers with any soul. "It's only normal," he writes, "when you're the daughter of Cissy Houston, a terrific gospel singer who belonged to The Sweet Inspirations, the group that accompanied Aretha Franklin back when she sang 'Respect' and 'Think,' and Elvis Presley when he sang 'In the Ghetto' and 'Suspicious Minds.'" He reminds his readers that Whitney is the niece of Dionne Warwick, a pop diva of the sixties. According to Cormier, soul is strictly a matter of genes. A question of race and skin color.*

Surprisingly, in the January 25 issue of Entertainment Weekly, *Jim Farber hands Céline Dion the prize for authenticity: "While Whitney and Mariah give us ersatz gospel and supper-club soul, Dion concentrates on mainstream, grown-up pop." So there we have it: different takes on the same reality.*

Actually, Céline is increasingly attracted to gospel. On all the stops of her American tour, she sang at least two songs, "Call the Man" and, from July 19 onward, "The Power of the Dream," the song from the opening ceremony of the Atlanta Olympic Games, backed up by a local choir.

Choreographer Dominique Giraldeau is responsible for locating and preparing the choir. She distributes sheet music to the eighteen women and twelve men, as well as the white tunics they will wear, and sets up the staging. After the performance, she evaluates and grades each one. The Detroit choir rates no better than a halfhearted B-. Houston walks away with an A+, as did Pittsburgh, Tampa and Memphis.

Chapter Thirty-Three
What Price Friendship?

The Colour of My Love may be a thirteen-time platinum worldwide winner, but it still couldn't get off the ground in England. In 1992, "Beauty and the Beast" had clawed its way up to the ninth spot on the British hit parade, but "Where Does My Heart Beat Now," released the following year, never made it past seventy-third place. They'd tried everything. They'd even rented a London theater, the Dominion, where Céline sang for 1,100 invited guests: disc jockeys, journalists, record librarians, recording industry and video professionals. They loved her, talked about her for a couple of days and promptly all but forgot her. *Unison* and *Céline Dion* never sold more than a few tens of thousands each. *The Colour of My Love*, complete with a full promotional campaign and positive notices from across the Atlantic, looked like it would have trouble cracking the 100,000 mark.

Her single, "The Power of Love," had pushed the album past the sixty-thousand level, then it ran out of gas. They tried other singles. Still no luck. Come spring, they booked her into a small theater, the Cambridge. It was the same story: everybody loved Céline. For a few days, everybody in the industry was talking about her, then they forgot her. In the fall, Paul Burger, who'd just taken over at Sony-UK., decided to start out fresh with another song, "Think Twice."

He quickly discovered that Céline had lots of die-hard fans in the London gay community. The same thing happened to Barbra Streisand, who began her career singing in a gay bar in Manhattan. One Sunday in October, Burger rented the Apollo Theater. His guests were the owners and DJs from London's gay clubs. It was a magical evening.

The next day, "Think Twice" was in the shops. On October 16 it had reached fifty-third on the charts; the following week, it was up to forty-second. Burger was starting to get excited. After a brief stumble at the beginning of November, the song began to climb steadily. In mid-December when Burger and his wife Ossi flew back to Montreal for Céline and René's wedding, "Think Twice" was in eighth spot. More than a year later, *The Colour of My Love* cracked the charts, in ninety-seventh position. Things were starting to happen, slowly but surely. The holiday period would be decisive.

In England, you can place bets on which song will be number one in London on New Year's Day. Through Burger, René bet several hundred pounds on "Think Twice." He didn't necessarily believe he'd win. After all, things were moving slowly. It was more like an offering to placate the gods.

By the holiday break, "Think Twice" was up to fifth, then slipped back to sixth, then seventh. But the following week, it nudged back up to fourth place. There was still hope. The video screened three times on England's top variety show, *Top of the Pops.* On January 1, "Think Twice" was in second place.

Céline and René were at Palm Beach, at the place they'd bought the year before. They arrived there the day after the wedding, the idea being to spend a month doing nothing. René spent his days on the golf course, Céline in the shops, or sunbathing. Most of the time, they spent their evenings at home alone, eating pasta and watching a film.

One Sunday afternoon, while Céline was cooking up some tomato sauce and René was watching the Super Bowl on the kitchen television set, Paul Burger called. The Sony PR people had just pulled off a spectacular coup. Céline was to make a personal appearance on *Top of the Pops.* Taped on Wednesday and broadcast on Sunday in prime time by the BBC, the show was the hit maker or breaker. The week's top ten was featured, either live or on video, and the producer would chose the artist most likely to emerge in the next two weeks. For Céline to sing "Think Twice" on *Top of the Pops* was a promotional masterstroke. Paul was nearly beside himself.

But René replied that he and Céline were on their honeymoon. They'd promised themselves they would do nothing for a whole month except relax and think of each other. Paul was rattled; he was apologetic but insistent: "I'll send the Sony jet to pick you up at the West Palm Beach Airport, and from there you can either fly direct to London, or to New York, and come by Concorde. You'll be back home on Friday night. Not even forty-eight hours."

René's refusal was final, Burger could see that. Céline would do *Top of the Pops* in a month. But a month later would be too late. And René knew it. Céline, who was listening to the conversation, stopped slicing her mushrooms. When René hung up, he could tell from her expression that she knew exactly what was going on. He told her, "I think I just hurt our friend. It would be too bad if Paul Burger came to us one day and told us it was our fault that we never made it in England. We've been together for ten years, and we've always done everything right. So far, our timing has been perfect."

She said, "Call Paul back and tell him to send the jet."

Burger would have to tell the show's producers, the people he'd been pushing for weeks, that his artist was would not be able to appear. At home, he turned in for the night. He was about to fall asleep when the telephone rang.

Ossi called out to him from downstairs, "Paul, it's for you."

He heard René's smooth voice.

"You're really upset, aren't you, Paul?"

"What do you think?"

"Céline and I talked it over. I told her I never heard you speak that way before. She told me we couldn't let you down. You've worked too hard. She told me to call you back and tell you we're coming."

Paul was moved. He got up and called his associates. They had to find an airplane as soon as possible. René wanted to leave Palm Beach on Tuesday night. Céline would sleep on the plane. She would tape the show on Wednesday afternoon and they would fly back immediately after the session.

Monday night, and still no plane in sight. Paul was looking for a jet that could fly from Palm Beach to London nonstop. And he would have to hire two crews; pilots couldn't fly a return journey with such a short stopover. The simplest solution turned out to be a private jet from Palm Beach to New York, and from there, the Concorde to London. Céline wouldn't be away from home for more than thirty-two hours.

Céline appeared on the January 19, 1995 edition of *Top of the Pops*. The following Monday, Paul was at his desk at seven o'clock in the morning waiting impatiently for the sweeps. "Think Twice" was still in second place. On the charts, the spread between first and second is as big as between second and fiftieth. Paul almost broke down. Then he glanced at the album rankings. There he got an unexpected surprise. *The Colour of My Love* had just vaulted into first place.

"Think Twice," a thoughtful, adult love song, quickly became a huge hit in the land of the Beatles. *The Colour of My Love,* with its 2.3 million copies sold, went on to become the album of the year for 1995. European sales which had leveled off at five million, began to roll again.

At Sony, there was great excitement. It was the first time that an in-house artist (Michael Jackson included) had sold more than a million singles in England. Jennifer Rush, a CBS artist, turned the trick in 1986 with "The Power of Love," a song Céline sang on *The Colour of My Love.* In 1968, Serge Gainsbourg and Jane Birkin with "Je t'aime, moi non plus" and Vanessa Paradis twenty-one years later with "Joe le taxi" had made it into the top ten of the British hit parade, but never number one. Since 1990, only three artists (on other labels) had hit the million mark, all three with film theme songs: Whitney Houston's version of "I Will Always Love You" (*The Bodyguard*), Bryan Adams in "Everything I Do I Do It For You" (*Robin Hood, Prince of Thieves*) and the group Wet Wet Wet, with "Love Is All Around."

Two weeks after Céline's appearance on *Top of the Pops,* she'd sold out five shows throughout the UK in less than an hour. And preparations were under way for a second tour in the fall, in larger halls, including the famous Wembley Arena.

Ever since his heart attack, René knew he was at risk. He took care of himself occasionally. He ate less, slept a bit more and even took the odd walk. Then he simply forgot. Aside from golf, one of the great loves of his life, he did little exercise. There were times when a record was being recorded, or when he was involved in long, complicated negotiations, that he got no exercise whatsoever. When he was alone, at the wheel of his car, or seated in the darkness among the crowd waiting for his wife's show to begin, he imagined what would happen to her if he died. One night, as he was speeding along the Laurentian Expressway, he heard Charles Aznavour's song "Qui?" He was bowled over. It was the story of his life, the story of a man in love with a much younger woman. They both knew that one day, he would no longer be there. What then? Who would look after her?

That February, Mia Dumont was visiting her parents at Fort Lauderdale. Céline and René invited her over to their place for dinner one evening. During the meal, René made her promise that if anything ever happened to him, she would take care of Céline. Céline should keep right on singing, he insisted. The career they'd built together was the only thing in his life. If they didn't keep it up, it would be like a second death for him.

Plenty of stars, women in particular, liked to come across as martyrs, to tell the story of their deprivation and unhappiness. "I was beaten, raped, betrayed, abandoned," they'd say, as though there was this irresistible urge to attract pity, to profit from the public's natural urge to side with the victim.

Céline would have nothing to do with that. Goldman knew what he was talking about when he had her sing, in "Je sais pas":

> J'suis pas victime, j'suis pas colombe
> Et pour qu'on m'abîme, faut qu'je tombe.
>
> (I'm no victim, I'm no dove
> I'll have to fall before I'm hurt.)

In her interviews and remarks to the audience from the stage, Céline made it clear that she was a happy person. In her field, people like her were becoming a real rarity. No complaints, no regrets, no self-pity. Quite the opposite. When she spoke of her childhood, she remembered the joys of being a little girl. For Céline Dion, life was beautiful. It always had been. She knew that with the passage of time, the people she loved would disappear, that she'd be sad, even brokenhearted.

She moved instinctively toward the wounded, the infirm, the sick. She helped them speak, made them laugh, especially children. She touched them, sat them on her lap, knelt down in front of them, held their hand. She gave them caps embroidered with her name and helped fit them on their head. She told them to hang on. And they believed they were alone with her and that no one else was watching.

On March 28, 1995, at 7:30 p.m., in Studio 42 at Radio-Canada, a broadcast coproduced by Canada's largest public network and MusiquePlus launched the new Dion-Goldman album, *D'eux*. Big, public launches with lots of media coverage were becoming an Angélil specialty. His strategy was to negotiate with the broadcasters himself, set the conditions, drive a hard bargain with one side while showing excessive generosity toward the other.

The show was to be aired Saturday, April 1 on MusiquePlus, and the following Sunday, on Radio-Canada's flagship program *Les Beaux Dimanches*. The whole listening spectrum would be covered.

MusiquePlus's young fans, the biggest record-buying group, and the not so young.

Angélil was convinced (and still is) that Céline's album with Goldman was her best to date. He was saying openly that it was unlikely she could do better.

Even though she expressed herself in English with remarkable self-assurance, she was more at ease in French. That was the language she used to speak of the things of the heart, of the soul, her language of poetry. Her English albums were producer designed. It was a totally different universe, where the sound was more important than the content.

In a matter of weeks, *D'eux* had broken the record of 350,000 set in 1981 by Ginette Reno's "Je ne suis qu'une chanson." In less than a year, it had gone platinum six times in Canada, and become the best-selling French album in the history of recorded music. "Pour que tu m'aimes encore" was the hit of the summer of 1995 everywhere in Europe.

Céline's voice had never been so radiant, so deep, so clear. Goldman had found a way to use the richest and most subtle nuances of her voice.

The *Falling Into You* Tour
Boston, July 23, 1996

Encore

As she takes the stage at the Great Woods Performing Arts Center, Céline feels nervous and tense. It was only four months earlier, in Atlanta, that she sang before the largest audience in history. Four billion people, so the media claimed. It was a great moment, but she felt dizzy and light-headed, like a prizefighter the day after a hard-fought victory. Still, Atlanta was only an appetizer.

It has been a month since she was the among supercharged crowds of the amphitheaters. Since June 23, in Toronto. That was where she wound up the Canadian leg of the Falling Into You tour, twenty-three shows in five weeks in nineteen halls in eight provinces.

Tonight, the tour is starting up again: twenty-six American cities in six weeks, then on to Europe in mid-September. There will be no letup until Christmas. The first shows of any tour are always the trickiest. It takes a while to get the kinks out of the music. And it's always back to square one with the crowd. You have to reestablish the connections and the confidence.

No sooner does Céline appear than the fans break out in a touching ovation, not only because they are happy to see her, but also because of her triumph in Atlanta.

She gave a good show, in spite of feeling a bit down for the past few days. Before she leaves the stage, she shouts out, "Good night, Boston! Sweet dreams! See you again soon!"

The audience is on its feet, driven by its own excitement. The stage becomes dark, illuminated by tiny flickering lights, a vacuum sucking in everyone's gaze. Suddenly there comes a crackling sound, and the blinding, opalescent glare of a dozen television screens light up the stage for a brief instant. In the darkness, Céline's voice rings out, sweet and throaty. Finally she appears high up, next to Paul Picard's percussion kit.

She leaves the stage and darts into a kind of tent at the foot of the steps, stage right. Loulou is waiting for her with a change of costume. She helps Céline slip off her leather trousers. Manon wipes the sweat from her back and shoulders, adjusting her hair. Céline pulls on a body-stocking and a long dress. She emerges from the tent, with Eric standing guard. Claude Plante, waiting for her at the foot of the steps, hands her the mike and guides her along the narrow catwalk behind Frulla's keyboards and Messier's drums. For her encore, Céline sits in the shadows, at the top of the risers that form the set. When she sings the first notes, the crowd falls silent. It is "Because You Loved Me," the theme song from the film Up Close and Personal *starring Michelle Pfeiffer and Robert Redford. Scenes from the film are playing on the screens.*

For all those times you stood by me
For all the truth that you made me see
"Because You Loved Me,"
Diane Warren

The film is the romantic love story of two American television journalists. She is inexperienced, naive, ready to try anything. He is a star reporter, a man of integrity and strength. When he is killed in combat, she goes on without him, for him.

"Sing for Robert Redford?" Céline said to René. "Any time."

A few days after the recording session, the actor-director-producer called in person to thank her and congratulate her. He loved her interpretation of Diane Warren's song. The public loved it too. It's pure velvet, soft as satin.

She repeats the last line, this time singing for the audience. "I'm everything I am because you love me." A voice cries out, "I love you, Céline." She hears it and answers back, "I love you too." Then she laughs and begins again, from the top, "I'm everything I am...." Again comes a torrent of applause, cries, laughter, shouts of "I love you." She is delighted, overjoyed. In a flash of inspiration, she asks the crowd to sing along with her. "I just had an idea. You sing the last line of the song along with me."

She asks Lapin to light up the crowd. He floods the hall with white light, shattering the intimacy of the stage lighting, the music, the scenes from the film. Intimidated, the crowd sings "I'm everything I am..." in a faint voice.

Céline pretends to be upset. The crowd laughs. "It's scarier for me to sing All By Myself in front of you than for you to sing in front of me." And the crowd picks up the tune again, much louder this time, Céline's voice mingling with theirs. "I'm everything I am..." The music stops to let her savor the pleasure. She sighs, "Because you loved me..."

Céline applauds. The fans do too. Through her, they enjoy a moment of bliss.

The script is simple. The trick is to carry it off every night with a partner who doesn't know what's coming. You've got to get a feel for the crowd, you've got to know that on the closing notes of "I'm everything I am," in the tiniest fraction of a second of silence, there will be shouts and applause. Someone may cry out from the back of the hall, "Céline, I love you," and she'll answer back, "I love you too." You've got to grasp the moment, motion to the musicians to stop, stretch out the silence for a second or two, then turn to the crowd and say, "I've got an idea. What if we sang that last line together?" Then make sure each of your lines creates the desired effect, and lets the fans know that their love makes you happy. And vice versa.

It is quite a discovery, this summer's night in Boston.

Chapter Thirty-Four
A Touch of Eccentricity

Phil Spector has been one of pop music's outstanding personalities for three decades. Single-handedly, he revolutionized recording techniques, and invented the "wall of sound," a new, rich, overpowering and exuberant style that won the hearts of young music listeners in the sixties and seventies. Spector could be called a colorist in the sense that he used sound textures more than rhythm or melody in the music he produced.

One night in August 1994, he was watching David Letterman's *Late Show* when he heard Céline Dion sing "River Deep, Mountain High," the song he'd produced for Tina Turner. He decided that one day Céline would sing his songs. A few months later, he got in touch with René Angélil to tell him he'd written some songs especially for his artist. René was so excited he couldn't sit still. Spector was a living legend, a man who'd worked with the greatest, including John Lennon, for whom he had produced "Imagine."

In the industry, and particularly at Sony, several people went out of their way to warn René about Spector. Tommy Mottola, who had the reputation of not taking any grief from anyone, claimed it was almost impossible to work with Phil Spector. "He wants everything, all the glory. He won't listen to anyone." René knew all that, but he was a

Spector fan. He'd read two books about the man, and Céline wanted to work with him, whatever the price.

> I'm a singer. I need to be directed, like an actress. A music producer is like a film director, or a copilot. Someone who tells me where to direct my voice. I've always gotten along fine with the producers who've worked with me. Even when they're terribly demanding, like David Foster. Each one has his own style, his habits. They're as important to the success of a song as the composer, the songwriter or the singer.
>
> I don't go around collecting producers, but I know that the more you have on an album, the more different colors and styles you have. I had the feeling that with Spector, it would be different from all the rest.

But Spector turned out to be more egocentric,, more stubborn, more paranoid than anyone could have imagined. Céline and René met him for the first time in Los Angeles in June 1995. He was a small, dark man with nervous tics and a feverish glint in his eyes. He was living in a rundown mansion in Hollywood, and driving the old Rolls John Lennon once gave him.

They motored over to the studio where Spector had recorded the Tina Turner song that Céline had made her own, "River Deep, Mountain High." When he went in, Spector advised the technical crew, whom he'd kept waiting more than two hours, that he wouldn't be speaking to them. His assistant would convey his orders. Noticing a wall that divided the studio in two, he said, "That wasn't here in my day. Knock it down, will you? I want all the musicians in the same room."

He took one look at the computers. "And clear all this stuff out of here while you're at it. I'll show you how to make a record. I don't need all this hardware. I've got ears."

He ordered the studio to be reconstructed so that six basses, six guitars, four drummers and two percussionists, brass and strings could all play at the same time. The next day, the wall was gone along with the computers. Angélil was astonished to see how much authority Spector still wielded in the trade, even though he had done almost nothing for the previous two or three years. There was an aura about the man, a hint of animal wildness.

The studio was packed. Spector asked that René and Céline not invite too many people, but he himself invited more than fifty, including Isaac Hayes and Ike Turner. When Tina was recording "River Deep,

Mountain High" with Spector several years before, the two men had been involved in a bitter feud. The place was so full of Spector's unusual friends that it was hard to move.

From behind the control panel, Spector chewed out the musicians as they waited for the parts to arrive. One of the bassists was off-key, a guitarist was muffing his riffs, a saxophone player didn't have any soul. During the session, he kept ordering sprays of red roses for Céline. He gave her looks that were so long and lingering that she could feel them on her skin. When she looked over toward him, he stared at her through squinting eyes, as if he wanted to look right inside her. René wasn't needed, he said. He could take the day off.

Meanwhile, Spector began to belittle the other producers who were scheduled to work with Céline. There was only one way of doing things — his way. If the others had the occasional success, it was because of him. They imitated him, copied him, stole his ideas.

> I don't know why, but I enjoyed the whole experience. Even though I was frightened of him … I'm still convinced he's a great artist.

They recorded four magnificent songs. But after those sessions, the tension became unbearable. One evening, Spector kept Céline waiting. It was three, then four, then five o'clock in the morning. Céline had to tape a video in a few hours. She had to look her best and be in top shape. Dave Platel dared to ask Spector when the tracks would be ready for Céline to sing to. Spector told him to take a walk in the back alley with his bodyguard. Through clenched teeth, he told Platel that he felt like pulverizing him. His reaction was so excessive that it almost sounded like a bad joke.

> I took one look at René and I knew exactly what he would think and what he would do. I was in complete agreement. I got up and walked out. I walked back and forth in the parking lot with Dave. The night was cool. I knew very well that I'd never set foot in that studio again, that I'd never work with Phil Spector as long as I lived. René came out to meet us in the car a few minutes later. He was calm. He's always calm when he's angry. He told me what happened. Spector hadn't even noticed I'd left. René went up to him. It was finished, he said. I was gone and I'd never be back. Spector said he was sorry. René never batted an eyelash. He'd never let anyone treat his friends that way, he said. Even the biggest artists don't have that right.

And so began — with a false start — the adventure of *Falling Into You*, Céline's fourth album in English. Vito Luprano, John Doelp from the New York office and René had brought together a few dozen songs for Céline to choose from. A handful had been recorded in the spring. But after the Spector episode, everybody needed some rest.

In July, Céline and René flew off to Fiji with Coco and Pierre Lacroix for a one-week stay at the Wakaya Club. It has to be one of the most beautiful spots on earth — the ideal place for recharging batteries. Almost uninhabited mountainous islands thick with vegetation are ringed by coral reefs marked by the spray from breaking waves. Within the reef, the waters lie calm and clear. Céline could have simply let the days slide lazily by, doing nothing.

It never failed. When she dropped everything, she fell ill the next day with a combination of intestinal flu, headaches and nausea.

Ever since the launch of *D'eux*, three and a half months before, she hadn't even stopped to catch her breath. Two days before the sessions with Phil Spector, she'd returned from a promotional tour in Australia. *The Colour of My Love*, six times platinum, had been at the top of the charts for six weeks, and the 125 employees of Sony Australia had signed a petition asking her to meet them. There'd been several public appearances and autograph sessions at Myers Records in Melbourne and at HMV in Sydney. Directly after the Spector episode, she'd begun recording for her upcoming album at the Record Plant in Los Angeles, at the Compass Point Studio in Nassau and at New York's celebrated Hit Factory. In the meantime, Angélil and Barry Garber were putting the finishing touches to an Australian tour scheduled to begin the following spring, in nine months. It was to be the start of the seemingly interminable *Falling Into You* tour that kicked off down under in March 1996, and ended in Zurich in June 1997.

Before the Australian campaign, she'd toured Scotland, the Netherlands and England, where *D'eux* had gone gold twice over. It was the first time in history that an album in French sold more than 100,000 copies in Great Britain. She sang "Pour que tu m'aimes encore" between "Calling You" and "Love Can Move Mountains." She also sang the Goldman song on June 14, on *Good Morning America* and a day later, on *The Tonight Show*, a significant breakthrough for French in English-speaking territory.

Nevertheless, as part of the Canadian tour, she did a show in Jonquière, a town in the Saguenay region of the province of Quebec. Two decorators transformed a concrete box with cinder block walls into a superb dressing room, with the comfort and luxury to fit a star. A few weeks later, when the decision was made to print T-shirts commemorating Céline's world tour, Jonquière took its place right alongside the world's great cities, and this would turn out to be one of Céline's most treasured moments onstage.

For these three months — on the road in Europe, the promotional tour in Australia, the top talk shows in the USA, recording sessions for her next album — she was happy, strong, rock solid. Everything was on track. There was nothing but activity, filling every minute of her life, day in, day out. She woke up slowly, then, after breakfast at about three o'clock, Suzanne or René or Barry or Dave would fill her in on the day's schedule. And they got down to work.

But here on Fiji, the inactivity threw her off. She had time to think. Her mind kept right on working. But there was nothing to concentrate on. She began to panic. Her dream of a huge house in the Laurentian mountains where she could take months off at a time suddenly lost its attraction. She'd come to love her nomadic existence and the action that got her adrenaline pumping. She was like the kind of athlete who couldn't stop, who had to push herself to the limit every day to keep in shape and stay happy. Maybe that's what life was like. Scary and intoxicating.

When she pulled herself out of her slump, she talked less and less about her work, and more and more about her search for happiness. You had to get the most out of life, she told journalists. "The difficult takes a while, the impossible, a little longer." She didn't like defeatists or people with negative vibes. The Spector incident had made her think. She knew she had to choose her partners cautiously. There was no time to lose, no energy to waste.

The band had changed a lot since the *Incognito* tour. Yves Frulla staked his claim to the keyboards in 1990, just before the release of *Unison.* Guitarist André Coutu took over from Pierre Gauthier two years later for the first tour with Michael Bolton. On August 6, 1995, Céline appeared at a huge outdoor festival in central Alberta, where three new musicians joined the band: Dominique Messier on drums, Marc Langis on bass and Paul Picard on percussion. A new backup singer, Rachelle Jeanty, also came on board.

Paul Picard had played with Céline back when she recorded "Une colombe" and on her first real tour in 1985. Then he returned to Montreal, where he played with Quebec stars Michel Rivard and Paul Piché. Picard had a reputation as a musician's musician, a man with taste, style and sensitivity. He also had an ear for trends. Now, ten years later, he came back to play for Céline. He found a stronger, more flexible voice. But she was still just as kind, playful and considerate as she'd always been. "That's one of the most impressive things I've ever seen in show business," says Picard. "Fame hasn't gone to her head."

Céline didn't know the two other musicians: Langis (who was trained in classical music and jazz at the University of Miami) and Messier (who had wide, hands-on experience). Both had been members of the house band on the Sonia Benezra Show. Mégo, who was still band leader and chief arranger, asked for a few extra days of rehearsal. "Impossible," answered Angélil. Céline was busy in Los Angeles, where they were working on the tracks for her next album. How about a few hours? Out of the question. The musicians had to rehearse alone. Everything clicked. But they were worried what would happen when Céline sang.

It was eight o'clock in the morning on August 6 when Rachelle Jeanty, Langis and Messier met Céline for the first time. Everybody was on edge during the sound check, even David Foster, who was in charge of the first half of the show. The presence of René Angélil and Vito Luprano, who would be evaluating the newcomers, only added to the pressure.

It was magic. As Messier put it, "It was wild up there onstage." It was one of the great moments in music, a meeting of the minds. They started off with "Everybody Is Talking My Baby Down." Everyone was charmed — Céline, the musicians, Vito, René and most of all, David Foster. Immediately, he asked the group to record "All By Myself" in the studio. It would become a part of Céline's new album.

The "All By Myself" session, at the Record Plant in Los Angeles, lasted three days. The day before, Foster told Céline that he'd changed the orchestration for the last part of the song. She would have to sing at a higher pitch, and hit a "D" that she had trouble reaching. It was at the upper limit of her range. Foster wanted her to hold that note on the "o" of "anymore" ("Don't wanna be All By Myself anymore") for several measures. She was afraid. And she knew she couldn't do it more than twice.

"Don't worry if you can't hit it," Foster said. "We'll find another way. I've got another arrangement ready if need be."

She was insulted. On recording day, she and René quarreled and René decided not to go to the studio with her. So off she went to the Record Plant all by herself. There she found Foster, cold, condescending, almost contemptuous.

Céline had already gotten the key, and as the technicians were laying down the tracks, she paced nervously up and down in the studio. Foster came up to her and told her, with a straight face, "If you can't hit the notes, don't worry. Whitney Houston can always do it. She's recording tonight in the next studio. I know she can hit high D and hold it as long as she has to."

Céline didn't say a word. She walked over to her mike and sang "All By Myself" with all her strength and soul, with fury and passion. And at the end, when time came to climb to high D, she gave her voice everything she had. It hurt, but she held the note, long and clear. When she came back down to earth, the musicians behind the glass wall were on their feet, applauding, tears in their eyes. She walked out without a word to Foster, or without asking the technicians if everything was okay. She knew. She knew she'd scored a hole in one. Picard and Frulla followed her out into the parking lot. The night was balmy. They were laughing like children. Céline thought of René. She tried to figure out the reason for her outburst of anger, but she couldn't.

As she climbed into the limo, she knew that Foster was already on the phone to René. She could imagine what they were saying.

"It's in the can," said Foster. "Good thing you weren't there. She was furious at everybody. Nobody, no singer in the world could hold a high D as long as she did. When she hit that note, her voice had a sound to it I've never heard before. It was better than I ever hoped."

When she got back to the hotel, René was waiting for her in the lobby with a broad smile on his face. She threw herself into his arms.

Céline barely had time to catch her breath after the album was recorded. Not that she wanted to. She made a rapid swing through Quebec. For the second year running, she participated in a fund-raiser for cystic fibrosis research on September 12. On October 12, she was off to Europe and a private show in Geneva, to be followed by her first full-scale tour of the continent. There would be fifty shows in two months, in twenty-one cities in eleven countries, in halls holding between six thousand and sixteen thousand spectators. Every show was a sellout.

Angélil was too busy wrapping up *Falling Into You* in Los Angeles and New York to attend the first show of the tour at the Zénith in Montpellier. He arranged with tour director Suzanne Gingue to catch it by phone. She promptly rigged up a receiver to pick up crowd reaction. There were a few flubs. René followed the tour by telephone — Toulon, Marseille, Nice, Toulouse, Bordeaux — until the show was perfect.

On October 18, they were in Brussels. After the last song, "Vole," the shouts and applause were still echoing in the amphitheater as the limousine carrying Céline, Eric, Suzanne and Barry Garber rushed toward the airport. It was all Céline could do to contain her joy. In an hour she would be in the arms of the man she loved, reunited in Paris.

In addition to her five Paris shows, she was slated to tape a television appearance and record an album in concert. A crew of twelve cameramen plus the producer attended the first shows to familiarize themselves with the artist. They were surprised at how consistent her movements were, how automatic, yet how fluid. But Céline always studded her presentations with hesitations and little "mistakes" that made the whole thing seem improvised and spontaneous. They were to film the October 24 and 25 shows. But on the twenty-fourth, Céline's voice broke.

In her dressing room, Céline collapsed in tears into Suzanne's and Manon's arms. René hovered tenderly nearby, trying to find the words to comfort her. There was only one night left for filming. The pressure would be enormous. But Céline had always given her best in situations like these. She loved live appearances, stage fright, pressure, walking the tightrope. The next show would be her best. She wanted it, and she worked for it, heart and soul.

The *Falling Into You* Tour
Hamburg, October 21, 1996

The Gift

It is almost dark when the Lear Jet from Amsterdam touches down on the rain-drenched runway of the Hamburg airport. Céline is happy. The tour is running on cruise control. Everybody is in top form, physically and mentally. They are together, a "band on the run" powering their way across Europe, a boisterous, good-hearted, good-humored beast overflowing with energy and joy.

In the month since Bercy, they performed eighteen shows. In between Grenoble and Nîmes, they made an appearance on Taratata, *France's most prestigious television variety show. Céline has kept silent for ten days. Everything was perfect, or so it seemed. Those long, unbroken, deep silences. And the shows: explosive, wild, marvelously exhausting.*

By now they have come to know the cities where they appear. They encounter familiar faces, the same drivers, the same dignitaries. A year ago, in late December 1995, they were all here in Hamburg, with the granddaddy of the show that was now taking them around the world.

Hamburg is all business, but it still manages to be attractive. Despite the season, the trees are still green. Céline is happy to be back at the same place she stayed the year before. When she steps into the room, the very same room with its view overlooking the park, with its heavy drapes and hunting scenes on the walls, she thinks back to all she has done in less than one year. She was just a little girl back then, she thinks. And now, she is a mature, responsible woman.

She has ideas, and people listen to her. Her relations with René have changed. He used to be her brain, the one who made all the decisions. Then, slowly, he began to ask her opinion on everything, from strategies to marketing. He is still the one with the fresh, new ideas, ideas that stimulate and excite her, ideas that make her love her show and her husband and her life. Like the one he came up with four days earlier.

She was doing her nails with Manon in their suite in Amsterdam. He called from Las Vegas and kept her on the phone for an hour, telling her about the Beatles, about their early days, their first dates in Liverpool, hard times in London, their bohemian existence in Hamburg where, he claimed, it all really began. "They even recorded a 45 in German, just like you."

She listened, and looked out the high windows at the busy canals of Amsterdam. René has told her the story so many times, but each time, he changes something, adds something, a little detail only he could imagine. That day, he talked long and lovingly about Pete Best, the drummer who quit the group because he didn't want to cut his hair like the others. It would not be long before the others, who were joined by Ringo Starr, became living legends. And millionaires.

"But it all started in Hamburg," said René. "When you do your show in Hamburg on the twenty-first, you ought to do an old Beatles song. Talk it over with Mégo. Something like 'Twist and Shout.' You could do it to wrap up the show. It would be like a gift to the people of Hamburg."

Mégo quickly located the music and arranged the orchestrations. Two days before, at the Ahoy Sportspaleis in Rotterdam, they rehearsed "Twist and Shout." Their version was fast and brief. A gesture that was sure to set the Hamburg Sportshalle on its ear.

There is only one thing on their minds now: Get to the end of the show, fast. After the first encore, they will send their version of "Twist and Shout" winging out into the crowd. That would get them on their feet. If it works out, they can do the Beatles' number after every encore. Just like on the last tour, with "Everybody Dance Now." It's always a good idea to leave the crowd excited, hungry for more.

Chapter Thirty-Five
The Price of Victory

René called Francine Chaloult from Atlanta on July 19, 1996. It was raining heavily in the Laurentians, she recalled. Angélil was almost beside himself with excitement, his nerves on edge. Underneath it all, she picked up the sense of accomplishment in his voice. It must be the same feeling that the great conquerors have when their goal was finally in sight; that scientists experience on the verge of a great discovery. It was a strong sense of satisfaction, mixed with a fond look back to the days when there was only hope, when pain and fear lay in wait along the road.

When you're on top, how much higher, how much further can you go? "You've got no choice," said René. "You've got to keep going. But it's scary. From now on, we're on our own. There are no more signposts, no more blueprints." They were like the athletes who, with each new world record, found themselves facing an even greater obstacle, a crossbar set even higher. Each time, the job got tougher. Céline was to sing that evening at the opening ceremony of the Atlanta Olympic Games. The potential audience was estimated at four billion people, more than half the human race. It was an enormous challenge. For her and for Angélil.

"Nothing seems to faze her," René told Francine. "Or else she doesn't realize what she's doing."

But he knew that deep down, she was terrified. He could spot it for a fraction of a second in her eyes, in her nervous laughter, in the little movements of her hands, in her tics, in the way she brushed her lips with her fingers as she stared off into space. But he had to get his own emotions under control.

That afternoon she rehearsed in front of eighty-five thousand people with the huge choir that was to accompany her in "The Power of the Dream." When she took the stage, she said a few words and made the crowd laugh.

Thousands of athletes and a fifteen thousand media corps from around the world gathered in Atlanta for the Games. The highway, railway and air transport hub of the southeastern United States, Atlanta was also one of the main interchanges on the information superhighway — the uncontested capital of the New South, close to Europe and the Americas. Here, in 1886, Dr. John Stythe Pemberton created Coca Cola. Here, Margaret Mitchell wrote *Gone with the Wind*, the masterpiece of the Civil War. Here, too, was where the Reverend Martin Luther King began his career, where he studied and hammered out his thoughts. On Sunday morning, the city's churches are filled to overflowing, throbbing with music. Atlanta is a musical town. And a believers' town. This is gospel country. Tourists visit the church, and snap up souvenirs printed with the great preacher's famous words, "I have a dream."

The song that Céline was to sing starts to play (was it simply coincidence, or was it planned?) the theme of empowerment and creativity. "The Power of the Dream" is a straightforward tune, right for the circumstances. Written by David Foster, Linda Thompson, and Babyface, it praises the virtues of solidarity, perseverance, blind faith in the future and in a world where anyone can succeed if they really want to.

> Appearances aside, it's not an easy song to like. As I was singing, I kept wondering just how powerful dreams really are. Can you really succeed in this world by wanting and dreaming? The truth is that for lots of people, it's not like that at all. Some people don't have the luck, the skill, the talent. Some kids are born healthy, some are born sick or crippled. Some people have the body of an athlete, others don't. I wondered what Karine would have thought of this song. What would the kids who live in poverty in India, in Haiti, or in Africa, or in the ghettos of Atlanta and Los Angeles think about it?
>
> When you get right down to it, dreams can carry you if you've already got what it takes to succeed. This is the story of my life, in a way. I had everything I needed. I had a voice, I had

René. And like Eddy Marnay used to say, I was born under a lucky star. But I had a dream of my own. I dreamed, and I still dream, of singing on the world's greatest stages. Before my wedding, Mia collected all kinds of quotes for me. One of them was from Charles de Gaulle. I've never forgotten it: "Glory comes only to those who have always dreamed of it." I can say that I dreamed of my own glory.

I know René told everybody that I wasn't afraid. That's not true. I was afraid. Going onstage in a huge stadium is always terrifying. It's like jumping off a cliff. Funny thing, the more people there are, the higher the cliff. I was afraid, but I wanted to ignore my fear. It only really hit me the day after. Afterward, I was scared to death. It came in spurts. Flashes. It took me two months to work it out of my system.

In the afternoon, after the rehearsal, she talked to her mother, who did everything she could to conceal how worried she was. She'd be watching her daughter that night from their house in Sainte-Anne-des-Lacs. All across Quebec, the rain was pelting down. As Céline reached the pinnacle of her triumph, one of the worst natural disasters in Quebec's history had begun to unfold.

A month later, on August 23 via satellite in Las Vegas, she sang Jacques Brel's "Quand on n'a que l'amour" for Radio-Canada television. The song was to be part of a benefit at the Molson Center in Montreal for the people left homeless by the devastating floods that ripped through the Saguenay region in the northern part of the province, in the very location that had been so dear to her on the last tour. She'd written a few words to tell the people that she was with them. She almost burst into tears. With Céline, you never can tell. Seeing people suffer, seeing people pulling together in times of crisis is touching. But there was more to it than that. She was exhausted. For almost a full year, she'd been on tour. Europe in January and February, Australia and New Zealand in March and April, Canada, from Vancouver to Halifax in May and June, the USA in July and August. And throughout it all, television shows and the recording of her album *Falling Into You*. By now, her career had taken on enormous proportions.

For the last few days, something was on her mind. She was waking up at night. In Denver it was more than she could take.

I dreamed I swallowed an apple and it got stuck in my throat, in my esophagus. It happened to me when I was a little girl, and it scared the daylights out of me. Then I dreamed that someone hit me in the chest. I woke up with this shooting pain over my breastbone. And it got worse. I was alone. Awake for hours. My mind was going around and around. Everything seemed dangerous to me. Then I stopped thinking. I was hurting. I was afraid. I couldn't eat. For a day or two, or sometimes three, I couldn't feel my weight. But I could feel a kind of bruise inside me. And it would come back, in the middle of the night.

Did you ever see *Alien* with Sigourney Weaver? The monster gets inside people, don't ask me how. And it grows and grows. Then suddenly it bursts out of them. That's the way I felt.

On the morning of August 29, in San Francisco, she had a bout of nausea, dizzy spells and fever. Suzanne phoned René, who had checked into a health spa the night before. Then and there, they decided to postpone the last three stops on the American tour, San Francisco, Portland and Seattle. The physicians at the hospital where she stayed for a few days of observation diagnosed the problem as gastric reflux caused by stress. They prescribed medication and rest.

Céline returned to Montreal to relax and be close to her mother, but she was facing a dilemma.

For me, resting and being inactive cause stress. I'm like my mother. I've got to find a balance between stress and rest.

When she left for Paris a few weeks later, she still had that queasy feeling. It wasn't painful, but she could feel it, at night most of all. It was keeping her awake. She could see it coming. It was almost inevitable. But there was no way she could avoid stress. The tour kept on growing, the halls were larger, the crowds bigger. Every day, things seemed to speed up.

The previous year's European tour had started out slowly in the outlying regions. When they finally hit Paris, the show was tight and finely tuned. But in spite of everything, one night at the Zénith, she lost her voice.

This year's *Falling Into You* tour kicked off in Europe with five shows in six days at Bercy, a hall that held twelve thousand people. On September 20, even though the show had been going well, even though the crowd seemed more than satisfied, Céline felt remote, far away, distracted. "Don't worry about it," René told her. On the twenty-first, as she left the stage, she felt the pain in her stomach. She slept badly, "drifting in and out," as she put it. At four o'clock on the twenty-second, when she left the hotel for a sound check, she'd eaten only two soda crackers and drunk a half glass of warm water. The blandest food, even a light chicken broth, made her stomach burn and cramp.

René was ready to cancel everything.

"No reason to suffer," he said. "It's crazy. You don't have to do it."

"I'll suffer just as bad if we cancel."

To show him that she would tolerate no discussion, she locked herself in her dressing room with Suzanne, Loulou and Manon.

During the sound check, René went onstage and let her know that he'd dropped two songs, "River Deep, Mountain High" and "Quand on n'a que l'amour," both physically demanding numbers. He was feeling a little weak himself. But they had to keep going. The halls were rented, eighteen concerts in October, nineteen in November. They were both on board a high-speed train, there was no getting off.

The fall tour of Europe turned out to be a tonic. On October 1, when she taped the *Taratata* show, she was still looking wan. In Nîmes, in Le Mans, in Caen, the pain was still there, but no sooner did she step onstage than it receded. No sooner had the show ended than there it was, back again. She managed to forget it for a few hours. But if you asked her how she felt, it would be there inside her, waiting ominously. Then, on October 21, in the Lear Jet flying from Hamburg to Amsterdam, she suddenly turned to Suzanne and Manon, as if she'd been stung by a bee. She just realized she felt no pain anywhere. It was gone. She sought it out deep inside herself. Not a trace.

From that moment on, the tour took off like a rocket. Copenhagen, Stockholm, Oslo, Berlin, Milan, Lausanne, Zurich. Never before had the musicians had so much fun playing with her. Every night she set the crowd ablaze. Her appetite was back. Her voice was strong, solid. Never had her connection with her public been so warm. Everyone — Céline and the band members, the technical crew, Suzanne and Barry — lived in a kind of euphoria that fall. On November 4, in Paris, she and René, who'd just arrived from Montreal that morning, were reunited.

Céline's career had grown to dimensions that Angélil could never have imagined, not even in his wildest dreams. To keep things from getting out of hand, he started to take a completely different approach from the one he'd used at the beginning. Now he spoke cautiously, reasonably, calmly. Like the mountain climber who keeps his eyes focused on the rock wall in front of him and avoids looking down into the abyss, he kept planning for the future.

Dave Platel and René Angélil met a woman named Suzie Sponder. She was the Sony representative for Latin America. With her, they wanted to draw up a plan of attack for the new market where Céline was a total unknown. She recorded "Sola otra vez," a Spanish version of "All By Myself." The experts and strategists agreed that its vocal fireworks would please the Latin audience. Soon she would start Spanish lessons.

Before sending Céline off on a campaign among the Latinos, Suzie suggested they bring Sony-Latin America's people to see her show in Montreal on December 16. She could kick off the promotional campaign during her swing down the east coast of the United States in the spring of 1997. Before that, she could dip down to Mexico City on January 26 to take part in a variety show called *Siempre el domingo* that was broadcast live throughout Spanish-speaking America, from the Rio Grande to Tierra del Fuego. The round trip from Los Angeles to Mexico City was already arranged. "What time is the show?" Angélil asked suddenly. "Six o'clock," said Suzie Sponger. "It won't work," he added. "Find another date. January 26 is the Super Bowl. The Mexicans won't be watching *Siempre el domingo.*"

The South American promotion project had to be put on the back burner. The immense Asian market was beginning to open its doors. In the space of a few weeks, after the launch of *Falling Into You* and plenty of hard work by the Sony-Asia staff, demand had become almost irresistible. A few days earlier, a delegation of young people from Taiwan met the woman they nicknamed "Slim" Dion. There were fan-club members from Taipei, radio hosts — disc jockeys and video jockeys — all young people her age, all intimidated out of their wits, standing in a semicircle at the back of the room. Turning on the charm, she stepped forward with a cheery "Hi, guys," shook their hands, made them laugh and had her picture taken with them. They came to tell her that they wanted her to stage a show in their country. Taiwanese television had been broadcasting the Japanese soap opera *Koi Bitoyo* with its theme song "To Love You More." In the previous six months, several hundreds of thousands of copies of *Falling Into You* had been sold. Céline promised, without committing herself. "I'll be coming to see you one of these days, that's for sure."

René, who was standing off to the side, knew it wouldn't be possible on this tour. Demand from the Asian front was so insistent that, as of October, as Céline continued her European swing, Barry Garber had already begun to plot an Asian tour for late January. But there just wasn't time for everything, not for Hong Kong, Singapore and Taiwan. Not this time. They would be concentrating on six Japanese cities: Tokyo, Yokohama, Fukuoka, Hiroshima, Osaka, Nagoya, then onto Korea for the first time, and finally Brunei.

Céline knew nothing of the plans and preparations. But she was beginning to wonder if that year's sabbatical they'd been talking about for months now would be postponed yet another time. In the limousine carrying them to the Lear Jet that flew them back to London after every show — from Cardiff, Sheffield, Birmingham or Manchester — René began entertaining the idea of having Céline do a stand-up comedy routine. He imagined Céline appearing on a TV show (Radio-Canada's satirical year-end roundup called *Bye-bye* or the Just for Laughs Festival) in disguise. No one would recognize her. She would impersonate a young singer talking about her favorites. After a tribute to Aretha Franklin and Barbra Streisand, she would zero in on Mariah Carey and Whitney Houston, then on Céline Dion. She'd make catty remarks and parody her tics and her little fetishes. And at the end, the viewers would learn that the young impersonator was none other than Céline Dion herself.

"It wouldn't take long," René concluded. "Nobody can imitate Céline Dion."

Céline shot back, looking straight ahead, "René, instead of looking for more ways to make me work, why don't you come up with something to entertain me while I'm taking my year off?"

Then, as if she regretted what she'd just said, she laughed, slid over close to him and laid her head on his shoulder. "I'll go where you go, you'll be the place I call home." But deep down, she wasn't really looking forward to that year off. There were too many unknowns, too much discomfort in inaction.

The following week in Paris, she appeared in the New Year's Eve special hosted by Michel Drucker, along with Alain Delon and Robert Charlebois. The taping lasted nearly twelve hours. At six o'clock in the morning, she stepped out of the TF1 studios bone weary but happy. She knew they'd just recorded a wonderful show. She and Delon sang "Parole parole," the song he used to sing with Dalida. Then she and Robert Charlebois sang one of her favorites, "Je reviendrai à Montréal."

She did return to Montreal a few days later, by way of Las Vegas and Los Angeles, where she took part in award galas. The flight from Paris to Vegas lasted nearly ten hours. No sooner did she arrive than Céline was whisked off to the studio for a sound check, then she got a few hours sleep, sang her bit and hopped back onto the same plane for Los Angeles. There, the next day, despite the severe jet lag, she made an appearance at the *Billboard* Awards banquet. Mariah Carey walked away with most of the prizes. Céline won nothing.

> You can't have everything. That evening, Montreal was on my mind. I hadn't seen my mother in two months. And I knew I'd be back in Montreal the next day. Last time I was there, it was September, and I was sick.

There was snow on the ground, and it was cold and damp when the aircraft touched down at Dorval Airport. But Céline was happy to be back home. In their kitchen in Montreal, she fixed sandwiches for herself and René.

René bought the Montreal papers. He was muttering through his teeth. Céline had bitten the dust at the *Billboard* Awards, they wrote.

"What were they supposed to say?" she asked.

"First off, they ought to know that at your level, there's no such thing as dust. Even being nominated is an achievement. That's what they should've said."

"That's what you always say, René. If you're so smart, why don't you fix it so you're a journalist in the next life?"

She was on vacation. Before the Quebec Cystic Fibrosis Association benefit at the Montreal Congress Center on December 15, they had six long days completely to themselves. There they were, in the Rosemere mansion, alone. Aside from her mother and father and René's kids, they didn't want to see a soul, not even the cleaning lady or the chauffeur.

But the next morning, when she woke up, René was already on the phone. Talking with Marc Verreault, Francine Chaloult, Michel Bergeron, Pierre Lacroix, with writers and translators David Homel and Fred Reed, with his associates at the Mirage Golf Club, with the architect who was designing their new offices. René never stopped. He didn't like being alone, doing nothing anymore than she did.

A few days later, at a press conference held before her show at the Molson Center, René informed Céline, and the Montreal media, that she would be leaving for an Asian tour at the end of January. There went their much ballyhooed vacation, which was supposed to start on January 1. Astonished, Céline turned to him, and they feigned an argument. "You're hiding things from me, my love." And René shot back with a laugh: "Too late. You can't back out now. Everybody knows about it."

She laughed. She pretended to be upset, but deep down she was happy. She really didn't want that year off. She didn't even understand why she'd ever wanted it in the first place. Why stop when everything was going great? The machine was in perfect order. The singer in full possession of her faculties and her talents. She knew she couldn't do without the stress, the excitement, the exhilarating tension.

> We never really talked it over. That's what's so wonderful about René. He makes up his mind, he organizes, he does it. He knows what I really want, he knows what I'm looking for. When you get right down to it, I was happy.
>
> René knew that going off to sing in Asia would make me happy. Besides, I really wanted to visit Brunei because it's so far away, completely outside the world I know, at the far end of the mysterious East. I imagined veiled princesses, sumptuously decorated palaces, landscapes straight out of *The Arabian Nights.* Another kind of sensibility. I imagined myself somewhere far away. I'd been to Asia a half dozen times, and I'd always had pleasant surprises.

So off she went to Asia, happy. Even if René wasn't with her. Even if, over the holidays, she discovered that there were bad feelings among her brothers and sisters.

> Maybe I'm an egotist, but I always dreamed of a perfectly united family who love and help each other. I always wanted to believe it, because it made me feel better. My family is my picture of the world. As long as I believed that my brothers and sisters were living together in harmony, I could imagine that peace in the world was possible. It made things easier for me. Singing love songs in a world of war and want, that takes an awful lot of energy.

At Christmas, she gave each of her brothers and sisters $100,000. A few days later, the generosity she hoped to keep secret was all over the front page of *Le Journal de Montréal.* Someone in the family had talked. The bad blood got worse. Mia had told Céline and René she had a hunch someone was telling the media about the Dion family and Céline's life. It had to be someone close. She'd read snippets in the French scandal sheets about Céline and René that could only have come from inside sources, "from someone you trust." Céline was dumbfounded. She was used to the paparazzi and the professional gossips. But being snitched on by one of her own, that was a low blow.

"If it's true, I don't want to know who it is," she said.

On tour, she could block out those sad realities. As soon as she was far away, she could reunite her family in her mind.

On Valentine's Day, she wrote René a love letter from Tokyo. She didn't like writing, or reading for that matter. "It's so complicated, and it takes so long. What counts is thc intention. That's what I have to say."

My treasure,

I'd love to make myself into a Queen of Hearts for the occasion.
I count the days, the shows, the nights and the hours that keep me from you.
I've burned so many candles projecting your face on the walls of my hotel rooms like shadow puppets.
And leaving some of my wildest dreams behind me.
In the sky above my bed, every night I play the silent film in black and white, where the King meets his Queen of Hearts.
They snuggle up against each other.
Until they become one.
How happy they are.

For Valentine's Day and for all eternity, I adore you,

Your wife,
Céline
xx

Udo Artists had been Céline's promoter in Japan ever since they took over hosting the tour three years ago. René and Barry met all the top producers early in 1994, spoke to them, listened to them. From the financial standpoint, there was little difference between their proposals. Feelings would make up their minds. René always worked with people who liked Céline. Seijiro Udo was a fan. He knew Céline's records. He had had lots of experience, and he'd given the matter a lot of thought. He had a plan and a strategy. In 1994, he insisted on starting out in medium-size halls to create demand among the young Japanese public.

Udo was a colorful character, a fast talker, a bit overbearing, a kind of gallic Japanese. He was sixty-eight years old, stocky, lively, hyperactive. A storyteller who loved being listened to. And like René, he had a passion for the history of show business.

"I've seen 'em all," he reminisced. "The Stones, Elton John, even the Beatles. Not to mention Kiss, Metallica, Pink Floyd, Bob Dylan, I've met 'em all." He produced the Beatles in 1966, at the Budokan.

After the 1997 tour, Udo invited Céline and her entire entourage to dinner in one of Tokyo's finest restaurants. There was nothing unusual about the invitation. All producers do the same thing after a show. What made it different was that Céline accepted this time. Often she met the people who produced her shows only briefly, for two or three minutes, just like the dignitaries who dropped by the dressing room to greet her.

On Tuesday, February 18, 1997 in Tokyo, Céline had been silent since Sunday. In the afternoon she was at Fuji television. Céline and Taro Hakase performed "To Love You More" against a psychedelic backdrop that reminded you of icy, polar landscapes. Mr. Udo came to say good-bye to Céline and to give her a gift she didn't even have time to unwrapin his presence. They had a train to catch. Everybody piled into the limousines and they hurried to the station where they boarded the Shinkansen, the Bullet Train, for Nagoya. Most of their luggage was already waiting for them. But Céline's entourage didn't exactly travel light. There were huge suitcases, and a stuffed frog as big as a St. Bernard. The passengers on the platform turned to stare while Eric and his assistants stood guard over the little flock.

On board the bullet train, Dave and Barry, seated across from Céline, were working on the upcoming tv special in Memphis. The idea, as they explained it, was to add a second show so they could get the best pictures from both. There would be twelve, fifteen or maybe eighteen cameras.

On the seat next to her, she laid out dozens of photos of her brothers and sisters, nieces and nephews, her brothers- and sisters-in-law. She was setting up a photo montage for her mother's room in the Palm Beach house. Her father had carried some of those photos in his wallet for more than twenty years. There was also a torn, creased slip of pink paper. It was the police report on the accident of April 27, 1970. She acted it out for Dave.

Céline has developed a remarkable talent as a mime ever since she was ordered to keep silent. In a matter of seconds, with a few precise gestures and glances, mimicry and facial expressions, she could tell an entire story without a word. She could make you laugh or make you think. On her feet in the corridor of the Shinkansen as it sweeps through the mountains at two hundred miles per hour, she acted out the story of someone everyone in the entourage knew well, a guy who slept around without thinking of the consequences (complete with classical pelvic thrusts). The girl got pregnant (a motion of the hand to illustrate a fat belly), rocked the baby in her arms, and the guy, crestfallen and terrified, waved good-bye. Then, with a little frown and a flick of her hand, Céline gave her opinion of the guy and showed her pity for the girl. A compact, silent drama that was over in five seconds.

That night in the Nagoya Hilton, in the suite Céline shared with Gilles and Manon, they unwrapped Mr. Udo's present. It was an *uchikake,* a ceremonial garment that the noble ladies of yesteryear (the Genroku period of the Edo era, between 1688 and 1703) wore over their kimonos.

Gilles and Eric shifted the furniture so that they could spread out the garment, and drape it over Céline's shoulders. She looked like a huge, flamboyantly colored bird. Gilles snapped some photos.

Meanwhile, in an adjoining room, Denis Savage and François Desjardins were examining the plans that a half dozen stadiums in Europe had faxed them. Suzanne Gingue now spent her nights on the phone with Montreal and Las Vegas, wherever René happened to be, and with Amsterdam, Dublin, London, Copenhagen. Everyone was hard at work on the last leg of the *Falling Into You* tour that would wind up in June in the largest venues in Europe.

By now, everyone knew there would be no one-year sabbatical. Some of them had never believed it in the first place. From time to time, Céline pretended to think so. She would take refuge in a dream and find shelter there. It was the dream of a quiet little life, all peaceful and serene — the kind of life she really didn't want to lead.

The *Falling Into You* Tour
Zurich, June 26, 1997

On the Run

More than a few shows on the tour end with what's called a "runner" in the trade. It happens when Céline and her entourage have to beat a hasty exit from the amphitheater. With the final chords of "Because You Loved Me," and while the stadium is still ringing with applause, everyone springs into motion. Céline comes dashing off the stage, pulling out her earphones and shouting to the band members and crew, "I love you all, thanks!" Someone throws a coat over her shoulders and everybody streaks for the cars that will speed off to the hotel or the airport. Sometimes, they even have a police escort to guide them through the city that's just given Céline a splendid ovation. They're like a river, unstoppable. Then they're airborne and they're all alone in the world, streaking across the sky in their deluxe jet — René, Céline, Barry, Dave, Eric, Gilles and Manon, Suzanne — the people close to her, her entourage.

Céline is often hyper after a show. She hums and sings in a soft voice that flits and darts around her.

The exit from the Olympic Gymnasium in Seoul will go down in the history of the tour as the tightest, most exciting and most stressful of all the runners. Céline's DC-8 was not allowed to take off after 11:30 at night. The airport was a full hour's drive away. There were huge traffic jams, and there was always the risk of getting caught in one, even at such a late hour. The show had to end no later than ten o'clock.

For starters, it had to get under way on time. But at eight o'clock, Patrick, Eric and Michel were still arguing with groups of young cameramen who'd plunked themselves down at various places in the hall to film the show. It took a long time, and some serious discussion, to convince them that it just wasn't done. Dave told Céline to cut the presentations short. The show started a little late, and with a bit of confusion.

It was electrifying. Céline made contact with the good-natured, young crowd with the very first songs. She was as surprised as she was delighted. But to everyone's dismay, she didn't want to leave the stage, doing one encore after another, talking with the audience, laughing. She'd forgotten they had a plane to catch.

> Sure I knew I shouldn't have. Sure, I was thinking that we'd be late. But I couldn't interrupt what was going on with the crowd.

They made it to the DC-8 just in the nick of time. As the plane was taking off, Céline, keeping to herself, murmured her little prayer. Then she said, "Now there's a show I'm really sorry my love missed."

But he did see the last show of this fabulous tour. One of the most beautiful and most moving was the unforgettable show in the Leitzegrund Stadion in Zurich. Many of her friends and collaborators had followed the final days of the Falling Into You *tour, in whole or in part. There was Marc Verreault, Ben Kaye, Lloyd Branet who, in spite of the rain all over Europe, managed to get in a round of golf every afternoon. Now, at the concert, along with Barry, Dave, René, Vito and Angélil's daughter Anne-Marie, they take in the show from the control booth right in the middle of the field. Patrick Angélil comes to get them during the encore, and they fly through the noisy crowd, flashing their passes and making their way backstage.*

Céline sings "Because You Loved Me" as an encore, while René leads Anne-Marie, Marc Verreault and Suzanne Gingue onstage. Standing there in the darkness, they see the breathtaking sight of the crowd head on — those tens of thousands of faces and upraised arms. They see Céline from behind, running back and forth across the stage like a surfer hurrying to catch the next wave. Then the musicians and backup singers join her, waving to the audience. Afterward, all around the stage, backstage and in the dressing rooms, for a good part of the night, people talk, kiss and cry. It is the finale. The next day, the whole crew will leave for Montreal. In Céline Dion's life, this is a historic moment.

Chapter Thirty-Six
Northern Lights

It was a long, long haul from Brunei to New York. They crossed the international date line, stopped at Anchorage the day *before* they left, then soared for hours on end across the frozen tundra of the Northwest Territories at an altitude of thirty-six thousand feet. That night, the aurora borealis shone in all its splendor. Everyone was hunched over their porthole on the starboard side of the aircraft, watching the opalescent, fluid movements that lit up the sky. Céline spotted them first, hurried to tell the others and pulled them over to look. They watched for the longest time. Céline moved from one person to another, explaining what the pilots had told her about the northern lights.

She talked to René who saw nothing, who wasn't even interested in such things, whose mind was far away.

One day, way back in 1986, they were returning from Europe. Far above the Atlantic, they spotted Halley's Comet off to the south. Céline went up to the cockpit where she spent several minutes learning about comets, their tails and their fuzzy heads. Then she called René. He came, leaned over and said, "That's nice!" Then he went back to his seat and picked up the magazine he was reading. He didn't have much fascination with the beauty of nature.

The moon rose over the icy expanses of the Northwest Territories.

Then, ahead of them, lights appeared. "It's Churchill, on Hudson's Bay," said the pilot. It was like a bubble of civilization afloat in a sea of wilderness. Céline Dion's DC-8 was rushing headlong toward New York.

She was still getting her papers in order, spreading out the photographs of her brothers and sisters as teenagers. She read aloud the list of quotations that Mia had drawn up for her in the summer of 1994 while she was preparing for the wedding. It included Shakespeare, Byron, Faulkner and Voltaire, Mother Theresa and Anonymous. A collection of lines to make you think. Céline liked reading from the list every now and again. Every time she read it, she'd find something new.

"The art of being now audacious, now prudent, is the art of success." Napoleon said that. "That which looks like love is always love," from Tristan Bernard. "The absence of love is the worst poverty," from Mother Theresa. "Today is the first day of the rest of your life," from Anonymous.

Oliver Cromwell: "One never travels so far as when one knows not where one goes." And Barbey d'Aurevilly, Céline's favorite: "To be beautiful and loved, is to be but a woman. To be unsightly and know how to make oneself loved, is to be a princess."

As soon as the DC-8 came to a stop on the tarmac at Newark Airport, a bus drove the musicians and technicians away, then two black limousines pull up at the foot of the gangway. The weather was bright and cold. Céline and Manon were in no hurry to leave the aircraft, although their entourage stood shivering on the tarmac. Far away in the cold, raw light of early morning, the skyscrapers of Manhattan were visible. The limo drivers were the first to hear of the long trip from Brunei, the stopover in Anchorage, the crossing of the Arctic, the northern lights.

Then she appeared, and all heads turned to look. For the briefest of instants she paused at the top of the gangway. She was freshly made up, her hair done, she was wearing dark glasses and a fur coat whose hem brushed against her bare legs. Slowly she came down the steps, her left hand clutching the mink coat closed. She placed her feet sideways on the narrow steps because of her stiletto heels. She looked every inch the star, confident in her beauty — "Céline" from top to bottom. The whole act was done with the wink of an eye, carried off with a knowing smile.

On that frosty February morning in New York, she was off to do a show — for the one and only man of her life whom she had not seen for more than three weeks. He was waiting for her now in one of the finest suites just blocks away from Central Park.

The entire day and night would be for him. She would see no one else. Then the fun would begin, starting with the Grammy Awards at Madison Square Garden, a little side trip in the middle of the *Falling Into You* tour. Then would come the rehearsals, the interviews, the song "All By Myself" that she would perform with David Foster. After that, there would be an appearance on *The Late Show* with David Letterman the following evening where she'd sing "Natural Woman," then *Good Morning America* a few hours later where, for the first time on television, she would do "Fly," the English version of Goldman's "Vole." And to wrap it all up, she would tape an hour-long special for the BBC with the venerable Sir George Martin, the man who produced every single Beatles record. And last, there would be a meeting with the people from Sony. All this in forty-eight hours, and with countless hours worth of jet lag in her system.

New York was a brutal, in-your-face kind of town. Encountering it could be harrowing the first couple of times. Céline was used to its particular euphoria, its manic disorder. The limousine came to a stop in the heavy rush-hour traffic, coincidentally, right under a huge poster: "Hottest tickets in AC. Tony Bennett, Tom Jones, Céline Dion."

"If you can make it there, you'll make it anywhere," as Sinatra and Liza Minelli once sang. Céline knows (Angélil's been harping on it long enough) that ultimately, it is here that her talent must be realized, here on the stage of Madison Square Garden, in front of the television cameras of the world's largest network, in front of that cavernous expanse of empty seats that tomorrow will be filled with celebrities and the movers and shakers of the recording industry. She knows that the paths of glory, the world being what it is, pass through the American Empire. And that the empire imposes its law on the entire world. It insists you speak English, no matter who you are or where you come from. If show business is a country, then New York, Hollywood and Las Vegas are its great capitals. If you can triumph there, you'll triumph anywhere in the world.

Quebeckers, living on the frontier of the American dream, were natural cultural participants in the experience. Thanks to her, they had close-up, prominent roles. At last, they existed. People talked about them. More than once, direct from Hollywood, Toronto or Paris, when she had won prizes at the Oscars or the Junos, she had greeted them in their language, in their accent: "A big how do you do to all you folks up there in Quebec. I love you all. You'll always be my inspiration." And in the living rooms and kitchens of Quebec, hearts would beat in unison.

To the Americans and the French, Céline Dion had an accent all her own. "For people outside Quebec, she was American and foreign at the same time," noted Christian Dufour in a long article in *La Presse* (March 27 and 29, 1997). Dufour, a professor at the National Institute of Public Administration, has written several books on the Quebec identity. He presented Céline as "a new kind of worldwide star" and wrote a detailed analysis of the phenomenon. Angélil read it, liked it and called up the writer.

The following afternoon, in Madison Square Garden, she would give interviews to a cross section of Canadian and American journalists. She already knew the kind of questions they would ask. She knew her answers by heart. Gently, calmly, she'd tell them exactly what they wanted to hear. To the television cameras of VH1, Much-Music, MusiquePlus, NBC, CTV and Radio-Canada, she would speak of her love for music. "Music is my life," she'd tell one. "Music is happiness," she'd confide in another. "If you sing, or if you play a musical instrument, you're never alone."

Someone might ask how she chose her songs. She received perhaps one thousand a year, and listened to fifty of them at most after the Sony artistic directors, Vito Luprano and John Doelp, weeded them out. In Paris, Melbourne and Dublin, famous or obscure musicians and songwriters would come backstage to visit Céline after the show and slip her a cassette. Then they would wait, hope, pray, with one thought in mind: "If she likes my song, I'll make a fortune." They know that Luprano, Doelp and René have already begun to search for songs for the next album.

Songwriter Diane Warren offered Toni Braxton a song she'd written in memory of her father, "Because You Loved Me." Braxton didn't go for it. Warren tried it on Céline, who made it into a great hit. Ironically, that evening at the Grammy Awards, that very song was in the running against one sung by Braxton.

When they came up with what they thought might become a song, a potentially happy mingling of words and music, John and Vito alerted Angélil. They had cut the number from one thousand to two hundred, then down to fifty songs. Céline would make the final choice, along with René. Some magic songs worked their charm immediately. Others, they would put aside once and for all, but then suddenly, they would come creeping back into their minds.

The tiny Madison Square Garden dressing room was crowded and overheated. Céline signed her autograph on the back of someone's guitar. The cameras moved in, focused on her, brutal and demanding. Her press attachés, Ellen and Kim, kept track of the time allocated to each journalist, and when time was up, they cut off the interview.

A young lady thrust her mike toward Céline and asked why she sang love songs, nothing but love songs. She was intimidated but proud of her question. Céline answered that love made the world go round. Love was what people wanted to hear about and would always want to hear about. "Love songs are always in style. People need them, especially these days. Don't you think so?"

She was tense. Everybody was. Vito, Doelp, René, the entire 550 team. What would happen at the Grammys? Céline had been nominated in four categories, including the most prestigious, Best Album of the Year.

Fortunately, executive producer Pierre Cossette, who had been televising the Grammys for more than twenty-five years, was on hand. His presence was reassuring. Cossette was one of the great names in American show business, a man who had rubbed elbows with and directed all the greats of the recording industry for the last three decades. He was a native of Valleyfield, a small town outside Montreal. Each summer, he came back to his home town to visit his family, to see the St. Lawrence River again, and the rolling fields of the Chateauguay Valley. In the summer of 1989, his family took him to a small theater in Chateauguay to hear a twenty-one-year-old marvel sing. Her name was Céline Dion. He'd forgotten her name, but he remembered the timbre and the power of her voice that had touched him to the depths of his soul.

Four years later, in February 1993, in the Shrine Auditorium in Los Angeles, he was conducting rehearsals for the Grammys when Céline took the stage with Peabo Bryson to run through "Beauty and the Beast." He recognized her voice and he went over to tell René that he'd heard her sing for the first time in Chateauguay four years before. He told René that he knew she would go far. "But I never thought it would happen so fast."

Since then, he'd followed her career closely. He loved René and Céline, who confided in him one day that she wanted to do a movie. Cossette had an inspiration: what about having Céline play Edith Piaf? Piaf was an idol, a legend even in the United States, where the industry could portray her as a charismatic personality.

There'd been other film suggestions too. With Gérard Depardieu, Mel Gibson. But for Céline and René, the Piaf project was the most attractive. Céline had always wanted to make a movie. She would tell journalists that when she sang, she was really acting. She slipped into the skins of the dreamy young girls that Eddy Marnay had endowed with such troubled feelings. She personified the vamps, the teases, the schizophrenics that Luc Plamondon had sketched out for her. They were roles. She didn't believe that she had to experience, in body and soul, the emotions she expressed in her songs, no matter what some critics said. It was play acting, all of it. She'd known it all along, ever since she'd started imitating Ginette Reno when she was seven years old.

With *D'eux* and *Falling Into You*, Céline Dion became, beyond a doubt, the world's top-selling singer for the previous year. She had at least one Grammy in her pocket already. The prize had been given off air, earlier in the afternoon. David Foster, who'd worked closely on the English album, was in a press conference at the time. He's just received the Grammy for best arrangement with vocal accompaniment for "When I Fall in Love," sung by Natalie Cole and her father, the late Nat King Cole. When he spotted Céline going onstage to accept her award, he declared that the girl from Quebec was the greatest voice he knew. Coming from a man with twelve Grammys to his credit, from a man who'd worked with Streisand and Houston, it was quite a compliment.

But the record counters' Grammy wasn't the one Céline coveted the most. She was nominated in three other categories: Best Female Vocal Performance for "All By Myself," Song of the Year for "Because You Loved Me," and Album of the Year for *Falling Into You*. The year before, Alanis Morissette and Shania Twain had taken home a half dozen trophies between them. The Canadian tidal wave had irritated some people, and that might have hurt her chances. In the corridors of American show business, people had begun to mutter and gnash their teeth. Americans had trouble digesting foreign cultural fare. Show business was going global, and Canadians were elbowing in on their act. For the past several years, not a single woman who had climbed to the top of the charts had been an all-American girl. Gloria Estefan was Cuban, Morissette and Dion were Canadians. Houston and Carey were African-Americans.

In the end, Toni Braxton, a gorgeous young black woman, claimed the Grammy for Best Female Pop Vocal Performance for "Unbreak My Heart." In the running, aside from Céline, were Jewel, Gloria Estefan and Shawn Colvin. Braxton was astonished. Later, at her press conference, she said that in her opinion, the award should have gone to Céline Dion, that it just didn't make sense, that she had so much more voice than all the other singers. People began to suspect that the wind had shifted, and that this year, products made in the USA would be getting the prizes. In spite of her disappointment, Céline had no right to feel bad. Being nominated for the Grammys and selling almost 40 million albums in one year was nothing to be ashamed of. She was seated in the first row, to René's right. She was smiling, but he wasn't. When he was tense or angry, René would bite his lower lip.

In the Song of the Year category, "Because You Loved Me" was up against "Give Me One Reason" by Tracy Chapman, Eric Clapton's "Change the World," "Ironic" by Alanis Morissette and "1979" by Smashing Pumpkins. The prize went to Clapton. Céline knew that *Falling Into You* would get chosen as Album of the Year. She knew her man was bitterly disappointed. She took his hand, turned to him. He'd bit his lip so hard it was bleeding. There was only one award left, the most prestigious of all, for Top Album of the Year. She was sure that René was still hoping, even though her chances were slimmer than ever.

Her *Falling Into You* was taking on the young, brilliant Beck, the Fugees, the Smashing Pumpkins and the soundtrack album from *Waiting to Exhale* with Whitney Houston, Brandy and Chaka Khan. Just before the award was to be announced, ten minutes before the end of the ceremony, the performers of *Waiting to Exhale* with Whitney Houston leading the way, took the stage. The applause was enthusiastic in spite of an uninspired performance.

From that moment on, no one in Céline's entourage believed that *Falling Into You* was still even in the running for Album of the Year. That's why there was astonished silence after the award was announced and people finally realized that the most prestigious Grammy of them all, the most coveted, had gone to *Falling Into You.*

The press conference that followed was tense. Some music reporters, undoubtedly closer to the Fugees or Smashing Pumpkins, seemed unhappy with the academy's choice. The following day's papers accused it of giving in to conservatism by handing such a prestigious award to such a conventional product. The headline in *USA Today* read, "More safe bets than gambles."

That same day, Céline was a guest on David Letterman's *Late Show.* Taping took place late in the day in an old Broadway theater where the temperature was set at a steady sixty degrees Fahrenheit to keep the public awake and clapping. A cheerleader harangued the crowd, which responded with clapping, shouting and laughter. Céline sang "Natural Woman." At the end of the song, Letterman came up to her. She threw herself into his arms flamboyantly. But Letterman didn't have time for Céline. He thanked her perfunctorily and wished the viewers goodnight. Angélil was furious. Getting his anger under control, he went off to tell the program researchers and producers what he thought of them.

"You missed out on an interview with the hottest girl in show business," he said. As far as he was concerned, they'd done it on purpose. Particularly since Letterman had taken some swipes at the Grammys at the beginning of the show. "Céline Dion won a Grammy or two. A

Grammy? Who wants that?" As a joke, it was in bad taste, and Angélil wasn't about to forgive him.

The same thing had happened on her previous appearance. Céline kept on smiling, treating everybody courteously. This time, Angélil asked her to be firm: as she left the stage to say goodbye she should say it coldly or, better still, not at all. But she couldn't care less about not being interviewed by Letterman. Her song had been fine, and for her, that was what mattered. She was incapable of being arrogant or short-tempered with anyone.

That evening in her room at the hotel, she received flowers and a message signed by David Letterman: "Sorry the show ran over. Please come back anytime you want."

For ten years, Céline Dion had been living in the fast lane. But there were still times when things got even faster. The last two weeks in March 1997 were a spectacular example.

On the night of the eighteenth, she sang at the Orlando Arena in Florida. Then she took a helicopter to the Disney World studios where she taped two songs for the Radio-Canada special benefit for the Quebec Cystic Fibrosis Association. At two o'clock that morning, the helicopter carried her to the airport where she boarded the Sony jet that would take her to Chicago. She didn't get to bed until five o'clock in the morning and was up at eight. An hour later, she was in the NBC studios where she joined Oprah Winfrey's talk show.

Taping began at around noon. For all her exhaustion, Céline talked, laughed and made Oprah and the studio audience laugh too. Her answers to Oprah's questions were graceful and humorous. She reached out, took her hostess's hands and asked her to talk about her own loves and dreams. The show was painstakingly prepared. There were pictures of Céline as a little girl, with Michel Jasmin, with Michel Drucker and at the Montreal Olympic Stadium singing for the Pope.

Céline sang "Because You Loved Me" in front of René. Usually when she does a television show, he stays in the control room or in front of a monitor. That day, she was a bit thrown when she spotted him in the first row of the studio audience. But she looked him straight in the eye and sang only for him. He was moved; everybody could see it. So was Oprah. That was what she was looking for: feelings, emotion. Then she sprang a surprise on Céline.

> I was expecting an appearance by David Foster, or maybe Diane Warren, who wrote the song. When I saw my dad and mom come onstage, I just about fell off my chair. And behind them came Michel, Ghislaine, Daniel, Clément, Linda, even Louise who came all the way from Sept-Iles. The only one missing was Claudette, who was in Barbados. When I spotted Liette, I just about broke down. I was supposed to sing "Fly," the English version of "Vole." I knew that if I let myself cry, the show would be over then and there. I could never sing Karine's song in front of her mother. So I kept myself under control.

All together, they sang "Ce n'était qu'un rêve." Then, as she sang "Fly," she saw a stagehand guide Liette to a seat directly in front of her, right beside the camera. It was all she could do to keep going, but she did. As she sang, big close-ups of her and her sister alternated on the screen. Liette stifled her tears until midway through the song. At the end, Oprah herself was weeping, so were René, Michel, Liette of course, and most of the people in the audience. Not Céline. She couldn't let herself be overcome.

Oprah was in seventh heaven. Her producer decided to postpone the interview with an up-and-coming comedian that was scheduled for the last fifteen minutes of the show. René Angélil marveled at how such a powerful machine could turn on a dime. To carry it off, you needed experience and know-how.

"In Quebec, no one would have done that. No one could have," he said. "It's always too complicated. But the Americans, they know how to seize the opportunity."

During the last commercial break, Oprah asked her if her family knew any other songs. In front of millions of American television viewers, Céline and her family sang "Les Cloches du hameau," an old French folk song. Before the song, Céline related how, when she was twelve or thirteen, she sang songs in English without knowing what the words meant. And now, she and her family were going to sing a song that no one in the audience would understand. The public was delighted. Never had a singer so powerfully introduced the French language into the very heartland of America.

After the show, Céline had only a half hour to talk to her folks. She was leaving for Los Angeles, where she was to record "Because You Loved Me" with a full orchestra. The song had been nominated for an Oscar. All in all, she spent less than twelve hours in Chicago.

In the Lear Jet, she sat close to the window and looked down over the now-familiar landscape of the American Rockies, the deep canyons, the snow-capped peaks, the ochre and reddish-brown deserts. Far off was a city, Las Vegas perhaps, where they had been so happy together.

"You're tired. Try to get some sleep," René said to her.

But she couldn't sleep. She felt no thirst, no hunger, no illness, no fear. No desire to do anything.

> A lot of the time when I'm all alone, I take refuge in a dream. The one where I'm old and all alone. Or the one where I build a house in the Laurentians and reunite my family. Or the one with all the children I'll have one day, my little three-year-old son who follows me everywhere I go, and my little girl who wants to be in the movies.... But that day, on the flight between Chicago and Los Angeles, I wasn't in the mood for dreaming. I had to force myself to eat a few bites of smoked salmon.
>
> "Sleep, my love."

She was leafing distractedly through a fashion magazine. She happened on a picture of a dress that had been the cause of a fight between her and René a few days before. She adored the dress, and intended to wear it at the Oscars. He found it too flimsy, too revealing, a bit vulgar.

For two days she gave him the cold shoulder, until she understood that she was hurting him. She regretted being so hard. They kissed and made up. She still didn't have an outfit for the Oscars, but she couldn't care less. There was nothing worth looking at in the magazines, and nothing in the smog-filled city of Los Angeles.

They made straight for Paramount Studios where they met their old pal Bill Conti. He was the band leader they had so much fun working with in 1992, when Céline recorded "Beauty and the Beast" with Peabo Bryson. It was a major production number that needed days of rehearsal. Gil Kates, the overbearing producer of the Oscar gala, was on hand as well. Kates and Conti were two of Hollywood's legendary figures. They knew everyone, they'd seen everything, and they still had passion and enthusiasm.

Céline's turn came at around four o'clock. She took up position in front of Kates's camera to sing "Because You Loved Me," Diane Warren's Oscar-nominated song. Each of the competing songs was prerecorded, both sound and picture, in case the performer were to break a leg, lose his or her voice or get too drunk. Céline's interpretation was impeccable.

Everything was seamless, perfect. The sixty-two members of the orchestra got to their feet to applaud. In the control booth, Kates and René watched via monitor as Bill Conti walked over and kissed Céline. Then he turned toward the camera, cracked a wide grin and gave an emphatic thumbs-up sign.

The sun was still high in the sky when Céline and René left the studio. In the limo that drove them to the hotel, she felt the same sickly sensation she'd experienced earlier in the afternoon. She'd just scored a direct hit, and won the admiration of an entire orchestra, but she seemed upset. René was all nerves, anxiety and fatigue. Everything's going to be all right, he told himself. The greater the pressure, the better Céline got. She would get some rest, then she'd be in top form for the Oscars.

Rehearsals were scheduled for the next day at four o'clock in the Shrine Auditorium. Céline had slept nearly twelve hours, but the queasiness was still with her, and that had René worried. Worse yet, he had the impression he was coming down with something himself — a case of the blahs, a sense of emptiness.

According to the rules, every singer was entitled to an hour of rehearsal time. But after Céline had gone through her song once, Bill Conti motioned to her politely that she was free to go. "You're a real pro," he said, taking her in his arms, but to his amazement, Céline asked him if she could run through the song one more time. "For the fun of it," was how she put it. René realized that she was looking for something, for some action. She'd been working so hard over the last months that nothing seemed hard for her anymore, nothing was dangerous or risky. Ever since Atlanta, she'd hardly stopped. And she hadn't come down from the highest, the most dizzying summits. There had been the Grammys, the Junos, the American Music Awards, the World Music Awards. She'd sung in some fifty cities on four continents, before crowds of all sizes. She appeared on all the variety shows you could imagine, in Tokyo, Paris, London, New York. And on David Letterman, Jay Leno and Oprah Winfrey's talk shows, on *Taratata* and more, many more.

Now, here in Hollywood, at the peak of her fame, in March 1997, Céline Dion, incredible as it sounded, was bored. She needed a touch of stage fright, some excitement, a jolt of activity. Contrary to what most people believed, she wasn't exhausted at all. She wanted more.

Finally she figured out what had been eating at her since the day before. René had told her the story of the young Boris Becker, who had won Wimbledon twice. His manager advised him to keep up the pressure if he wanted to keep winning. Becker promptly fired his coach to increase the sense of danger, add to the stress and fear. Today, Céline understood what was behind the story. She wasn't in danger anymore. She wasn't afraid of any microphone, camera, or crowd. She was deprived of stage fright and stress.

Stage fright is a funny thing. It's both unpleasant and satisfying — a senseless fear, a feeling of dread that dissipates only in the heat of action. When fear is overcome, you get the feeling of being extraordinarily alive. Victory over fear becomes the real reason for living. You look for fears to overcome, more and more terrible fears, more and more terrifying dangers. Like junkies, the great stage artists need an ever-stronger dose of stage fright.

"Here we are, getting ready for the biggest show of all, and there's no thrill to it," said René. "There's no challenge left."

There they stood, on the balcony of their suite at the hotel in the golden light of Beverly Hills. They were surprised and amused to realize that you could climb so high, and make all your dreams come true, and still feel dissatisfied and disenchanted. But, in the next few hours, they'd be getting more thrills and challenges than they'd ever bargained for.

At about seven o'clock, Ellen and Kim, Céline's American press agents, met them at the hotel. The four had a reservation for eight o'clock at the Matsuhisa, "the best Japanese restaurant in the world," according to René. They were to meet a representative from Chanel, who had some suggestions for the dress and jewelry Céline might wear at the gala.

Céline was in her room getting dressed and finishing her makeup. Ellen and Kim waited in the living room of the suite, while René zapped his remote control absentmindedly. When the phone rang, he motioned to Ellen to answer. He quickly understood she was talking to Danette Herman, Gil Kates's assistant, and that something startling had just happened. He switched off the sound on the TV when he heard the names of Whitney Houston, Mariah Carey and Toni Braxton. Then Ellen told Danette, "I'll talk it over with Kim. If we can think of somebody else, we'll let you know."

She hung up and turned to Kim and René. Kates had just gotten a call from Natalie Cole, on tour in Montreal, where she'd come down with a nasty case of the flu. She was scheduled to sing "I Finally Found Someone," the song from the film *The Mirror Has Two Faces*, starring Barbra Streisand. They had twenty-four hours to come up with a replacement.

René had stopped listening. He got up and went into Céline's room to tell her what was going on.

"What do you think of that?" he asked.

"The same thing you do, my love," she answered with a big smile, her first since they'd left Chicago.

At times like that, he loved her intensely — when they understood each other perfectly, when they came to the same decisions at the same time, without any discussion. Only she had the power, courage and intelligence in these extreme situations. Only she could reach out and catch luck as it passed. At times like this, they were truly alone in the world. It was a thrilling sensation.

"I think I can do their song," she told him.

He came up to her and took her in his arms.

"You'd better use a music stand," he suggested.

"And be seated on a stool. Great idea! Besides, I do 'Because You Loved Me' standing."

They imagined the staging. And the looks of surprise on people's faces, their reactions.

René returned to the living room and told Kim and Ellen, "Imagine the MC coming on after a commercial break and saying: 'Ladies and gentlemen, Natalie Cole, our next performer, is ill. Céline Dion has agreed to replace her on forty-eight hours notice.'"

"But it's never been done before," exclaimed Kim. "No one has ever sung twice at the Oscars."

"Exactly," said René. "We've got to do what's never been done before. That's what counts. Call Gil Kates. I want to talk to him."

When he heard René's idea, Kates shouted so loudly into the phone that Kim, Ellen and Céline heard his words. "I love it, René, I love it! That's a real Hollywood story."

Never in sixty-nine years had an artist sung twice at the same Oscar Awards ceremony. Hollywood is nuts about firsts like that, crazy about things no one's ever done before.

Bill Conti joined René and Kates on the telephone. He was just as excited, and relieved.

"I'm rehearsing until ten o'clock. Then I'll meet you at Matsuhisa's."

Céline had not seen the Streisand movie, nor had she heard the song, but she knew her voice, her repertoire, her favorite keys. She knew she'd like it. For her and René, Streisand was the world's greatest singer. René asked the chauffeur to stop at a record store, where they bought the sound track album of the movie. Céline listened to "I Finally Found Someone" three or four times, her eyes closed, standing in the tiny Japanese garden at the entrance to Matsuhisa's restaurant. It's a difficult song, full of nuances and half-tones. Streisand had recorded it as a duet with Bryan Adams.

At Matsuhisa's, the Chanel representative and a *Vogue* reporter, who'd been sworn to secrecy, joined the group. Céline asked them about the dress René disliked so strongly. Wear it, they encouraged Céline. René didn't say a word. He was happy. The queasiness, the draggy feelings, everything was gone. There was nothing but the thrill of action.

Bill Conti showed up a bit before midnight. He handed Céline a cassette with the arrangements he'd prepared for Natalie Cole. It was completely different from what she'd heard earlier in the evening. Conti had replaced Bryan Adam's voice with a trumpet. But, as luck would have it, his orchestrations fit Céline's voice perfectly. That night, they went over to Conti's place where Céline rehearsed with him a couple times. Back at the hotel, she listened to the song again, as she did the next day, when she got up. At last, she was excited, on top of the world.

She tried on several of the dresses that representatives from the leading designers had brought her.

"What do you think of this one, my love?"

"Magnificent," he answered.

"You never saw this dress anywhere else, my love?"

"No. Never."

She pulled out the magazine to show him that it was the famous Chanel dress he couldn't stand. Lucky for him, he laughed.

On Sunday afternoon, she was back in Paramount Studios to rehearsing "I Finally Found Someone" just as she'd prepared "Because You Loved Me." She'd gone over it time and again in her head. She knew the song perfectly, every note, every nuance she wanted to give her voice. Again, the musicians gave her an ovation, and Conti made a little speech insisting that they keep the secret.

On Monday evening, when they entered the Shrine Auditorium, René was looking from side to side, spotting the stars of showbiz and movies, and naming them in a loud voice. "Look, there are the Coen brothers. Quentin Tarantino, Tom Cruise and Nicole Kidman."

A few moments earlier, in the limo, they heard on the radio that Barbra Streisand had finally decided to attend the ceremony after all. The idea of singing in front of her idol, especially singing a song she'd performed for the first time, terrified Céline.

"I see her," said René. "To the left, two rows behind us, just behind Muhammad Ali." Later, as Céline took the stage to sing "Because You Loved Me," he turned to look at Streisand, but in the darkness he could not make out her features. He would have liked to know what she was thinking. What was she feeling when she heard Céline sing? She must have know that Céline would be singing her song.

During the fourth commercial break, as Céline was getting up again to sing "I Finally Found Someone," René noticed with astonishment that Streisand was leaving the hall. If she stayed out for more than three minutes, she would miss Céline. The doors were kept closed tight when the show was on. Why was she walking out? To keep from hearing Céline? Because she didn't want the cameras on her while someone else was interpreting the song she'd made famous?

Before she returned, the lights dimmed. René was disappointed because Céline had sung "I Finally Found Someone" beautifully. Not at all as Streisand sang it, just as romantic, but more playful, happier, younger. When Streisand returned to her seat her fiancé, James Brolin, leaned over and whispered in her ear. She tapped her forehead with her hand, visibly annoyed.

At a ceremony like the Oscars, the commercial breaks were always a scene of intense activity. With the cameras turned off, people got up, greeted and congratulated one another, shed a few tears of sorrow or joy.

A hefty, elegantly dressed, African-American man walked up to Céline and told her how much he liked her work. René saw he belonged to Muhammad Ali's entourage. Ali himself was a guest of the crew that had produced Leon Gast's magnificent film *When We Were Kings*, nominated for Best Documentary. René stood up with Céline and asked him to introduce them to Ali. "He's my idol, and we're both born on the exact same day." Truth is, René was born on January 16, 1942. Ali, on the seventeenth. But René Angélil was not the kind of man to let such minor details get in his way. Muhammad Ali smiled broadly and said something that René did not understand. Ali motioned to him to bend over. René's ear was up against Ali's mouth. In his low, muffled voice, Ali said, "We're getting old."

And he smiled even more broadly, giving René a wink.

Meanwhile, someone touched Céline's shoulder. She turned and saw, behind James Brolin, Barbra Streisand looking at her with a big smile and extended arms. Céline went to her. Barbra took her by both hands and said, "You sing beautifully. I really love what you do."

Céline wanted to ask her why, if that was true, she didn't stay in the hall to hear her song. But it was time to return to their seats. Besides, they were happy, fulfilled, not in the mood to be upset with anybody. They'd had more than their dose of stage fright and stress.

A few minutes later, Madonna received the Oscar for Best Song with "Evita." But Céline was to be the big winner in this 1997 edition of the Oscars.

After his heart attack, René would spend a few days at a spa getting some rest, losing weight and making resolutions he sometimes managed to keep for a few weeks. The Wednesday after the Oscars, he signed in at a health spa. It was the same place he'd been to in August when Céline fell ill and had to interrupt her West Coast tour. Now she was making up those canceled shows while René rested for a week.

A bare two hours after he checked in at the spa, René got a call from Marty Erlichman, Barbra Streisand's manager. He wanted to make sure Céline and René understood that, contrary to what the scandal sheets were saying, she hadn't walked out of the Shrine Auditorium to avoid hearing Céline, but because she really had to go to the ladies' room. In fact, she was sorry she missed the performance. Angélil told Erlichman how much Céline admired Barbra, and that she dreamed of doing a song with her one day.

At almost the same time, in her suite in San Francisco, Céline received a huge bouquet with a handwritten note from Barbra:

> I watched the tape of the show afterwards. And you sang my song beautifully. Thank you. I only wish I had been in the room to hear it. Next time, let's do one together.
>
> PS. I thought your song should have won. You are an incredible singer.

René kept the note in his wallet for weeks. Proudly, he showed it to his friends and to any journalist who crossed his path.

> One of the most wonderful things about my love is that he has this great capacity for amazement. I could give you a list of all the people he admires. The stars, of course, but also plenty of everyday people. People who do their jobs well. He knows how to recognize people who do good work. He knows how to trust, admire and love them.

René realized that Céline had truly become a superstar, a planetary pop diva hundreds of times bigger than anything they'd ever imagined. On April 8, in New York, she appeared in a benefit concert organized by Toys 'R' Us to raise funds for research into children's diseases. Among all the big shots, the stars of American politics, sports and motion pictures, she was the center of attention. At the airport, Arnold Schwarzenegger and Maria Shriver, who were also waiting for their private jet, came over to greet her and tell her how much they adored *Falling Into You.*

Céline did not plan to attend the World Music Awards in Monaco on April 17, even though she was to be awarded the trophy as the World's Best Female Vocalist. When the American television networks found out, they told the organizers that they wouldn't be broadcasting the event. It made no difference that big names like Bon Jovi or the Bee Gees were on the bill. Panic stricken, the producers were on the line to René every day. His artist was tired, he told them. She couldn't be everywhere at once. She couldn't spare more than forty-eight hours. Finally, they arranged for a private jet to fly nonstop from Palm Beach to Monte Carlo.

> Thank God for René. Me, I still have trouble saying no. I don't know how to ask for things either. Unless there's some direct connection with my songs or my shows. Then I don't let anything get by me. I've got very specific requirements, and I work only with the people I like, people I can trust. The rest of the time, I let people walk all over me.
>
> Some days, I feel like people think I'm some kind of poster, some kind of movie screen. People come to see me and they say, "You want a house? I'll build you one. You want to dress sharp? I'll look after it. I can do your hair, look after you, do your makeup, write your songs, your biography." I used to let them go ahead. I was like soft clay, easy to mold. But slowly, I'm learning to say no. Sure, I'm still afraid of hurting people.
>
> A few weeks ago, in Los Angeles, there was this photographer who wanted me to dye my hair black. Just for a photo. I told him no. It was a victory. Not over him, over myself. Two years ago I would've said yes. And I'd have been unhappy about it. You change as you get older. For the better, I think.

On May 6, 1997, Manon discovered Céline's first gray hair. They were in Céline's tiny dressing room at the Saint-Denis, in Montreal, where a dozen Quebec and French artists were paying tribute to Félix Leclerc, the beloved Quebec songwriter and singer. Céline would be singing "Bozo," the very song she'd sung fourteen years before at the opening of the short-lived Théâtre Félix-Leclerc.

After the rehearsal, she, Eric, Mégo, Manon, Gilles and René headed for the Mikado restaurant for sushi. For the first time in years, she was part of the hustle and bustle of the street. People on the sidewalks called out her name, waved to her, blew her kisses, smiled. It was a comfortable, happy feeling. But there was remembrance and sadness in the air. A few days before, Alice Angélil, René's mother, had died.

When they returned to the theater two hours before show time, Manon began combing Céline's hair. That's when she discovered the gray hair, just above her right temple.

"Pull it out," Céline said. "I want to show it to mom."

But Mrs. Dion never saw her baby's first gray hair. Manon mislaid it. "Don't worry," Céline told her. "With everything that's coming up, I'll be turning out plenty more."

Coming up was one final tour of the stadiums of Europe to wind up the *Falling Into You* tour that would ultimately take nearly two years of her life. She would record two albums, one in English, the other in French, that Vito, John Doelp and René had been working on for some time, followed by yet another tour, longer and even more ambitious than the last.

> My only goal is to keep moving forward. When people ask me what I want to do, I answer that I want to sing, make movies, keep on moving forward. One day, Mia faxed me this quotation from André Gide that she found in one of her books:
>
> "What are you looking for where you're going?
>
> I won't know until I get there."
>
> Bill Gates put it nicely in his book: "The journey is the reward."
>
> My life is my reward. It's a marvelous life, and scary too, when you realize that you've done more than you ever hoped or dreamed you would.

Céline had reached a point where there were no more models, no more signposts, She was all alone at the summit. Her voice was heard at the far corners of the earth, in palaces and in slums, in streets, schools and prisons. Her image was everywhere, copied by millions.

Everything was happening at a breakneck speed. Should she have aimed higher, sold more albums, given more shows in larger halls?

"Céline was born under a lucky star," Eddy Mornay used to say. "Whatever she wanted, she had. Or she will have. She wants to be in movies, and she'll do it." But she would have to choose carefully. At her level, at her speed, at her altitude, the slightest mistake could take on monstrous proportions. It would be up to her and René to weigh, evaluate and choose. They had luck and ambition going for them. She was endowed with enormous talent and energy. He had flair and visionary power.

> I know that one day I'll stumble, I'll make a mistake. They say a boxer is never complete until he's tasted defeat. It may be the same for an artist.

"If Céline had a major flop, a movie or an album that got shot down, she'd take it hard at first," says Paul Burger. "But I don't think it would change her career. Over time she had built up great personal strength. Her story was the story of a woman gaining her independence. Her power was that she loved to do what she was doing. Sure, she was happy to make money and win prizes and have the critics praise her. But I know that was not what made her tick. She had this fantastic talent, and thanks to René, she made it blossom. I think she would go on singing professionally until the end of her days."

Almost two dozen people were gathered around Céline and René in the Carnegie Deli late one night in October 1997. They were her close friends, the insiders, the indispensables — Manon, Gilles, Dave, Barry, Vito, Eric, not to mention Humberto Gattica, Walter Afanasief and David Foster. Just a few hours before, at the Hit Factory Studios, Foster had put the final touches on Céline's latest album, *Let's Talk About Love*. On Monday, photographer Michael Thompson would be taking the picture for the album cover. Céline already knew what she wanted: a big close-up of her face against a black background.

She was tired. Everybody was tired. Radiant too. A tiny fire burned in each of them. They were sure they'd accomplished something solid, something strong, something that would echo around the world for a long time to come.

René Angélil was a man who knew how to have a good time. He loved the kind of parties that brought together everyone who had taken part in the adventure, whatever their job — from secretaries to famous composers, from bodyguards to arrangers. When they were on tour, he would set up sumptuous banquets almost every day in their hotel suite or in the finest restaurants in the cities where Céline was singing. Often, he handled the preparations himself, making the reservations, planning the menu. The fare was always plentiful and varied. When it came to desserts, he avoided having to choose by simply ordering everything on the menu: ice cream, cakes, fruits flambé, raw, poached, sour, sweet....

Everything — "it's the Arab tradition," he said — had to be on the table at the same time, so that everyone could taste everything. It made for a mouthwatering foodscape and created a heightened sense of conviviality and friendship. The night at the Carnegie Deli was a fantastic moment, a magical night, full of romance. It was time for summing up and remembering.

René recalled how, the year before, in the fall of 1996, Barry told him of a young Dutch promoter who wanted Céline to appear in the Zuidoost in Amsterdam, a fifty-thousand-seat stadium. At first, he thought it had to be a prank. He asked Barry to feel out some other European producers. It wasn't long before the idea of a spring tour in the largest stadiums in Europe became a reality.

Requests and impatient demands came flooding in from all directions — Asia, Latin America, Eastern Europe, Mauritius, South Africa, the Maghreb, Lebanon and Israel. At the time, Céline was singing in amphitheaters with a capacity of ten thousand to twenty thousand seats. René had never imagined that she could appear in the largest stadiums, or that she would be in such great demand, far from the traditional itineraries of American show business. The demand was much stronger than his wildest dreams. For the first time, reality had outstripped his imagination.

Falling Into You did so well — selling more than 30 million copies around the world — that the Sony machine put enormous pressure on Céline, promising fabulous advances if she would record more albums. There would be the new one in November and a French album that Jean-Jacques Goldman was preparing for the spring of 1998. The *Let's Talk about Love* tour would wind up on the eve of the millennium. "Now there's a challenge," said Angélil, "for Céline Dion to be the number one singer in the world on January 1, 2000." Just for the fun of it, they started speculating on what stage she would sing on New Year's Eve, 1999. "We'll find the place," said René.

For most people, dreams and real life are two separate worlds. But for Céline Dion and René Angélil, the two have become one. They've worked long and hard to make their fantasies come true. They've been carried away by the raging torrent that their ambition has unleashed. It was exciting, troubling, thrilling, risky.

One night, the Bee Gees came to the Hit Factory to record the background voices for their song "Immortality," which they'd written for Céline. She sang them "Stayin' Alive," imitating the movements and steps of John Travolta. The Gibb brothers laughed. And when they heard what she'd done with their song, they shed tears of joy.

Joe Pesci, Billy Joel and Tommy Mottola, the big boss at Sony, all stopped by to watch the star at work. They listened quietly to several of the songs on the album. Then Billy Joel sat down at the piano. He, Céline and the Bee Gees belted out the old rock hits of the sixties and seventies for the pure hell of it. Filmmaker Scott Lochmus was doing a documentary about the recording sessions for the album, and now his cameras circled slowly around them as they played.

That same evening, in a nearby studio, Lochmus played the rushes from the California and London sessions. There was Céline, surrounded by friends and technicians, listening to the recording of "My Heart Will Go On," the theme song from the movie *Titanic.* Or working with Ric Wake on the tracks from "Treat Her Like a Lady," or alongside the venerable Sir George Martin, the man who created the sound — and a good measure of the legend — of the Beatles. Before he retired, Martin insisted on working with "the most intelligent, the most touching musical instrument of all" — Céline Dion's voice.

Sir George had produced "The Reason," with words and music by Carole King. It was supposed to be the title song until René Angélil happened on "Let's Talk about Love," an old Jean-Jacques Goldman tune that Bryan Adams had adapted into English. It had the tune and the words René had been looking for. "It's always like that now," he said. "We think of the music and the words, and they come to us. We dream of working with the artists we admire, and they call us up. Everything is happening exactly as we dreamed it would."

At the end of September, Céline Dion in New York and Barbra Streisand in Los Angeles listened simultaneously, via satellite, to the duet "Tell Him." They'd recorded it at different times and in different places. Barbra had recorded her part on a blank track, and hadn't even heard Céline's part, which was recorded a few days later.

After the playback, a tense silence swept over the main Hit Factory studio. Everyone was watching the telephone. It seemed to take an eternity, but it finally rang. A technician lifted the receiver and handed it to Céline. It was Barbra, calling from the other side of the continent to say how much she liked Céline's interpretation, how harmoniously she'd blended their voices.

"How do you do it?" she asked. "Your voice is like a butterfly, it's so agile and light. And then it's like a bird that flies so high that no one can touch it."

Céline replied that she worked hard like an athlete, every day.

She felt like she was all alone in the studio. She'd forgotten there was anyone else there.

"You'll have to teach me how," said Barbra.

"Teach you my routine?"

"No. To discipline myself."

"But there's nothing I can teach you. You're the greatest singer in the world."

"We can all learn something from one another. But you're a faster learner than any of us. Because you've got a great voice and a great soul. I'm so proud of you, Céline."

> That's when I started to cry. I knew it was going to be a violent outburst, a regular electrical storm of tears. I wanted to tell Barbra that, for me, she was a sister. That while I was singing, I felt our voices so close that you couldn't tell them apart. I didn't know who I was anymore. I couldn't tell which voice was mine. I wanted to tell her all that.

Overcome with emotion, René took the phone.

"You were always Céline's idol. She really thinks the world of you."

"I understand," said Barbra. "I felt the same way when I sang with Judy Garland. She'll get over it, let me assure you."

Then she asked to speak to Céline again.

"I want to get to know you better," she said. "Come visit me in Malibu as soon as you can. Tomorrow, if you can make it."

But the next day, a Friday, Céline would be working on "I Hate You, Then I Love You" with Luciano Pavarotti. And on Saturday night, she and René were invited to his Manhattan home for dinner. They agreed to go on the following Tuesday.

"I'll show you my rose garden," said Barbra, "and we'll go walking on the beach."

> Imagine being invited to dinner by your idol. Imagine her taking you in her arms. That was a great moment of happiness for me. Mind you, it's always scary to meet your idol face to face. You're not sure how to act. And you don't want to turn your back on the people you used to idolize.
>
> It's like with my dreams. Everything is happening so fast. Sometimes they come true even before I've had time to really dream them.
>
> No one wants to live without idols, and without dreams. Including me. I wouldn't do it for anything in the world.

Epilogue

At the time of going to press with this book, the love song from the movie *Titanic*, "My Heart Will Go On," had achieved the status of the most-heard song in the history of American radio. This unprecedented success has been a kind of sweet victory for Céline, René and the song's composer, James Horner. "My Heart Will Go On" was not the first time that James Horner had wanted to collaborate with Céline. In the summer of 1990, the composer and his lyricist, Will Jennings, had wanted Céline to sing "Dreams to Dream," the song they had written for Steven Spielberg's *An American Tail (Fievel Goes West)*. But after the suspense — and the numerous deals between recording companies — Spielberg finally asked Linda Ronstadt to sing the theme to his new movie. A few months later, however, Célinewas asked to record "Beauty and the Beast" with Peabo Bryson; this song was a major hit, won the Academy Award for Best Song and made a first-class star of the young Québécoise.

Although she had not been able to sing "Dreams to Dream" for the film, Céline still deeply loved James Horner's song, which she hummed to herself from time to time for her own pleasure. René, on the other hand, considered the loss a failure and could not help but feel somewhat bitter when he thought about it. A loss to him would always remain dreadful and inadmissible; he believed that he must never give up and must never resign — that he should trust his luck, believe in it and grab it when it presents itself.

And it was precisely his belief in his luck, and his determination to succeed, that led René back to James Horner. In the spring of 1997, Angélil learned that Horner was looking for a singer to interpret the love theme from James Cameron's *Titanic*. Already, the buzz was on about the film, which was reported to have a budget of more than $200 million US, and which people were calling "the movie of the century." René had only one goal: to have Céline associated with largest, and potentially most successful, of all Hollywood projects.

One night in Las Vegas, while he was watching, one more time, Francis Ford Coppola's *The Godfather*, René was reminded of the story of Marlon Brando's "audition" for that film. Brando, who was already a superstar, paid for a screen test of himself. He sent the test to Coppola, in the hopes of being cast as Don Corleone. And so René convinced Céline — already a superstar herself — to prepare a demo for presentation to Horner and Cameron, just as any novice would have done.

For the demo, Céline reached deep inside herself to find the voice best-suited to the lyrics of James Horner's song. The voice was warm and touching. Horner and Cameron were instantly seduced. "She perfectly understood what was the spirit of the movie," said Cameron. Horner declared the demo was "impeccable" — Céline did not need to rework it in the studio. "My Heart Will Go On" would be heard around the world in its very first version.

Céline's new album, *Let's Talk About Love,* was released in November of 1997. A month later, *Titanic* opened. By that time, December 1997, *Let's Talk About Love* had already sold more than 10 million copies. And, like *Titanic*, the album had staying power: by March 30, 1998 — Céline's thirtieth birthday — it was still on top of the charts.

On her thirtieth birthday, Céline was in Montreal. Patrick Angélil had organized a large surprise birthday party. The three hundred guests were treated to a retro-sixties theme: the world at the time of Céline's birth, in 1968. There were bell-bottom pants, platform shoes, afro wigs; people had their faces painted with stars and spangles, rainbows in their hair. There were strobe lights and mirrors everywhere.

Céline wore the wildest of three outfits designed for her to wear at the party. Céline entered the party, greeted the guests and danced away the better part of the night.

At this moment in time, Céline was radiant. She was surrounded by family and friends. She was happy. She was also pleased with her accomplishments and looking forward with true optimism to the future that awaited her and that she, with all her might, was prepared to meet and welcome. Ahead of her were new ventures and new passions. Passions like the one she had developed the previous summer, which would come as a surprise and which would bring her even closer — and create new bonds — with René. That passion was golf.

Upon their return in June from the European leg of the *Falling Into You* tour, René convinced Céline to take classes with Debbie Savoy-Morel, the pro at Mirage, the golf course in Terrebonne that they'd acquired just a few months earlier. Céline instantly fell in love. She liked the early mornings, the fresh air, the smell of grass covered with dew. She learned that golf is much more than a sport — it can become a way of life. It requires discipline, determination and rigor. It is a quest for balance and perfection. It brings intense moments of joy. The game of golf — like singing, like the pursuit of an art or profession — when practiced with seriousness and passion, helps you to learn more about yourself. In a short while, Céline became as enthusiastic about golf as René.

This enthusiasm for golf reached to such an extent that it became a priority when scheduling the next tour. Barry Garber was asked to ensure that there would be enough time between shows to allow Céline, René, and anyone from the crew who so wished, to play golf at least three times a week — no matter where in the world the next tour would take them.

But golf wasn't the only thing that made Céline so happy on this birthday.

A few days before, Céline had returned from Paris with a treasure: the demo from her second collaboration with Jean-Jacques Goldman, *S'il suffisait d'aimer*, which she had just finished recording. The album was originally scheduled to be released in the spring of 1998, but was delayed so as not to interfere with the success of *Let's Talk About Love*, which was still climbing the French charts. It was agreed that although *S'il suffisait d'aimer* was some of Céline's best work to date, that its release would be postponed to the fall of 1998.

While recording the new album, and working closely with Jean-Jacques Goldman for the first time in three years, Céline rediscovered the spirit she had shared with Goldman when they recorded *D'eux* — which she still considers among the best of her work. The collaboration had a special quality: it was vibrant and stimulating. Goldman's songs were about love, of course, but they were also about fear, about sorrow, about intolerance and anger, which must be overcome.

Aware that her success might make it impossible to see the world as it really is, Céline drew strength and reassurance from Goldman's songs. The lyrics bring the real world into sharp focus, they inspire compassion and tolerance; they provide a lucidity that isn't common to show business. The danger of becoming out-of-touch — of no longer feeling indignant when confronting injustice, of forgetting to marvel when in the presence of things that are pure, simple and beautiful — were addressed for Céline when she sang Goldman's songs.

Later, in the summer of 1998, René let a number of his friends and colleagues in Paris, New York and Montreal hear some of the twelve songs from the delayed album. He couldn't help but think how unfortunate it was to keep these wonderful songs a secret. But these doubts were balanced for him by his life. René and Céline played golf almost every day at Mirage; they were often alone and very happy. Life was indeed sweet and generous to them.

> I have remained in love with René like on the first day, in love with music, and in love with life. And at the same time, it seems to me, now more than ever, that everything around me is new: my house, my songs, my show, my passions and my loves. This is without a doubt my greatest luck and my finest achievement: to make life new every day. And to have enduring passions, friendships and loves.

In July of this year, Céline teamed up once again with her musicians to prepare the show for the *Let's Talk About Love* tour. The opening night was set: August 21, 1998, in Boston. The final night of the tour had yet to be determined, but it would end — in Europe? in Asia? in America? — at the turn of the millennium? The tour Céline and her musicians were planning in the Montreal rehearsal studios would be gigantic; it would be prepared with care, time, energy and money. Mégo wrote new arrangements for the globe-trotter songs from previous albums. There would be designer costumes for all onstage. On the south shore of Montreal, technicians under the direction of Lapin, began to construct a giant heart-shaped stage, two hundred meters square, which would become the platform on which Céline will sing. These are the same technicians who created the famous luminescent screen for U2's *Popmart* tour in 1997.

Once again, the Feeling machine was at work. The new show everyone had been anticipating would soon begin — "The most important of my life," said Céline. This would be the tour she'd always dreamed of, the show of a young woman, thirty years old, independent, free, caring and loving.